WISDOM AND WASTELAND

Bishop Jeremy Taylor, Bishop of Down and Connor

Wisdom and Wasteland

Jeremy Taylor in His Prose and Preaching Today

Thomas K. Carroll
with a foreword by
H.R. McAdoo

FOUR COURTS PRESS

Set in 10.5 on 13.5 point AGaramond for
FOUR COURTS PRESS LTD
Fumbally Lane, Dublin 8, Ireland
e-mail: info@four-courts-press.ie
http://www.four-courts-press.ie
and in North America
FOUR COURTS PRESS
c/o ISBS, 5824 N.E. Hassalo Street, Portland, OR 97213.

© Thomas K. Carroll 2001

A catalogue record for this title
is available from the British Library.

ISBN 1-85182-581-9

All rights reserved. No part of this publication
may be reproduced, stored in or introduced into
a retrieval system, or transmitted, in any form or by
any means (electronic, mechanical, photocopying,
recording or otherwise), without the prior
written permission of both the copyright
owner and publisher of this book.

Printed in Great Britain
by MPG Books, Bodmin, Cornwall

Contents

LIST OF ABBREVIATIONS	8
PREFACE	9
FOREWORD	15
INTRODUCTION: BIBLICAL AND POETIC PERCEPTION	
Word and Words	21
Poet and Priest	36
Prophet and Preacher	52
Preaching and Preachers	67
Catholic and Caroline	78
1. THE MINISTER OF THE WORD	
Introduction	93
The Minister's Duty in Life and Doctrine	99
2. MYSTICAL AND ASCETICAL	
Introduction	113
Via Intelligentiae	118
The Marriage Ring	133
3. BIBLICAL AND LITURGICAL	
Introduction	146
Advent Sunday: Christ's Advent to Judgment	151
Whitsunday: Of the Spirit of Grace	165
4. MORAL AND DOCTRINAL	
Introduction	180
Apples of Sodom; or The Fruits of Sin	185
The House of Feasting; or The Epicure's Measures	193
The Good and Evil Tongue	200
The Deceitfulness of the Heart	208

5. PREACHER AND PANEGYRIC
    Introduction   215
    The Countess of Carbery's Funeral Sermon   220
    Preached at the Funeral of the Lord Primate of Ireland   236

EPILOGUE: PANEGYRIC AND PREACHER
    Introduction   250
    The Funeral Sermon of Jeremy Taylor preached by the Most Reverend George Rust   256

TWO PRAYERS: BEFORE & AFTER SERMON   273

SELECT BIBLIOGRAPHY   277

INDEX OF BIBLICAL CITATIONS   281

INDEX OF PROPER NAMES   285

IN MEMORIAM

Henry Robert McAdoo

Abbreviations

ACW   Ancient Christian Writers, Newman Press, New York.
ANF   Ante-Nicene Fathers, W.B. Eerdmans, Grand Rapids, Michigan.
COWS   Classics of Western Spirituality, Paulist Press, Manwah, New Jersey and New York.
CS   Classical Series, London.
CUA   Catholic University of America, Washington, DC.
CSEL   Corpus Scriptorum Ecclesiasticorum Latinorum, Vienna.
EP   Enchiridion Patristicum, Barcelona.
ES   Enchiridion Symbolorum, Barcelona.
FOTC   Fathers of the Church series, CUA, Washington, DC.
LCL   Loeb Classical Library, London and New York.
LNPF   Library of Nicene and Post-Nicene Fathers, New York.
MFOC   Message of the Fathers of the Church, Liturgical Press, Collegeville.
PG   Patrologica Graeca, ed. Migne, Paris.
PL   Patrologica Latina ed. Migne, Paris.
SCBO   Scriptorum Classicorum Bibliotheca Oxoniensis.

Preface

Wisdom and Wasteland are the words of the prophet and poet for the mysterious reality unveiled in biblical revelation as Word and World. In the prologue of St John's Gospel the Word about which St John speaks was and is God, transcendent and immanent, present and real, pure and simple; 'all things were made through him, and without him was not anything made that was made.'[1] On the other hand, the World in St John is no less mysterious as the pattern of human life, or *spiritus mundi*, that is in rebellion against God and his Holy Spirit: 'he was in the world, and the world was made through him, yet the world knew him not. He came to his own home and his own people received him not.'[2] Unlike the mysteries of light and life, Word and World, in our order of being and becoming, are neither identical nor different, in either existence or essence. As concepts of reality they are from and for each other in a mysterious tension, and without their fullness of communion in giving and taking we are not for real: the consequent *carentia entis*, or deprivation of being, is unknown in science; however, it is known in theology as hell; in philosophy as evil; and in poetry as the wasteland.

This tension between the turbulence of the world, wherein Jesus faces death and his apostles persecution, and the peace of the Word he is in himself and bids his apostles to share, is felt increasingly as the Gospel of John unfolds the glorification of God and the transfiguration of Christ. The contrast stands out more plainly as the discourse becomes the Prayer of Jesus, the High Priest: here Jesus speaks from 'midst an historical crisis of human flesh and blood; yet he continues to speak as the Eternal Son of the Father: indeed, this Prayer of Consecration belongs both to the timeless communion of the Father and the Son in the Spirit, and to the conflict in time wherein the Son embraces the Father's will that he must die for the redemption of all. Nevertheless, the reader is in no way conscious of any unreality or discontinuity in the words of the Word made flesh; in fact in this drama of history and time the glory of God is revealed and the transfiguration of Christ is accomplished:

---

[1] Jn 1:3.   [2] Jn 1:11.

I pray not for the world, but for those whom thou hast given me; they are thine and I am glorified in them. I am no more in the world, but these are [...]. Holy Father, keep in thy name them thou hast given me that they may be one, even as we are [...]. I have given them thy word; and the world hated them, because they are not of the world. I pray not that thou shouldest take them from the world, but that thou shouldest keep them from the evil one. They are not of the world even as I am not of the world. Sanctify them in the truth; thy word is truth. As thou didst send me into the world, even so send I them into the world. And for their sakes I sanctify myself, that they also may be sanctified in truth [...]; they are thine and all that are mine are thine, and thine are mine.[3]

Paradoxically Calvary is our Tabor of Transfiguration and Glory; there the cross strikes the rock and the place of the skull becomes the Word of the Spirit; there, too, 'to all who received him, who believed in his name, he gave power to become children of God; who were born, not of blood nor of the will of the flesh nor of the will of man, but of God.'[4] There again, 'all things were restored in Christ',[5] and old words, like old skins, were filled with new wine or meaning to communicate to all the new mystery or pasch. Here the death of Jesus, like the flesh and blood of the passover victim and covenant priest, is the transfiguration or revelation of the Christ of God: 'from the side of Christ as he slept the sleep of death upon the cross there came forth the wondrous sacrament of the whole Church.'[6] This sacramental and sacrificial death, full of mystery and life, is described by John as the 'tradition of the Spirit;'[7] and this *paradosis* or *traditio* is for the transfiguration of every traitor like Judas, *who handed him over*, in the wrong direction, when *spiritus mundi* was in power.[8]

The Spirit, Word and words of the Hebrew Bible had earlier begun a revelation and revolution in vernacular Greek: the word *doxa*, for example, with its root in *dokein*, the verb 'to seem', is made in the Septuagint to translate the *kabod*, or *glory* of the temple, with words of kindred meaning, like majesty and beauty, fused into a greater fullness. Adaptable in its ability to express every aspect of the Hebrew *kabod*, the Greek *doxa* also served to express the Aramaic *shekinah* or presence of the Word, and thus proved itself to be in a striking way both servant and master: submitting itself to the service of Jewish theology it presses a variety

---

3 Jn 17:1-19; also cf. Michael Ramsey, *The Glory of God and the Transfiguration of Christ*, London, 1949, p. 78.   4 Jn 1:12-14.   5 Eph 1:10.   6 Augustine, *Enarratio in Psalm 138*; cf. 'Constitution on the Sacred Liturgy,' 5, *Documents of Vatican II*, ed. Flannery, Dublin, 1975, p. 3.   7 Jn 19:30; in Greek, *paradoken to pneuma*; in Latin, *tradidit spiritum*.   8 Jn 18:2; in Greek, *Ioudas, o Paradidous*; in Latin, *Judas, qui tradebat eum*.

of Hebrew and Aramaic words and ideas into a unity of a new and massive conception. This transignification of words continues in the Gentile world as the Jewish scriptures were now made to express the mystery of Calvary. In this world of Christ and the Church, Greek first, and Latin later, became the new words of the Word made flesh, and the official languages of the Churches, East and West, in their scriptures, liturgies, theologies and everyday commerce.

Dante was the first in his time, after nearly a thousand years of the Vulgate, to raise the possibility of literature in the vernacular. For Dante the vernacular was the language of the hearth, and consequently a more vital form of communication than the Latin of the schools. But this primary use of language must not be confused with the vulgar or prosaic of the common, in dialect or commerce; on the contrary the vernacular of Dante would be 'illustrious, cardinal, courtly and curial [...], exalted by discipline and power and exalting its followers with honour and glory.'[9] Thus it would be for Dante to create for his Italy, divided in region and tongue, one vernacular from the fourteen he reckoned around; but that one must be 'brilliant, illuminated and illuminating [...], a chosen instrument, elegant, complete, polished and clear.' This service to the speech of the common people he would render 'under the inspiration of the Heavenly Word.'[10] The Divine Comedy would be his, their and our reward.[11]

Renaissance in words and Reformation in Word would do for the English vernacular what Dante did for Italian, and in addition something more. Dante did not ever consider the possibility of the vernacular as a sanctuary or sacred language; for him Greek and Latin would remain for the Church the languages of grace that Hebrew was for the Redeemer to protect him from the evil confusion of Babel! On the other hand, the Reformers in England created from their vernacular a *new* language for the sanctuary in the Prayer-Book of Cranmer and the scriptures of King James. This sanctuary vernacular inspired the 'power of the pulpit'[12] in English for two hundred years, and in its written form Jeremy Taylor was its master. For him, as for the Carolines with their Renaissance taste, the Reformation would become much more than a political protest; in the Caroline appeal to antiquity the spiritual or living tradition of the Cross would inspire the scriptural, patristic and liturgical renewal of the Church. But in the politics of the Restoration the protest would prevail.

In the *via media* of the Anglican position tradition, Catholic and Caroline, is a presence, sometimes more, sometimes less, in every age. In our century the poet T.S.

---

9 Dante, *De Vulgari Eloquentia*, 'Literature in the Vernacular' trans. S. Purcell, Manchester, 1981, p. 34.   10 Ibid., pp 34ff.   11 Ibid., p.15.   12 *The Cambridge History of English Literature*, ed. Ward and Waller, Cambridge, 1920, vol.7, 'Caroline Divines and Jeremy Taylor,' pp 162ff; vol. 4, pp 225-42; 'Prose and Poetry – The Power of the Pulpit,' and G. Saintsbury, *A Short History of English Literature*, London, 1920, pp 439ff.

Eliot confronted the perception of our times and the wasteland of our world with the Caroline tradition of the Word and its Spirit, decades before the four major constitutions of the Second Vatican Council on Christ, the Church, Worship and the World. Without the Catholic and Caroline theology of tradition as the gift of the Spirit, *spiritus mundi* remains, and there can be no renewal in either Renaissance, Reformation or Second Vatican Council. Indeed the vernacular can mean little else than the contamination of the sacred with the secular, and without Renaissance taste in art and architecture, music and language, our recent Reformation, or Vatican Council, remains a surface protest against our past. Even ecumenism is little more than a search for the lost sheep, who have strayed from our institutions; seldom, if ever, do we begin the dig for the treasure buried in the Caroline field!

In the last eclipse of the sun of the second millennium the event was experienced by millions along the *line of totality*, and on the television screen by millions more with small wonder and no fear. For those who believe in the *marvels* of revelation, the words of the Prologue withstood the test of time, and retained their power and their glory to transfigure and transform; 'the light shone in the darkness, and the darkness did not overcome it.' Nevertheless, in our scientific analysis, media reporting, and prosaic or vulgar description of the phenomenon there was no place for the Word and words of poet or priest, preacher or prophet; nor was there any recognition of 'the tradition of God's Holy Spirit' for the transfiguration of our words and world. But this tradition is Divine – Catholic, Caroline and classical in God's way; his Word cannot be buried, neither in the past nor in the present – *Verbum Dei non est alligatum*;[13] unlike the mystery of the eclipse his Word is our World's true light and life. So the questions remain – What is the Word? Wisdom or Folly? What is the World? Wonderland or Wasteland?

Today, as never before, our world is our wilderness or wasteland, and without the Word or Wisdom, our words are its dead letters or lifeless language. In this world of words, without even the shadow much less the substance of the Word, language has lost the capacity for truth. For George Steiner, the Jewish critic, the *Logos* or organon of language has broken in our mouths; for Catherine Pickstock, a new Anglican theologian, the *event* of transubstantiation in the Eucharist is the only condition of possibility for all human meaning: for her, language has meaning only in the liturgical order of being: otherwise life is without language, meaning or mystery.

It was not ever thus: in the *polis* or sacred city of the ancients, language or orality was the talk of the town or life of the city. So too in the Catholic sanctuaries of the early Christian centuries, the language spoken there was always in praise of the *Mystery*, read and proclaimed, celebrated and communicated. Likewise, the

---

13 2 Tim 2:9.

renewal in Caroline England of this *Catholicism* of the Fathers, Greek and Latin, was no less radical in its orthodoxy and was equally lasting in its achievements. The King James or Authorized Version of the Bible, the Book of Common Prayer that became for these High Churchmen a cherished Catholic liturgy, and their Offices of Morning Prayer and Evensong are still the purest forms of worship to be found But the *Power of the Pulpit* in words as in Word, alone among their achievements, is now no more.

In his prose and preaching Jeremy Taylor belongs to that world that was, but as *the Shakespeare of English Prose* and *the Chyrsostom of English Preaching* his *beauty and truth* remain classical and eternal. Still the need to cut the prose of the preacher, or poetry of the bard, like the cloth to measure, is a feature of our times, and in this edition of sermons no more than half his words remain to express the Word of God. Certainly *beauty* is diminished in this loss of Taylor's words; but in the truth of the Word nothing is lost. The structure of each sermon as a whole has been preserved and as far as possible the magic of his sound. Nevertheless, elision and ellipsis, truncation and fragmentation, abound in this new and abridged edition; however, *the Word of God cannot be bound down*, either with or without the words of man; indeed, even on this earth, the *kingdom of God is not in words but in power*.[14]

In the Heber-Eden edition of Taylor's *Collected Works*,[15] not readily available today, his sermons are included in all their fullness *in words* and *in power*. On the other hand, the selection in this new edition is no random collection of Taylor's Sunday sermons but a structural reflection of his sacramental mind in praise of the *Mystery*, or Eternal Word, as heard in creation, in Christ, in scripture and in man. Accordingly, there is in Taylor's mode of knowing a clear distinction between poetic and biblical perception, and in the biblical liturgical awareness there are mystical, ascetical, doctrinal and moral dimensions. Even the Panegyric is in praise of the *Mystery*, as words and Word are his Beauty and his Truth – all on earth there is to know and all one needs to know!

The subtitle *Jeremy Taylor in His Prose and Preaching Today* was proposed by the late H.R. McAdoo, former Church of Ireland archbishop of Dublin, co-chairman of ARCIC 1 and still foremost of Caroline scholars, to complement his own sacramental work on *The Eucharistic Theology of Jeremy Taylor Today*, and to

---

14 1 Cor 4:20.   **15** The Taylor texts in this work are, except for minor adjustments in punctuation, from *The Whole Works of the Right Reverend Jeremy Taylor, DD, with a Life of the Author*, ed. Reginald Heber and Charles Page Eden, 10 vols., London 1847-52 and are cited as Taylor, followed by volume and page numbers. For notes on different editions of Taylor's Works see T.K. Carroll, *Jeremy Taylor: Selected Works*, New York, 1990, p. 80.

situate both within the ecumenical dialogue. In Taylor's understanding of sacramental representation, as in Dom Odo Casel's theory of the mystery-presence in the ritual, the sacrament was manifestly the visibility or corporality of the Word, while the Word was equally the invisibility or mystery of the sacrament. As a phrase *word and sacrament* must always be felt in its inmost unity, for in the sacramental order of being words and deeds are intrinsically intertwined and interwoven as natural symbols of revelation and faith. Henry McAdoo, like Jeremy Taylor, was by nature and grace an ecumenist in this sacramental way of hearing or knowing the Word of God:

> And so long as we know God only in the ways of man, by contentious learning, by arguing and dispute, we see nothing but the shadow of Him, and in that shadow we meet with many dark appearances, little certainty, and much conjecture. But when we know Him with the eyes of holiness, and the intuition of gracious experience, with a quiet spirit and the peace of enjoyment, then we shall hear what we never heard and see what our eyes never saw: then the mysteries of Godliness shall be opened unto us and clear as the windows of the morning.[16]

In dedicating this volume to the memory of Harry McAdoo I am no less mindful of his wife, Leslie, and our feasts of reason and flow of soul for over thirty years. In a particular way I am grateful to Michael Adams of the Four Courts Press whose prompt consideration and acceptance of my work was a consolation for the distinguished author of the Foreword the day before he died. Sincere thanks to June Gilleran and Maureen O'Driscoll, who prepared my manuscripts with great haste and greater skill, that I might finish the work, so to speak, within the appointed time; my thanks also to Father Mark Bennett, while still our deacon, for his careful preparation of every footnote and detail.

Already the spirit of ecumenism is abroad in all the Churches in a rich and wonderful way; for many years I have enjoyed the facilities of the Church Body Representative Library in Dublin, and in a very special way the friendship of the Librarian, Dr Ray Refaussé, and his staff. Similarly in Rome I have been made at home in the Anglican Centre since its foundation, and never more so than recently as I corrected there these Taylor proofs.

Finally, my deep and abiding gratitude to every friend and home caller – those domestic prelates of our household, many and varied, male and female, whose words and deeds in symbols, as in sacraments, keep fresh and well in its being that wonderful fullness of spirit and truth that is both Caroline and Catholic.

---

16 Taylor, vol. 8, p. 379.

Foreword

H.R. McADOO

Just as all preachers are not theologians so not all theologians are preachers. The truism leaves the realm of the platitudinous and becomes a realised truth for those who read and digest these sermons. For not only is Jeremy Taylor a theologian who can preach, as perceptive in the inspirational management of words and imagery as he is discerning in the observational assessment of the varieties of human experience. More than this, he is a teacher of spirituality whose primary and constant concern is with Christian practice, with believing and behaving. Mystery and sacramentality are at the heart of his religion but practicality is the form of it, and the recreation of the personality through grace, the *kainé ktisis*, its immediate objective. The ultimate goal is the unitive way, 'a prayer of quietness and silence [...], an immediate entry into an orb of light.'[1] These are sermons about being a Christian: 'Christianity is all for practice; make religion to be the business of our lives.'[2] Even in his funeral sermon for Primate Bramhall, Taylor insists that 'the inquiry here is, whether we are to be Christians or no? whether we are to live good lives or no?' This is the golden thread woven throughout his entire output. Dr Carroll has rightly divided his selection under different headings by way of help to the reader as he enters the mind and the world of Jeremy Taylor. To this necessary process of illustrative selection I would venture to add a footnote for the further understanding of Taylor as Minister of the Word. There appear to me to be two unifying factors in all these sermons and indeed in all his preaching. To appreciate this will be to concur with the judgment of his friend George Rust that 'those excellent discourses' are not only (as he says) brilliant, clear and profound but of 'general usefulness to all the purposes of a Christian' for 'it is not enough to believe aright, but we must practise accordingly.'[3]

The two factors which I would discern as giving its substance and distinctive colour to Taylor's preaching and to his writings generally are so interwoven as to be virtually one element. Their interaction is so mutual and reciprocal that they mesh together in a common purpose: 'Make religion our business.'[4]

---

[1] J. Taylor, *Works*, vol. 2, p. 139. [2] Ibid., vol. 8, p. 364. [3] Ibid., vol. 1, p. cccxxvi. [4] Ibid., vol. 4, p. 573.

The first factor is Taylor's widely and deeply pervasive moral/ascetic theology which is everywhere in these sermons. We recall that the Anglican name for it was *'practical divinity.'* Great though his range in theology is, as witness the variety of areas investigated from *Episcopacy Asserted* to the *Real Presence*, I would hold that first and foremost and in spite of the great ability and wide learning which he displays throughout his whole theological synthesis, Jeremy Taylor is before everything else a moral/ascetical theologian. It is not simply that he himself believed, as did his friend and successor George Rust, that his *Ductor Dubitantium* would 'alone [...] give its author immortality' (in which, of course, he was mistaken). Rather is it that the thinking, the aims, the concerns and the objective of moral/ascetical theology constitute the framework and create the context within which other subjects are viewed and expounded, whether it be *The Great Exemplar* or his eucharistic writings with their recurrent emphasis on 'Christ, who is our life.' Indeed, the clue to his thinking is given, were such needed, in the full titles, *The Great Exemplar of Sanctity and Holy Life according to the Christian Institution* and *The Worthy Communicant, or A Discourse of the Nature, Effects and Blessings consequent to the worthy receiving of the Lord's Supper*. For all the time it is Christian practice, believing and behaving, which is central to his thought and to his exposition. 'I have chosen,' Taylor wrote in the dedication of *The Great Exemplar,* 'to serve the purposes of religion by doing assistance to that part of theology, which is *wholly practical*; that which makes us wiser, therefore, because it makes us better.' Again, in the preface, he insists 'My great purpose, is to advance the necessity, and to declare the manner and parts of a good life.' The preface continues in a vein of moral theology which in places plainly foreshadows his major works yet to come in this field, *Unum Necessarium* and *Ductor Dubitantium*. What we have in *The Great Exemplar* is a melding of a Life of Christ with a related exposition of moral/ascetical theology. It is the work of one whose spirituality is profoundly sacramentalist and rich with affective devotion to Christ in his Sacred Humanity but whose realism and acute perception of the human condition completely justify the contemporary description 'practical divinity.'

In the same way, *The Worthy Communicant* merges eucharistic theology and moral/ascetical theology in a single form of preparation: 'Every worthy communicant must prepare himself by a holy life, by mortification of all his sins, by the acquisition of all Christian graces; and this is not the work of a day or a week.' 'Every time we receive the holy sacrament [...] we mend our pace,' he writes, linking the Christian's growing up into Christ with the regular reception of the blessed sacrament: 'Because, in the holy communion, we are growing up to the measures of the fulness of Christ, we can no otherwise be fitted to it, but by the progressions and increase of a man, that is, by the habits of grace and states and permanencies of religion.'[5]

5 Ibid., vol. 8, p.160; also cf. pp 44ff.

The fact is that Taylor, Robert Sanderson and others created a new kind of moral/ascetical theology through a deliberate fusing into one instrument of what had previously been reckoned and handled as two distinct instruments, moral theology and ascetic theology. In so doing they anticipated the twentieth-century reforms begun and continued by Gilleman, Häring, Fuchs, McDonagh, Waddams and others.

An inventory of these modern reforms reveals how they are anticipated in the Caroline reconstruction.[6] Today's view of the science, as reflected in Häring's 'We understand moral theology as the doctrine of the imitation of Christ' and in Waddams' 'moral theology is basically dealing with our life as it is lived in union with Christ', is identical with the Caroline concept of 'practical divinity.' In a sentence, Kevin Kelly's comment on Sanderson sums up the Anglican objective: 'For him moral theology is the science of Christian living.'[7]

What the Anglicans were doing was re-siting moral theology within the *kerygma*, the totality of the Gospel. It became therefore a moral theology of the new law, the new life and the new creature. Inevitably and in consequence it meshes inseparably with the second factor which I would discern as basic to Taylor's preaching and teaching, namely, the distinctive spirituality nurtured by Anglicanism with its constant emphasis on the *kaine ktisis*. The Anglican divines saw it as a moral theology of the kingdom, dealing with response and responsibility in discipleship. Its concern is with the Christian-in-the Church, with growth into personal maturity in the new life. Repentance and faith, twinned together as a constant in Anglican liturgy and spirituality, are of the essence in this, as Taylor, speaking for them all, stresses in *Unum Necessarium*: 'repentance is a whole state of the new life, an entire change of the sinner.' There is an emphasis too on the individual's responsibility for his own actions. But if every man is encouraged to be his own casuist, Taylor, and indeed Sanderson, Sharp and Baxter, all advise seeking spiritual guidance on occasion. Taylor proposes, 'I intend to offer to the world a general instrument of moral theology, by the rules and measures of which [...] men that are wise may guide themselves in all their proportions of conscience: but if their case be indeed involved, they need the conduct of a spiritual guide.'[8] It could be described as a Christocentric moral/ascetical theology dealing as it does with the imitation of Christ, with incorporation in Christ through the Word and Sacrament, so that the new life is both a gift and a quest. It is given in the baptismal gift of membership. It is realised, nurtured and striven for, through grace, in discipleship.

One can see why for Jeremy Taylor moral theology thus structured is 'the life of Christianity' and 'the life of religion'.[9] Sanderson's definition sums it all up: 'But

---

[6] P. Elmen, ed. *The Anglican Moral Choice*, Wilton Ct., 1983, cf. pp 34-7.   [7] K. Kelly, *Conscience, Dictator or Guide? A Study in Seventeenth Century English Protestant Theology*, London, 1967.   [8] J. Taylor, vol. 9 (Preface), p. xix.   [9] Ibid., vol. 7 (Preface) pp 7-20.

when all is done, positive and practical Divinity is it must bring us to Heaven: that is, it must poise our judgments, settle our consciences, direct our lives, mortify our corruptions, increase our graces, strengthen our comforts, save our souls [...]. There is no study to this, none so well worth the labour as this, none that can bring so much profit to others, nor therefore so much glory to God, nor therefore so much comfort to our own hearts as this.'[10]

Wilkins later borrowed the definition without acknowledgment and indeed it was the understanding of moral theology which became part of the Anglican ethos and to this transformation of the subject Jeremy Taylor was a major contributor. Martin Thornton put it in a single sentence: 'This Caroline method produced the integrated science of moral/ascetical theology, the art of full co-operation with grace, in a total Christian life. It emphasised progress towards perfection rather than keeping on the right side of the law.'[11] Taylor himself saw the close link between moral theology and the preaching office. In the introduction to *Ductor Dubitantium* he insists that preachers may retrench infinite numbers of cases of conscience if they will more earnestly preach and exhort to simplicity and love; for the want of these is the great multiplier of cases.

I have dwelt on this element in his preaching because of my conviction that no understanding of Jeremy Taylor as Minister of the Word is possible apart from it. Throughout Dr Carroll's representative choice of sermons we meet with it time and again: 'So in the new creation, Christ [...] intends to conform us to his image [...]; by the spirit of a new life we are made new creatures, capable of a new state [...]; we have new affections, new understandings, new wills.'[12] In a way, that says it all but the whole of that second Whitsunday sermon is a delineation of this moral/ascetical theology at work, as the Spirit creates in us 'a new principle, a new life [...] in all holiness and justice and sobriety.' The first Whitsunday sermon relates the 'new creature' to duty and to discipline but also to 'a certain joy and spiritual rejoicing,' for as a result of these graces this is 'another operation of the new birth.' To this end 'the consecrated and mysterious elements' are received so that men may be 'partakers of the divine nature' and so 'must dwell in Christ, and Christ in them.'[13]

The fact is that in the great majority of the sermons printed here the theme in one form or another is the out-working of the new nature or new birth in Christian practice. Whether he is preaching on prudence or patience, grace or sin; whether he is instructing the clergy or clerical students or the laity, Taylor wants to see us all 'transformed into a new nature'.[14] All the time, he is a moral theologian, not a moralist, for grace matches duty, and prayer and sacrament are the means to 'living

---

10 Sanderson, R.; cf. *Works* (ed. W. Jacobsen), vol. 3 *Sermons*, Oxford, 1854.   11 M. Thornton, *English Spirituality*, London, 1963, p. 239.   12 J. Taylor, vol. 4, p. 347.   13 Ibid., p. 332.   14 Ibid., p. 347.

such a life as Jesus taught, for this is [...] this new birth, the recovery of our nature'.[15] Constantly one is struck by Taylor's perceptiveness in respect of the varieties of the human experience. He is alive to the subtleties, the hindrances, the flawed motivations, the hopes and the difficulties of being human and seeking to be Christian. Probably he would not have recognised the term 'psychology' but in reality Taylor's sermons reveal genuine psychological insight, as, for example, those dealing with growth in grace and with sins of infirmity,[16] just as it is to be seen in the section on 'purity of intention' in *Holy Living*.

As his chief concern is with Christian practice so he is consequently concerned with the form this practice takes, the spirituality which clothes and enables it. It is a spirituality so profoundly influenced by this integrated science of moral/ascetical theology, it becomes virtually one by reason of the one goal: 'he that is grown in grace is not at ease but when doing the works of the new man'.[17] It is a distinctive spirituality, this Anglican piety of which Taylor is but one exponent for it is everywhere, moulded by the Book of Common Prayer, in the extensive devotional literature of the century. Elsewhere, I have characterised it as a spirituality of the five Ds – *devotion, duty, discipline, detail and doctrine*.[18] It is a sacramental spirituality, strong, even demanding, but with a warmth and richness of devotion and yet governed by Taylor's 'live by rule' and motivated by 'the walking in newness of life.' It is a piety for everyday use but it is neither earthbound nor moralistic, making much of meditation, of private prayer and of daily church-going. Faith and repentance are its twin foundations and sincere obedience to the law of love its goal, for its emphasis on duty depends on the Prayer Book Catechism's insistence that our duty to God and to the neighbour are each a duty to love. These two duties can only be performed, says the Catechism, with 'diligent prayer'and through 'special grace.'

This is the kind of spirituality which is both implicit and explicit in these sermons. To promote it is, for Taylor, one of the chief functions of the Ministry of the Word. Throughout these examples of his preaching we are made aware of these elements in this spirituality and all the time they are being linked in a sort of reciprocal causation with 'the new life,' 'the new creature,' 'the new possibility,' 'the new birth,' 'the new nature:' 'a man that is in a state of grace, who is born anew of the Spirit, that is regenerate by the Spirit of Christ, he is led by the Spirit, he lives in the Spirit, he does the works of God cheerfully, habitually, vigorously; and although he sometimes slips, yet it is but seldom, it is in small instances.'[19] The effects of this new life are visible, says Taylor, 'in all holiness and justice and sobriety.'[20] This reflection of Titus 2:12 is mirrored in the General Confession of the Prayer Book and

---

15 Ibid., p. 132. 16 Ibid.; cf. pp 496-506, 520-32, and 331-42 17 Ibid., p. 355. 18 H.R. McAdoo, *Anglican Heritage: Theology & Spirituality*, Norwich, 1991, p. 61. 19 J. Taylor, vol. 4, p. 355. 20 Ibid., vol. 4, p. 348.

in the overall structure of *Holy Living* and other popular devotional works of the period such as *The Whole Duty of Man*.

We can detect a certain austerity linked with an understanding of man's situation when Taylor says, 'It is true there is flesh and blood in every regenerate man, but they do not both rule: the flesh is left to tempt, but not to prevail.' No habitual sin can be excused as a sin of infirmity and the strength of a temptation is no excuse 'if it leaves the understanding still able to judge.' Sins of infirmity which must be 'small in their instance' must arise from an inculpable ignorance of our duty or a weakness of principle or a genuine inability to discern. But he grants that little unavoidable instances or faultless ignorance are 'always the allays of the life of the best men and for these Christ hath paid, and they are never to be accounted to good men, save only to make them more wary and more humble.' All the time, the Christian can rejoice because 'Christ is his pattern and support and religion is his employment.'[21] Taylor's overall rubric is 'Let us strictly follow a rule' in spite of what he calls 'the contradiction' when we 'pray against it and yet do it.'[22]

The second sermon on 'the flesh and the Spirit' is typical in the way in which it indissolubly links with 'the new nature:' *doctrine*, 'a firm belief [...] in the promises of the Gospel,' *duty*, 'if he perseveres in his duty,' *devotion*, 'The second great remedy of our evil nature [...], *discipline*, 'be [...] severe in our counsels,' and *detailed observance*, 'long for the day of communion and be pleased with holy meditation.'[23]

Perhaps it is enough by way of conclusion to remind the reader that this type of spirituality with its five characteristic emphases will be encountered everywhere in these sermons. Indeed Taylor himself tells us how we should hear and read sermons: men should come 'as to a school where virtue is taught and exercised, and none come but such as put themselves under *discipline*, and intend to grow wiser, and more virtuous to appease their passion [...] to have their faith established, and their hope confirmed, and their charity enlarged. They that are otherwise affected, do not do their *duty*'.[24] This distinctive spirituality he expresses with beauty and realism in the observation and perception of what it means to be human and striving through grace to be a practising Christian: 'Men, now-a-days, love not a religion that will cost them dear.'[25]

The inaccessibility of Taylor's works to the general reader today, *Holy Living* excepted, has meant that a great treasure has lain partly buried. By giving us this volume of sermons, showing Taylor as minister of the Word, as by his earlier book, *Jeremy Taylor: Selected Works* (1990), illustrating Taylor's basic theological synthesis, Dr Carroll has given us the opportunity of once more making creative and effective use of our inheritance. This is a large benefaction and Anglicans have every reason to be profoundly grateful for the gift.

21 Ibid.   22 Ibid., pp 408 and 419.   23 Ibid., cf. pp 132-5.   24 Ibid., p. 328.   25 Ibid., vol. 8, p. 372.

INTRODUCTION

Biblical and Poetic Perception

WORD AND WORDS

On a Good Friday retreat with a hundred others I heard a monk tell of his dark night and the search for light which brought him back to the world and words of man – those poems that were and are begotten and made outside the monastery, its sanctuary, and its light. Poets' souls, as a poet said, 'Are nearer to the surface of the body / Than souls that start no game and turn no rhyme.' In other words, poetic language brings into the clear light of day those dark secrets of the night that remain buried in the conscious or unconscious depths of lesser mortals. But can the poet speak from out the depths of his own being a word *of truth* that will make us free in the very depths of our own being? Can the poet grace, or redeem, our natures with his gift?

> I say that a Djinn spoke. A live-long hour
> She seemed the learned man and I the child;
> Truths without father came, truths that no book
> Of all the uncounted books that I have read,
> Nor thought out of her mind or mine begot,
> Self-born, high-born, and solitary truths,
> Those terrible implacable straight lines
> Drawn through the wandering vegetative dream.[1]

In spite of the theme of the retreat – 'Silence, the Empty Tomb and Poetry' – in the afternoon of that Good and Holy Day, the Gospel words of John about the trials and death of Jesus Christ were nonetheless felt and lived by all in the sanctuary of that monastery in a different sort of way. In that sacred space and for that sacred time I, for one, forgot the words of the poet, but I wondered much and marvelled more about the words of the prophet Isaiah; in the liturgy of that day, they preceded the proclamation of the Passion, as they had preceded in the history and worship of Israel the deadly deed of Golgotha, to reveal in greater

---

[1] W.B. Yeats, *The Poems: A New Edition*, ed. R.J. Finneran, New York, 1983: 'The Gift of Harun Al-Rashid,' pp 443ff.

depth, but in different detail, the mystery hidden, *once and for all*, in that darkest hour of history:

> He was despised and rejected by men; a man of sorrows, and acquainted with grief; and as one from whom men hide their faces he was despised, and we esteemed him not. Surely he has borne our griefs and carried our sorrows; yet we esteemed him stricken, smitten by God, and afflicted. But he was wounded for our transgressions, he was bruised for our iniquities; upon him was the chastisement that made us whole, and with his stripes we are healed. All we like sheep have gone astray; we have turned every one to his own way; and the Lord has laid on him the iniquity of us all; he was oppressed and afflicted; like a lamb that is led to the slaughter, and like a sheep that before its shearers is dumb, so he opened not his mouth.[2]

In the quiet peace of that paschal evening and night there was felt in that place a world of difference between the wisdom and words of the poet and the Word and words of the prophet. As in *The Gift of Harun Al-Rashid* the poetic truths of *night and light and the half-light* come from the *vegetative dream*, and great poets know this bodily origin of the soul's light: 'My lantern is too loyal not to show / That it was made in your great father's reign.' But the prophet's candle's bright, like the Dawn of Easter Day, comes from above to awaken in the soul the *gift* or grace of the Spirit; furthermore it penetrates the depths of darkness and death where no mortal one can live or see or hear, and brings to light and life the terrible reality or Word of God, really and truly present, in the long and lonesome silence of our Holy and Dreadful Sabbath in Hell:

> I descended as low as being casts its shadows; I looked into the abyss, and cried, 'Father, where are you?' But I heard only the everlasting ungovernable storm [...]. I looked from the unmeasurable world to the eye of God [...]; an empty socket without foundation stared back at me [...]. And Eternity rested on the chaos, gnawing at it ruminating.[3]

The centrality of the crucifixion, in the Easter season, as the revelation of a mystery ever present in the liturgical cycle of the years, more than an event of history vaguely remembered with the passage of time, was in art, architecture, music and words the inspiration of Western civilization, but in the sacred liturgy it is the Word that makes the symbol sacramental. Every work of art, written text

---

2 Is 53:3-7 RSV.   3 Romanos; cf. Von Balthasar, *Mysterium Paschale*, Edinburgh, 1990, p. 51.

or score of music incarnates a real presence of significant being, and its mystery is experienced whenever a melody comes to inhabit us, or a poem or passage of prose to engage us and to seize us: 'to be indwelt by music, art and literature in this way [...] is to experience the commonplace mystery of a real presence in that excess of significance [...] we call the symbol or agency of transparence.' But in the sacramental order of being, visible only to the eyes of faith, it is the biblical Word alone that takes us beyond our words into those heights and depths, the above and the below, that no earthly symbol can make real or communicate.

> The Lord God will swallow up death for ever and will wipe away tears from all faces, and the reproach of his people he will take away from all the earth; for the Lord has spoken. On that day it will be said 'Lo, this is our God; we have waited for him, that he might save us. This is the Lord; we have waited for him; let us be glad and rejoice in his salvation.'[4]

This vision of the *Word of the Cross* as the heart of the world, called by the theologian Hans Urs von Balthasar the theological *a priori*, and by his critics the Catholic standpoint, became for him his theology of literature. In the strict sense there can, of course, be no such person as a Catholic writer, and no Catholic standpoint as such, but there are those like Dante, and lesser mortals of the *renouveau catholique* like Peguy and Bernanos, who live and write in the reality or world that the *Word of the Cross* has expanded and enlightened. This space is also shared by writers of different visions and persuasions: in their different ways and varying degrees they too live between the Light's centre and those outer fringes that only gradually disappear into the total darkness of the extremities:

> Hear the voice of the Bard,
>   Who present, past and future sees;
> Whose ears have heard
> The Holy Word
>   That walked among the ancient trees.
>
> Calling the lapsed soul
>   And weeping in the evening dew;
> That might control
> The starry pole,
>   And fallen, fallen light renew.

[4] Is 25:7-9.

> 'O Earth, O Earth, return!
>   Arise from out the dewy grass;
> Night is worn,
> And the norm
>   Rises from the slumberous mass.
>
> 'Turn away no more;
> Why wilt thou turn away?
> The starry floor.
> The watery shore
>   Is given thee till the break of day.'[5]

Poets like Blake were already voicing their fears about the future of poetry in the new world structure of Newtonian physics, as Kant too had expressed his anxiety about philosophy with his infamous separation of man and the world, and his subsequent canonization of man. Blake, on the other hand, was content to state his case for the poet's *double vision* in a few poetic lines which perceives *an old man grey* with an *inward eye* much more than a mere sense perception of a *thistle across the way*. The *old man grey* is clearly an aspect of Blake himself, and stands for the fact that whatever we perceive is a part of us and forms an identity with us. When such perception takes place, the whole world is humanized; indeed, there must always be something human about an object, alien as it may at first appear, to which the perceiver is relating. This is the *double vision* or *fourfold* about which Blake speaks, although it is essentially twofold in contrast to the scientific view from which he prays to be delivered:

> For double the vision my eyes doth see,
> And a double vision is always with me,
> With my inward eye 'tis an old man grey,
> With my outward a thistle along the way.
>
> 'Tis fourfold in my supreme delight,
> And threefold in soft Beulah's night,
> And twofold always. May God us keep,
> From single vision and Newton's sleep.[7]

Unlike Blake in his sanctuary of biblical being, Hoffmannsthal, a young German poet of promise in the 1890s, fell suddenly silent in the Vienna Circle of

---

[5] W. Blake, *Complete Writings*, ed. Geoffrey Keynes, Oxford, 1972, p. 210; cf. his letters to Thomas Butts with reference to the double vision, pp 816-19.   [6] Ibid., p. 818.   [7] Ibid.

his European mainland with its endless analysis of words, words, words. Then doubt was cast on the adequacy or accuracy of language to communicate the truth of human experience, and the infectious nature of every word that is, has been, or ever will be, written or spoken was underscored. This New World crisis in language or words, as in God or the gods, installed self-consciousness as the immanent centre of real being, and condemned language to the depths of that interior darkness. At this very time, the poet William Butler Yeats was coming of age, and safe and secure on the island reality of his Celtic myth and twilight, as in his use of biblical and poetic language, was confidently confronting this darkness of man's own making with the divine light or twilight of his God or gods, their power in his every word:

> All the words that I gather
> And all the words that I write
> Must spread out their wings untiring
> And never cease in their flight
> Till they come where your sad sad heart is
> And sing to you in the night
> Beyond where the waters are moving
> Storm darkened or starry bright.[8]

Whatever the significance in these few lines should be of the *night*, the *Beyond*, the *Storm* or the *star*, in the biblical and poetic tradition of Blake and Yeats, the Easter break of day, brightness and breeze remains the revelation in history, even now, of the divine mystery that it was, even then, for those first witnesses, who had the eyes to see and the ears to hear. Without this presence of the Word or Action, that was in the beginning to separate light from darkness and in the tomb to bring life to death, there is neither mystery nor meaning in sacred scripture, nor rhyme nor reason in the secular feast. Like a biblical fundamentalist or historical critic, who search and research the empty tomb for angels or bones, philosopher and poet can likewise hide in their platonic cave, as the one *terms* the universality of evil a problem, and the other *recycles* at will the words of the sacred scriptures, once they are emptied of their Word. Thus the poet has nothing to say to the *Silence* in that *Tomb* and less than nothing to do about its *Emptiness*; he may, of course, articulate in his words all the human questions he can, but only God the Father, in his Word and Spirit, can give the Divine Answer that He alone can be.

In our new experience of mystery and meaning, or rather in the substantive absence of both, the death of man as man completes and compliments the death

---

[8] Yeats, op. cit., 'Where My Books Go'; not included in many editions; cf. the 'Additional Poems', p. 529.

of God as God. Here again is the problem of the real absence of the Word of God that should be a real presence in the words of man; without this Word that *was in the beginning*, before time began, to separate light from darkness, and *is now and ever shall be*, till the end of time, to enlighten those *who sit in darkness and in the shadow of death*, poets, or makers of forms, are searching for the living among the dead. In those circumstances there is no contact between Christianity and culture, scripture and literature, theology and philosophy, for God is dead and man is dead.

For Yeats this turning point in time and thought was his *widening gyre* of confusion in a world without centre or Word: as *things fall apart* and as *anarchy* gives rise to a tide of blood, the *innocence* and *conviction* of the *best* gives way to the *passionate intensity* of the worst. Like a prophet of doom our greatest poet read the signs of his times, and his poem *The Second Coming*, an apocalypse in the images and words of the scriptures without their Word, brings to light, so to speak, this darkness and its hour:

> Surely some Revelation is at hand;
> Surely the Second Coming is at hand.
> The Second Coming! Hardly are those words out
> When a vast image out of *Spiritus Mundi*
> Troubles my sight: somewhere in sands of the desert
> A shape with lion body and the head of a man,
> A gaze blank and pitiless as the sun,
> Is moving its slow thighs, while all about it
> Reel shadows of the indignant desert birds.
> The darkness drops again; but now I know
> That twenty centuries of stony sleep
> Were vexed to nightmare by a rocking cradle,
> And what rough beast, its hour come round at last,
> Slouches towards Bethlehem to be born?[9]

As a theme 'Silence, the Empty Tomb and Poetry' can be stating no more than the division of all Gaul or, at best, admitting the silence of the poet at the empty tomb of Christian revelation today. But in our secular society critics, in their piety, may sometimes confuse the poet's gift with the mystic's grace: for example, the poet who sees 'Mass-going feet crushing the wafer ice on the potholes' may be wrongly considered as the Angelic Doctor of the Christian faith who relished 'beneath the twofold sign, symbols of the gifts divine:'[10] nor indeed does geo-

---

9 Ibid, p. 187.   10 Aquinas; cf. the Lauda Sion sequence of the Corpus Christi feast.

graphical or historical knowledge of Clonmacnois make one a Christian any more than the experience of Stonehenge should make one a pious pagan. Homer was a poet and not a mystic, and Yeats may have simply been lamenting the death of the poet's gods when he saw 'a staring virgin stand / Where holy Dionysus died,/ And tear the heart out of his side,/ And lay the heart upon her hand / And bear that beating heart away:' without the gods the poet was left 'to sing of Magnus Annus at the spring,' and since then nothing has been 'more beautiful than spring.'[11]

For Yeats biblical language, like the poetic language of Homer, has its own power apart from its revealed mystery. Like Vico he is much aware of the passing of Troy and Rome, but in keeping with his theory of history he may well be blaming the event of Christianity for the destruction of Greek civilization: at the same time the force for change seems to come from within and not from without; perhaps from below, certainly not from above: 'Whatever flames upon the night / Man's own resinous heart has fed.' Indeed, in retrospect, man would seem to be the measure of all that he is, and yet at the same time no more than the psalmist thought him to be: 'Everything that man esteems / Endures a moment or a day.' Word and words! 'What is man, O Lord, that you are mindful of him?' for 'The painter's brush consumes his dreams'[12] and again, 'O Lord, what is man that thou dost regard him?' for 'Love's pleasure drives his love away:'[13]

> In pity for man's darkening thought
> He walked that room and issued thence
> In Galilean turbulence;
> The Babylonian starlight brought
> A fabulous, formless darkness in;
> Odour of blood when Christ was slain
> Made all Platonic tolerance vain
> And vain all Doric discipline.[14]

Poetry may make nothing happen, as another poet suggests, and may be more an expression of our times than an influence upon them, but the poetic vision cannot be denied, and in this century the worst fears of our best poets have been verified, and are visible in the ordinary signs of our culture and audible in the rhetoric of our social and political order; 'political rhetoric, the tidal mendacity of journalism and the mass media have made of everything modern urban men and women say or hear or read an empty jargon, a cancerous loquacity. Language has lost the very capacity

---

11 Yeats, op. cit., 'Two Songs from a Play', p. 213.   12 Cf. Ps 8:4.   13 Cf. Ps 144:3.   14 Yeats, op. cit., p. 213.

for truth: it has marketed and mass-marketed its mysteries of prophetic intuition and operates self-doubtingly on the sharp edge of silence; it were as if the quintessential, the identifying attribute of man – *the Logos* – the organon of language had broken in our mouths.'[15]

What is the word

folly –
folly for to –
for to –
what is the word –
folly from this –
all this –
folly from all this –
given –
folly given all this –
seeing –
folly seeing all this –
what is the word –
this this –
this this here –
all this this here –
folly given all this –
seeing –
folly seeing all this this here –
for to –
what is the word –
see –
glimpse –
seem to glimpse –
need to seem to glimpse –
folly for to need to seem to glimpse –
what –
what is the word –
and where –
folly for to need to seem to glimpse what –
where –
what is the word –

[15] G. Steiner, *Real Presences*, Cambridge, 1986, p. 5.

there –
over there –
away over there –
afar –
afar away over there –
afaint –
afaint afar away over there what –
what –
what is the word –
seeing all this –
all this this –
all this this here –
folly for to see what –
glimpse –
seem to glimpse –
need to seem to glimpse –
afaint afar away over there what –
folly for to need to seem to glimpse
    afaint afar away over there what –
what –
what is the word –
what is the word –[16]

Here Beckett seems to have run full circle: the primeval darkness of *Genesis*, that was in the beginning, is now or *drops again*, and one wonders shall it ever be world or words without end! Western literature, from Homer to Eliot, has always addressed itself to either the presence or absence of the gods or the God. Every great artist has had Jacob as his model wrestling with creative power and Job as his patron to sustain him in the dark night of his soul or effort: 'I am God, said Matisse, when he had finished painting the chapel at Vence; God, the other craftsman, said Picasso in open rivalry.' But today, however, our darkness is different, as Steiner goes on:

> indeed it may well be that modernism can best be defined as that form of music, art and literature which no longer experiences God as a competitor, a predecessor or an antagonist; in fact, there may well be in atonal [...] music, in non-representational art, in certain modes of surrealist, automatic, concrete

---

16 S. Beckett; cf. J. Calder, *As the Story Was Told. The Uncollected and Late Prose of Samuel Beckett*, New York, 1990, pp 131-4.

writing, a sort of shadow-boxing. Form would now seem to be the only adversary of the modern artist; the sovereign challenger as creator is gone; and God is dead in our day to day living.[17]

This preoccupation with form as the exclusive matter of modern art began to be in the philosophy of Immanuel Kant (d.1804) whose 'empty forms of the understanding' were imposed *a priori* on the given of the senses or on our *a posteriori* perceptions. Thus Kant's conviction that the thing in itself, the ultimate reality out there, could not be analytically defined, let alone be articulated, led quite naturally to the dissociation of designation from perception, and ultimately to that separation of language from reality, which is our peculiar crisis. In literature Mallarmé was first to seize upon this separation in philosophy of words and world, and to create his own world of words in which the texture and odour of the rose was fixed in the word and its verbal associations and not in some fiction of external correspondence. Afterwards there came and went Rimbaud to make form and structure in words, or form pure and simple, the core of all reality. Thus poetic discourse became in itself a literal construction, or animation, for the endless unfolding of conceptual possibilities, and 'replaced that *Adamic conceit*, or *naming of the world*, which is the primal myth and metaphor of all Western theories of language.'[18]

This separation in poetry and poetics of words and world, or subversion and rejection of any naive correspondence between the written or spoken word and the empirical word or reality, was shortly afterwards accentuated and intensified by the beginnings and development of psychoanalysis. In particular the Freudian emphasis on the unfathomable and deepest structures, or substructures, of the nocturnal and the subconscious, put meaning in chaos or in perpetual motion, and put ultimate or final meaning, the Light of the Word, beyond every realm of possibility. Philosophy too, at the turn of the century, especially logical positivism, and linguistic analysis to a lesser extent, excluded the world from their consideration of words as truth and meaning, and distinguished between the *clear and distinct* words, or truth-functions, of grammar and science and the make-believe words of poetry, or myth and metaphor.

Positivism, in this strict sense, holds that there is nothing in human experience about which one must be silent, and that the effable, or that about which one can speak, is all that matters in life: hence in the name of logic their endeavour to purge language of its metaphysical impurities and of its facile phantasms of unexamined inference. Wittgenstein, on the other hand, was more philosophic in a metaphysical way, and believed passionately in the primary articles of his own faith: in his view we

17 Steiner, op. cit., p. 22.   18 Ibid., p. 3.

must be silent about the things that matter most in human life. This intuitive awareness of a mystical world made Wittgenstein distinguish between the ability of words to say (*sagen*) what is effable and their ability to show (*seigen*) what is ineffable: thus, when he takes immense pains to delimit the unimportant (i.e. the scope and limits of ordinary language), it is not the coastline of that island which he is bent on surveying with such meticulous accuracy but the boundary of the ocean. Thus in linguistic analysis, as in logical positivism, our *pedestal gods* – Homer and Virgil, Dante and Shakespeare – are thrown, and *Finnegans Wake*, our world's song of songs, or canticle of canticles, is canonized as the apocalypse and revelation of every Ulysses or Aeneas, who walk again in darkness and in the shadow of death without that Word that was in the beginning to say and to do – to separate light from darkness and to light the way to eternal life.

Today this real absence is our real presence – the *mysterium tremendum* in a new form to be felt and lived in our search for meaning and mystery. For Steiner this naked exposure to the unknown is man's final experience of his self-revelation and his last hope for his future or survival: 'one day, Orpheus will not turn around, and the truth of the poem will return to the light of understanding, whole, inviolate, life-giving, even out of the dark of omission and death.'[19] Like despair such presumption is surely a sin against hope! Nevertheless, the distinction is clear, and the separation of Word and words remains; in music, as in poetry, *the falcon cannot hear the falconer* and in Schoenberg's *Moses und Aron* the despair of our times before the limitations of our words is heard and heartfelt in the final cry – *O Word, O Word, which is lacking to me*.

The poet's *glimpse* of the Word – *afaint afar away* – may be more intuitive than the analysis of the critic, and hopefully more prophetic, as it is conceivably, at least, more expressive of the Word's rising than of its setting. In his way of *Waiting for Godot* Beckett felt and lived the *mysterium tremendum* of the real absence without presumption or despair: in the cycle of his words are the end and the beginning; *the darkness drops again* – but – *Orpheus (may) not turn around – yes, the time had come for him to set out on his journey westward* according to Joyce! Unlike Hopkins, who was writing before modern darkness overpowered our poetry, Beckett may be the first among the poets of the real absence to acknowledge as folly – *all this this here* – like the folly in Corinth the Greeks called *wisdom* (1 Cor 1:22), and Paul called the *Word of the Cross* (1 Cor 1:17): indeed the words of Hopkins may be quite apt to describe the Word – or *glimpse – afar afaint away* – of Beckett:

> And though the last lights off the black West went
> Oh, morning, at the brown brink eastwards, springs –

---

[19] Ibid., p. 24.

Because the Holy Ghost over the bent
World broods with warm breast and with ah! bright wings.[20]

As in poetry and literature, so too in biblical studies and in theology in recent times there are signs or stirrings – *afaint afar away* – of searching again for the Word of God in the inspired books of sacred scripture, and of seeking afresh for a Word of transcendence in the classical texts of the living tradition; *at the brown brink eastwards*, the hour of Augustine, preacher and rhetor, exegete and theologian, *may come around at last* with the familiar beginning of many a sermon – *we have heard the words, now let us seek the Word*. Already eminent critics like George Steiner, whom we are here considering, and Northrop Frye, in his *Words with Power* and *Great Code* are holding the critics up to criticism, and reminding them of the origins of hermeneutics and criticism in the ageless probing of the sacred scriptures for their divine and transcendent secrets: 'our grammars, our explications, our criticisms of texts, our endeavours to pass from letter to spirit, are the immediate heirs to the textualities of western Judaeo-Christian theology and biblical-patristic exegetics.' In such insights or signs are our hopes born again in this hour of darkness for the Light of the Word which alone has the words of Eternal Life.

The darkness of our hour, or 'Silence, the Empty Tomb and Poetry' in a literal and real sense, was foreseen, a century before Yeats, by Johann Wolfgang Goethe (d.1832), 'the German poet and author of *The Four Ages of Man* – 1) the Age of Poetry; 2) the Age of Theology; 3) the Age of Philosophy; and 4) the Age of the Prosaic or Vulgar.'[21] In this astonishingly perceptive work Goethe tried to give back to language something of the vitality of its origin in poetry and myth: then, in source and origin poem and myth were one and the same, but their separation in subsequent cultural epochs, and for different reasons, impoverished our language or words, deprived them of their original significance and ultimately emptied them of their Word of Light and Life:

> It is here that Goethe once again stands alone, and never more lonely, against his age and contemporaries experiencing not without bitterness their lack of understanding. His aim was to combine the cool precision of scientific research with a constant awareness of the totality apparent only to the eye of reverence, the poetic-religious eye, the ancient sense for the cosmos. But the scientists had gone over to Newton, his arch-enemy, and the Idealists preferred to deduce nature as an *a priori* system, or if they were Romantics, to feel a vague irrational feeling of the whole. Goethe was just as much a lone

---

20 'God's Grandeur', in *The Poems of G.M. Hopkins*, London, 1953, p. 27.

fighter in his age as Thomas Aquinas had been when he sought to combine exact research and intellectual work with a reverentially pious perception of the divine presence in the cosmos. For without a union of the two, there can be no attitude objective enough to do justice to existence.[22]

In these sentiments there is a remarkable affinity between the method of von Balthasar, a modern theologian, and that of Goethe, our earliest critic: each in its own way seeks for the unity of the subjective and objective principle within the appearance: in other words, literature and scripture are preserved in the fulness of their being and difference as objective texts or words of the Word in our world. Thus Balthasar admires Goethe's refusal to collapse the analogical distinction between God and the world. Similarly, in their understanding of language, as in the way of analogy, the words of man and the Word of God are similar and dissimilar in their being and significance. In poetry, as in myth, there is a real presence in the words of a Word that is Other, and those words are the appearance or sound of that Other Word. But in the words of the sacred scriptures that Other Word 'was in the beginning with God, was God [...] and is the Word of God [...] now [...] and forever more [...] world without end [...].' Amen:

> Without him was not anything made that was made. In him was life, and the life was the light of men. The light shines in the darkness, and the darkness has not overcome it.
>
> There was a man sent from God whose name was John. He came for testimony, to bear witness to the light, that all might believe through him. He was not the light, but came to bear witness to the light.
>
> The true light that enlightens everyman was coming into the world. He was in the world and the world was made through him, yet the world knew him not. He came to his own home and his own people received him not. But to all who received him; who believed in his name, he gave power to become children of God: who were born, not of blood nor of the will of the flesh nor of the will of man, but of God.
>
> And the Word became flesh and dwelt among us, full of grace and truth; we have beheld his glory, glory as of the only Son from the Father [...]. And from his fulness have we all received – grace upon grace.[23]

Word and words, prophecy and poetry, the existence of God and the essence of man, is the conundrum of our intelligibility or being, and ever was and will be.

21 E.T. Oakes, *Pattern of Redemption. The Theology of Hans Urs von Balthasar*, New York, 1994, pp 81-8.
22 Ibid. p.96.   23 Cf. John's Prologue, RSV.

As the Word is one in being with the Infinite Father, so too our words are of our finite essence. Every critic since the time of Goethe has focused on the nature of language and history. According to Vico, the most important critic since Goethe, and Frye, the disciple of Vico, there are three ages in a cycle of history – the mythical or age of the gods; the heroic or age of the aristocracy; and the demotic or age of the people; and correspondingly three types of verbal expression – the poetic, the heroic and the vulgar. Is there, as Vico thought there was, a *ricorso* or return to restart the process? That indeed is the problem of God and man, of Word and words.[24]

According to Frye, history moves in a cyclical rhythm which never forms a complete or closed cycle: a new movement begins, works itself out to exhaustion, and something of the original state then reappears, though in a quite new context, presenting new conditions. This vision of history, in keeping with Freye's Christian faith, seems more spiral than cyclical and is the light of Genesis and Apocalypse on the other biblical books, Old and New, for Christ is the Alpha and Omega, our beginning and our end. Thus a single vision of language, nature, history and God is an impoverished one leading to the destruction of everything that makes human or divine sense; the double vision on the other hand releases our imaginative and creative energy to see through our own minds and hearts that all things, through love, are possible. In Frye's 'Double Vision of God', as in *Little Gidding* for Eliot, the golden longing for peace is present:

> We shall not cease from exploration
> And the end of all our exploring
> Will be to arrive where we started
> And know the place for the first time.[26]

Without this biblical perception of language, nature, time and God we are left with *The Four Ages* of Ovid's *Metamorphoses*, the treasure-house of myth and legend, which was read with delight in his day, and has continued to charm succeeding generations, providing a source from which the whole of Western European Literature has derived inspiration.

> And the first Age was Gold.
> Without laws, without law's enforcers,
> This age understood and obeyed

---

24 M. Lilla, *G.B. Vico*, Cambridge, Mass., 1994: cf. chapter 4, 'An Ideal History of the Eternal City', , pp 152ff.   25 N. Frye, *The Double Vision Language and Meaning in Religion*, Toronto, 1991.   26 Ibid.; cf. Eliot's *Little Gidding*, p. xvi.

What had created it.
Listening deeply, man kept faith with the source [...]

After Jove had castrated Saturn,
Under the new reign the Age of Silver –
(Lower than the Gold, but better
Than the coming Age of Brass) –
Fell into four seasons [...]

After this, third in order,
The Age of Brass
Brought a brazen people,
Souls fashioned on the same anvil
As the blades their hands snatched up
Before they cooled. But still
Mankind listened deeply
To the harmony of the whole creation,
And aligned
Every action to the greater order
And not to the moment's blind
Apparent opportunity.

Last comes the Age of Iron.
And the day of Evil dawns.
Modesty,
Loyalty,
Truth,
Go up like a mist – a morning sigh off a graveyard.[27]

Goethe, the sage of Eliot, who condemned the world that Newton made, and the man that Kant created, was the first of our critics to mend the mythical garment of scripture and poetry, of Daniel and Ovid, that our times had rent in two, like the veil of the Temple, in the darkness of our hour and being. As a convert to the cause Eliot was late in coming but in his essay on Dante, Shakespeare and Goethe, called *The Three Europeans*, he makes his amends as he acknowledges the liberality of their genius: 'we cannot get very far with Dante, or Shakespeare, or Goethe, without touching upon theology, and philosophy, and ethics, and politics, and in the case of Goethe,

---

27 T. Hughes, *Tales from Ovid*, London, 1997; cf. E. Moore, *Studies in Dante*, New York, 1968. Earthly Paradise was for Dante the Golden Age of Ovid's poets; cf. *Purg.* xxii, 148-50; *Purg.* xxviii, 139-44 ; cf. Dan 2:26-47 for prophetic vision of the gold, silver, bronze, iron statue with feet of clay.

especially, penetrating in a clandestine way and without *legitimation papers*, into the forbidden territory of science.'[28] Unlike Dante and Shakespeare in their criticism of their times, Goethe was as opposed to Newtonian mechanism and Kantian dualism as the spirit of this age of enlightenment was opposed to his type of consciousness: 'so perhaps,' says Eliot, 'the time has come when we can see that there is something in favour of being able to see the universe as Goethe saw it, rather than the scientists have seen it, now that the *living garment of God* has become somewhat tattered from the results of scientific manipulation.'[29]

> O world of spring and autumn, birth and dying!
> The endless cycle of idea and action,
> Endless invention, endless experiment,
> Brings knowledge of motion, but not of stillness;
> Knowledge of speech, but not of silence;
> Knowledge of words and ignorance of the Word.
> All our knowledge brings us nearer to our ignorance,
> All our ignorance brings us nearer to death,
> But nearness to death no nearer to God.
> Where is the Life we have lost in living?
> Where is the wisdom we have lost in knowledge?
> Where is the knowledge we have lost in information?
> The cycles of Heaven in twenty centuries
> Bring us farther from God but nearer to the Dust.[30]

POET AND PRIEST

The divisions of history in *The Four Ages of Man* are probably more useful in structuring ideas than accurate in recording the facts; nevertheless, Goethe's generalizations are not without some degree of recovery in modern studies of ritual, or without growing significance in recent considerations of language. The identity in the age of origins of poetry and myth is appearing afresh in much that is being written today on the nature of religious language. Once again myth means a tale to be told and to be verified by nothing other than the telling of it, and it neither requires nor includes any possible verification outside of itself. Stories about God and man, of Jesus dying and Christ rising, and many other stories in different religious and cultural traditions, have a verifiable or dogmatic content. But from a hermeneutical point of view we

---

28 Ibid. 29 Oakes, op.cit., fn. 30; Eliot's *Goethe as the Sage*, pp 218-19; and Oakes, pp 83-5. 30 T.S. Eliot, *The Complete Poems and Plays*: Choruses from 'The Rock,' New York, 1971, p. 96.

must abstract from this dogmatic content, and concentrate on narration as one of the characteristic features of religious experience. Like music, the narrative, myth or story can never exhaust all that is to be told; it retains a certain *floating wordlessness*: it is not just like a lack of words; 'it is more like a door that is waiting for the key Word that will open its meaning.'[1]

There are echoes here of the 'Age of Poetry,' when the spirits of myth and poetry emerged from the primeval chaos and were the head and heart of the community they formed and sustained. Then the poet was priest, prophet and king: he possessed, expressed and preserved the popular faith, and ruled as the supreme legislator of the tribe or clan. His words were the Word of their gods. That halcyon memory, evoked by Goethe, may be more dormant than dead in our studies of literature and scripture today, and is, perhaps, recovering something of its former vitality in the works of critics like Steiner and Frye, and theologians like Barth or von Balthasar, with their renewed emphasis on mythical hermeneutics.[2]

Secondly, the 'Age of the Holy' emerges as theology subjects the gods of poetry to the authority of the One and the Absolute: 'it is in this era, and only in this era that God can be revealed, purifying the fear and tremor of the poetic stage into a reverence that is simultaneously love and awe.'[3] This is the monotheism and transcendence of the God of Abraham, Isaac and Jacob, and in the biblical expression of this revelation the role of the poet as prophet surpasses that of the priest: furthermore, in language the prophet remains no less mythical and no less poetic, for always in his words it is the Lord God who speaks; like a priest of magical powers he may even act out in symbolic actions the words he is announcing, for the Word of God will do what it was spoken to do and prosper in the doing.

In Greek literature and philosophy, as in biblical literature and theology, the Homeric myths were a form of revelation, more divine than human, in their analysis of man in the depths of his soul, but differ essentially from the folktale or fable which recount man's antics here, there and everywhere. Poetry as a purposeful creation of the imagination lies somewhere in between; on the one hand, its tragedies distinguish the poet of the myth, like Sophocles, and, on the other hand, its comedies do the fabulous poet, or poet of the fable, like Aristophanes. But in each case their material comes from their traditions, and not simply from the fertility of their own imaginations. In his *Republic* Plato recognised this distinction of the mythical and fabulous poet, but questioned their respective roles in religion without the wisdom of philosophy as dialectic to guide them: 'on the highest level, myths are the instrument of knowledge about the intelligible world [...] the wise man's untroubled vision of reality. Such myths are removed from the obstacle myths or silly stories which offend

---

[1] N. Frye, *The Double Vision*, Toronto, 1991, 'The Double Vision of Language,' pp 3-21 [2] E. Oakes, *The Pattern of Redemption*, New York, 1994, cf. 'J.W. Goethe,' pp 83-5. [3] Ibid., p. 36.

our sense of reality and moral decorum. Thus Plato makes the distinction between myth and fable as wide as he can get it, one being at the top and the other at the bottom of his vision of reality.'[4]

In the New Testament, myth and fable become identical, as a more rational conception of truth developed, and *fabulous* poetry acquired the quality of the imaginary, of fiction more than fact.[5] Such *bebelous mythos*, or profane stories, were what other religions had, whereas Christians had *logoi* or true stories. In early Christian tradition this platonic hierarchy of myths continued as 1) scripture or revelation; 2) theology or dogma; 3) pious legend or preaching, and 4) literature, secular or profane. Nonetheless, antiquity did not completely pass away in this new order of being and transcendence, scripture and meaning: for one thing, Aristotle's emphasis on *poieisis*, that is, on the poem as an artistic creation in itself, and Plato's on the *daimon* or the divine power that takes possession of the artist gave poem and poet a new lease of life when Chrysostom was at his best in Constantinople in condemnation of both.

In this new world of biblical mythology there came to be a new blend of East and West that was a beginning in the fourth century of that new culture called Catholic: a second look at this mythology shows us that it actually became, for medieval and later centuries, a vast mythological universe, stretching in time from creation to apocalypse, and in metaphysical space from heaven to hell. This universe of Catholic culture had its origins in the world of the Greek and Latin Fathers, poets in poetry like Gregory Nazianzus, and poets in prose like Augustine of Hippo. In European literature since then and down to the last couple of centuries, the myths of the bible have continued to form a special category as a body of stories with a distinctive authority. Poets who attach themselves to this central mythical area, like Dante and Milton, have been thought of as possessing a special kind of seriousness. On the other hand, in the tales of Chaucer, as in the comedies of Shakespeare, the motif of entertainment prevails and the folktale appears as the obvious literary ancestor. But whenever the note of tragedy is struck in *Anno Domini* there is little difference in the poems of any poet, mythical or fabulous:

> Christ's place indeed is with the poets. His whole conception of humanity sprang right out of the imagination and can only be realized by it. What God was to be pantheist, man was to him. He was the first to conceive the divided races as a unity. Before his time there had been gods and men, and feeling through the mysticism of sympathy that in himself each had been

---

4 Frye, op. cit., 'The Double Vision of God,' pp 59-85; also cf. N. Frye, *Words with Power*, New York, 1990, 'Concern and Myth,' pp 30-62.   5 Ibid., 'Concern and Myth,' *mythous bebulous*, or *silly myths*, condemned in the New Testament,. pp 34-5.

made incarnate, he calls himself the Son of the one or the Son of the other, according to his mood [...]. I had said of Christ that he ranks with the poets. That is true. Shelley and Sophocles are of his company. But his entire life also is the most wonderful of poems. For 'pity and terror' there is nothing in the entire cycle of Greek tragedy to touch it. The absolute purity of the protagonist raises the entire scheme to a height of romantic art from which the sufferings of Thebes and Polops' line are by their very horror excluded, and shows how wrong Aristotle was when he said in his treatise on the drama that it would be impossible to bear the spectacle of one blameless in pain. Nor in Aeschylus nor Dante, those stern masters of tenderness, in Shakespeare, the most purely human of all the great artists, in the whole of Celtic myth and legend, where the loveliness of the world is shown through a mist of tears, and the life of a man is no more than the life of a flower, is there anything that, for sheer simplicity of pathos wedded and made one with sublimity of tragic effect, can be said to equal or even approach the last act of Christ's passion.[6]

In the third epoch of *The Four Ages of Man* comes the 'Age of Philosophy,' of Rationalism or Enlightenment in the eighteenth and nineteenth centuries. In this age reason does to the Holy One what theology did to the gods: however, the notion of the One is now an abstract concept, not derived from the revelation of God, but from reflection on the meaning of religion as such: 'in its greatest energy and purity, the understanding honours its earliest beginnings and rejoices in the poetic faith of the people, highly esteeming this noble need of man to recognize a highest realm. The only trouble is, [that] the man of understanding strives to appropriate everything thinkable to terms of his clarity and to dissolve even the most mysterious of phenomena. This in no way means that the faith of the people and the priests has been rejected, but behind that same faith what the man of understanding assumes is something conceivable, commendable, useful.'[7] Against this philosophy of religion one can hear in every age the poetic voice, mythical or fabulous, crying out for a vision of God or the gods, transcendent or immanent, in nature or grace, that will make man free from the bondage of being physical: 'Great God! I'd rather be / A Pagan suckled in a creed outworn; / So might I, standing on this pleasant lea,/ Have glimpses that would make me less forlorn.'[8]

The 'Age of the Prosaic' is the fourth and final stage of the *Four Ages of Man* as the masses visit on their own culture a terrifying revenge of vulgarity: 'instead of

---

6 O. Wilde, *The Complete Works of Oscar Wilde*, ed. J.B. Foreman, London, 1948, 'De Profundis', p. 923.
7 Oakes, op. cit., pp 86-7; the age of Hegel and philosophy.   8 W. Wordsworth, 'The World Is Too Much with Us,' in *The Norton Anthology of Poetry*, New York, 1970, p. 588.

instructing its age with its understanding and serenely sinking its roots into the past, the people of this age randomly strew good seed and bad in all directions. There is no centre of gravity any more from which perspective can be gained. Every individual steps forth: sets up shop as teacher and leader, and purveys the most utter nonsense as if it were the well-rounded perfection of the whole. Thus the value of each individual mystery has been destroyed, and the faith of the people desecrated.'[9] This reading of the signs of the times by Goethe, so accurate in its prophetic power, anticipates *The Apocalypse of the German Soul*, with Hegel representing the 'Age of Philosophy' and Nietzsche frantically warning against the pathetic misery that would visit man in our century – the most Prosaic Age of all. Now *the darkness drops again*: 'the human spirit [...] leaps backwards over all hurdles reason has erected, clinging here and there to remnants of tradition, then plunges headlong into pools of insipid mythologies, bringing to the top the muddy poetry of the depths as the creed of our age.'[10] *What is the Word* [...] !

The poet T.S. Eliot in the poem he called Ash Wednesday (1930) confronted this *Age of the Prosaic*, the meaning of man's words and world, with the Light of the Divine Word. Earlier in *The Waste Land* (1922) and later in *The Hollow Men* (1925) he began his consideration of the real absence our critics have been calling a real presence – the *mysterium tremendum*, or substantive absence of Steiner's naked unknowing, and the *reductio ad crucem*, or positive negativity in von Balthasar's *Apocalypse of the German Soul*. In the 'Age of Philosophy', and the 'Age of the Prosaic,' that followed the hour of Goethe, so to speak, Eliot, as poet and critic, stands apart, as a voice crying in the wilderness, and with New England clarity and diction speaks afresh and anew the mythical words of the 'Age of Poetry' and the biblical Word of the 'Age of the Holy.' In a sense, *La Figlia che Piange* (1917) announced his arrival and vision of life and love – *O quam te memorem virgo*: in this 'garden of sunlight and flowers,' of 'fugitive resentment' and 'autumn weather,' of 'troubled midnight' and 'the noon's repose,' sex was his symbol, and will remain throughout his works (seen here as one continuous poem), his mode of expression and criticism.[11] On the one hand there will be the negative way of Phlebas, the Phoenician sailor of *The Waste Land*, who turns the wheel westwards, and is drowned among the rocks, washed clean of his lust and greed; a painful purgation! on the other hand, there will be the positive way of Dante in the *Vita Nuova*, or way of the final cause or calling, in demonstration of the Spirit and the power of the Word, of conversion and conviction, of decision and determination, of spiritual life and love, pure and simple:

---

9 Oakes, op. cit., p. 87, Nietzsche and our age of the prosaic.   10 Ibid., p. 88, cf. E. Heller (ed.), *Goethe and Nietzsche*, London, 1975, p. 93,.   11 T.S. Eliot, *T.S. Eliot. The Complete Poems and Plays*, New York, 1971.

> So I would have had him leave,
> So I would have had her stand and grieve,
> So he would have left
> As the soul leaves the body torn and bruised,
> As the mind deserts the body it has used.
> I should find
> Some way incomparably light and deft,
> Some way we both should understand,
> Simple and faithless as a smile and shake of the hand.[12]

Like Dante, Eliot lived in a vast mythological and biblical world stretching in time from creation to apocalypse, and in metaphorical space from heaven to hell: he, too, was a pilgrim on the face of the earth as he journeyed in time to eternity well aware of the *hell, purgatory,* and *paradise* dimensions of human experience. Furthermore, the writers of his Anglo-Catholic tradition in England, like those of the *renouveau catholique* in France, also lived and wrote in a reality or world that the *Word of the Cross* had enlightened and expanded: accordingly they understood, *sub specie aeternitatis,* the tensions of the temporal: 'human passions against eternal laws that is the eternal conflict, and human passions use every device to get the best of it, and set themselves above the laws. All very tragic and pitiful, but writers about it should be on the right side – if they can.'[13] In his understanding of sexual life, as either the negative expression of earthly despair and death, or else the positive experience of heavenly life and love, Eliot, like von Balthasar, cuts sharply and finely between the soul and the spirit to isolate the dead centre, if not the living heart, of the *Waste Land* that is our world, and the *Hollow Men* who are its citizens. His aesthetic judgment like all critical theory is ultimately a politics of taste; *de gustibus non disputandum*; but in his range of inferred or cited reference, in the lucidity and rhetorical strength of his style, as in the genius of his creativity, are fulfilled those objective criteria of aesthetic judgment that made him, in his time and beyond, as great a critic as he was a poet.

In his name there arose in the thirties, forties and fifties the New Criticism with its emphasis, first and foremost, on the *objective-correlative*, or that reality of metaphor, that separates the poem from the poet, the more perfect the artist, the more completely separate in him will be the man who suffers and the mind which creates. Secondly, this emphasis on the structure of the poem, its own emotion and movement, distinct from the life or tragedy of the poet, gave a new significance to the text as text, and the phrase *explication de texte* was launched to describe the word for word, or phrase by phrase, analysis; the search was, rather, for architecture and

---

12 Ibid., 'La Figlia Che Piange,' p. 20.   13 Rose Macaulay, *Letters to a Friend,* ed. C. Smith, vol. 1, *1950-1952*, London, 1961, p. 172.

texture – or call it resonance and intricacy, the responsive webwork between the words. Thirdly, in Eliot's understanding of poetry and criticism the classics of Western Civilization remained normative as a canon for, in his opinion, the poet needed to be inspired by the past as the critic needed to be directed: 'the historical sense compels a man to write not merely with his own generation in his bones, but with a feeling that the whole of the literature of Europe from Homer, and within it the whole of the literature of his own country, has a simultaneous existence and composes a simultaneous order.'[14]

As a poet and critic Eliot was uniquely and distinctively Catholic and Caroline, and his work can never be separated, not even in this 'Age of the Prosaic' and the secular, from the Word of Genesis that separated light from darkness (Gen 1:1-4); the Word of the Prologue that was in the beginning with God and was God, the life and light of men (Jn 1:1-4) and the Word of Revelation or Alpha and Omega, the beginning and end (Rev 21:6). John's *Life* was Eliot's *Light*, and without that *Light* and *Life*, the cycle turns full circle; *the darkness drops again*; the *formless void* returns, and in *The Waste Land* the scriptures are fulfilled again: 'he was in the world, and the world came into being through him; yet the world did not know him [...]. But to all who received him [...] he gave power to become children of God, who were born, not of blood or of the will of the flesh, or of the will of man, but of God'(Jn 1:10-13).

In the very title of *The Waste Land* there are echoes not only of the return of the *formless void* in this 'Age of the Prosaic', but also of the fertility rites of the Lance and the Cup, the youth and the maiden, that in our secular society of sexual promiscuity replaces the medieval legend of the Holy Grail or cup of salvation. Now the Fisher-King represents the fate of man that originates in sex, or in the will of the flesh, and cannot transcend it; his maimed condition is reflected in the land that is laid waste. Unlike the Phoenician sailor, the Fisher-King of our degenerate society has an awareness of his calling and the possibility of his transcendence, but he lacks the positive will necessary for the *Vita Nuova*, or new life that is the spiritual love of God. He can be kept going, so to speak, by the music and magic of the moment, but the people of his *Waste Land* have no desire to be restored to a life that is worse than death. Hence the paradox of the seasons with which *The Waste Land* begins, as it reverses the significance of the vegetation myth: 'indeed it inverts the normal attitude to the cycle of life and gives an ironic twist to the office of *The Burial of the Dead* as spring disturbs the sleep of the dead world, and stirs in man the uneasy memories and disturbing desires that winter had buried deep and laid to rest.'[15]

---

14 C. Ozick, 'A Critic at Large. T.S. Eliot at 101,' cf. *New Yorker*, 20 Nov. 1989, pp 119-54 and Anthony Lane, 10 Mar. 1997, pp. 86-92.   15 E. Drew, *T.S. Eliot*, 'The Design of His Poetry', New York, 1949; cf. *The Waste Land*, pp 58-91.

> April is the cruellest month, breeding
> Lilacs out of the dead land, mixing
> Memory and desire, stirring
> Dull roots with spring rain.
> Winter kept us warm, covering
> Earth in forgetful snow, feeding
> A little life with dried tubers.[16]

Death is the ultimate meaning of *The Waste Land* for a people without the *Holy Grail*, or cup of salvation, for whom the sexual union and significance of the Lance and the Cup is more destructive than creative, and in whom the will to believe is frustrated by the fear to live. At this point in 'The Burial of the Dead' the Tarot deck of cards is introduced to shed its magic light in the darkness of life. Again there is the sexual significance as the diamonds and spades of the magic deck have no more to offer to the hearts and clubs than the male lance to the female cup; Madame Sosostris, the famous clairvoyante, cannot even find in her magic deck the 'Hanged Man', or figure of the dead God, that might offer life in a land of death. In these circumstances the sex-game continues in life like 'A Game of Chess', and becomes in 'The Fire Sermon' the principle of death, of life without love and of love without life. In its simplest form *The Waste Land* is a statement about the futility of earthly love that never transcends its origins in the flesh to become in the spirit the life and love of divine revelation: consequently, people are driven in desperation to the fortuneteller; to believe in the earthly fortunes that are foretold, and to experience the passing of this empty moment:

> She turns and looks a moment in the glass,
> Hardly aware of her departed lover;
> Her brain allows one half-formed thought to pass:
> 'Well now that's done: and I'm glad it's over.'
> When lovely woman stoops to folly and
> Paces about her room again, alone,
> She smoothes her hair with automatic hand,
> And puts a record on the gramophone.[17]

Modern biographies have broken the code of Eliot's reticence and revealed the secrets of his dark side, but such snippets have only enhanced the power of *The Waste Land* as a metaphor of reality. Its evocations of loss and lamentation, *its empty cisterns and exhausted wells*, are broken sketches of the ruins that remain

---

16 Eliot, op. cit., p. 37, '1. The Burial of the Dead.'   17 Ibid., p. 44, '3. The Fire Sermon.'

when the traditional props of civilization have failed; for some, as for Eliot, a world without God; for others a world without even an illusion of intelligibility or restraint. However, in 'What the Thunder Said', or final part of *The Waste Land*, Eliot recognized the presence of the 'Hanged Man, wrapped in a brown mantle and hooded:' his Word is silence and his chapel is in ruins, but he is always the third one in every company of two 'walking beside you,' on the way to Emmaus:

> In this decayed hole among the mountains
> In the faint moonlight, the grass is singing
> Over the tumbled graves, about the chapel
> There is the empty chapel, only the wind's home.
> It has no windows, and the door swings,
> Dry bones can harm no one.
> Only a cock stood on the rooftree.[18]

Eliot, among the poets and critics of his time, was popularly known as 'the Pope of Russell Square': in fact, he was more a monk of St Stephen's, the Anglican community of celibate priests, where he spent some six years or more in penance, and in prayer, suffering the very isolation circumstances had forced upon him, and which he once prized as the poet's reward. Here the daily liturgy of the Catholic and Caroline tradition extended his frontiers of sense and feeling, of space and time, and his words began to express the inner, wider and loftier world of the Word. In the liturgical life of St Stephen's, as in the visionary and symbolic landscape of Dante, he sensed the concentrated framework of mythology and poetry, philosophy and theology, which he found lacking in the music of Blake's language, as he did in the hallucinations of his vision.

In this Catholic experience of life and liturgy Eliot's works began to form one continuous poem, and in the canon of Western literature his poetry, like the *Confessions of Augustine*, and unlike the *Apologia pro Vita Sua* of a Newman, is modernism's metaphor of transcendent reality. Appropriately, *Ash Wednesday* with its liturgical antiphon – 'Remember, man, thou art but dust, and unto dust thou shalt return'- begins the creation of the spiritual man from the flesh of the earth with a new *anima*, or life-principle, that marks the beginning of the *Vita Nuova*, or positive way of sexual love: 'the new dominating figure is that of a Lady, but inseparable from her is a garden, a rose, a fountain and two yew trees. These all form a new symbolic centre, in which the poet finds a renewal of life. They alternate with a desert of sand and of blue rocks, and there are further contrasting

---

18 Ibid., p. 49, '5. What the Thunder Said.'

images of sounds and silence; of movement and stillness; of disintegration and reintegration; of light and darkness; of loneliness and companionship.'[19] Fragments of liturgy, appearing in most of the separate parts of the poem, also take on the character of a symbol of unity and direction, as the whole is controlled by images of transition, of turning from one condition to another: indeed, it is obvious that the whole poem is coloured by religious and literary tradition but its particular quality is entirely its own:

> And I pray that I may forget
> These matters that with myself I too much discuss
> Too much explain
> Because I do not hope to turn again
> Let these words answer
> For what is done, not to be done again
> May the judgement not be too heavy upon us ...
> Pray for us sinners now and at the hour of our death
> Pray for us now and at the hour of our death.[20]

As a metaphor, or poem with a life of its own, the objective correlative of *Ash Wednesday* is in constant rotation between states of feeling that are centered in the presence or absence of a Lady, or vision in life that corresponds in the *Divine Comedy* to that of Beatrice. For Eliot this vision too had its origin in a childhood memory, but belongs to what he calls 'the world of the high dream,' or positive way of sex, whereas the modern world seems capable of only 'the low dream,' or negative way of the Phoenician sailor. In origin this dream may appear physical and sexual, but in the true human being, it is spiritual and mystical: indeed, this fundamental human experience can be understood only by finding meaning in final causes rather than in origins, for the final cause of man is his attraction towards God. In this mode of perception, classical mysticism, unlike that of the Romantics, is seen as the expansion of adolescent love through the mature contemplation of the One, the Good, the True and the Beautiful, and is the only source of authentic Christian humanism and peaceful communion or prayer:

> The single Rose
> Is now the Garden
> Where all loves end
> Terminate torment

---

[19] Drew, op. cit., p. 98 on *Ash Wednesday*.   [20] Eliot, op. cit., p. 61.

> Of love unsatisfied
> The greater torment
> Of love satisfied
> End of the endless
> Journey to no end
> Conclusion of all that
> Is inconclusible
> Speech without word and
> Word of no speech
> Grace to the mother
> For the Garden
> Where all love ends.[21]

In the first part of *Ash Wednesday*, the *blessed face* and the *voice* are renounced in an act of faith which accepts their loss as creative patience. On the other hand, in the second part the presence of the Lady [...] *withdrawn in a white gown to contemplation* [...] is the prayer-life and happiness of a land, divided by lot, but neither division nor unity matters [...] *we have our inheritance*. The third part, however, requires again more than submission and singing: *the deceitful face of hope and despair* appear, and so the creative effort is necessary to climb the steep stairs from the distractions of the lilac and the brown hair – *Blown hair is sweet, brown hair over the mouth blown* [...] but *speak the word only*. There is by way of contrast and rotation in the fourth part a brief vision of this garden: this is the only place where the poet actually meets the Lady, but there she remains veiled and silent – *Between the yews, behind the garden god [...] And after this our exile*. The exile quickly follows in the fifth part as contact is again lost with the only Word that can reconcile all the opposing forces held in tension in the struggle, and *gathers up all things*, 'things in heaven and things on earth' (Eph 1:10):

> If the lost word is lost, if the spent word is spent
> If the unheard, unspoken
> Word is unspoken, unheard;
> Still is the unspoken word, the Word unheard,
> The Word without a word, the Word within
> The world and for the world;
> And the light shone in darkness and
> Against the Word the unstilled world still whirled
> About the centre of the silent Word.
>
> O my people, what have I done unto thee.

[21] Ibid., p. 62.

> Where shall the word be found, where will the word
> Resound? Not here, there is not enough silence
> Not on the sea or on the islands, not
> On the mainland, in the desert or the rain land,
> For those who walk in darkness
> Both in the day time and in the night time
> The right time and the right place are not here
> No place of grace for those who avoid the face
> No time to rejoice for those who walk among noise and deny the voice[22]

In the final part of the poem, the time of tension between dying and birth, the conflict remains – 'human passions against eternal decrees' – the pattern and the core of Christianity. Among the rocks the poet remains far from paradise, but his prayer is still for patience and humility: 'it is the simple prayer that he may express his love in contemplation of the beloved [...] and guiding figure who is the spirit of life and love, the spirit of the fountain, of the garden, of the river and of the sea.'[23] And like all other dwellers among the rocks he turns to the Lady and her Word with the words of the Church at prayer – 'And let my cry come unto Thee.'

> Love has her priests in the poets,
> And sometimes you will hear a voice
> Which knows how to hold her in honour;
> But not a word will you hear about faith!
> Who is there who can speak
> In honour of this passion?[24]

In his *Fear and Trembling*, Kierkegaard never foresaw in his tradition a poet and critic like Eliot, nor a theologian and priest like Karl Rahner. However, nearly fifty years have now passed since Rahner set out to do for theology what Eliot was already doing for poetry: 'Alas, that there should still be no theology of the Word! Why has no one yet set about gathering together, like Ezekiel, the scattered members on the fields of philosophy and theology, and spoken over them the Word of the Spirit, so that they rise up a living body!'[25] Since then much has been done, and more must yet be done, to develop Rahner's seminal articles on 'Poetry and the Christian', and on 'Priest and Poet', in which he set out to effect that symbiosis of Word and words without which the Word of God cannot be heard, and, *a fortiori*, can never be preached. In the article on 'Poetry and the Christian'[26] his method was that of the transcendental school of

---

[22] Ibid., p. 65.   [23] Ibid., p. 67.   [24] Drew, op. cit., p. 98 = a quote from Kierkegaard.   [25] K. Rahner, *Theological Investigations*, vol. 3, London, 1974, p. 294; cf. 'Priest and Poet,' pp 294-317.   [26] Ibid., *Theological Investigations*, vol. 4; cf. 'Poetry and the Christian,' pp 357-67.

theology, which he had so developed and shaped, and which von Balthasar had so dogmatically opposed: 'Rahner's principal objective is pastoral. He sees people of our time estranged from biblical truth and, stressing the essentially transcendent nature of man, he seeks to show how closely Christian truth conforms to the boldest hopes and expectations of humankind [...]. Thus anthropology becomes inchoate or deficient Christology.'[27]

This preference of von Balthasar for the primacy and priority of the Word of Revelation as Love, more given in grace than discovered in theology, would certainly simplify Rahner's laborious efforts to develop a theology of the divine Word through his ponderous considerations of the poetic word. Nevertheless his philosophical and linguistic reflections on the luminosity of the poetic word, and its capacity to reflect the Word of God as Word, are in themselves rare exposures of the poet that was in this priest and the critic that was in this theologian. In his usual philosophical and transcendental way Rahner argues with unusual poetic and mystical feeling that a Christian must first be able to hear the word through which the silent mystery of existence is present; secondly, he must be able to perceive the word which touches the heart in its inmost depths; thirdly, he must be initiated into the human grace of hearing the word which gathers and unites, and finally he must be open to the word which in the midst of its own finite clarity is the embodiment of the eternal mystery. From these four characteristics of the poetic word, symbolic in their very being of a reality that is transcendent and other, disposed towards it and pointing towards it, Rahner argues to the theology of that Divine Word or transcendent reality.

The 'Priest and Poet' article, however, is more descriptive than analytical of the distinct roles of poet and priest in the orders of creation and redemption, and less inclined to confuse by fusing together poetry and Christianity into the gospel of the anonymous Christian. In fact his philosophy of the human word and his theology of the divine Word remain throughout the article as distinct as von Balthasar could wish them to remain: his theology of the Word, however, remains within Heidegger's tradition of German idealism more than Balthasar's vision of biblical revelation as the pouring forth of the overpowering love of a personal Father. Revelation for von Balthasar is infinitely more than the fulfilment of man's transcendent longing: nevertheless, Rahner's philosophy of the human word, consciously or unconsciously the fruit of his theology of the divine Word, is a unique contribution to revelation as Word, poetic and biblical: someone may be a priest and in addition also a poet. But this is very far from saying that he is the one in the other and that both are in him the same. But the fulfilment of the future towards which we journey answers in advance that the perfect priest and perfect poet are one and the same – Jesus Christ, priest and victim, or poet and poem.

27 Oakes, op. cit., p. 95 = *Communio* 5/1 (1978), p. 79.

In this article on the 'Priest and Poet,' Rahner considers in the first place the poet and his primordial words; secondly, the priest and the divine Word; thirdly, priest and poet; fourthly, the Church and the priest; and finally he offers his concluding remarks. Beginning with his philosophy of the human word as an embodied thought, more than the embodiment of the thought, he makes his fundamental distinction between utilitarian and primordial words: 'Some words are clear since they are shallow and without mystery; they suffice for the mind: other words are obscure as they invoke the blinding mystery of things. Such words, which spring up out of the heart, which hold us in their power, which enchant us, I should like to call primordial words; the remainder could be named fabricated, technical; or utility.'[28]

But primordial words cannot be defined, for in a sense they are ultimate; as the basis of man's spiritual existence they are children of God, possess something of the luminous darkness of the Father and are filled with the soft music of infinity. Such words are like sea-shells in which the sound of the ocean can be heard, no matter how small they are in themselves.

Primordial words, like *the pity beyond all telling that is hid in the heart of love*, belong to the poet and constitute for Rahner the language of poetry, although poets and critics may disagree about the very name and nature of poetry: even when poetry has a meaning, as it usually has, it may be inadvisable to draw it out. 'Poetry gives more pleasure,' said Coleridge, 'when only generally and not perfectly understood; and perfect understanding will sometimes almost extinguish pleasure.' For Rahner, on the other hand, primordial words have always a literal meaning and an intellectual-spiritual meaning as well, and without the latter the verbal sense cannot ever be what is fully meant: 'thus primordial words reflect man in his indissoluble unity of spirit and flesh, transcendence and perception, metaphysics and history. It means that there are primordial words, because all things are interwoven with all reality, and therefore every genuine and living word has roots which penetrate endlessly into the depths.'[29]

Furthermore, the primordial word, in the strict sense, is the presentation and presence of the reality pronounced, for when such a word is spoken, like a word of love, something happens: the reality known takes possession of the knower and the lover through the word. Through the Word the object known is transferred into man's sphere of existence, and its entry is a fulfilment of the reality of the object known. It is to the poet, and the word of the poet, that this power has been given, for poets speak primordial words in powerful concentration: 'he has the power to speak in such a way that, by means of his word, things move as though set free into the light of others who hear the words of the poet.' Thus the primordial word, before

---

[28] Rahner, op. cit, vol. 3, p. 296. [29] Ibid., pp 298-9.

all other artistic expressions, is the primordial sacrament of all realities, and the poet is the minister of this sacrament: 'to him is entrusted this word, in which realities come out of their dark hiding place into the protective light of man to his own blessing and fulfillment.'[30]

Secondly, in his consideration of the Priest as a minister of the Word (Acts 6:4), Rahner relies on the New Testament as the unique source of the efficacious Word of the Eternal God in the flesh of the man Jesus. Hence all the words of God previously spoken are only the advance echoes of the Word of God in the world: so much therefore is the Word possessed of divine nobility, that we can call the Son, the self-comprehension of the Father, nothing else but the Word. It was precisely this person who is the Word, who became in the flesh the Word of God directed to us. Thus the Word, the primordial sacrament of transcendence is capable of becoming the primordial sacrament of the conscious presence in the world of the God who is superior to the world: this word has been spoken by God. 'He has come in grace and in the word. Both belong together: without grace, without the communication of God himself to the creature, the Word would be empty; without the Word, grace would not be present to us as free and spiritual persons in a conscious way. The Word is the bodiliness of God's grace.'[31]

Consequently, the word is an event or sacred action that comes from above, and must be spoken to the world through Christ, or through those whom he sends. Christianity is therefore a message and the priest is a herald or a messenger that must be sent; what he says is a proclamation or *kerygma*, and not just a *didache* or doctrine: his words are not his own and point to the Word spoken by another; like John the Baptist, he must be submerged and unseen behind this message he preaches and prays. This is particularly true as he speaks the efficacious words of the consecration at Mass: 'here everything is present – Godhead and manhood, heaven and earth, body and blood, soul and spirit, life and death, Church and individual, past and eternal future; all is gathered together into this word, and everything that is evoked in this world really takes place.'[32] This efficacious Word has been entrusted to the priest and makes him a priest. Every other word that he speaks is merely an echo of that one Word of Consecration – the handing over in life and death of the Son, and with him of the world to the Father in glory.

In the third section of his article, he contrasts the poet's ministry with the priest's mission: 'to the true poet, a god,' said Goethe, 'has given the power to express his experience, while others remain silent in their agony and in their bliss.' He experiences that communion with himself which is in fact a poetic and concentrated expression where everything is given in one; spirit and body, what is far and what is near, what is infinitely profound and what is finitely simple. This is the grace of the

30 Ibid., p. 302.   31 Ibid., p. 305-6.   32 Ibid., p. 307.

poet and the priest does not have it. His words come from the immeasurable remoteness of the distant God and not from the intimate proximity of the human heart. God's words humble the priest and demand too much of him: 'they are the judgment upon his sinfulness which is never completely done away with as long as we have to speak with human words about this thrice holy God. They pierce his heart like a sword, especially when he puts his heart into these words which his mouth is uttering. They unmask him [...] for the priest is always more and mostly less than the poet.'[33] Nevertheless these modes of existence appeal to each other, and mutually condition each other; indeed, in a real sense, the priesthood releases poetic existence and sets it free to attain its ultimate purpose in the world, the *Word of the Cross* has expanded and enlightened.

Fourthly, 'the priest must call upon the poet if the scriptures of the Church are to penetrate his own heart, and fill him with primordial words to penetrate the heart of darkness about him. Who is capable of calling upon another man in such a way that he is roused in his inmost being, which he often does not know himself [...], if not the poet?' Here Rahner acknowledges the power of the primordial word in the mouth of the poet; at the same time he knows all too well that 'the Word of God in its descent to the level of the human word has entered also those spheres where the laboured, humble, daily word of man is heard. For all its truth and dignity the Word of God has emptied itself and taken on the form of the slave, and consequently must be heard in the all too human words of the street, simple, without pretension and almost worldly wise. Similarly in the sacred science the utilitarian word has dominated and the primordial words of the ancient Fathers are scarcely audible.'[34] Still theology is doubtfully more divine because theologians are certainly more prosaic! So the priest must call upon the poet that the poet's primordial words may be the consecrated vessels in which he will effectively proclaims the Word of God.

Fifthly and finally, the poet calls upon the priest, as Dante and Eliot did on revelation, or the Word of the Cross, that widened their world and gave it light. In this new world of universal grace the primordial words, which poets, knowingly or unknowingly, speak, are words of longing. They call upon that which has no name and seek for that which cannot be grasped: their words are acts of faith in the spirit and in eternity; acts of hope for a fulfillment which they can never give themselves; acts of love for unknown gods. This something more which belongs to art and from which art lives is the Mystery that transcends art. The poet is driven by his nature towards this Mystery or transcendence of the spirit: 'he has already been overpowered secretly and quite unknown to himself by the longing which the grace of the Holy Spirit has implanted in the human heart,' so he speaks words of divine longing and

---

33 Ibid., pp 308-9.   34 Ibid., pp 310-16.

love, even when he speaks of the love of two human hearts and longs for the definitive transfiguration of all reality. His words cry out to the efficacious Word and expect an answer: 'only where the intimate faith in the possibility of such an answer has been suffocated in the hellish agony of desperate disbelief, would the human poetic word also be dead; only there, but there absolutely, idols are dumb as the scriptures say.'[35] But on the other hand, where there is faith in God and grace in man the words of the poem and poet speak to a High Priest and Victim, who has made answer to both God and man. Indeed, the words of man, like the Word that was made flesh, is not just a sort of silent signal pointing the finger – *afaint afar away* – from what it delimits and illuminates into the infinite distance of the incomprehensible: rather, in the region encompassed by the human word Infinity has pitched its tent; Infinity itself is there, really and truly present, in the finite; the Word is in the words. The poet, George Mackay Brown, in his final poem, 'A Work for Poets,' carves out, in a clear and simple way, all that the poet can do and say:

> To have carved on the days of our vanity
> A sun
> A ship
> A star
> A cornstalk
> Also a few marks
> From an ancient forgotten time
> A child may read.
> That not far from the stone
> A well
> Might open for wayfarers.
> Here is a work for poets –
> Carve the runes
> Then be content with silence.[36]

PROPHET AND PREACHER

The immanence of the biblical word explicit in Eliot's poetry, and the transcendence implicit in Rahner's theology of poetic words, raises, in our search for mystery and meaning, profound questions about divine revelation and human perception; in other words, there is the question about God or the gods and our different ways of knowing what is for real – cosmological, scientific, poetic in the

---

35 Ibid., pp 316-17.   36 G.M. Brown, *Following a Lark*, London, 1996.

broadest sense of the artistic, philosophical, historical, biblical and mystical as well. In particular there is the phrase *knowledge of God* and its polyvalent senses; more precisely there is the biblical use of this phrase which distinguishes it in its significance from every other mode of knowing. In Israel *the knowledge of God* was the correlative or pre-eminent fruit of the Word of God, and consequently there was a very clear distinction between the knowledge of which God is the subject and the knowledge of which God is the object. The first can be understood only from the second; indeed, Paul's phrase, 'then I shall know as fully as I am known' is a clear expression of this awareness or revelation.[1]

In the literature of Dante, Shakespeare and Goethe – *The Three Europeans* – there is a traditional mode of seeing and saying that is at once both Western and Catholic.[2] The philosophy of immanence from Kant to Hegel, and the theology of transcendence from Heidegger to Rahner, was a departure from this Catholic tradition of Western civilization; in the one the separation of Word and world understands all that is from within human experience, and in the other the separation of biblical Word and poetic words makes each one a potential hearer and divine revelation the fulfillment of human expectation. On the other hand, in the turmoil of our times, there is in certain schools a turning away from man as the measure of all that he is and a turning towards *Glory* as the source of all that he might be; this decisive turning point in our theology of revelation as salvation, a new dawn and hope, is the work of Hans Urs von Balthasar, 'the most cultured man of our times,' according to one, and, to another, a man 'overwhelmed by the Word of God:'[3]

> My main argument against Rahner and the entire school of transcendentalism is this: it might be true that from the beginning man was created to be disposed towards God's revelation, so that with God's grace the sinner can accept all revelation. *Gratia supponit naturam.* But when God sends his own living Word to creatures, he does so, not to instruct them about the mysteries of the world, nor primarily to fulfill their deepest needs and yearnings. Rather he actively demonstrates and communicates such unheard-of things that man feels not just satisfied but awestruck by a love he never could have hoped to experience. For who would have dared describe God as Love, without having first received the revelation of the Trinity in the acceptance of the cross by the Son?[4]

---

[1] L. Bouyer, *The Eucharist*, Notre Dame, Ind., 1968, pp 30-40. [2] T.S. Eliot, *On Poetry and Poets*, 'Goethe as the Sage', London, 1957, pp 207-27. [3] P. Henrici, 'Balthasar', *Communio*, 16 (1989), p. 306.
[4] H.U. von Balthasar, 'Current Trends in Catholic Theology,' *Communio*, 5/1 (1978), p. 79.

This biblical answer to the poetic question, contained for Balthasar in the transcendent and revealed mysteries of the Trinity and the Incarnation, is categorically refused by the immanence of a human reason that makes itself absolute; likewise it is no less diminished by a transcendence of no grace which makes everyone that is, at the very least, an anonymous Christian. For Balthasar, however, the Trinity and Incarnation are doctrines of revelation and faith, of grace and graceful vision, to continue in the here and now of time the light and life of eternity: 'in the Trinitarian dogma God is One, Good, True and Beautiful, because He is essentially Love; and Love supposes the One, the Other, and their Unity. And if we must suppose the Other, the Word, the Son, in God, the 'otherness' of creation is then not a fall, but an image of God, even as it is not God.'[5] Revelation is from above; discovery from within!

Such is the vision of Balthasar about the Word of God and the world of man: for him God is the answer to man; the biblical answer to the poetic question; the real presence of the Word of God that is a real absence in the words of man. But this Word, that was in the beginning, is present in the here and now of our every age, and ever shall be for those who are being made and remade to see and to hear. 'Man is not alone' ever, because always 'God is in search of man:' present in the scriptures that are, in a sense, a record of those things that were; and present too in the every day of every *Anno Domini* to make our sinful history as sacred and as saving as that of chosen Israel. In our cycles of grace God walks once again with Adam, the everyman of every time and place, to question and make answer in the ever present Easter mystery : 'Adam, where art thou? I have risen: I am with you once more; you placed your hand upon me to keep me safe. How great is the depth of your Wisdom, alleluia?'[6]

In Balthasar's theology of the Word, as in his philosophy of language, the analogy of being is primary; consequently, the Word is of the Infinite Being of God just as words are of man's essence or finite being: 'thus, in appearing in being the Word gives itself; it delivers itself to us; it is good. And in giving itself up, it speaks itself, it unveils itself; it is true in itself and in the other to which it reveals itself.'[7] This understanding of the Word of God as similar and dissimilar to the words of man is not based on the concept of being in the abstract, but on the concrete concept of being as encountered in its attributes of unity, goodness, truth and beauty.

On this understanding of the Word of God as the starting point of his trilogy Balthasar constructs, in the first place, his theological *Aesthetics* on the glory of God as it appeared from Abraham to the cross and resurrection of Christ 'a glory that is

---

[5] *Hans Urs von Balthasar: His Life and Work*, ed. D. Schindler, San Francisco, 1991, pp 1-7, 'A Resume of my Thought' .   [6] *Missale Romanum*; cf. Easter Sunday antiphon = Gen 3:9; Ps 139:18.   [7] Schindler, op. cit., p. 4.

revealed and different from all other glory in our world;' [8] secondly, there is his *Theo-Dramatique* or mystery of God in the history of man, paschal in its every aspect – 'the unfolding of the battle, the mortal struggle, the final victory;'[9] and there is thirdly *his Theo-Logique*, the incarnation of the infinite Word in finite flesh, and the restoration of all creation in the Word of the eternal Trinity: 'as the Son in God is the eternal Son of the Father, he can without contradiction assume in himself the image that is the creation, purify it, and make it enter into the communion of the divine life without dissolving it in a false mysticism. It is here that one must distinguish between nature and grace.'[10]

Hans Urs von Balthasar has appeared in our times as a man with a message that is as profound as it is simple. For him neither God nor man are dead: the Word of God is alive and active, and man alive is, was and ever will be, the glory of God. This is the sum and substance of von Balthasar's thought, but he is different and original in his understanding of metaphysics, anthropology and revelation: for him the true response to philosophy can only be given by Being, infinite and personal, revealing himself from himself, and this posits a counterpart: to be able to hear and understand the auto-revelation of God man must be in himself a search for God, a question posed to him. Thus there is no biblical theology without a religious philosophy; no water without a thirst. Reason must be open to the infinite:

> It is here that the substance of my thought inserts itself. Let us say above all that the traditional term *metaphysical* signified the act of transcending physics, which for the Greeks signified the totality of the cosmos, of which man was a part. For us physics is something else: the science of the material world. For us the cosmos perfects itself in man, who at the same time sums up the world and surpasses it. Thus our philosophy will be essentially a meta-anthropology, presupposing not only the cosmological sciences, but also the anthropological sciences, and surpassing them towards the question of the being and essence of man.'[11]

This rethinking of tradition, Western and Catholic, in the face of modernity, secular and scientific, was brought about, on the one hand, by his experience in literature of the abyss into which the German soul had been drawn, its metaphysical despair and apocalyptic inclinations; on the other hand, there was the French experience of his studies as a Jesuit which brought him into the *oecumene* of the Greek and Latin Fathers of the first Christian ages. For the young Balthasar there was then in the early Greek East Origen (d.253), who was for him 'the most

---

[8] Ibid., p. 4. [9] Ibid. [10] Ibid., p. 5. [11] Ibid., pp 2-3.

open and inspired of all those who interpret and love the Word of God,' and later in the Latin West Maximus the Confessor (d.622), for whom 'the Word was at once the revealer and the whole revelation of God, the divine sacrament of the ineffable God.' [12]

In this tradition of Word and words, described by de Lubac in the book he called *Catholicism*, the boundaries of reality are expanded, and Dante, a pilgrim on the face of the earth, can be guided through Hell, Purgatory and Paradise, by Virgil, Beatrice and Bernard to the Virgin-Mother of the eternal Word in the Trinity of God. In this harmony of scripture and poetry which is Catholic tradition Balthasar saw the only constructive approach possible and restorative synthesis which could lay the mystical foundation necessary to enlighten and enliven our times: 'if the immanent presence of God in this world reveals to us something of the divine essence itself and helps us comprehend why all creation aspires to rejoin its Creator, then the Word of God, the saving Logos, reveals to us the divine existence, the pure act of absolute love which draws God to the very heart of this world on the Cross. In fact this world takes its real meaning only in the Christocentric perspective.' [13]

In the second part of the sixteenth century, those fifty troubled years of Revolution more than Reformation, our present crisis in Word and words began to be. Then the scriptures, more the words of men than the Word of God, were powerless to practise what they preached. In the more historical than sacramental approach to scripture at this time there was little awareness of the mystery and presence of its Word, and none of the mythogical and metaphorical nature of its words; consequently, historical conflict put asunder the marriage of scripture and poetry God had joined together and, for the most part, laid the foundations for that empty searching historical criticism would continue. In the fulness of time the mystery of Israel had been made the revelation of the Gentiles; their poets became its prophets and brought into being those schools of intrepretation or mediaeval exegesis Aquinas preached and Dante practised. But neither Renaissance nor Reformation prepared us well for our brave new world, and Revolution won what Reformation began.

The seventeenth century in England began in theological dismay with theologians questioning much of Reformation innovation. Since Hooker, the Caroline Divines, theologians who flourished around the time of Charles I (1625-48) made scripture, tradition and reason the source and norm of reform and change. In this *appeal to tradition*, as it is now called, the Church of England then was anticipating what the Church of Rome now is intending in the scriptural, patristic and liturgical renewal of the Second Vatican Council. Each in its way was responding to the turmoil of the

---

12 E. Oakes, *Pattern of Redemption. The Theology of Hans Urs von Balthasar*, New York, 1994, pp 127-9.
13 Ibid.; cf. 'Balthasar and the Church Fathers', p. 102.

times and in the Catholicism of the Fathers recognized the fulness of revelation more than the universality of an institution. But for theologians like de Lubac and von Balthasar Catholicism remains the problem that it was for Caroline divines like Andrewes and Taylor in the Protestantism of their times. Then as now the sacramental mode of knowing was in doubt and in the words of man the Word of God was a real absence.

In the symbolic world of the ancients the Jewish Word of God was a veritable revelation, and Jewish Word and natural symbol became the sacrament of Christian worship. In this sacramental order of being, the biblical Word gave a new significance and presence to the metaphysical symbol, and this reality became the new world of the Greek and Latin Fathers. In their appeal to this tradition, Catholic and sacramental, the Carolines found new meaning in words of the ancient faith like *mystery* and *sacrament*, *similitude* and *symbol*, *type* and *representation*, which gave to their own words a real presence of significant being just as metaphysics was going out of fashion. But Jewish Word and patristic symbol, the thunder and lightning of God's presence in every age, then as now, was neither heard nor seen in the world of political noise and religious enthusiasm.

In the Jewish understanding of the Word of God, as in the tradition of the Fathers it would inspire, the divine Word, like the human word, is always the experience of someone else entering one's life – a fact, an event, a personal intervention in one's existence. 'The lion has roared,' says Amos, 'who will not fear? The Lord God has spoken, who can but prophecy?' [14] Here God bursts into our world by his Word or action and intervenes as the master in our existence: indeed, on every page of the Bible the divine Word defines and manifests itself in this way:

> Hear, O Israel: The Lord our God is one Lord; and you shall love the Lord your God with all your heart, and with all your soul, and with all your might. And these words which I command you this day shall be upon your heart; and you shall teach them diligently to your children, and shall talk of them when you sit in your house, and when you walk by the way, and when you lie down, and when you rise. And you shall bind them as a sign upon your hand, and they shall be as frontlets between your eyes. And you shall write them on the doorposts of your house and on your gates.[15]

This conviction in Israel about the power of the Word to assert and impose itself is so strong that even the ungodly kings beg the prophets not to prophesy unless it be in their favour; and for their part the prophets themselves, especially Jeremiah, Amos and Ezekiel, illustrate a similar conviction about the power of the

[14] Amos 3:8. [15] Deut 6:4.

Word, which surpasses their words, to go straight towards its fulfilment. This means that the Word, once it has made itself heard, takes possession of man and his history to accomplish the plan or mystery of salvation: 'It is truth that goes forth from my mouth,' says Isaiah, 'a Word beyond recall:'

> For as the rain and the snow come down from heaven, and return not thither but water the earth, making it bring forth and sprout, giving seed to the sower and bread to the eater, so shall my Word be that goes forth from my mouth; it shall not return to me empty but it shall accomplish that which I purpose, and prosper in the thing for which I sent it. [16]

In Israel, therefore, the *knowledge of God*, always and primarily the knowledge that God has of us, will go hand in hand with his preferential election of a people for the revelation of his plan of salvation. Ultimately, this knowledge is that merciful love he pours into our sinful selves; more precisely, for Hosea, God behaves towards Israel like a man in love with a harlot; and for Ezekiel, it is to the child of adultery, abandoned from birth, a true waif, that the unmerited love of God goes out to set her on her feet, bring her up and make her into a queen. The royal epithalamion of Psalm 45 is a figured description of this union under the guise of a marriage between an Israelite king and a foreign princess; and the Song of Songs was only received into the canon of inspired books when the Shulammite woman was seen as the daughter of Zion called to a union of love by and with the King of Heaven.

As a consequence of the knowledge God has of us the knowledge that we are called to have of him will be a participation in his very being and love. Hence the nuptial imagery in Genesis where 'Adam knew his wife Eve' continues in Israel the life-giving action of the Word, and in Christ, the Word made flesh, or spouse of the Church, 'loved the Church and gave himself up for her, that he might sanctify her, having cleansed her by the washing of water with a word; that he might present the church to himself in splendour, without spot or wrinkle or any such thing, that she might be holy and without blemish.'[17] Such is the verb or action of the Word made flesh in spirit and in truth: indeed, the union of two lives expressed and accomplished in bodily oneness is *knowledge of God* in the full sacramental sense of the biblical term. Ultimately to know God as we have been known is to acknowledge the love with which he loves us and pursues us to the ends of the earth and to the end of time.

In this understanding of *knowledge of God* as Word of Revelation and obedient faith we are simply meant to be what He simply is – one, true, good and beautiful

---

[16] Is 55:10-11. [17] Eph 5:27.

in His being, as von Balthasar would have us say. We can therefore unmistakably understand how the Word of God in Jewish piety came to be identified with the Torah or Law of Life,[18] which impresses on the Israelite the seal or image of the One who communicates it. Thus neither *lex* in the narrow Latin sense, nor *nomos* in the broader sense of the Greeks can mean what Torah meant for the Israelite – the revelation of what God himself is in what he wills to do with the people he has chosen. 'Be Holy as I am Holy' is His Law.[19]

In the other historical books of the Bible the Law of the Pentateuch is seen to develop as Torah or that presence of God or *Shekinah* which is a union of God with his people; indeed, the observance of the Law places God in the life of those whom he has known and who know him in return. 'This interiorization and humanization of the Law as Torah is seen in the transformation of literature from the ancient East after its contact with the Word of God in Israel. In the East Wisdom was a practical knowledge that focused on the art of living; however, in Israel Wisdom becomes the gift of the Spirit and projects the light of heaven onto the experience and rational reflection of man.'[20]

The seven wisdom books of the Old Testament, or first fruits of the Spirit, are the beginning in Israel of a literature, more sacred than profane. In Job, Proverbs, Ecclesiastes, Sirach and Wisdom the human condition is considered in its joy and sorrow, suffering and success, happiness and vanity; then versified by the skilful use of parallelism it is expressed in the balanced phrases peculiar to Hebrew poetry. 'But in the Psalms of David, as in the Song of Songs, there is manifestly more in Jewish sacred literature than the symmetrical phrase of a Hebrew poet.'[21] In the Psalms, or *Gospel according to the Holy Spirit*, Wisdom is identified with the *Shekinah* and the presence is made to dwell, not in a sanctuary made by man but in the reconciled heart of Israel made by God. And so from a Wisdom that seemed to come from the poetic words of man we pass over to the apocalypse and prophecy of the Word – the expectation and revelation of God's impenetrable ultimate plan, purpose or mystery in which he will reveal himself to his people in the flesh so that he might soon be revealed to the whole world in a definitive and final way.

Mystery, or divine purpose, is of the essence of biblical Wisdom and progressively revealed and communicated in history, as at Passover and Covenant, it is constantly renewed and celebrated in the worship of praise, petition and thanksgiving. In the chanting of the psalms, as in the *berekoth* of house and home, synagogue and Temple, the Word of God was kept *alive and active* to revive the Law and beget the Prophet; more specifically the Psalms of David, written over a seven hundred year span, kept repeating and fostering the hope of the promised Redeemer, and preserved

[18] Cf. Ps 119. [19] Mt 5:48; cf. Lev 19:2. [20] Bouyer, op. cit., pp 39ff. [21] L. Bouyer, *The Meaning of Sacred Scripture*, Notre Dame, Ind., 1958; cf. 'The Word of God in Israel,' pp 1-14.

that unity of the Law and the Prophets that is known to us as the Old Testament. As in Israel's sacrifice of praise where the psalms spoke for them as the scriptures spoke to them, so too in ours, and the bond of the Testaments, Old and New, is now preserved as was the unity of the Law and the Prophets then.

Prophecy, the other side of the mystery-coin in the history of Israel, is the fulfilment of the Law, as the Logos will be of Moses and Elijah, the Law and the Prophets. Again in the span of some eight hundred years no more than eighteen in all were chosen to read the signs of their times and announce the Word of the Lord, although the phenomenon of inspiration or prophecy was widespread. In the Hellenic world, as in the Semitic, there was the *heiros logos*, or sacred word, of the Pythian oracle; even today, in the valley of Delphi there is the irresistable sense of a divine presence ready to speak! But in Israel the God of the prophets, who takes possession of his chosen, is no cosmic power, no simple reflection of the sub-human world, but the Lord of all things and free in relation to his creation. He reveals himself in fire from heaven, but he does so ever more clearly in the faint undefinable murmur by which Elias, the man of God, perceives his personal presence and prostrates himself before the Holy and Infinitely-Other. With these prophets there is revealed, from age to age, the mysterious design of the Almighty, who is the Lord of history, as he is of creation.

The prophets of Israel, unlike the ecstatics or *enthusiasmoi* of Plato, were the first to be struck by the absolute originality of their own experience: 'I am no prophet, nor a prophet's son,'said Amos in the eighth century, 'I am a herdsman, and a dresser of sycamore trees; the Lord took me from following the flock, and the Lord said to me, 'Go, prophesy to my people Israel;'[22] and then the uncultured shepherd is made the mouthpiece of the Divine Judgment for himself and for the people: 'you yourself shall die in an unclean land, and Israel shall surely go into exile away from its land.' In the same way Hosea, a husband profoundly in love with an unworthy wife, is made the prophet of the divine love for an unfaithful people: she shall pursue her lovers, but not overtake them; then she shall say, 'I will go and return to my first husband, for it was better with me then than now.'[23] Thus Israel is made to grow in her knowledge of God by the words of her prophets; in her own sinfulness she is made aware of the holiness of her God.

Later in Juda a different kind of man, the aristocratic Isaiah, is possessed by the same divine Word in the Temple sanctuary: 'And one called to another and said, Holy, Holy, Holy is the Lord of Hosts; the whole earth is full of his Glory.' [24] This idea of the holy as the glory or mystery of the *kabod*, at once *tremendum* and *fascinans*, is a real radiation of light, a kind of fire of which the Seraphim are, as

[22] Amos 17:15-16. [23] Hos 2: 7-8.

it were, the condensation. In the Bible whatever God touches reflects this light like the shining face of Moses; it is as it were his stamp or seal on the things and beings he has made his own. And the Seraphim with a burning coal from the altar touched the unclean lips of the prophet and he answered, 'Here am I. Send me.'[25] This knowledge of God in the holiness of his being cannot be reduced to any moral teaching or psychological notion; nor can it be separated from the justice of Amos or the mercy of Hosea that are the bread and wine of the Temple sacrifice.

Jeremiah, a century later, with his 'God of the heart'[26] will follow Isaiah and the God of holiness, as the mercy of Hosea followed the justice of Amos. Unlike Isaiah he was reluctant to accept his call: 'Ah, Lord God! Behold, I do not know how to speak, for I am only a youth.' Then, 'the Lord put forth his hand, touched my mouth and said to me, 'I have put my words in your mouth.'' [27] His vocation was to experience in his own heart the destruction of the Temple, the desertion of the city and the dispersion of the people: in these trials and tribulations he would prefigure the suffering servant on the cross, whose sufferings would be for the healing of the nations. In this way he would lay the foundation of the new and eternal covenant in the heart of man; God would demand his heart but in return would promise him His. 'I will give them a heart that knows me, aware that I am Yahweh: they shall be my people and I will be their God, for they shall return to me with their whole heart.' And again he says: 'I will put my Law within them, and I will write it in their heart, and I will be their God, and they shall be my people.'[28]

Like Jeremiah, Ezekiel too experienced the ruination of Israel in her hour of glory; he also experienced the *kabod* of Israel departing the Temple and leaving the sanctuary of its own accord. Then, borne on the wings of the Cheroubim the Glory abandons the city and goes away above the Mount of Olives. It is from there that it departs to rejoin the faithful in exile: 'I have sent them afar among the nations and scattered them among the countries; but I will be to them as a sanctuary in the countries where they have gone.'[29] Then follows the promise of the return, of the restoration, of the covenant renewed along the lines Jeremiah had laid out: [30] 'somehow the departure of the Presence, the *Shekinah*, makes this new covenant possible for the 'remnant'; it would prepare them to become the people of God in its definitive form.' [31] Indeed, 'it is better for you that I go!': the death of Israel with the heart of stone was the resurrection of the spiritual Israel with the heart of flesh. The real absence would become the real Presence in the final phase of the mystery – the Hour of Jesus:

24 Is 6:3. 25 Bouyer, op. cit.; 'Isaiah and the God of Holiness', pp 69-81. 26 Jer 1:6ff; cf. Bouyer, op. cit., 'Jeremiah and the God of the Heart', pp 82-90. 27 Jer., 24:7. 28 Ibid., 31:31-33; also 32: 38-40. 29 Ezek 8:10-12. 30 Ezek 11:16.

> The Lord is King; let earth rejoice;
> Let all the coastlands be glad.
> Cloud and darkness are his raiment;
> His throne, justice and right.
>
> The mountains melt like wax
> Before the Lord of all the earth.
> The skies proclaim his justice;
> All peoples see his Glory.
>
> Light shines forth for the just,
> And joy for the upright of heart;
> Rejoice, you just, in the Lord;
> Give Glory to his Holy Name. [32]

At the end of the Old Covenant, as in the biblical position of the Minor Prophets after the Law and before the Logos, there is the expectation of a supreme revelation in an unprecedented outpouring of the Word and its Spirit. Joel calls for penance to avert the Day of the Lord, just as Nahum passes judgment on Nineveh; similarily, Habakkuk inveighs against the enemies of Juda, and for Obadiah the Kingdom of the Lord, like the Day of the Lord and the Doom of Edom, is at hand. But the remnant of Zephaniah and the Second Temple of Haggai would be the *fons et origo* of the salvation, universal and messianic, announced by Jonah and Micah, the prophet of Bethlehem. A contemporary of Haggai in the sixth century, Zechariah, the penultimate book of the Law and the Prophets, will announce the Prince of Peace and his coming. Finally there is Malachi, the last of the minor prophets, to announce at the end of the Old Testament the sacrifice of the New: 'for from the rising of the sun to its setting [...] and in every place, incense is offered to my name, and a pure offering.'[33] Then comes John, Elijah, the prophet of God, the Most High, to prepare his ways and to guide us into the way of peace – the Hour of Christ in history.

In Judaic and Christian tradition the different positioning of our eighteen prophetic books of the Old Testament, called major and minor according to their length, has its own significance. In the Hebrew Bible Isaiah, Jeremiah and Ezekiel are grouped together but followed immediately by the Twelve Minor Prophets. Both groups are known as the Later Prophets and distinguished with a certain historical significance from the Former Prophets of Joshua, Judges, 1 & 2 Samuel, and 1 & 2 Kings. The Greek Bible with a certain liturgical significance places

---

[31] Bouyer, op.cit.; 'Ezekiel and the Temple,' pp 91-7. [32] Ps 97:1. [33] Mal 1:11.

those prophetic books after the Psalms and the books of Wisdom, and adds to the collection of major prophets Lamentations, Baruch and the exile Daniel, more apocalyptic than prophetic. In the Latin Vulgate this arrangement continues but places the twelve minor prophets after the six major ones with a very definite Christological or messianic significance. In fact the structure of the Christian Bible as a whole, centered on Christ as the revelation of the apocalyptic mystery, takes us, at its beginning as at its end, out of time and into eternity: in Genesis, protology, the study of our origins, is our focus as is eschatology, the study of our destiny, in Revelation; but always God's mystery creates our history as we learn in time to read the signs of eternity.

In the pious practices of Roman Catholics the Annunciation, Visitation, Nativity, Presentation in the Temple and the Finding there of the Christ child are commonly known as the Joyful Mysteries. But in the scriptures these mysteries are markers to speed us through the historical distractions of thirty years to the hour of Jesus, the Christ of God and the Mystery of our Pasch. In historical criticism there are many questions about the census of Quirinius which Joseph, a just man, may, or may not, have been observing; but there is seldom any question about the prophecy of Micah which Joseph, son of David, may also, or may not, have been consciously fulfilling. Never is this guardian of the Word made flesh ever considered within the prophetic tradition as a man possessed by that very Word, and this is surely strange. Obsession with the details of the shadows may indeed blind us to the light of the reality.

In the Gospels, mystery and history, as reality and shadow, are usually expressed in the word and symbol of the hour of Jesus. At Cana his hour had not yet come for the messianic sign; again according to John, when they sought to arrest him, no one laid hands upon him, because his *hour* had not yet come; at the Last Supper the *hour* had come for the Father to *glorify* the Son and the Son to *glorify* the Father; and for Matthew the *hour* was at hand when Judas came and kissed him. So is history the temporal unfolding of the eternal mystery of our passover and covenant, for Jesus is no mere moralist, or contriver of metaphysics: 'he came to transform us and the world by a divine action that no created intelligence could have foreseen or even conceived. Since the death of Socrates men may be more enlightened about reality than they were before; but since the death of Jesus, reality itself is wholly transformed or transfigured.' [34] Christ Jesus is indeed the sacrament of man's encounter with his God.

The apparitions of Christ in Jesus, in the fulness of time and its hour, brought to its end the age of the biblical prophet: 'the Law and the Prophets were until

---

34 L. Bouyer, *The Paschal Mystery*, London 1951, 'The Hour of Jesus', pp 37ff; Jn 2:4; Jn 17:1; Jn 7:30; Mt 26:45.

John; since then the Gospel of the Kingdom of God is preached, and everyone enters it violently.' Like John, 'a man sent from God,' the Nazarean of Isaiah, or 'Branch of Jesse,'[35] was also 'more than a prophet,' and Infinitely more so. In Matthew he came 'not to abolish the Law and the Prophets, but to fulfil them;' and in Paul are found the words to say what must be said about that Word:

> Now to Him who is able to strengthen you according to my Gospel and the preaching, of Jesus Christ, according to the Revelation of the Mystery, which was kept [...] secret [...] for long ages, but through the prophetic writings is now made known to all, according to the [...] decree [...] of the eternal God for the obedience of faith [...] to the Wisdom of God,' *Glory* for evermore through Jesus Christ! Amen. [36]

The presence of the Word of God in the words of the apostles, and the preservation of their words as our scriptures continues in time the mystery of the Incarnation: 'here the *Verbum Caro* attains its perfection; flesh has become wholly a word at the disposition of the eternal Word.' This presence of the eternal Word in our temporal words, like the Word of God in the mouth of the prophet, fills with a fulness which is infinitely more than the words of history or poetry can ever possess. Scripture then is the full flower and fruit of the Word made flesh, and the Old and New Testaments are now our 'Word of Christ' (Rom 10:17) and 'river of life' (Rev 22:1), kerygma or Gospel. Thus the entire Old Testament, and not just certain messianic texts, was so prophetically opened out towards the New that for Christ and the apostles it was their sacred source, and became the words of the Word made flesh – indeed, in the words of the New the Word of the Old was made flesh again, came to be and is preserved in its being for the healing of the nations.

In this new context or experience the specific meaning of the old phrase, Word of God, became that of 'the Good News' or the Gospel – the announcement of the fact of Christ, including his teaching and redeeming action. In the Acts of the Apostles the office of the Twelve will be described interchangeably as 'the ministry of the Word' (6:4) or 'preaching – testifying to the Jews that the Christ was Jesus' (18:5). In this sense the Word proclaimed by the Apostles to the world will be called 'word of Salvation' (13:26), 'word of grace' (14:3), 'word of the cross' (1 Cor 1:18), 'word of reconciliation' (2 Cor 5:19), 'word of truth' (2 Cor 6:7; Eph 1:13; Col 1:5; 2 Tim 2:15; Jas 1:18) 'word of life,' or 'living word.' (Phil 2:16; Heb 4:12; 1 Pet 1:23) This Word, of which Christ is source and summit, is fused with the New Law, the New Covenant, the new creation (Lk 22:20; Jn 13:34; 2 Cor 5:17) brought about by Him and brought to us in Him. And so the Glory that departed the Temple is seen to dwell again in the words of John – *the Word was made Flesh*, or pitched his tent among us.

[35] Is 11:1-10. [36] Rom 14:25-26.

Scripture in this light is easily seen as the primary source of revelation in the Church, a sort of rock upon which the Church is built. As the twelve foundation stones of the Church there can be no successors to the apostles other than their own living words. As ministers of the Word of God, bishops, priests and deacons are ordained in every age and place to proclaim the words of those apostles. In the sanctuary of the Church they perform this priestly ministry and speak the Word of Salvation. There as in the cloud of darkness, they feel the Word of God, and there too, as in a cloud of light, they hear the words of the apostles; less priestly functions, like governing and teaching, may be performed elsewhere and are for our times and making. But the Word of God alone is fixed and lasts for ever; for all time too that Word is fixed to the words of the apostles, as it was fixed for a moment in time to the flesh of the Word.

Criticism, textual and historical, may help the student to appreciate the complexity of scripture's being and becoming; but for the mature believer, the bible, whole and complete, and regardless of the protraction of its completion, is now the Glory or, *kabod*, Presence or *shekinah*, of *Emmanuel*, or God with us, and its existence and endurance in time can neither be fully explained nor explained away. This source of wisdom, divine and human, simply is; it exists and is the Word of God; He who is: it reveals God's grace in history or time, and in Genesis, its prologue, as in Revelation, its epilogue, it lets in the light of eternity on man's origin and destiny. Glory, sin and grace are the words of its mystery and salvation: from a human point of view, no text of secular literature presents such a bewildering wealth of perspectives; one single word may have hundreds of echoes and the religious experience of many ages are accumulated in such a word; indeed its words come to us from far away, charged with a kind of Infinity, much meaning, and innumerable reflections, stratum upon stratum.

In the New Testament there are no prophets in the Old Testament sense, although Paul mentions them with apostles, teachers and the other gifts; in this sense they would seem to be Christian preachers, as prophet and preacher were revealed as one and the same in the synagogue at Nazareth: 'today this scripture is fulfilled in your hearing.' This understanding of preaching as the fulfillment of scripture makes the homily prophetic in the deepest sense; indeed, the essential nature of prophecy speaks to the present with divine authority, transforms the historical revelation into a contemporaneous dynamic reality and does not merely foretell the future in some vague vision or other. At Nazareth Isaiah was the inspiration of the prophetic Word and the worship of the synagogue its source; in the generations that would follow those synagogal dimensions of preaching would develop in the Gentile world as Greek homily and Latin sermon; in the course of time other forms of preaching would arise – less exegetical, less liturgical, less prophetic; more often than not those other forms would be that beating about the *bush* that puts the *burning* out.

In this new Christian world of Greek homily and Latin sermon the influence of prophecy in preaching would be seen in a new form of scriptural exegesis or interpretation. In traditional exegesis, biblical or classical, the interpretation of a text ranged from the crudest literalism to the wildest flights of fancy. But in the new order of Christian faith and exegesis, called typology, mystery and history were sacramentally one, and both Testaments, Old and New, were seen as successive stages in the progress or revelation of the one divine mystery or plan. Thus Christian exegesis corresponds neither to literal exegesis, or hermeneutics, concerned with the characters, institutions and events of the Old Testament in themselves, nor to allegorical exegesis, which covers the many possible uses to be made of scripture considered as a complex of symbols. But in the causal connection or interrelation of those intertestamental events one can read the signs of those saving times and sense and see the presence and power of the Word of God, acting according to the divine plan and creating our history and its redemption.

On the other hand, preaching as a contemporary term in English had its origins in Reformation theology and not in the New Testament notion of *kerygma* or proclamation as the sacrament of the Word. As a result the separation of Word and words remains and can be seen in our traditions of Western Christianity. Catholicism. for example, developed its doctrines as *kerygma* and *didache* grew further apart: indeed for nearly a thousand years, the *kerygma* was proclaimed to the masses in a dead language, and where the scriptures do not speak teaching can become the dogma of an institution. Protestantism, on the other hand, recovered the scriptures and to some extent their primacy, but without a corresponding emphasis on *kerygma* and liturgy instruction is easily tied to a dead book. In these circumstances demonic literalism can prevail and the language of myth and metaphor, which tells of things no eye has seen nor ear has heard, is soon forgotten. Without myth and metaphor we can do little to broaden our horizons, and without the typology of biblical faith less to light our path through Genesis and Revelation; so we remain prisoners of history without mystery. Even a sedate local Church can easily lose its pilgrim soul and degenerate into an hierarchical institution, content with its doctrines and laws and the mores of its tribe. Scripture alone can preserve the people of God from the dangers of arrival; it is always a departure, a journey from the image to the truth, from the promise to fulfillment, from the Word to the Word made flesh; it is also a pasch from physical death to spiritual life [...], a journey from the physical presence, through the absence, caused by his death and resurrection and ascension, towards the eschatological presence. All this truth is made up of tension, *diastasis*; it is the truth of the *cor inquietum*, hope and longing love [...] to relieve the devouring stress of existence.[37]

---

37 H. Urs von Balthasar, ed., *Liturgy and the Word of God*, Collegeville, Minn., 1959, p. 42.

PREACHING AND PREACHERS

The Septuagint (LXX) and the Vulgate (VG) were cardinal points in the history of language and civilization, of words and the Word, for the Hebrew scriptures, even on the natural level, were a revelation and inspired first in Greek (c.250 BC) and later in Latin (c.350 AD) new structures of thought and new modes of expression. Similarly, the renaissance of Hebrew, Greek and Latin after the century of Dante, Aquinas and the Gothic, marks another moment in human awareness, another harmony in nature and grace, and, consequently, another expression in language and literature as in architecture and art. In those circumstances, the scriptural reformation of the Church in England and the use of the vernacular in worship influenced the development of Elizabethan English and eventually occasioned the Authorized Version of the scriptures (AV, 1611) commonly called the King James Bible. Like the Greek Septuagint and the Latin Vulgate, the English James was a new text in a new world and it also inspired its own golden age of pulpit oratory and English literature: 'indeed, in a certain qualified sense, it may be broadly said that the Septuagint, the Vulgate and the James gave rise respectively to the Greek Homily, the Latin Sermon and English Preaching. In our English speaking parts of the world this period of Renaissance in words and Reformation in Word ought not be ignored, as all Churches are in need of a sanctuary language in our secular worlds.'[1]

While English preaching flourished in the early seventeeth century, its origins go back to the friars of Dominic and Francis in the early thirteenth century, and more specifically to the Council of Oxford in 1222, presided over by Stephen Langton, archbishop of Canterbury. There an attempt was made to bring into force in England the decrees of the Fourth Lateran Council (1215). Accordingly, preaching and visiting of the sick were placed on an equal footing and 'rectors and vicars were obliged by decree to be diligent instructors of the people in the Word of God.'[2] Thus, for the first time, a decree on preaching became part of the canon law of the Church in England; hitherto, as in an age of teaching, parish priests were merely obliged to expound and explain the Creed, Commandments, Pater and Ave three or four times a year. In this practice the exegetical, liturgical and prophetic exposition of the scriptures is no more as once it was in Jewish synagogue, Greek homily and Latin sermon.

The emergence of the friar, or itinerant preacher, in the provinces and parishes of the late middle ages was a veritable revelation in itself: 'here was a man trained in the schools [...] traveller, friend of the outcast, master alike of the ecclesiastical and the

---

1 T.K. Carroll, 'The Genius of the Latin Sermon', *Irish Theological Quarterly* 63:4 (1999), pp 341-61.
2 Ibid., p. 359.

popular tongue, with intimate knowledge of the world as well as of books, he could mingle in his discourse the latest narration with the mysteries of nature, to please in method and invent by rule – *joculator Dei* of St Francis and sacred pedlar rolled into one – for ever bringing forth out of his treasures things new and old.'[3] In the cities and towns, he was no less a marvel and the huge nave-shaped churches at such places as Blackfriars in Norwich or Austin Friars in London are monuments to the popularity of their preaching revolution. Such churches were built, fitted and furnished for congregations of listeners: 'for the first time the pew was introduced where Mass worshippers had previously knelt, and the stone pulpit, sometimes elaborately carved, became an integral and well positioned part of the whole structure, and was no longer a mere wooden and moveable lectern as it was in the days of teaching and as it is again in our restructured sanctuaries.'[4]

The influence of the friars on the matter and form of English Preaching has endured for better and for worse, like their use and abuse of the schema and the exempla. The construction of a sermon according to a fixed and rigid scheme of divisions and sub-divisions, and its adornment according to the conventions of scholastic eloquence, reflects the sphere and influence of the University, where the friars enjoyed many of their preaching triumphs; on the other hand, their use of the exempla by way of anecdote or illustration shows their understanding of the medieval congregation and what has been described as 'either their genius for the common touch or their pernicious habit of playing to the gallery: in all ages of the Church's history, the line between the two is perilously thin, and it is only the resources of his secret and interior life that can save the popular preacher from transgressing it.'[5]

This new style of preaching or sermon, pedantic in the school and popular in the parish, was a deviation from the exegetical dimension of the Greek homily, and the liturgical dimension of the Latin Sermon, and was aimed at the evangelization of the masses. Now there was chosen from the gospel of the day, or from the epistle, or indeed from any place in scripture, a single text which was developed theme-like according to the rules of medieval rhetoric. Following the 'Rule of Three', the new type of sermon had three parts: (i) the introduction, explaining the text, describing the occasion, and presenting the subject to the imagination; (ii) the body, giving the exempla, answering objections and appealing to the understanding; (iii) the conclusion, making the application, pointing out the consequences, and appealing to the will: 'single things said are soon forgotten. Too many confuse. Arrangement in three binds them together, and a threefold cord is not swiftly broken.'[6]

---

3 C. Smyth, *The Art of Preaching. A Practical Survey of Preaching in the Church of England, 747-1939*, London, 1953, p. 15.   4 Ibid., p. 17.   5 Ibid., p.18.   6 Ibid., '1. The Sermon Scheme', pp 19-54.

The thirteenth and fourteenth centuries were the golden age of the exemplum in the history of the English pulpit. Hitherto, anecdotes and illustrations were an accessory to the homily or sermon and were sparingly used by the Cistercians of the previous century to drive home their message, and to encourage their congregation to emulate the good deeds of holy men and women; but with the friars the exemplum became an integral, and, at times dangerous, part of the sermon as a whole, and all and sundry were made grist to the preacher's mill: 'similes drawn from characters and scenes of everyday life; figures of allegory, often scriptural in origin but non-scriptural in development; bible stories and legends of the saints; and, commonest and most popular of all, the rich and varied class of moralized anecdotes, whether true or fictitious, drawn from sources both ancient and contemporary, secular as well as religious.'[7] Autobiographical reminiscences are, strangely enough, comparatively rare, and personal exempla are usually introduced at second or third hand and in a set form: 'This is a story which I learned from the lips of a certain very truthful and holy man, who asserted that he had himself witnessed the fact which he narrated to me.'[8] Collections of such exempla – forerunners of such modern compilations as *A Thousand and One Things to Say in a Sermon* – were published without interruption in those centuries, and survive to tell the tale of medieval preaching and should encourage the revival of the Greek homily and the Latin sermon.

In this form of preaching, the Word of God played no vital part, for the scripture text was little more than a peg for the preacher's theme. There is here no wrestling with the Word, 'no preaching as of a dying man to dying men.'[9] Consequently, people like John Wycliffe (d. 1384) at Oxford called for a return to the older method of expounding a portion or chapter of the bible, instead of extracting a text and constructing a sermon around it: 'this ornamental style of preaching is little in keeping with God's Word [...] for heroic declamation and scholastic eloquence, devoid of evangelical content, is like a nurse presenting a dry breast to a bairn.'[10]

Renaissance and Reformation in words and Word produced in English 'the power of the pulpit,' and that golden age from Fisher to Taylor, which is part and parcel of England's literary heritage. In this new harmony of Antiquity and Christianity, of classical letters and sacred scriptures, the schema and the exempla of the medieval friars were restrained and refined, and from the mid-sixteenth century English preaching flourished for over a hundred years. Bishop Lancelot Andrewes (1555-1626) is the best example of this renaissance and reformation, and of the medieval *artes praedicandi* influencing the renewal of the sermon or the schema of English preaching in his day: 'Andrewes placed the "exordium" with a closing

---

[7] Ibid., '2. The Exemplum', pp 55-94. [8] Ibid., pp 61ff. [9] H. Davies, *Worship and Theology in England*, vol. 2, Princeton, N.J., 1975, p. 162. [10] Smyth, op. cit., p. 54; cf. H.B. Workman, *John Wyclif. A Study of the English Medieval Church*, vol. 2, London, 1926, pp 211-12.

prayer ahead of the text and the beginning of the sermon proper. He excelled in a minute division of his theme, he loved Latin and Greek citations and an ingenious play on words, but at the same time he did not worship form for its own sake. He was a devout man and a serious theologian and the Spinozistic subject arrangement was usually a real expression of a thoughtful and laborious dialectic.'[11] Likewise, in the "illustrative" sermons of Bishop Jeremy Taylor (1613-67), the medieval *exempla* of the friars are much refined by this great master of the simile, as he makes use of the whole of Noah's Ark: 'the silkworm is an illustration of the development of the soul, the bee's busy life illuminates the blessing of marriage, and the crocodile who is always growing exhibits the danger of sinful habits.'[12]

The changes in the liturgical life of the Church of England, in this time of renewal, had a profound effect on English Preaching as homily or sermon, for it continued and promoted the non-liturgical preaching of the medieval friars more than the homilies and sermons of the Greek and Latin Fathers: 'as long as the service of the Lord's Supper retained its character as a high mass, as was the case in the First Prayer Book of Edward VI (1549) it was natural for the sermon to maintain its place in the service and to be based upon the established pericopes. The collection of model sermons, Book of Homilies, edited by Thomas Cranmer in 1547, was based upon these pericopes and was a parallel exhibit to the Lutheran postils. Its influence on the later history of preaching was meagre. But when the mass became a communion service, as in the Books of Common Prayer of 1552 and 1559 (also 1662), the service no longer offered a natural place for a sermon directed at the whole congregation [...] and later developments pushed aside the communion mass (completely) and made morning and evening prayer the best-attended worship services on Sunday. No organic place for the sermon was found in these prayer offices. The sermon became a non-liturgical addition even though it was set in the framework of hymn singing, itself a later addition to the old liturgical order.'[13]

In these circumstances, the liturgical dimension of English preaching was much diminished, but not, however, entirely lost. There remained the Church's Year, and certain other liturgical elements like the constant use of the psalms, to continue at least the language of preaching if not to express the presence and power of its mystery. Secondly, the exegetical dimension, so characteristic of the Greek homily, was equally diminished, when the pericopes or fixed liturgical readings were no longer used as preaching texts: 'Instead, the later Reformed custom of speaking on a short passage of Scripture, which had the character of a word of introduction or motto rather than of an actual text, was introduced. A great portion of the extant homiletical literature exhibits this character and is hardly distinguishable

---

11 Ibid., p. 123.   12 Ibid., p. 115; = Taylor, vol. 4, pp 221 and 285.   13 John Donne, *Sermons, Devotions and Prayers*, ed. J. Booty, Classics of Western Spirituality Series, New York, 1900, pp 45ff.

in any formal sense from the Reformed practice.'[14] Nevertheless, in English preaching in particular, as indeed in the preaching of the Reformers in general, there was struck at this time a new and distinctive note, and in the preaching of Donne, the Carolines and the Puritans, there is a clear sounding of the preacher's role as prophet: 'To them thou shall be a Tuba or Trumpet. Thy preaching shall awaken them and so bring them to some sense of their sins.' But then for Donne, who was more Caroline than Puritan, more Catholic than Protestant, the preacher shall become 'Carmen musicum [...] a musical and harmonious charmer, to settle and compose the soul again in a reposed confidence, and in a delight in God.'[15]

Jeremy Taylor, the Shakespeare of English prose according to Coleridge, was the *carmen musicum*, par excellence, of the Caroline Divines. Pastor, poet and preacher, 'his words have the timeless quality of the eternal Word, which he heard (a) in creation, the Word made mystery; (b) in Christ Jesus, the Word made flesh; and (c) in Scripture. the Word made words. In the words of Jeremy Taylor, Renaissance and Reformation man alike, the Word of God 'charms ever so wisely (Ps 58:5) the pilgrim's inner ear in every age.'[16]

> There is in the things of God to them which practise them a deliciousness that makes us love them, and that love admits us into God's cabinet, and strangely clarifies the understanding by the purification of the heart. For when our reason is raised up by the Spirit of Christ, it is turned quickly into experience; when our faith relies upon the principles of Christ, it is changed into vision. And so long as we know God only in the ways of man, by contentious learning, by arguing and dispute, we see nothing but the shadow of Him, and in that shadow we meet with many dark appearances, little certainty, and much conjecture. But when we know Him with the eyes of holiness, and the intuition of gracious experience, with a quiet spirit and the peace of enjoyment, then we shall hear what we never heard and see what our eyes never saw; then the mysteries of godliness shall be opened unto us, and clear as the windows of the morning.[17]

These primordial words, like those of a poet, are filled with the soft music of infinity; spoken by Taylor, the preacher, such words are sacramental like those of Chrysostom and Augustine, and communicate directly to the pilgrim's soul a presence and a peace that is transcendent and real:

---

14 W.F. Mitchell, *English Pulpit Oratory from Andrewes to Tillotson*, New York, 1964; 'Preaching as a branch of rhetoric,' pp 93-101.   15 J.W. Blench, *Preaching in England in the Late Fifteenth and Sixteenth Centuries*, New York, 1964, pp. 102-3; 106-7; cf. *John Donne*, ed. Booty, op. cit., p. 46.   16 Carroll, *Jeremy Taylor*, op. cit., p. 5.   17 Taylor, vol. 8: p. 379.

> There is a sort of God's dear servants who walk in perfectness; [...] and they have a degree of clarity and divine knowledge more than we can discourse of, and more certain than the demonstration of geometry, brighter than the sun and indeficient as the light of heaven [...] This is called by the apostle the *apaugasma tou theou*. Christ is this 'brightness of God,' manifested in the hearts of His dearest servants [...] But I shall say no more of this at this time, for this is to be felt and not be taked of; and they that never touched it with their finger, may secretly perhaps laugh at it in their heart, and be never the wiser. All that I shall now say of it is, that a good man is united unto God, as a flame touches a flame, and combines into splendour and to glory: so is the spirit of a man united unto Christ by the Spirit of God. These are the friends of God, and they best know God's mind, and they only that are so know how much such men do know. They have a special unction from above so that now you are come to the top of all; this is the highest round of the ladder, and the angels stand upon it: they dwell in love and contemplation, they worship and obey, but dispute not: and our quarrels and impertinent wranglings about religion are nothing else but the want of the measures of this state. Our light is like a candle, every wind of vain doctrine blows it out or spends the wax, and makes the light tremulous; but the lights of heaven are fixed and bright and shine for ever.[18]

Taylor, like his predecessor Donne, was more than a poet and more than a prophet: in his mystical moments, his sermons were meditations on 'those secrets of spiritual benediction,' that are deep down and heartfelt by any disciple who is grown old in religion and in conversations with the Spirit: 'This man best understands the secret [...] and feels this unintelligible mystery, and sees with his heart what his tongue can never express and his metaphysics can never prove.' This vision of the heart – 'what heart heard of, ghost guessed' – and which not even the poet's tongue can express – 'nor mouth had, no nor mind expressed' – is God-given. God opens the heart and creates a new one, and without this new creation, this new principle of life, we may hear the sounds of God's Word but never feel its spirit: Taylor is a high-priest of this new mystical way that Renaissance and Reformation paved and prepared:

> Unless there there be in our hearts a secret conviction by the Spirit of God, the gospel in itself is a dead letter and worketh not in us the light and righteousness of God, [...] for [...] the Scriptures [...] are written within and without [...] and unless there be a light shining within our hearts, unfolding

---

18 Ibid., p. 380.

the leaves and interpreting the mysterious sense of the Spirit, convincing our consciences and preaching to our hearts, to look for Christ in the leaves of the gospel is to look for the living among the dead.[19]

This mystical dimension of English preaching inspired in Taylor a combination of sound and image, which enchants the ear and fascinates the eye. But side by side with this magic of style, which flourished and faded in Caroline times, there was the cult of 'scriptural and christian plainness' favoured by preachers like George Herbert, which was no less inspired by Renaissance taste and Reformation belief. The religious dimension of the Renaissance in England brought to life not only the words of Cicero and Seneca, but also those of Chrysostom and Augustine and the tradition of the Fathers and the Reformation made all those masters of words, classical and patristic, to be servants of the Word. James Ussher (1581-1656), Church of Ireland archbishop of Armagh, and earliest, if not foremost, master of the Fathers in the English language, was seen during his residency in Oxford in 1642 as the protagonist of 'scriptural and christian plainness' in the pulpit: 'nothwithstanding the learnedness of most of his hearers, he rather chose a plain substantial way of preaching, for the promoting of piety and virtue than studied eloquence, or a vain ostentation of learning; so that he quite put out of countenance that windy, affected sort of oratory which was then much in use, called 'floride preaching or strong lines.'[20]

Ussher's contemporary, John Wilkins (1614-72), bishop of Chester. continued in his preaching the plain and direct style of the Irish primate: 'He spoke solid truth, with as little show of art as possible. He expressed all things in their true and natural colours, with that aptness and plainness of speech that grave natural way of elocution that showed he had no design upon his hearers [...]. In his writings, too, he was judicious and plain, like one that valued not the circumstances so much as the substance.' His book *Ecclesiastes, or the Gift of Preaching* (1646) began a new era in English preaching which began to flourish at the time of the Restoration (1660). Other promoters of the new style, like Robert South (1634-1716) and Herbert Croft, bishop of Hereford, in his pamphlet entitled *The Naked Truth or, The True State of the Primitive Church* (1675), were loud in their denunciations of the Carolines and the medieval tradition which they inherited and renewed: 'they take here or there a sentence of Scripture, the shorter and more abstruse the better, to show their skill and invention; this they divide and subdivide into generals and particulars, the quid, the quale, the quantum, and such like quaksalving forms; then they study how to hook in this or that quaint sentence of Philosopher or Father, this or that nice speculation, endeavouring to couch all this in most elegant language; in short, their main end is to show their wit, their reading, and whatever else they think is excellent in them [...].

19 Ibid., p. 379. 20 Mitchell, op. cit., pp 228ff.; see also Smyth, op. cit. p. 100.

And I verily believe this is the reason why Preaching hath so little effect in these days, because they labour to speak the wisdom of this world, which is foolishness with God, nor do they preach in demonstration of the spirit, but in demonstration of their learning.'[21]

John Tillotson (1634-94), who died as archbishop of Canterbury after a long life of preaching in the plain and simple style, and a short primacy of three years which he never desired, is considered the master of this cult of plainness, which has survived in both traditions of English preaching, Anglo-Catholic and Puritan alike, and is still called 'The triumph of Tillotson': it was Tillotson whose pulpit manner first attracted universal admiration, and finally secured the universal triumph of the plain and edifying style in preaching; by persuading men that a plain equable, and judiciously modulated prose was not only a possible medium, but the most proper medium for the sermon, he was largely instrumental in diffusing a taste for plainness and perspicuity in prose in general. 'He was not only the best Preacher of the age', wrote Bishop Burnet, 'but seemed to have brought preaching to perfection; his sermons were so well heard and liked, and so much read, that all the nation proposed him as a Pattern, and studied to copy after him [...]. By the study of the ancients, and the classical authors, whom he had made his models, he had formed a style and acquired a just way of thinking, with a simplicity and easiness of expression, before his time unknown in England. This justly gave him the character of an excellent preacher.'[22]

The significant fact for us in the triumph of Tillotson is the emphatic condemnation of two particular and characteristic aspects of the medieval tradition of pulpit oratory, its popularity and its pedentary, or in other words, the use of exempla, and the verbal elaboration of the scheme. But while English preaching under Tillotson returned to the text of the bible, 'to scriptural and christian plainness,' it remained for the most part outside the liturgical or cultic context and was seldom, if ever, exegetical in the way of Origen and the early Fathers, be they Greek or Latin. Consequently, through Tillotson, who was neither a liturgist, an exegete, nor a prophet, the essay type of sermon became the model of Anglican spiritual oratory for more that a century: as a result, the sermon lost its heroic note and became a moral essay, the mediator of a sober, utilitarian, prudential ethic rather than a proclamation of the gospel of the Kingdom of God.

Against this background of English preaching as an oral essay – objective, general and impersonal – on a religious or ethical topic, credible attempts were made to give preaching a greater spiritual depth in the eighteenth century by the Evangelical Revival Movement and in the nineteenth century by the Tractarian and Oxford

---

[21] Mitchell, op.cit. pp 107-9; Smyth, op. cit., pp 99-100. [22] Ibid., cf. 'Restoration Preachers and the Reform of Style,' pp 308-46: Smyth, op. cit., pp 99-166, 'The Triumph of Tillotson'.

Movement. For example, the early Methodists, who restored the preaching of the Cross, were characteristically and emphatically personal, and the pulpit style of John Wesley (1703-91) and George Whitefield (1714-70) has been characterised in a single phrase as 'individualising': it is a missionary style not suited to all times or to all circumstances, but it was demanded by the circumstances of their time:[23]

> My message is to thee sinner! I stand here to-day to bring thee to bethink thyself of thy past ways. Thou who dost now appear in the presence of thy God loathsome in thy sins – I challenge and command thee to bow thy stubborn neck, and to bend thy knee. Dost not thou though ungrateful as thou hast been these many years – yea a hardened rebel from thy mother's breast until now – dost thou not hear the Saviour calling to thee to repent and turn? Was it not for thee that he shed his blood? Did he not carry thy sorrows to Calvary, even thine? Was he not wounded for thy transgressions? Did he not think of thee, of thy soul, and of all its abominations, that dark night when he lay in agony on the ground? Yes. It was none other than thy sins that made him sweat blood in that garden. But now, with a purpose of mercy in his heart toward thy wretched soul, he calls thee to himself; and says, yes he says it to thee, 'Come now let us reason together'.[24]

The Tractarian Movement, on the other hand, in the nineteenth century, with its characteristic doctrine of the Church and her sacramental ministry, marks the second wave of the reaction against the merely ethical preaching of the eighteenth century. Indeed, the Catholic Renewal in the Church of England was heralded when Hugh James Rose, the Christian advocate in the University of Cambridge, challenged Tillotsonian piety and held up to criticism the very words the primate had preached before the House of Commons in 1678: 'For God's sake, what is religion good for,' asked Tillotson, 'but to reform the manners and dispositions of men, to restrain human nature from violence and cruelty, from falshood and treachery, from sedition and rebellion?' 'Its utility in this view', observed Rose, 'is today perhaps condescendingly recognized, and even that of a ministry sometimes acknowledged, as being a body of men whose business it is to enforce the obligations to good order and moral duty, and to terrify those who might hope to evade human laws, by holding up to their imagination and their fears an invisible power, and a future retribution. But any belief that God has himself instituted certain means, through the medium of which he confers internal and spiritual grace, any belief that through these means he seeks to open that communion with his crea-

---

[23] J. Downey, *The Eighteenth Century Pulpit. A Study in the Sermons of Butler, Berkely, Secker, Sterne, Whitefield and Wesley*, Oxford, 1969: cf. 'Pulpit oratory, a general view', pp 1-29; 'Wesley', pp 189-225.
[24] I. Taylor, *Wesley and Methodism*, London, 1851, p.159; cf. Smyth, op. cit., p. 171.

tures without which the high gifts of reason, of genius, of the soul itself, if not as worthless and as dead as this fair bodily frame when the spark of life is gone, yet subsist in a low and degraded state, any such belief, I fear, exists not, in the present day, with any large portion of mankind.'[25]

Among the Tractarians, John Henry Newman (1801-90) won his position of spiritual leadership by his preaching in the University Church of St Mary the Virgin, in Oxford, what are now the eight volumes of the *Parochial and Plain Sermons* (1834-43). There are many descriptions of this legendary priest in his pulpit, including Matthew Arnold's nostalgic evocation of 'the charm of that spiritual apparition, gliding in the dim afternoon light through the aisles of St Mary's, rising into the pulpit, and then, in the most entrancing of voices, breaking the silence with words and thoughts which were a religious music, – subtle, sweet, mournful.'[26] This religious setting certainly contributed to the mysterious power of Newman's preaching: nevertheless, the liturgical dimension of the Latin Sermon is as absent in the preaching of Newman as it was in that of Taylor or Tillotson. Likewise, the exegetical dimension of the Greek homily is equally absent, although there is that biblical sense that pervades all English preaching since the Reformation. But, on the other hand, there is present in the sermons of Newman, as in English preaching in general, that intense conviction about the world of God and that zeal for the care of souls which gives the academically constructed lecture, be it of Taylor, Tillotson, Wesley or Newman, the character of a prophetic message:

> One further remark I will make about these professedly rational Christians; who, be it observed, often go on to deny the mysteries of the Gospel. Let us take the text; – 'Our God is a consuming fire.' Now supposing these persons fell upon these words, or heard them urged as an argument against their own doctrine of the unmixed satisfactory character of our prospects in the world to come, and supposing they did not know what part of the Bible they occurred in, what would they say? Doubtless they would confidently say that they applied only to the Jews and not to Christians; that they only described the Divine Author of the Mosaic Law; that God formerly spoke in terrors to the Jews, because they were a gross and brutish people, but that civilization has made us quite other men; that our reason, not our fears, is appealed to, and that the Gospel is love. And yet, in spite of all this argument, the text occurs in the Epistle to the Hebrews. written by an Apostle of Christ [...]. Think of this, I beseech you, my brethern. and lay it to heart, as far as you go with me, as you will answer for having heard it at the last day. I would not

---

[25] Smyth, op. cit., pp 168ff.   [26] I. Kerr, *The Genius of John Henry Newman*, Oxford, 1989, 'The Preacher', pp 121-74.

willingly be harsh; but knowing 'that the world lieth in wickedness', I think it highly probable that you, so far as you are in it (as you must be, and we all must be in our degree), are, most of you, partially infected with its existing error, that shallowness of religion, which is the result of a blinded conscience; and, therefore, I speak earnestly to you. Believing in the existence of a general plague in the land, I judge that you probably have your share in the sufferings, the voluntary sufferings, which it is spreading among us. The fear of God is the beginning of wisdom; till you see Him to be a consuming fire, and approach Him with reverence and godly fear, as being sinners, you are not even in sight of the strait gate. I do not wish you to be able to point to any particular time when you renounced the world (as it is called), and were converted; this is a deceit. Fear and love must go together; always fear, always love, to your dying day [...].[27]

In this sermon of Newman on 'The Religion of the Day' he spoke on the text of Hebrews: 'Let us have grace, whereby we may serve God acceptably with reverence and Godly fear. For our God is a consuming fire' (Heb 12:28-29). In his philosophical, commonsense, manner of exposition he explains the world's partial acceptance of the Gospel in all ages, in one sense or other, but always on its own terms, and then comments as only he could comment: 'he who cultivates only one precept of the Gospel to the exclusion of the rest, in reality attends to no part at all.' Then in this manner of the good and holy man he continues:

Think, too, of Christ's own words: 'What shall a man give in exchange for his soul?' Again, He says, 'Fear Him, who after He hath killed, hath power to cast into hell; yea, I say unto you, fear Him.' Dare not to think you have got to the bottom of your hearts; you do not know what evil lies there. How long and earnestly must you pray, how many years must you pass in careful obedience, before you have any right to lay aside sorrow, and to rejoice in the Lord? In one sense, indeed, you may take comfort from the first; for, though you dare not yet anticipate you are in the number of Christ's true elect, yet from the first you know He desires your salvation, has died for you, has washed away your sins by baptism, and will ever help you; and this thought must cheer you while you go on to examine and review your lives, and to turn to God in self-denial. But, at the same time, you never can be sure of salvation, while you are here; and therefore you must always fear while you hope. Your knowledge of your sins increases with your view of God's mercy in Christ. And this is the true

---

[27] Ibid., p. 143.

Christian state, and the nearest approach to Christ's calm and placid sleep in the tempest; – not perfect joy and certainty in heaven, but a deep resignation to God's will, a surrender of ourselves, soul and body, to Him; hoping indeed, that we shall be saved, but fixing our eyes more earnestly on Him than on ourselves; that is, acting for His glory, seeking to please Him.[28]

The sermons of Newman., like those of English preaching in general, were essays that were orally delivered in their time and are now preserved in their written form as part of a great literary and religious heritage. But the content of Newman's sermons, more that the quality of their masterful prose, gave them that mysterious power that makes Newman, both before and after his conversion to Rome, one of the greatest preachers in the history of the Church. As preacher, his mysterious power sprang from his awareness of the Holy Spirit as indwelling in the hearts of that faithful that was his congregation. This doctrine of the indwelling of the Holy Spirit was the most fundamental theological discovery which Newman had made in his study of scripture and the Fathers: 'it is at the heart of the stress that the Tractarians placed on 'mystery,' and is opposed to the 'enthusiasm' of the Evangelicals and to the 'coldness'of the liberal and 'high-and-dry' Anglicans.'[29] This awareness or doctrine of the Holy Spirit compensates, perhaps, in the sermons of Newman for their lack of the liturgical dimension, as it makes Newman in his preaching to be that combination of priest and prophet that is wanting in much English preaching, be it Anglican or Roman. This relationship of liturgy and preaching has been a constant problem in the history of English preaching: in the Anglican tradition, preaching has prevailed at the expense of liturgy: in the Roman tradition, liturgy has prevailed at the expense of preaching. Now, the liturgical movement has brought both traditions to recognise the liturgical dimension of preaching and the preaching dimension of the liturgy that the Greeks called 'homily,' and the Latins called 'sermon.' But strangely there is little in writing from Newman's days as a Roman Catholic to show the influence of the Liturgy on his preaching!

CATHOLIC AND CAROLINE

The liturgical changes of the past forty years in the Roman Catholic Church are now being acknowledged, even by those in the highest places, as a cultural revolution more than a genuine reformation of the old religion: 'what happened after the Second Vatican Council could itself almost be called a cultural revolution, if you think of the false zeal with which Church buildings were cleared out.'[1] The hierarchical structure of the Church can alone explain the extent of this revolution: what

[28] Ibid., p.144. [29] Ibid., p.121. [1] J. Ratzinger, *Salt of the Earth*, San Francisco, 1996, p. 256.

is not explicable is the hierarchical consensus achieved for its widespread execution, since the theological intention of the Council was in no way as radical, about the externals of worship, as was its pastoral interpretation; even the Vatican itself, in its directions for renewal, seemed helpless in the face of the episcopal avalanche for change. Nor is the silence of the laity understandable, especially in these heritage-conscious times, for the destruction of liturgical tradition in art and architecture, language and music, has surpassed with a violence the worst excesses of Cromwell and his times. The comparison is not palatable but it must be made. Only an honest narration of the stripping of our altars, done in the name of renewal, will prepare us for the liturgical revival intended.

The revisionism in which scholars of the great Reformation are at present involved should be an incentive for students of our more recent reformation or revolution to consider critically the quality of what was done by a careful analysis of the resolve with which it was done. Nowadays historians like Scarisbrick, Bossy and most recently Eamon Duffy are seeing the *Anglican Way* of the sixteenth century as an outward innovation and departure from traditional observances. In his monumental work. *The Stripping of the Altars: Traditional religion in England from c.1400-c.1580*,[2] a most positive account is given of that religion's dynamism in practice and in prayer up to the very eve of the Reformation. In the first part the Protestant picture of a corrupt and ignorant clergy undermining the faith of the laity with its excessive sacerdotal claims is firmly rejected. The second part of this 700-page volume is a lengthy narrative in great detail; there is no other way by which the bitter tale can be told of the political and theological attack on the time-honoured ritual with its rood screens, images, paintings and sculptures of great beauty – done in the name of renewal.

Duffy's story is a poignant one of great relevance for our times and told for our benefit with scholarly integrity. For over a thousand years Catholicism flourished liturgically in medieval England, and everywhere the Latin of the Sarum rite was perceived sacramentally as a language higher and holier than the vernacular. At the same time early printers, like Caxton and Wynkyn de Worde, mass-produced Primers or Books of Hours to meet the enormous demand of an increasingly literate laity for private prayer books. Most of these Primers centered around the Little Office of the Virgin in Latin but included vernacular paraphrases of rites, texts and prayers. At this time too a growing body of religious writing in English became available to the laity such as meditations on the life of Jesus and catechetical instructions on doctrines and practices of the medieval Church, such us Purgatory and prayers for the dying and dead. The vogue of new feasts and cults,

2 E. Duffy, *The Stripping of the Altars. Traditional Religion in England, 1400-1580*, New Haven & London, 1992.

such as those of the Holy Name and the Five Wounds, together with the centrality of the parish Mass and its ceremonies, all affirm the hold of Catholic tradition on the people on the eve of the Reformation.

Nevertheless, all this and much more, between 1530 and 1580, was swept away brutally and with relatively little protest. According to Duffy, and in keeping with the other revisionists, the English Reformation was political and set off by a king's need to deny Roman supremacy for his own benefit. Therefore it was directed from the top, and its ecclesiastical leaders, like Cranmer, Ridley and Latimer, were willing politicians of the *Injunction* and the *Visitation*, and accordingly disobedience was likely to prove disadvantageous, if not dangerous. In these circumstances pragmatism in matters of externals became the *modus vivendi* of Tudor folk, as they put aside their nostalgia for the old ways and bowed to the royal injunction. Yet in 1584 there was the puritan complaint that 'three parts at least of the people were still wedded to their old superstitions.' In Duffy's *Stripping of the Altars* the facts would seem to speak for themselves; however, in their interpretation the balance can be very easily tilted over; perhaps, as Keen argues, 'he says a little too much for a strictly even balance about the heart-warming aspects of the piety of late medievalism, too little of its coolnesses [...], a little too much about the heart-chilling aspects of reform, and too little about the new insights of the Reformers.'[3]

As the stripping of the altars continued, after the compromise of the Elizabethan Settlement of 1559, the new insights of the English Reformers became more clearly those of the continental Protestants. In theory the Act of Supremacy and the Act of Uniformity had solved the two great problems of the English Reformation, but in practice the religious and political issues continued to aggravate one another, as both sides sought to bring each other within the influence of either Rome or Geneva. The Elizabethan Settlement. while establishing Protestantism, did not immediately produce either a developed theology or a polity, and so the religious and political issues smouldered on, and nearly one hundred years later, William Laud, the archbishop of uniformity, and some few years later, King Charles, 'the only supreme authority in matters spiritual and temporal,' were both executed. During those fifty years of Elizabeth's reign the Reformation that began in England as a struggle among Catholics about loyalties to pope or king, continued as a religious conflict in the Church of England between Catholic tradition and Protestant reform.

Historians of the Reformation in England, revisionists or status quo, Catholic and Protestant, must focus more on the first fifty years of the seventeenth century when the issues were more theological, and less on the last fifty years of the sixteenth century when they were more political. The controversies of these times gave

---

[3] M. Keen, in the *New York Review of Books*, 23 Sept. 1993, pp. 50-1.

rise, at the turn of the century, to a group of scholars who were pre-eminently capable of imbuing the Elizabethan compromise with a soul that was both Catholic and Reformed. Of these, Richard Hooker (d. 1600) was first to lead the way back to the living tradition of the early Christian centuries and to find there the patristic sources for all Reformation. There followed poets and preachers like John Donne and Jeremy Taylor; bishops and spiritual writers like Andrewes and Cosin; country parsons like George Herbert, and devout and learned laymen like Sir Thomas Browne, Nicholas Ferrar, Thomas Vaughan, Evelyn the diarist, and Izaak Walton. These either set out spontaneously along similar paths, or else deliberately followed the path of Hooker, and having flourished in the reign of Charles I, and afterward in the time of his son Charles II, are now known to us as the Caroline Divines.

The makers of the Second Vatican Council with its four major constitutions on Christ, the Church, Worship, and the World, were theologians reaping the full fruits of their research studies, for over fifty years, in the renewed disciplines of scripture, liturgy, patristics and medieval synthesis and exegesis. On the other hand, the Caroline Divines were, for the most part, the parish priests of those disturbing times when Catholic and Protestant minds were locked in conflict; yet they were the first to see that true reformation lay neither in Protestantism nor in the Baroque mentality of the Counter-Reformation. These divines, like the theologians of Vatican II after them, saw in the scriptures, the liturgies and the preaching of the early Greek and Latin Fathers, the living tradition of the apostolic Church and, in keeping with the principle *acqua purior manet a fonte quam per rivos*, a constant source of Church renewal or revival. Hence their insistence on the vernacular and on a systematic course of liturgical instruction; hence too their attempt to read the whole bible during the course of the Church year in its traditional context of worship, and in constant reference to the mysteries of Christ as permanently actual and living in and for the Church. Those men were the first to see Reformation as Church renewal, but then as now the times were not favourable and they had to sail against the tide of protest.

In spite of those times of compromise and conflict, Protestant and Catholic, the Caroline achievement in the life of the Church was considerable and lasting in its essentials; first and foremost is the King James Bible; secondly, in the hands of those High Churchmen, as they are commonly called, the Book of Common Prayer became a cherished Catholic liturgy as they gave it form and meaning, discovered its beauties, came to love it and were prepared to die for it; and thirdly, the Offices of Morning Prayer and Evensong, as they are still performed in the great Anglican Churches, are among the purest forms of Christian common prayer anywhere to be found, even today. This transformation of the vernacular for sanctuary use could have saved modern Roman Catholics from the banality of their English prayer books and prepared them for a more sacred utterance of the sacramental mysteries, but alas! 'there is something strangely unreal in the prevalent neglect of the heritage of Anglicanism. Barthianism, Thomism, and even Counter-Reformation thought possess a following in the English Church, but the study of the Fathers of Anglicanism has received only a fraction of its rightful need of attention.'[4]

With the death of Elizabeth (1603) and the reign of James I there began in the Church of England a new awareness of being Catholic, scriptural and reformed, and a new method of doing theology with its emphasis on scripture, tradition and reason as forming a trinity of sources. In this new beginning the scholar-bishop, so typical of the Church of Chrysostom and Augustine, was born again, so to speak, and names like Lancelot Andrewes, William Laud and John Cosin began to flourish in England. and in Ireland, John Bramhall, James Ussher and Jeremy Taylor are but the first names in a litany that is long and living. Nourished and moulded by the being and texture of the King James Bible, as the Latin Fathers were by the Vulgate, and the Greek Fathers by the Septuagint that was the Precursor of the Gospels in Greek, these scholar-bishops are the Anglican Fathers of a spirituality and theology that is the *great code* of our literary and cultural heritage in English. In this appeal to the Church as it was before its more institutional form in the Middle Ages, the role of the scholar was accepted, the place of the bishop confirmed, and the unity of teaching and authority preserved. Indeed, the scholar-bishop was a mark of that Church when *Catholicism* referred more to the fulness of revelation than to the universality of an institution.

In this new trinity of sources the patristic studies of these High Churchmen made their theology quite different from the scientific treatises of the Counter-Reformation and from the biblical literalism of continental Protestantism; 'one finds in them something of the Catholicity, the wide-mindedness, the freshness, the suppleness and sanity of Christian antiquity.'[5] Similarly, freed from the syllogism of the schoolmen, reason can wander at will and wonder all the more: 'the reason of man is a right judge always when she is truly informed, but in many things she knows nothing but the face of the article [...] and though you see the revelation clear, and the article plain, yet the reason of it we cannot see at all [...] the whole knowledge which we can have here, is dark and obscure.' [6] Reason and religion, continues Taylor, are like Leah and Rachel: 'reason is fruitful indeed, and brings forth the first-born, but she is blear-eyed, and oftentimes knows not the secrets of her Lord; but Rachel produced two children, faith and piety, and obedience is midwife to them both, and modesty is the nurse.'[7] In this way of

---

4 H.R. McAdoo, *The Structure of Caroline Moral Theology*, London, 1949, p. 1.   5 Ibid., pp. 316-54.
6 Taylor, vol. 9, p. 64   7 Ibid., p. 65.

doing theology lies the spirit of Anglicanism. These Caroline Divines, or first Fathers of the Church in English, were soon recognised as a very vital branch of the Catholic Church and their presence as such was felt in Rome. Pope Clement VIII, after he had read what was most important in the *Ecclesiastical Polity* of Richard Hooker, is quoted as follows: 'there is no learning that this man has not searched into; nothing too hard for his understanding; this man indeed deserves the name of an author; his books will be reverenced as they grow in age, for there is in them such seeds of eternity that if the rest be like this they shall endure until the last fire shall consume all learning.'[8] Furthermore, according to Jeremy Taylor Pope Pius Quartus was prepared to acknowledge the Book of Common Prayer, if Elizabeth in turn would recognise him as the Supreme Head of the Church. In a sense, these Fathers were their own magisterium and their influence has continued over the centuries, and is still felt wherever or whenever a T.S. Eliot can be heard to speak: 'at the end of Elizabeth's reign, liturgy began to live again in the persons of Hooker and Andrewes. They brought into the Church a breadth of culture and an ease with humanism and renaissance learning, both hitherto conspicuously lacking. Their intellectual achievements and prose style did for the Church of England what thirteenth-century philosophy did for medieval Christianity – they completed its structure and gave it form and shape.'[9] However, Rome and the Puritans had yet to raise philosophical and political difficulties.

During the reign of Elizabeth neither Papist nor Puritan entertained any hope of toleration, but with the advent of James from Scotland the Puritans took heart. However, 'the humble petition of the thousand ministers', presented to the king on his way to England, concerned Protestant modifications of the Prayer Book but received scant attention at the Hampton Court Conference (1604), to be associated for ever with the King James Bible. For his entire reign the High Churchmen were in his favour, and for twenty years more remained in the favour of his son, Charles I (1625-49) Meanwhile the Puritan cause was on the march, and soon the king and his archbishop were out of touch with the People and Parliament: their glorification of the episcopacy, and Erastian conception of royalty were simply ill-suited to the puritan temper of the times. By 1642 civil war had begun, and monarch and bishop were overthrown; in 1645 Laud was beheaded and Charles in 1649, and for nearly twenty years Parliament was in power and the Church of England in hiding until the restoration of Charles II in 1660.[10]

Behind the religious and political events of those fifty years lay the philosophical bankruptcy of the leading High Churchmen. Their sacramental theology came into

---

8 L. Bouyer, *Life and Liturgy*, London, 1956, p. 44.   9 *Selected Prose of T.S. Eliot*, ed. Kermode, London, 1975, p. 180.   10 Carroll, *Jeremy Taylor*, op. cit., pp 38-59.

being as metaphysics went out of fashion with the passing of the Middle Ages. They were unanimous in rejecting the Roman doctrine of transubstantiation but had no category of thought to express the *real presence* in which they one and all firmly believed. The keystone of their Catholic arch had been removed, but the collapse of the edifice was only apparent to those who stood outside. Attacked on all sides by Papists, Puritans and Freethinkers, the High Churchmen retained the ritual of the eucharist, but in their theology of it vacillated between Virtualism and Receptionism. In their thinking the Middle Ages of the Vulgate and the Schoolmen were missing, and without that centre nothing holds together from antiquity, classical and Christian, and modernity, Christian and secular, to constitute and continue the living tradition that is Western Civilization. In the Christian understanding of this tradition, a thousand years is an integral part of the life of the Church and her Holy Spirit, and therefore it matters little whether that Millennium be the first or the second.

Born in 1613 in Cambridge and dying in Ireland in 1667 Jeremy Taylor, lived throughout those fifty troubled years. Educated at Gonville and Caius College, Cambridge, and in Ely, the diocese of Lancelot Andrewes, Taylor's future in Church and State was predictable. In 1638 he became rector of Uppingham; married Phoebe Langsdale; preached his first surviving sermon; and was appointed chaplain to Charles and Laud the archbishop. Here the young priest, for he was only twenty-five, began his ministry of preaching. Already in his language there is clear evidence of the symbolic mind of the ancients, classical and Christian, for the Laudian churchman was sounding more patristic than the more medieval Andrewes. For him Golgotha was the place of Adam's skull, and the Cross a shoot from the Tree of Life, mysteriously secured by Seth from Paradise and planted on Calvary, flourished there for a thousand years, died and was revived by the Blood of Christ. These sermons were published as 'Discourses, Considerations and Prayers' in a massive volume of a thousand pages; as *The History of the Life and Death of the Holy Jesus* it was the first of its kind to appear in the English language; commonly known as *The Great Exemplar*, it was the beginning in English of a spirituality that is at the same time Christological and biblical, ecclesial and sacramental.

> The *Great Exemplar* is a celebration of the beauty of the Lord Jesus – God and Man. The up-raised, ecstatic movement of the paragraphs betrays the enthusiasm of the writer; he is Christ-possessed. The most gracious voice then to be heard in England is lifted like that of a nightingale above the frogs and ravens of the age. The form he adopts is interesting; the great family of Man is described, the necessity of discipline in its organism demonstrated and

Christianity shown to be the most perfect law conceivable for its direction [...] after an exhortation to the imitation of Jesus, the romance begins.

The string on which the whole sequence of pearls is hung is the narrative of the life of Christ on earth. The author tells the story as he chooses. There is no attempt at Biblical criticism, even as in those days it was understood; no dealing with difficulties of parallel Evangelists; no weighing of evidence.

Taylor selects such versions of the narrative as best suits his purpose, not shrinking from the traditions of a later age, if they attract him. For instance, he accepts without a question the legend of the prostration of the Egyptian gods when the Infant crossed the border. If an incident inflames his imagination, he lingers over it as long as he chooses; he weaves his fancy, for instance, for page after page, around the apparition of the Star of the Epiphany. What he dwells upon, exclusively, is the imaginative and the pathetic. He wishes to draw men away from the weariness of controversy to the exquisite mysteries of pure religion.[11]

Taylor's sacramental mode of seeing and saying, or *sacramental representation*, as he everywhere calls it, in the first place transformed theologically and liturgically what he saw and said of Christ and his Church, and secondly, what he saw and said of man and his world. The former he did for the most part as a theologian and priest; the latter, again for the most part, as a poet and preacher. But just as seeing and saying, from the philosophic perspective are rooted and grounded in being, so too Taylor's sacramental mode is no less rooted and grounded, from the theological perspective, in the new being of the risen Christ and the ever-Rising Church: 'For the meaning of these mysteries and sacramental expressions, when reduced to easy and intelligible signification is plainly this; by Christ we live and move and have our spiritual being in the life of grace and in the hopes of glory.'[12]

In May of 1642 the death of his son was recorded in the parish register, and in the summer of the same year he left Uppingham and joined the king's forces at Nottingham. For three years the country was plunged in a bloody conflict that ended with the rout of the royal forces at Naseby in 1645. The two issues of the Elizabethan Settlement, (1559) or compromise were still at stake in this war – the political, in which the Lords was opposed to the Commons, and the religious, in which the bishops were opposed to the Puritans. Sometimes those same interests cut across family ties so that it can be said of that conflict that a man's foes were those of his own household, and civil war was the name of that game. Imprisoned at Cardigan Castle in the south of Wales, Taylor, on his release, was to remain in Wales and to find there his sanctuary for nearly a decade.

11 Gosse, *Jeremy Taylor*, op. cit., pp 58-9.   12 Carroll, op. cit., pp 193-9.

At Golden Grove, the estate of Richard Vaughan, earl of Carbery, Taylor found refuge for his wife and family and a means of living, while in Frances, Lord Carbery's young and saintly wife, he found his muse and inspiration. It was for her he wrote his devotional works, and, at her suggestion, published the sermons she so devoutly heard: in *Holy Living* and *Holy Dying*, and in *A Yearly Course of Sermons* he shows the variety of his astounding mind. At last the fruit of his tremendous reading comes pouring out; Greek philosophy, Latin historians and poets, the Church Fathers, all march across his pages. The most curious and bizarre stories rub shoulders with God-impelled flights of thought and with vivid and sensitive descriptions of external nature. Indeed, these devotional works, like many of his sermons, owe their inspiration to the place around him: 'the odour and colour of flowers, the hum of insects and the song of birds, the raging wind, the forest bending beneath the storm, even the worm crawling across the path and stretching out its elastic length after a shower, are all put under contribution to point his moral or adorn his doctrine.'[13]

Unlike the sermons preached to the congregations at Uppingham, where for four years Taylor was the parish priest, those at Golden Grove were preached, in the peace and quiet of the place, to Lady Carbery amd her household who persuaded Taylor, against his wishes, to have them published. The *Eniautus*, as it is known, is a one-year collection of fifty-two sermons, but without any reference to the liturgical year, or life of Christ, which in the *Great Exemplar* had been already covered. In its sub-title it is described as *A Course of Sermons for all the Sundays of the Year, fitted to the great necessities and for supplying the wants of preaching in many parts of this nation*, and that it is: it gives us a general survey of human life and the mortal condition, the vanity of our desires, the folly and emptiness of our ambitions, and the misery of our lives; 'man is a lump of folly and unavoidable necessities: and our hearts, so intricate and various and trifling, so full of wantonness and foolish thoughts, come in for many a well deserved if not altogether novel castigation.'[14] We are, indeed, made of dust.

Taylor's view of the world, its vanities and temptations, was derived from what Coleridge called 'his oceanic reading of the ancients,'[15] and was more classical than Christian. But that Platonic philosophy, which the early Greek Fathers absorbed from the Neoplatonism of their day, and which was so potent an influence in the Anglican theology of Taylor's times, opened for him another world of which the existing world is but an evanescent shadow and which we apprehend not with the senses but with the mind. The recognition of this unseen eternal

---

13 L.P. Smith, op. cit., pp xlv-xlvii.   14 H.R. McAdoo, cf. *First of Its Kind: Jeremy Taylor's Life of Christ.* op. cit., pp 123ff; also Carroll, op. cit., p. 348 = J. Taylor, vol. 3, p. 266.   15 L.P. Smith, op. cit., p. lv.

world behind the flux of phenomena is the vision that inspires Taylor's preaching as he lifts man out of the darkness of time and up to the brightness of eternity.

To pass from shadow to substance, from the pleasures of the senses to the contemplations of heavenly realities, from dwelling on the transitory earth to residence amid intellectual and eternal essences, was for Jeremy Taylor the progress from earth to heaven and the purpose of his preaching. 'Children and fools,' he wrote, 'choose to please their senses rather than their reason, because they still dwell within the regions of sense, and have little residence amongst intellectual essences.'[16] The growth in grace was for him the growth in this life of the spirit; for it was possible, he said, to taste of this perfection while in our mortal state on earth; a man's heart and eye may be in the state of perfection, that is, heaven, before he sets his feet upon that golden threshold; and God, 'the eternal essence,' would now and then grant his worshippers 'little antepasts of heaven,' opening for him 'little loopholes of eternity'; 'God sometimes draws aside the curtains of peace, and shews man his throne, and visits him with irradiations of glory, and sends him a little star to stand over his dwelling, and then covers it with a cloud.'[17] Here indeed the preacher is priest and shares in those divine communications; Taylor's appealing discourse brings forth the only-begotten Word, which is the source in man of eternal life.

Here, 'far from the madding crowd's ignoble strife', charity preserved the quality of his life and work: 'let me look about me. They have left me the sun and moon, fire and water, a loving wife, and many friends to pity me, and some to relieve me, and I can still discourse; and unless I list they have not taken away my merry countenance, my cheerful spirit and a good conscience: they still have left me the providence of God, and all the promises of the Gospel, my religion, my hopes of heaven, and my charity to them too; I read and meditate; I can walk in my neighbour's pleasant fields, and see the varieties of natural beauties, and delight in all that in which God delights, in virtue and wisdom, in the whole creation and in God himself.'[18] And yet, like Hopkins' Margaret grieving there over Golden Grove *unleafing*, for Taylor too *sorrows' springs were the same*: in the Fall of 1650 Lady Carbery died, and in the Spring following he buried his wife Phoebe. There and then *Holy Dying* was published, Taylor's unique contribution to English spirituality, theology and literature. Here Taylor reached divine heights and depths of understanding and expression, new in the English language, and still salutary whenever or wherever death calls:

> Since we stay not here, being people but of a day's abode, and our age is like that of a fly and contemporary with a gourd, we must look somewhere

16 Ibid.   17 Ibid.; also cf. Carroll, op. cit., p. 348.   18 Taylor, vol. 4, p. 291.

else for an abiding city, a place in another country to fix our house in, whose walls and foundation is God, where we must find rest, or else be restless for ever. For whatsoever ease we can have or fancy here is shortly to be changed into sadness or tediousness: it goes away too soon, like the periods of our life: or stays too long, like the sorrows of a sinner: its own weariness, or a contrary disturbance, is its load; or it is eased by its revolution into vanity and forgetfulness; and where either there is sorrow or an end of joy, there can be no true felicity: which because it must be had by some instrument and in some period of our duration, we must carry up our affections to the mansions prepared for us above, where eternity is the measure, felicity is the state, angels are the company, the Lamb is the light, and God is the portion and inheritance.[19]

In a diary entry for 15 April 1654 John Evelyn, Taylor's new patron and protector, records his going to London 'to hear the famous Doctor Jeremy Taylor at St. Greg: Matt. 6:48, concerning evangelical perfection.' [20] By this time Taylor was married again to Joanna Bridges, left Golden Grove, already Evelyn's *ghostly Father* and again a pilgrim, priest and preacher in a Church driven underground by the army of Independents who replaced Parliament in 1653. Another entry in Evelyn's diary records 'the funeral sermon of preaching for Christmas Day 1655: 'in a private house in London [...] I was given the Blessed Sacrament – the first time the Church of England was reduced to chamber and conventicle.' [21] In 1656 Taylor was the most active and outspoken priest in England, and imprisoned in Chepstow Castle. Released on the intervention of Evelyn he kept ministering to private congregations who were loyal to king and Church. Like William Byrd, who satisfied the musical needs of Roman congregations at the beginning of the Reformation in the private homes of the great, so now at its end Jeremy Taylor composed his *Collections of Offices* when the Prayer Book was proscribed. The publication was discovered and again Taylor was imprisoned in the Tower. The final entry in Evelyn's diary is for 7 March 1658: 'to London to Dr Taylor in a private house on Lk 13:23-24. After the Sermon followed the Blessed Communion of which I participated.'[22]

In June 1658, on his release again from prison, Taylor in his forty-fifth year departed London to begin the last decade of his life an exile in Ireland and far from the England, where he had buried his first wife and five sons. Like Golden Grove in Wales, Portmore in Northern Ireland, the Inigo Jones home of Lord and Lady Conway, would be his new shelter and sanctuary. Friends of John Evelyn and Henry

19 Ibid., vol. 3, p. 276. 20 W.J. Brown, *Jeremy Taylor*, London, 1925, p. 20. 21 Gest, op. cit., p. 21. 22 Ibid.= Carroll, op. cit., p. 28.

More, the Cambridge Platonist, the Conways too were members of Taylor's London congregations and made him chaplain to their household. Here, however, the political scene soon changed with the death of Cromwell, the very year of Taylor's arrival, and the Presbyterians of Ulster lost no time in taking full advantage of it. By adopting a double policy of intriguing, on the one hand, for the king's return, and on the other hand, of standing stoutly for the principles of the Reformation, they took political advantage of the Puritans and religious advantage of the Anglicans, and again on both scores Jeremy Taylor was vulnerable and suffered.

In 1659 Ulster was a province of political and religious unrest as Puritan and Presbyterian fought viciously for property and belief, while pockets of Anglo-Catholic gentry and Roman Catholic peasants held on doggedly to whatsoever of each they possessed. In 1660 the restoration of Charles II set the fires of Puritan power and Presbyterian zeal ablaze and Ulster was on the march. A deputation of ministers from the diocese of Down and Connor congratulated the new king on his preservation and restoration, but reminded him of the rule of the Reformation against popery, episcopacy and heresy. In these circumstances, Taylor's appointment as their bishop was a questionable prize for the theological defender of the monarchy and episcopacy. Indeed, a storm of protest greeted his appointment and explains his letter to the lord lieutenant about 'being thrown into a place of torment'; about 'the implacable ministers [...] preaching vigorously and constantly against episcopacy and liturgy;' and about accusations against him as 'an Arminian, a Socinian, and a Papist, – or at least half a Papist.'[23]

The consecration of Taylor as bishop took place nonetheless; with him nine other bishops and two archbishops had been appointed after the Restoration to the vacant sees, and as several of the pre-Commonwealth Irish bishops were still alive, the new were consecrated by the old in a single ceremony in St Patrick's cathedral in Dublin on 27 January 1661. The aged bishop of Derry, John Bramhall, was the new primate of Armagh; he planned the service and presided. Civil and military leaders, ecclesiastical and academic figures, all took part in the grand public procession to the cathedral, while the choir sang music specially composed for the occasion; Jeremy Taylor was accorded the exceptional honour of preaching at his own consecration. His sermon on the *Faithful and Wise Steward* of Luke 12:42 was a defence of episcopacy on the lines of his earlier work, *Episcopacy Asserted*, but he dealt at great length with a bishop's responsibility for the lost sheep of his flock.[24]

The quiet of Portmore was soon consumed in the agitations of Down and Connor, which had neither cathedral nor residence. At Hillsborough Castle, in Lisburn, they found temporary sanctuary but again little is known about their family

---

23 C.J. Stranks, *The Life and Writings of Jeremy Taylor*, London, 1952, p. 221 = Gosse, op. cit., p. 173 = Carroll, op. cit., p. 31.   **24** Carroll, op. cit., p. 33.

life there except that it began with the burial of their two-year old son, the sixth of his seven sons to die; in fact the seventh son was buried one week after the death of his father Jeremy Taylor on 13 August 1667. Meantime in the diocese the theologian of tolerance was soon perceived as the bishop of tyranny, for his Presbyterian ministers were given no quarter. Soon the institutional Church that he so masterfully defended theologically and politically distanced itself from his uncompromising stand, but he remained nonetheless useful for his controversial contributions, like his *Discourse on Confirmation*. Similarly, he was soon forgotten by friends like Evelyn: 'only Henry More had time to keep in touch, sometimes by affectionate messages, letters and books enclosed in packages for Lady Conway.' [25]

Although the eminent Caroline Divine was now firmly established in institutional darkness, he was still the brightest light in the Irish hierarchy and remained indispensable to adorn the great occasions with his sermons. In May 1661, after the Restoration in London, he preached at the opening of the new Parliament in Dublin, a sermon on the duty of obedience, in which his attitude to nonconformity was conditioned by his own bitter experience: 'My eyes are almost grown old with seeing the horrid mischiefs, which come from rebellion and disobedience.' [26] Yet one year later, in the most glorious of all his sermons, 'Via Intelligentiae', preached to the scholars of 'the little, but excellent' University of Dublin, there are moments of transcendence when the bishop of Down and Connor escapes his 'place of torment' and speaks of divine experience and vision: 'Divine knowledge more than we can discourse of; more certain than the demonstrations of geometry, brighter than the sun, and indeficient as the light of heaven [...] to be felt and not to be talked of [...] for a good man is united unto God as a flame touches a flame and combines into splendour and to glory.'[27]

The death of Archbishop Bramhall in June 1663 brought Taylor at least to the pulpit, if not afterward to the cathedra or the episcopal chair, of Armagh. Once again he fuses the human and the divine, the mystery in history, so to speak; the sermon is partly a rhapsody on the sure and certain hope of resurrection, and partly a very skilful and picturesque biography. There are echoes here of Golden Grove as he weaves his way through nature's reflections of the resurrection: 'Night and day, the sun returning to the same point of east; every change of species the eagle renewing her youth, the snake her skin, the silkworm and the swallows, winter and summer, fall and spring.'[28] But there is also the mortal wound of Down and Connor; and when he turns to the portrait of Bramhall, he insists with indignant zeal upon the primate's 'heroic passion for the Church, and upon all

---

[25] Stranks, op. cit., p. 248 = Carroll, op. cit., p. 34.   [26] Gosse, op. cit., p. 188.   [27] Gest, op. cit., p. 114 = J. Taylor, vol. 8, p. 379.   [28] Gosse, op. cit., p. 198 = J. Taylor, vol. 8, p. 403.

that he was called upon to suffer, for he was driven into exile and poverty by that wild storm by which great Strafford and Canterbury fell.'[29]

Isolation and rejection in Church and State by Presbyterian and Puritan, Anglican and Roman, made this Catholic and Caroline High Churchman grow up in Christ, the Head, so to speak, more than in his Body, the Church. The *kenosis* of the Son of God emptying himself of his divinity to be a man like us in all things except sin alone gives meaning and mystery to the pilgrim people of the Old Testament and the biblical language of *wandering, desert, exile* and *dispersion*: similarly in the New Testament 'the Son of Man hath not whereon to lay his head'[30] and the language of the pilgrim people is continued, for the Church of Christ is a gathering together of the dispersed, those exiles from Paradise, journeying together through the wilderness of sin and division – 'the place where she is to be nourished for a time, and times, and half a time.'[31] Early in his time at Portmore, Sally Island on Loch Beg, 'where the things of the spirit are so plainly seen in the lights and shadows, the colour and shapes of every common day,'[32] became his place of retreat and from there he wrote to Evelyn, his former patron:

> My retirement in this solitary place hath been, I hope, of some advantage to me as to this state of religion, in which I am yet but a novice, but by the goodness of God I see fine things before me whither I am contending. It is a great but a good work, and I beg of you to assist me with your prayers, and to obtain of God for me that I may arrive at that height of love and union with God. which is given to all souls who are very dear to God.[33]

In *Muskets and Altars*,[34] a recent study of Taylor and his period, Reginald Askew, a theologian, would seem, at first glance, to be taking up where historian Eamon Duffy left off, and ready to present Cromwell around 1650 completing what Cranmer began around 1550. But Askew is not simply writing as an historian; he is concerned, rather, with the complex present, sacred and secular, that is for ever at odds, if not always at war, with itself, whether it be called Church and State, Pulpit and Press, Religion and Science, Spiritus Dei or Spiritus Mundi, and the century from Cranmer to Cromwell is its symbol. For the most part Askew's haunting words and their peculiar spellings are those of Jeremy Taylor, 'the Shakespeare of English prose', but his voice and its authority is Catholic and Caroline. In some 200 pages, beautifully presented with well-structured and lengthy quotations, and worthy of him in classical allusion and literary elegance, Askew, the theologian, writes about sanctity and spirituality in our sequestered Church and secular world.

29 Taylor, vol. 8, p. 414. 30 Mt 8:20. 31 Rev 12:6. 32 M. Cropper, *Flame Touches Flame*, London, 1949, p. 142. 33 Ibid., p. 143, = Carroll, op. cit., p. 78. 34 R. Askew, *Muskets and Altars. Jeremy Taylor and the Last of the Anglicans*, London, 1997.

The subtitle of this work, 'Jeremy Taylor and the Last of the Anglicans,' revives the apocalyptic fears of Taylor's times, and establishes their continuity with the *blood-dimmed tide* and *Second Coming* of today's confusion and anarchy. Then Taylor's *Holy Living* and *Holy Dying* were written for believers living without a ministering Church, and after the compromise of the Restoration continued to nourish the Catholic and Caroline tradition in the Church of England as spiritual classics. Now those classics of Taylor speak from the past, but their voice is that of Askew who believes in the Word and its words, and remembers the good order of the ancients. Indeed, he sheds afresh the 'Tears of Achilles', because 'the religious sensibility common to Homer and Sophocles, Horace and Cicero, and to Jeremy Taylor's Church of England, is no longer plain to our society, in which Greek, Latin and Divinity are hardly known to anyone.'[35] *Sic transit gloria mundi!*

The assimilation, on the other hand, by Reginald Askew, of Taylor's voluminous writings creates a unity in mind and heart that is a powerful expression of truth and tradition, classical and Christian, Catholic and Caroline. In this light he sees our muskets and our altars: on the one hand, Parliament does not persecute; it merely disposes of our Sunday; neither is the Church prohibited, it simply continues to dwindle without any prospect of a glorious restoration: on the other hand, our altars have not the Word of Eternal life; 'the mealymouthed [...] all-embracingly secular Church [...], about hell-fire is evasive; about divine judgement bashful; about the struggle between love's endeavour and perdition politely open.'[36] Like Taylor, Askew challenges our apocalyptic darkness with the Word of *Very 'Heaven or hell'*[37] here not even Milton is spared for he confused Revelation and mythology, prophecy and poetry, and hastened the *Enlightenment* of our darkness. In theological writing in English today this publication is a welcome respite, for scripture is its source, tradition its stream, and our world its wasteland. *Pusillus Grex*, or remnant of Isaiah! *O tempora! O mores!*

---

35 Ibid., op. cit., p. 45. 36 Ibid., p. 155. 37 Ibid., p. 160.

CHAPTER I

The Minister of the Word[1]

INTRODUCTION, BY H.R. McADOO

When Jeremy Taylor picked the title, 'The Whole Duty of the Clergy' for his pair of sermons on Titus 2:7-8, he was making a play on the title of 'The Whole Duty of Man' (1658/9) which with *Holy Living* (1650) were the most popular devotional books of the age [...], keeping the spirit of Anglicanism alive when the Church's outward system had been dismantled under the Commonwealth [...]. If so much is expected of us all it follows that the clergy are to be first in this kind.[2] They are called 'to be examples even of the examples themselves.'[3]

The 'Whole Duty of the Clergy' first appeared in *Ten Sermons* (1667); taken with his *Rules and Advices to the Clergy* (1661) and *Clerus Domini* (1651), which is theologically more important because of its analysis of priesthood in respect of the eucharist, we have a complete picture of his understanding of the ministry and of the life of those called to serve in it.

The nature of the clerical vocation is such that so much of it having to do with the personal problems of others, it can only be a half-told story of years that are largely hidden and of valued help which in the nature of things can never be known. Yet the form and shape and some of the content of the clerical life are known and we recognize its clear outlines in books which delight and encourage the clerical descendants of the authors of the Woodforde diary, the Kilvert diary, the Armstrong diary, and we see it more sombrely depicted in the Skinner diary.[4] The setting changes from century to century; people's ideas change. Yet of their pastors, humanly inadequate though they may be, men and women will require, as Taylor stresses, integrity in life and in teaching:[5] 'You must be so for yourselves, and you must be so for others.'[6]

So we ask ourselves, knowing that essentially human spiritual needs do not change very much for cybernetic man, what sort of pattern for the clerical life did

---

1 H.R. McAdoo, 'The Whole Duty', *Search*, 16:1 (Dublin, 1993), pp 39-47.   2 J. Taylor, vol. 8, pp 502-4   3 Ibid., p. 505.   4 H.R. McAdoo, op. cit., p. 48.   5 J. Taylor, vol. 8, p. 505.   6 Ibid., p. 502.

Taylor see who had himself been through the mill of persecution, sequestration, imprisonment, misunderstandings, poverty and dependence on others but who yet stood firm through national catastrophe and civil war, through personal loss and many bereavements. Out of such an experience the pattern of ministry he outlines is not an idealized one in an unreal setting [...]. 'The Whole Duty' deals with the content of the clerical vocation while *The Rules and Advices* is concerned with its form, but for Taylor form and content are mutually supportive. Given then that, in his day, belief and acceptance were stronger in a society which had not yet seen religion marginalized, the question for us is: To what extent, if at all, Taylor's view of the whole duty of the clergy is relevant to us and to the reality of ministry today?

The content of the pattern was that the young clergyman then as now and in company with his fellow-members of the Church was seeking through grace to grow despite sins and setbacks in the new life in Christ, and striving to keep in mind that ministry is an enabling service which like charity begins at home (Eph. 4:12-13). Probably it would be the experience of most clergymen that this form and content supplement and vivify (St Bernard's word) each other. It is striking how Jeremy Taylor sees all this in terms of a pattern, 'the pattern in his life and conversation,'[7] and applies it individually, 'he must be a pattern.'[8] This is at the heart of how he understands the whole duty of the clergy and he is well aware of how daunting this can be so he constantly stresses humility which in itself, he says, is 'the greatest of all miracles [...]. You can never truly teach humility, or tell what it is, unless you practice it yourselves,'[9] and so 'Let every curate of souls strive to understand himself best; and then to understand others.'[10]

Obviously, generalisation is of only limited validity but on the whole I would imagine that within wide variations dictated by local conditions much the same pattern obtained elsewhere fifty years ago, more intricately designed and more intensively worked in great and populous parishes, but basically the same understanding of the whole duty of the clergy.

What of the pattern of the whole duty today? The form in respect of day-to-day parochial activity will have been modified to varying extents by the impact of the changing social context and by other linked factors. The hospital, the sick-call, the liturgical commitments, religious education, study and prayer groups, confirmation classes, no doubt remain constants in the overall design of the pattern even if in some respects technique as in teaching and in group-dynamics has changed [...]. Also increased involvement in civic concerns in the wider community and the growth of ecumenical contacts and occasions, both welcome, make inroads on time and further modify the pattern. Widespread change in moral perceptions and practice and the

---

7 Ibid. p. 506.   8 Ibid.   9 J. Taylor, vol. 1, p. 102.   10 Ibid.

growth of the so-called permissive society are factors which, as well as altering the context of the work and affecting the doing of it, will have made, together with the devastating effects of the drug problem, heavier demands on counselling than was formerly the case. Not, of course, that 1940 or 1640 were golden ages of idyllic innocence and pastoral peace – our own experience and the reading of history and of the clerical diaries referred to show that this was far from being the case. Yet one must conclude that the last half-century has resulted in a stretching and a complicating of the form of the pattern [...]. Does this continuing similarity of pattern mean that those responsible for training are devoid of all imagination and adaptability? Or could it be that history is telling us to concentrate on proven essentials while being open to new thinking but not over-hospitable to passing fashions? Thoughts like this cross the mind as one analyses what Taylor considers to be the whole duty of the clergy.

As to the content, I would imagine that nobody believes the pattern to have changed in its essentials since George Herbert, prostrate before the altar in the little church at Bemerton on the day of his institution, prayed: 'I will always condemn my birth, or any title or dignity that can be conferred on me, when I shall compare them with my title of being a Priest and serving at the Altar of Jesus my Master.'

In spite of the many new insights [...] on vocation and function, the clergyman knows that he is the servant of all because of Christ the Servant who 'emptied himself and took the form of a servant[...] and was obedient' (Phil 2:7,8). As Michael Ramsey put it, 'We are servants, called upon to obey. Has not the idea of obedience as a Christian virtue rather slipped out of our contemporary religion? [...] But it has an ineradicable place in the New Testament.' [11]

The clergyman knows, as the clergy always and in deliberate disavowal of any personal worthiness have known, that he lives unworthily at a grace-point of intersection where the vertical and the horizontal aspects of the whole duty meet and cross, because he is both the servant of all and the minister of God's word and sacraments. Through the Spirit abiding in the Church he is enabled to be, in spite of his own inadequacies, an enabler of others: 'It is only a humble priest who is authoritatively a man of God, one who makes God real to his fellows.'[12] This too is how Taylor so uncompromisingly puts it: 'You must be a man of God, not after the common manner of men, but "after God's own heart", and men will be strive to be like you.' Yet with all this he is always aware of and shares in the poignant human realisation of the gap between our ideal and our real and the gap that this creates: 'Our nature is too weak, in order to our duty [...] if it be not helped by a mighty grace but the Spirit enables the church with gifts and graces. And from these there is another operation of the new birth.'[13]

[11] M. Ramsey, *The Christian Priest Today*, London, 1972, p. 62.   [12] Ibid., p. 78.   [13] J. Taylor, vol. 8, p. 517.

Reflections such as these are occasioned by reading again 'The Whole Duty of the Clergy' which was probably preached in the summer of 1663 when Taylor was visiting Connor parishes and the *Rules and Advices* which was certainly delivered to the clergy of Down and Connor in 1661 at his visitation in 'Lisnegarvey' or Lisburn. Taylor's outline of the ministerial pattern gives occasion for self-criticism to every generation of his successors by its blunt simplicity: 'Here then is, 1. Your duty. 2. The degrees and excellency of your duty. 'The duty is double:' 1. Holiness of life. 2. Integrity of doctrine. Both these have their heightenings, in several degrees.'[14] He builds his case by describing first the calling of all Christians, what he terms 'the first separation' since 'all that profess themselves Christ's disciples, all that take his signature, they and their children are the church, an ecclesia, called out from the rest of the world'.[15] The goal to be aimed at is that all 'must acquire all the graces of the holy Spirit of God.' This is no soft option, for the gifts of the Spirit have to be sought with diligence, 'no lazy worker is a good Christian.' The call is insistent, so 'you see how severe and sacred a thing it is to be Christian.' Further still, 'God requires of us perseverance' and 'a constant thrusting all this forward.'[16] This, says Taylor, is what is implied for all within the called community, the Church. But for the clergy there is involved a second separation: 'a separation of you even beyond this separation: he hath separated you yet again.'[17]

For Taylor, the implications of this reach far and deep into the clerical life and office: 'You are to be the first in this kind, and consequently the measure of all the rest' and 'you are the ministers of Christ's priesthood, under-labourers in the great work of meditation and intercession.' This profoundly theological view of ministerial priesthood is further worked out in the eucharistic context of *Clerus Domini*, but here he emphasises to the clergy that in the eucharistic action the people are the Church: 'Thus, in the consecration of the mysterious sacrament, the people have their portion; for the bishop or the priest blesses, and the people, by saying 'Amen' to the mystic prayer, is partaker of the power, and the whole church hath a share in the power of the spiritual sacrifice.'[18]

'The double duty' of such a life and calling, says Taylor, requires that 'Ye must be patterns, not only of knowledge and wisdom [...] but of something that is more profitable [...], something by which mankind shall be better [...], a pattern of good works [...]. Indeed, the duty appears in this, that many things are lawful for the people which are scandalous for the clergy[...]. The integrity of life means that you are tied to more abstinences, to more severities, to more renunciations and self-denials [...] others must relieve the poor, you must take care of them.'[19] According to Taylor, this double standard of more being required of the clergy is clear in scripture and in 'the concurrent sense of the whole Church, and

---

14 Ibid., p. 505.   15 Ibid., p. 503.   16 Ibid.   17 Ibid.   18 Ibid., p. 504

expectations of all the world.' It is not enough to be 'innocent': the clergy are expected to be zealous in life and devotion: 'but if you be not this, you are not good ministers of Jesus Christ [...] and this is infinitely your duty [...]; none do their duty but those who, by an exemplar sanctity, become patterns to their flocks.'[20]

To our ears this strikes an austere note, though it is hardly more than the charge and examination in the Ordinal to be 'wholesome examples and patterns to the flock of Christ'. Yet here is the paradox; Taylor, the man, was neither austere nor forbidding but 'courteous and affable and of easy access'; George Rust tells us that his 'long hours of prayer' resulted in a personality, winning and attractive, a delightful and witty conversationalist and a sought-after counsellor and confessor. Though vastly learned in theology he was also a 'rare humanist' and what 'did captivate and enravish' was his poetic quality which matched 'his indefatigable industry'. He penetrated deeply into the art of meditation and sacramental life. This discipline produced a life as beautiful as his voice which was 'strangely musical'. 'He was,' says Rust, 'of most sweet and obliging humour, of great candour and ingenuity' and he who knew what it was to be poor died poor because of his 'large and diffusive charity.' The fact is that Taylor is deliberately evoking a salutary self-depreciating assessment from his readers as he did from his fellow-clergy when he began his visitation with 'Remember that it is your great duty, that you be exemplar in your lives and patterns to your flocks: lest it be said unto you, Why takest thou my law into thy mouth, seeing thou hatest to be reformed thereby'.[21]

The second sermon treats of the other part of 'the double duty', namely, doctrine, and its central theme around which all else revolves is 'that you teach nothing to the people, but what is certainly to be found in scripture.'[22] He is alive to the danger of 'so many interpretations' by partisans and lists for scripture study books that are 'not infrequent in all public libraries.' But he allows that there can be 'too laborious methods of weary learning' so he recommends to the preacher concentration on the literal sense of scripture and 'the prime intention of the speaker;' 'a spiritual interpretation or mystical is not ruled out if the literal is not contradicted.'[23]

Rust assures us that 'he would never be governed by anything but reason', the core value in all his works, and example of the classical Anglican appeal to scripture, antiquity and reason. Then 'how shall our reason be guided that it may be right [...] and direct us to the place where the star appears [...], where the babe lieth?' Firstly, he says, 'let the fundamentals of faith be your light to walk by, and whatever you derive from thence, let it be agreeable to the principles from whence they come [...]. Next to this analogy or proportion of faith, let the consent of the Catholic Church be your measure, so as by no means to prevaricate in any

---

19 Ibid., pp 505-6   20 Ibid.   21 Ibid., vol. 1, p. 101.   22 Ibid., p. 519   23 Ibid., p. 525.

doctrine, in which all Christians have consented.'[24] He is at pains to point out that this does not mean that the doctrine of the church should be the rule of faith distinctly from, much less against, the scripture: 'he holds that the appeal to antiquity is the safer, because it cannot go far being limited in its application[...], in the creed, in ecclesiastical government, and in external forms of worship and liturgy [...]; the practice of the Catholic Church is the best commentary', or great rule of truth: *Quod ubique, quod semper, quod ab omnibus*, and what cannot be proved by these measures, cannot be necessary.'[25]

He concludes 'The Whole Duty:' 'Do not trouble your people with controversies [...]. Let not your sermons [...] be busy arguing about hard places in scripture; preach good works as the fruit of faith working through love. Learn them to be sober and temperate, to be just and to pay their debts, to speak well of their neighbours and to think meanly of themselves; it is the new life [...], so dress your people into the imagery of Christ.'[26]

In the *Rules and Advices* his counsel on preaching becomes pastoral and practical [...]. We meet the familiar framework for the day: 'Every minister is obliged, publicly or privately, to read the common prayers every day in the week, at morning and evening [...] and in populous places it must be read in churches [...]; every minister ought to be well skilled and studied in saying his office.'[27] The importance of preaching cannot be overestimated for 'it is the one half of his great office and employment [...]. Let the business of your sermons be to preach holy life, obedience, peace, love among neighbours [...]. Press those graces most that do most good and make the least noise; such as giving privately and forgiving publicly.'[28] No jargon, no cant: 'Use primitive, known and accustomed words, and affect not new, fantastical, or schismatical terms.'[29] He is all the time pressing the practical, an external practice of religion which issues inwardly in what he variously calls 'the new life,' 'the new creature,' 'the new birth,' 'the new possibility.' One of his *Whitsunday Sermons* says it all: 'So in the new creation, Christ [...] intends to conform us to his image [...]; by the spirit of a new life we are made new creatures, capable of a new state [...]; we have new affections, new wills and understandings [...]. So build them up in a most holy faith to a holy life [...]. Let no preacher envy any man that hath more fame in preaching than himself [...]. If you meet praise[...], stand upon your guard, and pray against your own vanity.'[30]

Catechising, parochial visiting, individual instruction and regular study are all extensions of the ministry of the Word. 'Let a bell be tolled when the catechizing is to begin [...]. Let every minister teach his people the use, practice, methods, and

[24] Ibid., pp 528-30. [25] Ibid., p. 531. [26] Ibid., p. 533. [27] Ibid., pp 113-14. [28] Ibid., p. 108. [29] Ibid., p. 110. [30] Ibid., vol. 4, pp 347ff.

benefits of mental prayer [...], for by preaching, catechizing. and private intercourse, all the needs of souls can best be served; but by preaching alone they cannot.'[31] Central to Christian practice is the Holy Communion, treated in full, devotionally and doctrinally, in a number of his books; so here he confines himself to recommending frequent attendance.

His general rubric is 'Pray much and very fervently for all your parishioners' but sick-visiting is a priority and Taylor himself died of fever after visiting the sick in Lisburn. The pattern of 'The Whole Duty' and of the *Rules and Advices* is today relevant; what is essentially a matter of relationships is not fundamentally altered by changing structures. With all this, 'strive to get the love of the congregation; but let it not degenerate into popularity.'[32] There is much else besides, but let Taylor's be the conclusion forged out of his personal and often bitter experience in troubled and tumultuous times: 'I end this with the saying of St Austin, Let your religious prudence think, that, in the world, especially at this time, nothing is more laborious, more difficult, or more dangerous, than the office of a bishop, or a priest, or a deacon [...]; but nothing is more blessed, if we do our duty, according to the commandment of our Lord.'[33]

The Minister's Duty in Life and Doctrine[1]

JEREMY TAYLOR

> In all things shewing thyself a pattern of good works:
> in doctrine shewing uncorruptness, gravity, sincerity;
> Sound speech that cannot be condemned, that he that is
> of the contrary part may be ashamed, having no evil
> thing to say of you. (Tit 2:7-8)

As God in the creation of the world first produced a mass of matter, having nothing in it but an obediential capacity and passivity, [...] so God hath also done in the new creation; all the world was concluded under sin, it was a corrupt mass, all mankind had corrupted themselves, but yet were capable of divine influences, and of a nobler form, producible in the new birth: here then God's spirit moves upon the waters of a divine birth, and makes a separation of part from part, of corruption from

---

[31] Ibid., vol. 1, pp 111-2.   [32] Ibid., p. 106.   [33] Ibid., vol. 8, p. 518.   [1] Sermon X, in J. Taylor, vol. 8, pp 499ff.

corruption, and first chose some families to whom He communicated the divine influences and the breath of a nobler life; Seth and Enoch, Noah and Abraham, Job and Bildad: and these were the special repositories of the divine grace and prophets of righteousness to glorify God in themselves, and in their sermons unto others. But this was like enclosing of the sun: he that shuts him in, shuts him out; and God who was and is an infinite goodness, would not be circumscribed and limited to a narrow circle; goodness is His nature, and infinite is His measure, and communication of that goodness is the motion of that eternal being: God therefore breaks forth as out of a cloud, and picks out a whole nation; the sons of Israel became His family, and that soon swelled into a nation, and that nation multiplied till it became too big for their country, and by a necessary dispersion went, and did much good, and gained some servants to God out of other parts of mankind. But God was pleased to cast lots once more, and was like the sun already risen upon the earth, who spreads his rays to all the corners of the habitable world, that all that will open their eyes and draw their curtains, may see and rejoice in his light. Here God resolved to call all the world; He sent into the highways and hedges, to the corners of the gentiles and the highways of the Jews; all might come that would; for 'the sound of the gospel went out into all lands;'[2] and God chose all that came, but all would not; and those that did, He gathered into a fold, marked them with His own mark, sent His Son to be the great 'Shepherd and bishop of their souls,' and they became 'a peculiar people' unto God – a 'little flock,' a 'new election.'[3]

And here is the first separation and singularity of the gospel; all that hear the voice of Christ's first call, all that profess themselves His disciples, all that take His signature, they and their children are the church, an *ekklesia*, 'called out' from the rest of the world, the 'elect' and the 'chosen of God.'

Now these being thus chosen out, culled and picked from the evil generations of the world, He separates them from others, to gather to Himself; He separates them and sanctifies them to become holy; to come out (not of the companies so much, as) from the evil manners of the world: God chooses them unto holiness, they are *tetagmenoi eis zoen alonion*, 'put in the right order to eternal life.'[4]

All Christians are 'holy unto the Lord,' and therefore must not be unholy in their conversation; for nothing that is unholy shall come near to God: that's the first great line of our duty, but God intends it further; all Christians must not be only holy, but eminently holy. For 'John indeed baptized with waters'[5] but that's but a dull and inactive element, and moves by no principle, but by being ponderous; Christ 'baptizes with the holy Ghost and with fire,' and God hates lukewarmness; and when He chooses to Him a 'peculiar people,' He adds, 'they must be zealous of good works.'[6] [...] This is a great height, and these things I

2 Ps 19:4.   3 1 Pet 2:25.   4 Acts 13:48.   5 Mt 3:11.   6 Tit 2:14.

have premised, even of all Christians whatsoever, that you may not depart without your portion of a blessing, but also as a foundation of the ensuing periods, which I shall address to you my brethren of the clergy, the fathers of the people, for I speak in a school of prophets and prophets' sons; to you who are or intend to be so.

For God hath made a separation of you even beyond this separation. He hath separated you yet again, He hath put you anew into the crucible, He hath made you to pass through the fire seven times more. For it is true that the whole community of the people is the church, *ecclesia sancta est communio sanctorum*, 'the holy catholic church is the communion of saints,' but yet by the voice and consent of all christendom, you are the church by way of propriety, and eminency, and singularity. 'Churchmen-' that's your appellative: all are *andres pneumatikoi*,[7] 'spiritual men,' all have received the Spirit, and all walk in the Spirit, and ye are all 'sealed by the Spirit unto the day of redemption,' and yet there is a spirituality peculiar to the clergy. 'If any man be overtaken in a fault, ye which are spiritual restore such a one in the spirit of meekness:'[8] you who are spiritual by office and designation, of a spiritual calling, and spiritual employment, you who have the Spirit of the Lord Jesus, and minister the Spirit of God, you are more eminently spiritual; you have the Spirit in graces and in powers, in sanctification and abilities, in office and in person, the 'unction from above' hath descended upon your heads and upon your hearts; you are *kat' exochen*, by way of eminency and prelation, 'spiritual men.'

'All the people of God were holy;' Corah and his company were in the right so far, but yet Moses and Aaron were more holy and stood nearer to God.[9] All the people are prophets: it is now more than Moses' wish, for the Spirit of Christ hath made them so. 'If any man prayeth or prophesieth with his head covered,' or 'If any woman prophesieth with her head uncovered,'[10] they are dishonoured, but either man or woman may do that work in time and place, for 'in the latter days I will pour out of My spirit, and your daughters shall prophesy:'[11] and yet God hath appointed in His church prophets above these, to whose spirit all the other prophets are subject, and as God said to Aaron and Miriam concerning Moses, 'To you I am known in a dream or a vision, but to Moses I speak face to face;'[12] so it is in the church: God gives of His spirit to all men, but you he hath made the ministers of His spirit. Nay, the people have their portion of the keys of the kingdom of heaven, so said St Paul, 'to whom ye forgive any thing, to him I forgive also,'[13] and to the whole church of Corinth he gave a commission, 'in the name of Christ, and by His Spirit, to deliver the incestuous person unto Satan;' and when the primitive penitents stood in their penitential stations, they did *caris*

---

[7] 1 Cor 2:15; 3:1.   [8] Gal 6:1.   [9] Num 16:3.   [10] 1 Cor 11:5.   [11] Joel 2:28.   [12] Num 12:6ff.   [13] 2 Cor 2:10.

Dei adgeniculari, et toti populo legationem orationis suae commendare[14] and yet the keys were not only promised, but given to the apostles to be used then, and transmitted to all generations of the church; and we are 'ministers of Christ, and stewards of the manifold mysteries of God;'[15] and 'to us is committed the word of reconciliation.'[16] And thus in the consecration of the mysterious sacrament, the people have their portion; for the bishop or the priest blesses, and the people by saying 'Amen' to the mystic prayer is partaker of the power, and the whole church hath a share in the power of spiritual sacrifice; 'ye are a royal priesthood,' 'kings and priests unto God;'[17] that is, so ye are priests as ye are kings, but yet kings and priests have a glory conveyed to them, of which the people partake but in minority, and allegory, and improper communication: but you are, and are to be respectively that considerable part of mankind by whom God intends to reign in the hearts of men, and therefore you are to be the first in this kind, and consequently the measure of all the rest. To you therefore I intend this, and some following discourses in order to this purpose; I shall but now lay the first stone, but it is the corner stone in this foundation.

But to you, I say, of the clergy, these things are spoken properly; to you these powers are conveyed really; you are the choicest of his choice, the elect of his election, a church picked out of the church, vessels of honour for your Master's use, appointed to teach others, authorized to bless in His name; you are ministers of Christ's priesthood, under-labourers in the great work of mediation and intercession, *medii inter Deum et populum*, you are 'for the people towards God,'[18] and convey answers and messages from God to the people. These things I speak, not only to magnify your office, but to enforce and heighten your duty; you are holy by office and designation; for your very appointment is a sanctification and a consecration, and therefore whatever holiness God requires of the people, who have some little portions in the priesthood evangelical, He expects it of you, and much greater, to whom He hath conveyed so great honours, and admitted so near unto Himself, and hath made to be the great ministers of His kingdom and His spirit: and now as Moses said to the levitical schismatics, Corah and his company, so I may say to you, 'Seemeth it but a small thing unto you that the God of Israel hath separated you from the congregation of Israel to bring you to Himself, to do the service of the Tabernacle to the Lord, and to stand before the congregation to minister to them? And He hath brought thee near to Him.'[19] Certainly if of every one of the christian congregation God expects a holiness that mingles with no unclean thing, if God will not suffer of them a lukewarm and an indifferent service, but requires zeal of His glory, and that which St Paul calls the *ponos tes*

---

[14] Tertullian, *Penance*, 9 = ANF, vol. 3, p. 657.   [15] 1 Cor 4.1.   [16] 2 Cor 5:19.   [17] 1 Pet 2:9: Rev 1:6; 5:10.   [18] Ex 18:19.   [19] Num 16:9.

agapes, the 'labour of love;' if He will have them to be without spot or wrinkle, or any such thing, if He will not endure any pollution in their flesh or spirit; if He requires that their bodies, and souls, and spirits be kept blameless unto the coming of the Lord Jesus; if He accepts of none of the people unless they have within them the conjugation of all christian graces; if He calls on them to abound in every grace, and that in all the periods of their progression unto the ends of their lives, and to the consummation and perfection of grace, if He hath made them lights in the world, and the salt of the earth, to enlighten others by their good example, and to teach them and invite them by holy discourses, and wise counsels, and speech seasoned with salt, what is it think ye, or with what words is it possible to express what God requires of you? They are to be examples of good life to one another, but you are to be examples even of the examples themselves, that's your duty, that's the purpose of God, and that's the design of my text, that 'in all things ye shew yourselves a pattern of good works, in doctrine shewing uncorruptness, gravity, sincerity, sound speech that cannot be condemned; that he that is of the contrary part may be ashamed, having no evil thing to say of you.'

Here then is your duty and the degrees and excellency of your duty:

1. Holiness of Life.
2. Integrity of Doctrine.

1. The very first words of the whole psalter are an argument of this necessity. 'Blessed is the man that walketh not in the counsel of the ungodly, nor standeth in the way of sinners, nor sitteth in the chair of the mockers'[20] the seat of the scornful [...]. These words are greatly to be regarded: the primitive church would admit no man to the superior orders of the clergy, unless among other prerequired dispositions, they could say all David's psalter by heart, and it was very well, besides many other reasons, that they might in the front read their own duty, so wisely and so mysteriously by the Spirit of God made preliminary to the whole office [...].

It will be more useful for us to consider those severe words of David in the fiftieth psalm, 'But unto the wicked God saith, What hast thou to do declare My statutes, or that thou shouldst take My covenant in thy mouth, seeing thou hatest instruction and casteth My words behind thee?'[21] The words are a sad upbraiding to all ungodly ministers, and they need no commentary; for whatever their office and employment be to teach God's people, yet unless they regard the commandments of God in their heart, and practise themselves, they having nothing to do

---

20 Ps 1:1.   21 Ps 50:16.

with the word of God, they sin in taking the covenant, a testimony of God, into their mouth [...]. Indeed, if none could be admitted to this ministry but those who had never sinned, the harvest might be very great, but the labourers would be extremely few, or rather none at all, but after repentance they must be admitted, and not before [...].

'But thou when thou are converted,' said Christ to Peter, 'strengthen the brethren.'[22] The primitive church had a degree of severity beyond this, for they would not admit any man who had done public penance to receive holy orders; [...] 'none of the public penitents must be ordained, for who will esteem that priest venerable, whom a little before he saw dishonoured by scandalous and public crimes.'[23]

But in all cases, *turpe est doctori cum culpa regardi ipsum*.[24] The guilt of the sin which a man reproves, quite spoils his sermon: 'a sick conscience spoils the tongue of the eloquent, and makes it stammer,' said St Ambrose;[25] [...] 'nothing confounds a man so much as to be judged out of his mouth: the hand that means to make another clean, should not itself be dirty,' said St Gregory.[26]

But all this is but in general: there are but yet considerations more particular and material.

(a) A minister of an evil life cannot do much good to his charges; [...] 'a good sermon without a good example, is no very good sermon,' said the Jews' proverb; [...] 'he that preaches mortification and lives voluptuously, propounds the duty as if it were impossible'[27] [...]. But if your charges see you bear your sickness patiently, and your cross nobly, and despise money generously, and forgive your enemy bravely, and relieve the poor charitably, then he sees your doctrine is tangible and material, it is more than words, and he loves you, and considers what you say [...]. Furthermore, a minister of an evil life cannot preach with that fervour and efficacy, with that life and spirit, as a good man does.

(b) Secondly, a wicked minister cannot with success and benefit pray for the people of his charges; and this is a great matter, for prayer is the key of David; and God values it at so high a rate, that Christ is made the prince of all intercession, and God hath appointed angels to convey to His throne of grace the prayer of the saints, and He hath made prophets and priests, even the whole clergy, the peculiar ministers of prayer. *Orabit pro eo sacerdos*, 'the priest shall pray for him,' 'the priest shall make atonement for his sin, and it shall be forgiven him.'[28] [...] This I say is the priest's office, and if the people lose the benefit of this they are undone. To bishop Timothy St Paul gave it in charge 'that supplications, and prayers. and intercessions be made for all men;'[29] and St James advised the 'sick' to 'send for the elders of the church,'

22 Lk 22-32. 23 Hormisda (Pope), *Letters*, 25 = CSEL 35. 24 J. Taylor, vol. 1, p. ccclxv. 25 Ambrose, *On Psalm 118*, Ser. 6 = PL 16. 26 Gregory (Pope), *Moralia*, 7:36 = EP 2302/17 27 Talmud. 28 Num 15:25; Lev 4:35. 29 1 Tim 2:1.

the bishops and priests, 'and let them pray over them' and then 'their sins shall be forgiven them.'[30] But how? That is, supposed the minister prays fervently, and be a righteous man; for the effectual fervent prayer of a righteous man availeth much, it is promised on no other terms: *Qualis vir talis oratio* is an old rule, 'As is the man, such is his prayer.'[31]

'The prayer of the wicked is an abomination to the Lord,'[32] said Solomon; he cannot prevail for himself, much less for others [...]. Believe it or not; a man that is ungracious in his life can never be gracious in his office, and acceptable to God [...]. In short, if so much holiness as I formerly described be required of him that is appointed to preach to others, to offer spiritual sacrifices for the people, to bless the people, to divert judgments from them, to deprecate the wrath of God, to make an atonement for them, and to reconcile them to the eternal mercy, certain it is, that though the sermons of a wicked minister may do some good, not so much as they ought, but some they can; yet the prayer of a wicked minister does no good at all, it provokes God to anger, it is an abomination in His righteous eyes [...].

(c) Thirdly, every minister that lives an evil life is that person whom our blessed Saviour means under the odious appellative of a 'hireling.' For he is not the hireling that receives wages, or that lives of the altar; *Sine farina non est lex*, said the doctors of the Jews, 'Without bread-corn no man can preach the law,' and St Paul, though he spared the Corinthians, yet he took wages of other churches, of all but in the regions of Achaia;[33] and the law of nature and the law of the gospel have taken care that 'he that serves at the altar should live of the altar,'[34] and he is no hireling for all that; but he is a hireling that does not do his duty, he that 'flies when the wolf comes,'[35] says Christ, he that is not present with them in dangers, that helps them not to resist the devil, to master their temptations, to invite them on to piety, to gain souls to Christ; to him it may be said as the apostle did of the gnostics, 'gain to them is godliness;'[36] and theology is but *artificium venale*, 'a trade of life,' to fill the belly and keep the body warm [...]; then thou dost but sell sermons, and give counsel at a price and, like a fly in the temple, taste of every sacrifice, but do nothing but trouble the religious rites: for certain it is, no man takes on him this office, but he either 'seeks those things which are his own,' or 'those things which are Jesus Christ's:' and if he does this, he is 'a minister of Jesus Christ,' if he does the other, he is the 'hireling,' and intends nothing but his belly, and 'God shall destroy both it and him.'

(d) Lastly, 'these things I have said unto you that ye sin not;'[37] but this is not the great thing here intended; you may be innocent, and yet not 'zealous of good works;'[38] but if you be not this, you are not good ministers of Jesus Christ[39] [...]. *Ad majorem Dei Gloriam*, 'to do what will most glorify God,' that's the line you

---

30 Jas 5:14. 31 Seneca, *On Anger*, 2:25, LCL, vol. 2. 32 Prov 15:8. 33 2 Cor 11:8. 34 1 Cor 9:13. 35 Jn 10:12. 36 1 Tim 6:5. 37 1 Jn 2:1. 38 Tit 2:14. 39 1 Tim 4:6.

must walk by: for to do no more than all men needs must, is servility, not so much as the affection of sons; much less can you be fathers to the people, when you go not so far as the sons of God: for a dark lanthorn, though there be a weak brightness on one side, will scarce enlighten one; much less will it conduct a multitude, or allure many followers by the brightness of its flame [...].

Remember your dignity to which Christ hath called you [...]. Severe were the words of our blessed Saviour, 'ye are the salt of the earth; if the salt have lost his savour, it is therefore good for nothing, neither for land, nor yet for the dunghill;'[40] a greater dishonour could not be expressed; he that takes such a one up will shake his fingers. I end with this saying of St Austin, 'Let your religious prudence think [...] that in the world, especially at this time, nothing is more laborious, more difficult, or more dangerous than the office of a bishop or a priest, or a deacon; nothing is more blessed if we do our duty according to the commandment of our Lord.'[41]

1. I have already discoursed of the integrity of life, and what great necessity there is, and how deep obligations lie upon you, not only to be innocent and void of offence, but also to be holy; not only pure, but shining; not only to be blameless, but to be didactic in your lives, that as by your sermons you preach in season, so by your lives you may preach out of season, that is, at all seasons, and to all men, 'that they seeing your good works may glorify God' on your behalf, and on their own [...]. Now by the order of the words and my own undertaking, I am to tell you what are the rules and measures of your doctrine which you are to teach the people - *in doctrine shewing uncorruptness, gravity, sincerity, &c.*

Firstly, be sure that you teach nothing to the people, but what is certainly to be found in scripture [...]. Whatsoever is not in and taken from the scriptures, is from a private spirit, and that is against scripture certainly, for 'no scripture is *idias epiluseos*,'[42] said St Peter; 'it is not, it cannot be 'of private interpretation'.[...]

This rule were alone sufficient to guide us all in the whole economy of our calling, if we were not weak and wilful, ignorant and abused [...]. 'How can I understand unless some man should guide me?' and indeed in St Paul's epistles 'there are many things hard to be understood,[43] and in many other places we find that the well is deep, and unless there be some to help us draw out the latent senses of it, our souls will not be filled with the waters of salvation; [...] you may therefore make great use of the labours of those worthy persons whom God hath made to be lights in the several generations of the world, that a hand may help a hand, and a father may teach a brother, and we all be taught of God: for there are many who have by great skill, and great experience, taught us many good rules for the interpretation of scripture [...].

40 Mt 5:13; Lk 14:34. 41 Augustine, *Letters*, 148 = PL 33. 42 2 Pet 1:20. 43 2 Pet 3:16.

And so it is in the interpretation of scripture, there are ways of doing it well and wisely without the too laborious methods of weary learning, that even the meanest labourers in God's vineyard may have that which is fit to minister to him that needs:

(a) In all the interpretations of scripture, the literal sense is to be presumed and chosen, unless there be evident cause to the contrary. The reasons are plain; because the literal sense is natural, and it is first, and it is most agreeable to some things in their whole kind, not indeed to prophecies, not to the teachings of the learned, nor those cryptic ways of institution by which the ancients did hide a light, and keep it in a dark lanthorn from the temeration of ruder handlings and popular preachers: but the literal sense is agreeable to laws, to the publication of commands, to the revelation of the divine will, to the concerns of the vulgar, to the foundations of faith, and to all the notice of things in which the idiot is as much concerned as the greatest clerks [...].

But then remember this also, that not only the grammatical or prime significance of the word is the literal sense; but whatsoever is the prime intention of the speaker, that is the literal sense, though the word be to be taken metaphorically, or by translation signify more things than one. 'The eyes of the Lord are over the righteous;'[44] this is literally true; and yet it is as true that God hath no eyes properly: but by 'eyes' are meant God's providence; and though this be not the first literal sense of the word 'eyes', it is not that which was at first imposed, and contingently; but it is that signification which was secondarily imposed, and by reason and proportion [...]. In this case the rule of Abulensis is very true, *Sensus literalis semper est verus*, 'the literal sense is always true,'[45] that is, all that is true which the Spirit of God intended to signify by the words, whether He intended the first or second signification; whether that of voluntary and contingent, or that of analogical and rational institution. 'Other sheep have I', said Christ, 'which are not of this fold:'[46] that He did not mean this of the *pecus lanigerum* is notorious; but of the gentiles to be gathered into the privileges and fold of Israel. For in many cases the first literal sense is the hardest, and sometimes impossible, and sometimes inconvenient; and when it is any of these, although we are not to recede from the literal sense, yet we are to take the second signification, the tropological or figurative. 'If thy right eye offend thee, pluck it out,'[47] said Christ: and yet no man digs his eyes out [...]. In this, common sense and a vulgar reason will be a sufficient guide, because there is always some other thing spoken by God, or some principle naturally implanted in us, by which we are secured in the understanding of the divine command [...].

44 Ps 34:15.   45 Cf. Taylor, vol. 1, p. cccclxv.   46 Jn 10: 16.   47 Mt 5:29.

But I shall not insist longer on this; he that understands nothing but his grammar, and hath not conversed with men and books, and can see no farther than his fingers' end, and makes no use of his reason, but for ever will be a child; he may be deceived in the literal sense of scripture, but then he is not fit to teach others: but he that knows words signify rhetorically as well as grammatically, and have various proper significations, and which of these is the first is not always of itself easy to be told; and [that] remembers also that God hath given him reason, and observation, and experience, and conversation with wise men, and the proportion of things, and the end of the command, and parallel places of scripture in other words to the same purpose; [he] will conclude, that since in plain places all the duty of man is contained, and that the literal sense is always true, and (unless men be wilful or unfortunate) they may with a small proportion of learning find out the literal sense of an easy moral proposition: will I say, conclude, that if we be deceived, the fault is our own; but the fault is great, the man so supine, the negligence so inexcusable, that the very consideration of human infirmity is not sufficient to excuse such teachers of others, who hallucinate or prevaricate in this [...].

But then take in this caution too; although there be but one principal literal sense, yet others that are subordinate may be intended subordinately, and others that are true by proportion, or that first intention, may be true for many reasons, and every reason applicable to a special instance; and all these may be intended as they signify, that is, one only by prime design, and the other by collateral consequence. Thus when it is said, 'Thou art My son, this day I have begotten Thee,'[48] the psalmist means it of the eternal generation of Christ; others seem to apply it to His birth of the blessed Virgin Mary; and St Paul expounds it of the resurrection of Christ: this is all true, and yet but one literal sense primely meant; but by proportion to the first the others have their place, and are meant by way of similitude. Thus we are the sons of God, by adoption, by creation, by favour, by participation of the Spirit, by the 'laver of regeneration,'[49] and every man for one or other of these reasons can say, 'Our Father which art in heaven,' and these are all parts of the literal sense, not different, but subordinate and by participation: but more than one prime literal sense must not be admitted [...].

The sum is this; he that with this moderation and these measures construes the plain meaning of the Spirit of God, and expounds the articles of faith, and the precepts of life, according to the intention of God signified by his own words, in their first or second signification, cannot easily be cozened into any heretical doctrine, but his doctrine will be *adiaphthoros*, the pure word and mind of God - in *doctrine shewing uncorruptness*.

48 Ps 2:7. 49 Tit 3:5.

(b) There is another sense or interpretation of scripture, and that is mystical or spiritual; which the Jews call *midrash*; and this relates principally to the Old testament. Thus the waters of the deluge did signify the waters of baptism; Sarah and Agar, the law and the gospel; the brazen serpent, the passion of Christ; the conjunction of Adam and Eve, the communion of Christ and His church; and this is called 'the spiritual sense' [...]. This sense the doctors divide into tropological, allegorical, and anagogical [...]. This spiritual sense is that which the Greeks call *uponoian*, or the 'sense that lies under' the cover of words: concerning this I shall give you these short rules, that your doctrine be *adiaphthoros*, pure and without heretical mixtures, and the leaven of false doctrines, for above all things this is to be taken care of.

(i) Although every place of scripture hath a literal sense, either proper or figurative, yet every one hath not a spiritual and mystical interpretation, and Origen was blamed by the ancients for forming all into spirit and mystery [...].

(ii) Whoever will draw spiritual senses from any history of the Old or New testament, must first allow the literal sense, or else he will soon deny an article of necessary belief [...]. I have seen all the revelation of St John turned into a moral commentary, in which every person can signify any proposition, or any virtue, according as his fancy chimes: this is too much, and therefore comes not from a good principle.

(iii) In moral precepts, in rules of polity and economy there is no other sense to be enquired after but what they bear upon the face; [...] therefore let no man tear those scriptures to other meanings beyond their own intentions and provisions. In these cases a spiritual sense is not to be enquired after.

(iv) If the letter of the story infers any undecency or contradiction, then it is necessary that a spiritual or mystical sense be thought of, but never else is it necessary [...]. But if the spiritual sense be proved, evident and certain, then it is of the same efficacy as the literal; for it is according to that letter by which God's holy spirit was pleased to signify His meaning [...].

These are the two ways of expounding all scriptures; these are as 'the two witnesses of God' [...] and are sufficient to guide us from destructive errors. It follows in the next place that I give you some rules that are more particular according to my undertakings, that you in your duty, and your charges in the provisions to be made for them, may be more secure.

(c) Although you are to teach your people nothing but what is in the word of God; yet by this word I understand all that God spake expressly, and all that by certain consequences can be deduced from it. Thus Dionysius Alexandrinus argues, 'He that in scripture is called the Son and the word of the Father, I conclude He is no stranger to the essence of the Father;'[50] and St Ambrose[51] derided them that called

---

50 Athanasius. *On the Opinion of Dionysius*, 20 = LNPF, vol. 4, p. 18.   51 Ambrose, *The Faith*, 1:19 = PL 16, p. 847

for express scripture for *omoousios*, since the prophets and the gospels acknowledge the unity of substance in the Father and the Son, and we easily conclude the holy Ghost to be God, because we call upon Him, and we call upon Him because we believe in Him, and we believe in Him because we are baptized into the faith and profession of the holy Ghost. This way of teaching our blessed Saviour used when He confuted the sadducees in the question of the resurrection, and thus he confuted the pharisees in the question of his being the Son of God. The use I make of it is this, that right reason is so far from being an exile from the enquiries of religion, that it is the great insurance of many propositions of faith [...]. All that is to be done here is to see that you argue well, that your deduction be evident, that your reason be right: for scripture is to our understandings as the grace of God to our wills; that instructs our reason, and this helps our wills, and we may as well choose the things of God without our wills, and delight in them without love, as understand the scriptures or make use of them without reason [...].

(d) In the making deductions, the first great measure to direct our reason and our enquiries is the analogy of faith: that is, let the fundamentals of faith be your *cynosura*, your great light to walk by, and whatever you derive from thence, let it be agreeable to the principles from whence they come [...].

(e) To this purpose it is necessary that you be very diligent in reading, laborious and assiduous in the studies of scripture: not only lest ye be blind seers, and blind guides, but because without great skill and learning ye cannot do your duty. A minister may as well sin by his ignorance as by his negligence [...]. Christ did not say 'read,' but 'search the scriptures;'[52] turn over every page, enquire narrowly, look diligently, converse with them perpetually, be mighty in the scriptures: for that which is plain there, is the best measures of our faith and of our doctrines [...]. Take this rule with you, do not pass from plainness to obscurity, nor from simple principles draw crafty conclusions, nor from easiness pass into difficulty, nor from wise notices draw intricate nothings, nor from the wisdom of God lead your hearers into the follies of men [...].

(f) Next to this analogy or proportion of faith, let the consent of the catholic church be your measure, so as by no means to prevaricate in any doctrine in which all christians always have consented [...] in the creed, in ecclesiastical government, and in external forms of worship and liturgy; [...], in these things all Christians ever have consented, and he that shall prophesy or expound scripture to the prejudice of any of these things, hath no part in that article of his creed, he does not believe the holy catholic church, he hath no fellowship, no communion with the saints and servants of God [...] for we speak according to the Spirit of God, when we understand scripture in that sense in which the church of God hath always practised it.

---

52 Chyrysostom, *On John*, Hom. = FOTC, vol. 33, p. 415.

Quod pluribus, quod sapientibus, quod omnibus videtur, that's Aristotle's rule: [53] and it is a rule of nature; every thing puts on a degree of probability as it is witnessed 'by wise men, by many wise men, by all wise men;' and it is Vincentius Lirinensis' great rule of truth, *quod ubique, quod semper, quod ab omnibus* [...] [54] and he that goes against 'what is said always, and everywhere, and by all Christians' had need have a new revelation, or an infallible spirit, or he hath an intolerable pride and foolishness of presumption [...].

And now it is time that I have done with the first great remark of doctrine noted by the apostle in my text; all the guides of souls must take care that the doctrine they teach be *adiaphthoros*, 'pure' and 'incorrupt,' the word of God, the truth of the Spirit *in doctrine shewing uncorruptness, gravity &c.*

Secondly, doctrine must be *semnos*, grave and reverend, no vain notions, no pitiful contentions, and disputes about little things;[...] a controversy is a stone in the mouth of the hearer, who should be fed with bread, and it is a temptation to the preacher [...]. Christian religion loves not tricks nor artifices of wonder, but, like the natural and amiable simplicity of Jesus, by plain and easy propositions leads us in wise paths to a place where sin and strife shall never enter [...]. The kingdom of God consists in wisdom and righteousness, in peace and holiness, in meekness and gentleness, in chastity and purity, in abstinence from evil and doing good to others; in these things place your labours, preach these things, and nothing else but such as these [...], for these things are profitable to men, and pleasing to God [...]. That's the second rule and measure of your preaching that the apostle gives you in my text.

Thirdly, your speech must be *ugies*, 'salutory and wholesome:' and indeed this is of greatest concern, next to the first, next to the truth and purity of that doctrine; for unless the doctrine be made fit for the necessities of your people, and not only be good in itself, but good for them, you lose the end of your labours, and they the end of preachings; 'your preaching is in vain, and their faith is also vain' [...]; you must not give your people words, but things, and substantial food [...].

Lastly, the apostle requires of every minister of the gospel that his speech and doctrine shall be *akatagnostos*, 'unreprovable:' [...] that is, 'such as deserves no blame,' and needs no pardon, and flatters not for praise, and begs no excuses, and makes no apologies; a discourse that will be justified by all the sons of wisdom: now that yours may be so, the preceding rules are the best means that are imaginable. For so long as you speak the pure truths of God, the plain meaning of the Spirit, the necessary things of faith, the useful things of charity and the excellencies of holiness, who can reprove your doctrine? [...]

---

53 *The Basic Works of Aristotle*, ed. R. McKeon, New York, 1941. 54 Vincent of Lerins, *Commonitorium*, 2, 5 = PL 50.

But above all things nothing so much will reproach your doctrine, as if you preach it in a railing dialect; [...] if you comment upon the gospel, and revile your brethren that are absent, you imprint hatred and enmity in your people's hearts, and you teach them war when you pretend to make them saints [...].

Frame your life and preachings to the canons of the church, to the doctrines of antiquity, to the sense of the ancient and holy fathers; [...] in christian religion they that were first were best, because God and not man was the teacher, and ever since that, we have been unlearning the wise notices of pure religion, and mingling them with human notices and human interest [...].

Quod primum, hoc verum;[55] the same I say concerning authority and antiquity; never do anything, never say or profess anything against it; for [...] no man is able to bear the reproach of singularity [...]. These rules if you observe, your doctrine will be *akatagnostos*, 'it will need no pardon,' and *anegkletos*, 'never to be reproved in judgment.'

I conclude all with the wise saying of Bensirach, 'Extol not thyself in the counsel of thine own heart, that thy soul be not torn in pieces as a bull straying alone.'[56]

---

[55] Tertullian. *The Prescription of Heretics*, 31 = ANF, vol. 3, p. 24.　[56] Eccles 6:2.

CHAPTER 2

Mystical and Ascetical

INTRODUCTION

The sermons of Jeremy Taylor are those of a priest who preached the eternal Word, ineffable in itself, in the words of his time and place. Divine mystery is the message of the preacher, and the presence of that mystery in the *kerygma* or words of the preacher, as in the *appealing discourse* in the synagogue at Nazareth (Luke 4:20), was no less real in the homilies and sermons of the Greek and Latin Fathers. In England this unique form of rhetoric was commonly called the *power of the pulpit*, and found new life with John Fisher of Rochester, at the turn of the sixteenth century and new heights with John Donne, dean of St. Paul's, towards its end. Almost all great preachers, from Fisher to Donne, preached without a written text; William Perkins in *Art of Prophesying*, first published in 1592, speaks of 'the received custom for preachers to speak *memoriter* or by heart before the people.'[1] Afterward these free and easy discourses, good talking rather than set speeches, were written down, usually by other hands and probably without revision by the preacher. Taylor was later and, by then, style was a part of persuasion: so Bacon, describing the happiness of England in the reign of James I, could mention the good fortune of that Church enlightened with its preachers as a heaven with stars.

Taylor was distinguished from those English preachers who had most prominently preceded him in that he was in no sense an improvisator, and his sermons exhibit all the embellishments of literary style and oratorical technique. He exercises every legitimate art of finished literary oratory, from the abrupt beginning to the solemn and stately close. In a sermon *The House of Feasting* he cites the proberb, 'Let us eat, drink, and be merry, for tomorrow we die,' and abruptly comments, 'this is the epicure's proverb, begun upon a weak mistake, started by chance from the discourses of drink, and thought witty by the undiscerning company.'[2] By contrast, with this abrupt beginning he almost invariably ends in a studied verbal harmony that promotes its own peculiar peace. As he developed his text, which took about an hour, but never more, to deliver, the pithy and pungent phrases of a Plutarch or an Ovid are copiously used to summarize and make the point in a memorable manner.

1 T.K. Carroll, *Jeremy Taylor, Selected Works*, op. cit., pp. 347-53. 2 Ibid., p. 349.

113

But metaphor and simile, more than classical quotation, are his preferred forms of communicating the Word of God in the words of man, as images from light and colour, like living creatures on the wing, fly to God this mystical and ascetical man; always he is at the service of grace as his words present the Word, for he was as sensitive to Heaven, as the poet is to the earth:

> Jesus was like the rainbow, which God set in the clouds as a sacrament to confirm a promise and establish a grace. He was half made of the glories of the light, and half of the moisture of a cloud. In His best days, He was but half triumph and half sorrow. [3]

At Trinity College in Dublin, while he was bishop of Down and Connor, Taylor preached a sermon entitled *Via Intelligentiae* or 'On the Way of Understanding', included here in its abridged form. He is at his best in this sermon as poet and priest, prophet and preacher, as he expounds on the text of John: 'If any man will do his will, he shall know of the doctrine, whether it be of God. or whether I speak of myself' (Jn 7:17). In this youthful hall of learning Taylor speaks about the knowledge of God, but has clearly in mind that knowledge of God of which God is the subject more than the knowledge of man of which God is the object:

> My text is simple as truth itself, but greatly comprehensive, and contains a truth that alone will enable you to understand all mysteries, and to expound all prophecies,' and to interpret all scriptures, and to search into all secrets, which concern our happiness and our duty: and it being an affirmative hypothetical, is plainly to be resolved into this proposition: The way to judge of religion is by doing of our duty; and theology is rather a divine life than a divine knowledge. In Heaven indeed we shall first see, and then love; but here on earth we must first love, and love will open our eyes as well as our hearts, and we shall then see and perceive and understand [...] for nothing makes us fools and ignorants but living vicious lives [...]. No man understands the Word of God as it ought to be understood, unless he lays aside all affections to sin; the sweet wine that Ulysses gave to the Cyclops put his eye out; and a man that hath contracted evil affections and made a league with sin, sees only by these measures and likes your reasoning well enough if you discourse of *bonum jucundum* [...], the mirth and songs of merry company; but if you talk to him of the joys of the Holy Ghost and of rest in God [...], after your long discourse and his great silence his cry is 'What's the matter?' He knows not what you mean; you must either fit his humour or change your discourse.[4]

3 Ibid.   4 Taylor, vol. 8, p. 363.

In the *Via Intelligentiae* the clear distinction between human and divine learning is expressed in the words of the prophet Isaiah as a book that is sealed: 'he that is no learned man, who is not bred up in the schools of the prophets, cannot read God's book for want of learning. For human learning is the gate and first entrance of vision; not the only one indeed, but the common gate.' But beyond this, there must be another learning; 'he that is learned, bring the book to him, and you are not much the better as to the secret part of it, if the book be sealed, if his eyes be closed, if his heart be not opened, if God does not speak to him in the secret way of discipline.' Human learning is an excellent foundation; but the top-stone is laid by love and conformity to the will of God; 'to a man that is good in his sight He giveth wisdom, knowledge and joy.'[5]

Vision and style, or Word and words, are here made one, like a painter's colouring and the world of his unique perception. Furthermore, this vision of faith confers on the words of scripture and tradition the timeless quality of the Eternal Word: Taylor's language has this timeless quality, and his words mellifluously flowing from image to image, and 'falling faintly [...], faintly falling' from cadence to cadence, tell of that Eternal Word, which he heard a) in creation, the first sacrament of the Word; b) in Christ, the Word made flesh; c) in scripture, the Word made text; and d) in man, the flesh made spirit. He is at all times a preacher of this Word and its Spirit and presence in his words *charms ever so wisely* (Ps 58:5) man's inner ear as he speaks of 'a sort of God's dear servants who walk in perfectness.' This 'brightness of God, manifested in the hearts of his dear servants,' is, he says, 'to be felt and not talked of.' But then he does talk and has this to say: 'a good man is united unto God as a flame touches a flame, and combines into splendour and unto glory; so is the spirit of a man united unto Christ by the Spirit of God.'[6]

In the language of this sermon 'On the Way of Understanding' one can easily sense the symbolic world of the ancients, which the biblical words of the Greek and Latin Fathers made sacramental: deadened by the definitions of the later schoolmen, sacramental language was revitalized by the Anglican appeal to tradition, and found fresh expression in the Elizabethan prose of the Carolines. This period, rich in faith and utterance, is of significance today in a world where the Word of God and the words of man are in crisis: it is of particular importance for modern spiritual writers, preachers and theologians, since the Roman Church by its recent acceptance of the vernacular has made English more widespread as a theological and liturgical language. Taylor was of this time of theological renewal in Word and words, but his concept of theology and spirituality is traditional in words as in Word; 'from meditation man rises to devotion, and mental prayer,

5 Ibid., p. 385. 6 Ibid., p. 381.

and intercourse with God; and after that, he rests in the bosom of beatitude and is swallowed up with the comprehensions of love and contemplation.'[7]

These primordial words, like those of a poet, are filled with the soft music of infinity; spoken by Taylor, priest, prophet and preacher, such words are sacramental and communicate to man's soul a presence that is transcendent and real. Taylor's sermons tell of this presence, which becomes on every page a possession, a pleasure and a prayer. Indeed, there is scarcely a preacher or a writer in the tradition of English spirituality, since Taylor or before him, whose words reveal with so much music and peace the secrets of God's Word alive in man's heart. In this sacramental use of language Taylor is in the tradition of Christian mysticism as heartfelt knowledge of the Christian mystery, and in the same tradition asceticism, as a theological praxis, refers to the practices of self-denial or spiritual combat involved in this Christian struggle, as asceticism and mysticism are the alpha and omega of the pilgrim's progress.

From the beginning of his Irish exile Taylor found his mystical and ascetical sanctuary on Sally Island in Loch Beg, which was overlooked by the Great House of Portmore. There, 'where the things of the spirit are so plainly shown in the lights and shadows, the colours and shapes of every common day,'[8] he saw 'fine things' before him, and prayed to arrive 'at that height of love and union with God, which is given to all those souls who are very dear to Him.'[9] In the quiet and peace of this island retreat Taylor's spirit advanced in the wisdom and grace of God, while his many afflictions, religious, political and domestic, continued to torment him in soul and body: 'there is in every righteous man a new vital principle; the Spirit of grace is the Spirit of wisdom, and teaches us by secret inspirations [...], and as the soul of man is the cause of all his vital operations, so is the Spirit of God the life of that life [...]. God opens the heart and creates a new one; and without this new creation, this new principle of life, we may hear the Word of God, but we can never understand it; we hear the sound but are never the better; unless there be in our hearts a secret conviction by the Spirit of God, the gospel in itself is a dead letter and worketh not in us the light and righteousness of God.'[10]

Taylor preached two sermons on *The Marriage Ring*, which were published in the *Eniautos*, or 'Collection of Sermons' in 1653, the year his first wife died. At this time Milton's acrimonious pamphlets on divorce were already in circulation, and different theories of marriage were being discussed. The sectaries, who were now strongly in power, hated all religious ceremonies and would soon enact that only marriages performed by a justice of the peace would be legal. Already in his *Apology for Liturgy* or 'Collection of Offices' (1649) Taylor had denounced the Cromwellian *Directory*, which replaced the outlawed Prayer-Book because 'it joins

---

[7] Ibid., vol. 2, p. 135.   [8] M. Cropper, *Flame Touches Flame*, London, 1949, p. 142.   [9] Ibid., p. 143.
[10] Taylor, vol. 8, p. 375.

in marriage as Cacus did his oxen, in rude, inform and unhallowed yokes.'[11] But the sermons, on the contrary, avoiding the controversies, were delightful outpourings of a heart happily married in spite of worldly misfortunes. These two sermons have attracted a good deal of attention, both because of the unusual charm of the thought and the carefully wrought literary beauty with which they abound. In them, we get one of those all too rare glimpses into his own home life:

> Above all the instances of love let him preserve towards her an inviolable faith, and an unspotted chastity; for this is the marriage-ring, it ties two hearts by an eternal band; it is like the cherubim's flaming sword set for the guard of paradise; he that passes into that garden, now that it is immured by Christ and the church, enters into the shades of death. No man must touch the forbidden tree, that is in the midst of the garden, which is the tree of knowledge and life. Chastity is the security of love, and preserves all the mysteriousness like the secrets of a temple. Under this lock is deposited security of families, the union of affections, the repairer of accidental breaches. This is a grace that is shut up and secured by all arts of heaven, and the defence of laws, the locks and bars of modesty, by honour and reputation, by fear and shame, by interest and high regards; and that contract that is intended to be for ever, is yet dissolved and broken by the violation of this; nothing but death can do so much evil to the holy rites of marriage, as unchastity and breach of faith can.[12]

In such symbolic words there is a much more sacramental view of marriage than was believed in either Church or State in that Erastian age. For Taylor, on the other hand, marriage was man's first blessing from the Lord. For him marriage was ordained of God and instituted in Paradise as the seminary of the Church to bring forth sons and daughters unto God and for the relief of a natural necessity. Although the Lord was born of a maiden, 'yet was she veiled under the cover of marriage,'[13] and was married to a widower, for Joseph, the supposed Father of the Lord, had children by another wife. In Taylor's view marriage was in the world before sin, and 'in all ages of the world was the greatest and most effective antidote against sin, in which all the world, had perished, if God had not made a remedy.'[14] His theological interpretation of marriage, expressed in traditional language, scriptural and sacramental, is mystical almost in the extreme:

> 'This is a great mystery,' but it is the symbolical and sacramental representation of the greatest mysteries of our religion. Christ descended from his Father's bosom, and contracted his divinity with flesh and blood, and married

11 Ibid., vol. 7, p. 253.   12 Ibid., vol. 4, p. 226.   13 Ibid., p. 210.   14 Ibid.

our nature, and we became a Church, the spouse of the Bridegroom, which he cleansed with his blood, and gave her his Holy Spirit for a dowry and Heaven for a jointure; begetting children unto God by the Gospel. This spouse he hath joined to himself by an excellent charity, he feeds her at his own table, and lodges nigh his own heart, provides for all her necessities, relieves her sorrows, determines her doubts, guides her wanderings, he is become her head, and, she as a signet upon his right hand [...] the indissoluble knot, the eternal conjunction, the communicating of goods, the uniting of interests, the fruit of marriage, a celestial generation, a new creature. *Sacramentum hoc magnum est* [...] this is the sacramental mystery, represented by the holy rite of marriage [...] divine in its institution, sacred in its union, holy in its mystery, sacramental in its signification, honourable in its appellative, religious in its employments; it is advantage to the societies of men, and it is to the Lord holiness. *Dico autem in Christo et Ecclesia*, It must be in Christ and it must be in the Church.[15]

Via Intelligentiae[1]

JEREMY TAYLOR

If any man will do His will, he shall know of the doctrine, whether it be of God, or whether I speak of myself. (Jn 7:17).

The ancients in their mythological learning tell us, that when Jupiter espied the men of the world striving for truth, and pulling her in pieces to secure her to themselves, he sent Mercury down amongst them, and he with his usual arts dressed error up in the imagery of truth, and thrust her into the crowd, and so left them to contend still: and though then by contention men were sure to get but little truth, yet they were as earnest as ever, and lost peace too, in their importune contentions for the very image of truth. And this indeed is no wonder: but when truth and peace are brought into the world together, and bound up in the same bundle of life; when we are taught a religion by the Prince of peace, who is the truth itself, to see men contending for this truth to the breach of that peace; and when men fall out, to see that they should make christianity their theme: that is one of the greatest wonders in the world. For christianity is *hemeros*

---

15 Ibid., p. 212.   1 Sermon VI, in J. Taylor, vol. 8, pp 363ff.

kai philanthropos nomothesia, 'a soft and gentle institution;' [...] it was brought into the world to soften the asperities of human nature, and to cure the barbarities of evil men and the contentions of the passionate. The eagle seeing her breast wounded, and espying the arrow that hurt her to be feathered, cried out - *pteron me ton pteroton alluei*: 'the feathered nation is destroyed by their own feathers;' that is, a Christian fighting and wrangling with a Christian; and indeed that's very sad: but wrangling about peace too; that peace itself should be the argument of a war, that's unnatural; and if it were not that there are many who are *homines multae religionis, nullius paene pietatis*, 'men of much religion and little godliness,' it would not be that there should be so many quarrels in and concerning that religion which is wholly made up of truth and peace, and was sent amongst us to reconcile the hearts of men when they were tempted to uncharitableness by any other unhappy argument. Disputation cures no vice, but kindles a great many, and makes passion evaporate into sin: and though men esteem it learning, yet it is the most useless learning in the world. When Eudamidas the son of Archidamus heard old Xenocrates[2] disputing about wisdom, he asked very soberly, 'If the old man be yet disputing and enquiring concerning wisdom, what time will he have to make use of it?' Christianity is all for practice, and so much time as is spent in quarrels about it is a diminution to its interest: men enquire so much what it is, that they have but little time left to be Christians. I remember a saying of Erasmus, that when he first read the New testament with fear and a good mind, with a purpose to understand it and obey it, he found it very useful and very pleasant: but when afterwards he fell on reading the vast differences of commentaries, then he understood it less than he did before, then he began not to understand it. For indeed the truths of God are best dressed in the plain culture and simplicity of the Spirit; but the truths that men commonly teach are like the reflections of a multiplying glass: for one piece of good money you shall have forty that are fantastical; and it is forty to one if your finger hit upon the right. Men have wearied themselves in the dark, having been amused with false fires: and instead of going home, have wandered all night *en hodois abatois*, 'in untrodden, unsafe, uneasy ways;' but have not found out what their soul desires. But therefore since we are so miserable, and are in error, and have wandered very far, we must do as wandering travellers use to do, go back just to that place from whence they wandered, and begin upon a new account. Let us go to the truth itself, to Christ, and He will tell us an easy way ending of all our quarrels: for we shall find christianity to be the easiest and the hardest thing in the world: it is like a secret in arithmetic, infinitely hard till it be found out by a right operation, and then it is so plain, we wonder we did not understand it earlier.

[...] I know I am in an auditory of inquisitive persons, whose business is to study for truth, that they may find it for themselves and teach it unto others: I

---

2 Plutarch, *Moralia*, LCL, vol. 3, p. 319.

am in a school of prophets and prophets' sons, who all ask Pilate's question, 'What is truth?' You look for it in your books, and you tug hard for it in your disputations, and you derive it from the cisterns of the fathers, and you enquire after the old ways, and sometimes are taken with new appearances, and you rejoice in false lights, or are delighted with little umbrages and peep of day. But where is there a man, or a society of men, that can be at rest in his enquiry, and is sure he understands all the truths of God? where is there a man but the more he studies and enquires, still he discovers nothing so clearly as his own ignorance? This is a demonstration that we are not in the right way, that we do not enquire wisely, that our method is not artificial. If men did fall upon the right way, it were impossible so many learned men should be engaged in contrary parties and opinions. We have examined all ways but one, all but God's way. Let us (having missed in all the other) try this: let us go to God for truth; for truth comes from God only, and His ways are plain, and His sayings are true, and His promises Yea and Amen: and if we miss the truth it is because we will not find it: for certain it is, that all that truth which God hath made necessary, He hath also made legible and plain, and if we will open our eyes we shall see the sun, and if 'we will walk in the light,' we shall 'rejoice in the light:' only let us withdraw the curtains, let us remove the impediments and the sin that doth so easily beset us: that's God's way. Every man must in his station do that portion of duty which God requires of him, and then he shall be taught of God all that is fit for him to learn: there is no other way for him but this. 'The fear of the Lord is the beginning of wisdom, and a good understanding have all they that do thereafter?'[3] And so said David of himself, [4] 'I have more understanding than my teachers, because I keep Thy commandments.' And this is the only way which Christ hath taught us: if you ask, 'What is truth?' you must not do as Pilate did, ask the question, and then go away from Him that only can give you an answer: for as God is the author of truth, so He is the teacher of it; and the way to learn it is this of my text: for so saith our blessed Lord, 'If any man will do His will, he shall know of the doctrine whether it be of God or no.'

My text is simple as truth itself, but greatly comprehensive, and contains a truth that alone will enable you to understand all mysteries, and to expound all prophecies, and to interpret all scriptures. and to search into all secrets, all (I mean) which concern our happiness and our duty: and it being an affirmative hypothetical, is plainly to be resolved into this proposition, - The way to judge of religion is by doing of our duty; and theology is rather a divine life than a divine knowledge. In heaven indeed we shall first see, and then love; but here on earth we must first love, and love will open our eyes as well as our hearts, and we shall then see and perceive and understand.

3 Ps 111:10. 4 Ps 119:19.

I. In the handling of which proposition I shall first represent to you that the certain causes of our errors are nothing but direct sins, nothing makes us fools and ignorants but living vicious lives; and then I shall proceed to the direct demonstration of the article in question, that holiness is the only way of truth and understanding.

(a) No man understands the word of God as it ought to be understood, unless he lays aside all affections to sin; of which because we have taken very little care, the product hath been that we have had very little wisdom, and very little knowledge in the ways of God. *Kakia esti phthartike tes arches,* [5] saith Aristotle, wickedness does corrupt a man's reasoning, it gives him false principles and evil measures of things: the sweet wine that Ulysses gave to the Cyclops put his eye out; and a man that hath contracted evil affections, and made a league with sin, sees only by those measures. A covetous man understands nothing to be good that is not profitable; and a voluptuous man likes your reasoning well enough if you discourse of *bonum jucundum*, the pleasures of the sense, the ravishments of lust, the noises and inadvertencies, the mirth and songs of merry company; but if you talk to him of the melancholy lectures of the cross, the content of resignation, the peace of meekness, and the joys of the holy Ghost, and of rest in God, after your long discourse and his great silence he cries out, 'What's the matter?' He knows not what you mean: either you must fit his humour, or change your discourse.

I remember that Arrianus tells of a gentleman that was banished from Rome . and in his sorrow visited the philosopher, and he heard him talk wisely, and believed him, and promised him to leave all the thoughts of Rome and splendours of the court, and retire to the course of a severe philosophy; but before the good man's lectures were done, there came *pinakides apo Kaisaros*, 'letters from Caesar,' to recall him home, to give him pardon, and promise him great employment. He presently grew weary of the good man's sermon, and wished he would make an end, thought his discourse was dull and flat; for his head and heart were full of another story and new principles; and by these measures he could hear only and he could understand.

Every man understands by his affections more than by his reason: and when the wolf in the fable went to school to learn to spell, whatever letters were told him, he could never make any thing of them but *agnus*; he thought of nothing but his belly; and if a man be very hungry, you must give him meat before you give him counsel. A man's mind must be like your proposition before it can be entertained: for whatever you put into a man it will smell of the vessel: it is a man's mind that gives the emphasis, and makes your argument to prevail.

---

5 Aristotle, *Nicomachean Ethics*, LCL, vol. 19, p. 420.

And upon this account it is that there are so many false doctrines in the only article of repentance. Men know they must repent, but the definition of repentance they take from the convenience of their own affairs: what they will not part with, that is not necessary to be parted with, and they will repent, but not restore: they will say *Nollem factum*, 'they wish they had never done it:' but since it is done, you must give them leave to rejoice in their purchase: they will ask forgiveness of God; but they sooner forgive themselves, and suppose that God is of their mind: if you tie them to hard terms, your doctrine is not to be understood, or it is but one doctor's opinion, and therefore they will fairly take their leave, and get them another teacher.

What makes these evil, these dangerous and desperate doctrines? Not the obscurity of the thing, but the cloud upon the heart; for say you what you will, he that hears must be the expounder, and we can never suppose but a man will give sentence in behalf of what he passionately loves [...] So that it is no wonder we understand so little of religion: it is because we are in love with that which destroys it; and as a man does not care to hear what does not please him, so neither does he believe it; he cannot, he will not understand it [...]. Where is the fault? The words are plain, the duty is certain, the book lies open; but alas, it is 'sealed within,'[7] that is, 'men have eyes and will not see, ears and will not hear.' But *obedite et intelligetis*[8] (saith the prophet), 'obey' and be humble, leave the foolish affections of sin, and then 'ye shall understand.' That's the first particular: all remaining affections to sin hinder the learning and understanding of the things of God.

(b) He that means to understand the will of God and the truth of religion must lay aside all inordinate affections to the world. St Paul complained that there was 'at that day a veil upon the hearts of the Jews in the reading of the Old testament:'[9] they looked for a temporal prince to be their Messias, and their affections and hopes dwelt in secular advantages; and so long as that veil was there, they could not see, and they would not accept the poor despised Jesus.

For the things of the world, besides that they entangle one another, and make such business, and spend much time, they also take up the attentions of a man's mind, and spend his faculties, and make them trifling and secular with the very handling and conversation. And therefore the Pythagoreans taught their disciples [...] 'a separation from the things of the body, if they would purely find out truth and the excellencies of wisdom.'[10] Had not he lost his labour that would have discoursed wisely to Apicius, and told him of the books of fate and the secrets of the other world, the abstractions of the soul and its brisker immortality, that saints and angels eat not, and that the spirit of a man lives for ever upon wisdom, and holiness and contemplation? The fat glutton would have stared a while upon the preacher, and

---

6 Lactantius, *The Divine Institutes*, PL 6.722. 7 Rev 5:1. 8 Jer 5:21; Ezek 12:2. 9 2 Cor 3:14.
10 Plotinus, *Enneads*, LCL, vol. 1, p. 204.

then have fallen asleep. But if you had discoursed well and knowingly of a lamprey, a large mullet, or a boar, – *animal propter convivia natum*[11] – and have sent him a cook from Asia to make new sauces, he would have attended carefully, and taken in your discourses greedily. And so it is in the questions and secrets of christianity: which made St Paul, when he intended to convert Felix, discourse first with him about 'temperance, righteousness and judgment to come.'[12] He began in the right point; he knew it was to no purpose to preach Jesus Christ crucified to an intemperate person, to an usurper of other men's rights, to one whose soul dwelt in the world, and cared not for the sentence of the last day. The philosophers began their wisdom with the meditation of death, and St Paul his with the discourse of the day of judgment: to take the heart off from this world and the amabilities of it, which dishonour and baffle the understanding, and made Solomon himself become a child, and fooled into idolatry, by the prettiness of a talking woman. Men now-a-days love not a religion that will cost them dear: if your doctrine calls upon men to part with any considerable part of their estates, you must pardon them if they cannot believe you; they understand it not [...]. When men's souls are possessed with the world, their souls cannot be invested with holy truths. *Chre apo touton auten psuchen psuchousthai*, as St Isidore said: the soul must be informed 'insouled,' or animated with the propositions that you put in, or you shall never do any good, or get disciples to Christ. Now because a man cannot serve two masters; because he cannot vigorously attend two objects; because there can be but one living soul in any living creature; if the world have got possession, talk no more of your questions, shut your bibles, and read no more of the words of God to them, for they cannot 'tell of the doctrine whether it be of God,' or of the world. That is the second particular: worldly affections hinder true understandings in religion.

(c) No man, how learned soever, can understand the word of God, or be at peace in the questions of religion, unless he be a master over his passions; [...] said the wise Boethius,[13] 'a man must first learn himself, before he can learn God.'[14] *Tua te fallit imago*: nothing deceives a man so soon as a man's self; when a man is (that I may use Plato's expression) *sumpephurmenos te genesei*, 'mingled with his nature and his congenial' infirmities of anger and desire, he can never have any thing but *amudron doxan*, a knowledge partly moral and partly natural: his whole life is but imagination; his knowledge is inclination and opinion; he judges of heavenly things by the measures of his fears and his desires, and his reason is half of it sense, and determinable by the principles of sense. *Euge hoti philopheis en tois pathesi*, 'then a man learns well when he is a philosopher in his passions.'[15]

---

11 Juvenal. *Satires*, 1:141, CS (Ferguson), p. 12. **12** Acts 24:25. **13** Boethius, *Consolation of Philosophy*, 1. m.7, LCL, pp 168-70. **14** Ovid, *Metamorphoses*, LCL. vol. 1. p. 156. **15** Gregory Nazianzen, *Letters*, PG 37.70.

Passionate men are to be taught the first elements of religion: and let men pretend to as much learning as they please, they must begin again at Christ's cross; they must learn true mortification and crucifixion of their anger and desires, before they can be good scholars in Christ's school, or be admitted into the more secret enquiries of religion, or profit in spiritual understanding. It was an excellent proverb of the Jews, *In passionibus Spiritus sanctus non habitat,* 'the holy Ghost never dwells in the house of passion.' Truth enters into the heart of man when it is empty and clean and still; but when the mind is shaken with passion as with a storm, you can never 'hear the voice of the charmer though he charm very wisely:' and you will very hardly sheath a sword when it is held by a loose and a paralytic arm. He that means to learn the secrets of God's wisdom must be, as Plato says, *kata ten logiken zoen ousiomenos,* 'his soul must be consubstantiated with reason,' not invested with passion: to him that is otherwise, things are but in the dark, his notion is obscure and his sight troubled; and therefore though we often meet with passionate fools, yet we seldom or never hear of a very passionate wise man.

I have now done with the first part of my undertaking, and proved to you that our evil life is the cause of our controversies and ignorances in religion and of the things of God. You see what hinders us from becoming good divines. But all this while we are but in the preparation to the mysteries of godliness: when we have thrown off all affections to sin, when we have stripped ourselves from all fond adherences to the things of the world, and have broken the chains and dominion of our passions; then we may say with David, *Ecce paratum est cor meum, Deus,* 'my heart is ready, O God, my heart is ready:'[16] then we may say, 'Speak, Lord, for Thy servant heareth:'[17] but we are not yet instructed. It remains therefore that we enquire what is that immediate principle or means by which we shall certainly and infallibly be led into all truth, and be taught the mind of God, and understand all His secrets; and this is worth our knowledge. I cannot say that this will end your labours, and put a period to your studies, and make your learning easy; it may possibly increase your labour, but it will make it profitable; it will not end your studies, but it will direct them; it will not make human learning easy, but it will make it wise unto salvation, and conduct it into true notices and ways of wisdom.

II. I am now to describe to you the right way of knowledge: *Qui facit voluntatem Patris mei,*[18] saith Christ, that's the way; 'do God's will, and you shall understand God's word.' And it was an excellent saying of St Peter, 'Add to your faith virtue,' &c. 'If these things be in you and abound, ye shall not be unfruitful in the knowledge of our Lord Jesus Christ.'[19] For in this case 'tis not enough that our hindrances of knowledge are removed; for that is but the opening of the covering of the book of

---

16 Ps 57:7.   17 1 Sam 3:9.   18 Jn 7:17.   19 2 Pet 1:5.

God; but when it is opened, it is written with a hand that every eye cannot read. Though the windows of the east be open, yet every eye cannot behold the glories of the sun; *ophthalmos me helioeides ginomenos helion ou blepeio*, saith Plotinus, 'the eye that is not made solar cannot see the sun;'[20] the eye must be fitted to the splendour; and it is not the wit of the man, but the spirit of the man; not so much his head as his heart, that learns the divine philosophy.

(a) Now in this enquiry I must take one thing for a praecognitum, that every good man is *theodidaktos*, he is 'taught of God'[21] and indeed unless He teach us, we shall make but ill scholars ourselves, and others. *Nemo potest Deum scire nisi a Deo doceatur*,[22] said St Irenaeus. If God teaches us, then all is well; but if we do not learn wisdom at His feet, from whence should we have it? It can come from no other spring. And therefore it naturally follows, that by how much nearer we are to God, by so much better we are like to be instructed.

But this being supposed, as being most evident, we can easily proceed by wonderful degrees and steps of progression in the economy of this divine philosophy; for,

(b) There is in every righteous man a new vital principle; the Spirit of grace is the Spirit of wisdom, and teaches us by secret inspirations, by proper arguments, by actual persuasions, by personal applications, by effects and energies: and as the soul of a man is the cause of all his vital operations, so is the Spirit of God the life of that life, and the cause of all actions and productions spiritual: and the consequence of this is what St John tells us of: 'ye have received the unction from above, and that anointing teacheth you all things:'[23] all things of some one kind; that is, certainly, 'all things that pertain to life and godliness;'[24] all that by which a man is wise and happy. We see this by common experience. Unless the soul have a new life put into it, unless there be a vital principle within, unless the Spirit of life be the informer of the spirit of the man, the word of God will be as dead in the operation as the body in its powers and possibilities. *Sol et homo generant hominem*, saith our medieval philosophy – a man alone does not beget a man, but a man and the sun; for without the influence of the celestial bodies all natural actions are ineffective: and so it is in the operations of the soul.

[...] The Spirit of God makes us 'wise unto salvation' [...]. He opens the heart, not to receive murmurs, or to attend to secret whispers, but to hear the word of God; and then He opens the heart and creates a new one; and without this new creation, this new principle of life, we may hear the word of God, but we can never understand it; we hear the sound, but are never the better; unless there be in our hearts a secret conviction by the Spirit of God, the gospel in itself is a dead letter, and worketh not in us the light and righteousness of God.

20 Plotinus, *Enneads*, LCL, vol. 1, 6:9, p. 258. 21 Is 54:13. Jn 6:45; 1 Thess 4:9. 22 Irenaeus, *Against Heresies*, PG 7.989. 23 1 Jn 2:27. 24 2 Pet 1:3.

Do not we see this by daily experience? Even those things which a good man and an evil man know, they do not know them both alike [...]. They both read the scriptures, they read and hear the same sermons, they have capable understandings, they both believe what they hear and what they read, and yet the event is vastly different. The reason is that which I am now speaking of; the one understands by one principle, the other by another, the one understands by nature, and the other by grace; the one by human learning, and the other by divine; the one reads the scriptures without and the other within; the one understands as a son of man, the other as a son of God; the one perceives by the proportions of the world, and the other by the measures of the Spirit; the one understands by reason, and the other by love; and therefore he does not only understand the sermons of the Spirit, and perceives their meaning: but he pierces deeper, and knows the meaning of that meaning; that is, the secret of the Spirit, that which is spiritually discerned, that which gives life to the proposition, and activity to the soul. And the reason is, because he hath a divine principle within him, and a new understanding; that is, plainly, he hath love, and that's more than knowledge; as was rarely well observed by St Paul. 'Knowledge puffeth up, but charity edifieth;'[25] that is, charity makes the best scholars. No sermons can edify you, no scriptures can build you up a holy building to God, unless the love of God be in your hearts, and 'purify your souls from all filthiness of the flesh and spirit.'[26] For there is in the heart of man such a dead sea, and an indisposition to holy flames, like as in the cold rivers in the north, so as the fires will not burn them, and the sun itself will never warm them, till God's holy spirit does from the temple of the New Jerusalem bring a holy flame, and make it shine and burn.

(c) Sometimes God gives to His choicest, His most elect and precious servants, a knowledge even of secret things, which He communicates not to others. We find it greatly remarked in the case of Abraham, 'And the Lord said, Shall I hide from Abraham that thing that I do?'[27] Why not from Abraham? God tells us [...], 'For I know him, that he will command his childen and his household after him, and they shall keep the way of the Lord, to do justice and judgment.'[28] And though this be irregular and infrequent, yet it is a reward of their piety, and the proper increase also of the spiritual man. We find this spoken by God to Daniel, and promised to be the lot of the righteous man in the days of the Messias; [...] 'Many shall be purified, and made white, and tried; but the wicked shall do wickedly:' and what then? 'None of the wicked shall understand, but the wise shall understand.'[29] Where besides that the wise man and the wicked are opposed, plainly signifying that the wicked man is a fool and an ignorant; it is plainly said that 'none of the wicked shall understand' the wisdom and mysteriousness of the kingdom of the Messias.

---

25 1 Cor 8:1. 26 2 Cor 7:1. 27 Gen 18:17. 28 Gen 18:19. 29 Dan 12:10.

d) A good life is the best way to understand wisdom and religion, because by the experiences and relishes of religion there is conveyed to them such a sweetness, to which all wicked men are strangers: there is in the things of God to them which practise them a deliciousness that makes us love them, and that love admits us into God's cabinet, and strangely clarifies the understanding by the purification of the heart. For when our reason is raised by the Spirit of Christ, it is turned quickly into experience; when our faith relies upon the principles of Christ, it is changed into vision; and so long as we know God only in the ways of man, by contentious learning, by arguing and dispute, we see nothing but the shadow of Him, and in that shadow we meet with many dark appearances, little certainty, and much conjecture: but when we know Him *logo apophantiko, galene noera*, with the eyes of holiness, and the intuition of gracious experiences, with a quiet spirit and the peace of enjoyment; then we shall hear what we never heard, and see what our eyes never saw; then the mysteries of godliness shall be opened unto us, and clear as the windows of the morning, and this is rarely well expressed by the apostle, 'If we stand up from the dead and awake from sleep, then Christ shall give us light.'[30]

For although the scriptures themselves are written by the Spirit of God, yet they are written within and without: and besides the light that shines upon the face of them, unless there be a light shining within our hearts, unfolding the leaves, and interpreting the mysterious sense of the Spirit, convincing our consciences and preaching to our hearts; to look for Christ in the leaves of the gospel is to look for the living amongst the dead. There is a life in them, but that life is, according to St Paul's expression, 'hid with Christ in God:' and unless the Spirit of God be the *promocondus*, we shall never draw it forth.

Human learning brings excellent ministries towards this: [...] but there is something beyond this, that human learning without the addition of divine can never reach [...]. Pythagoras read Moses' books, and so did Plato; and yet they became not proselytes of the religion, though they were learned scholars of such a master. The reason is, because that which they drew forth from thence was not the life and secret of it – *Tradidit arcano quodcunque volumine Moses*.[31]

There is a secret in these books, which few men, none but the godly, did understand: and though much of this secret is made manifest in the gospel, yet even here also there is a letter and there is a spirit: still there is a reserve for God's secret ones, even all those deep mysteries which the Old testament covered in figures, and stories and names, and prophecies, and which Christ hath, and His spirit will yet reveal more plainly to all that will understand them by their proper measures. For although the gospel is infinitely more legible and plain than the

---

30 Eph 5:14.   31 Juvenal, *Satires*, 14:102, CS, p. 95.

obscurer leaves of the law, yet there is a seal upon them also; 'which seal no man shall open but he that is worthy.'[32] We may understand something of it by the three children of the captivity; they were all skilled in all the wisdom of the Chaldees, and so was Daniel: but there was something beyond that in him; 'the wisdom of the most high God was in him,'[33] and that taught him a learning beyond his learning.

In all scripture there is a spiritual sense, a spiritual *cabala*, which as it tends directly to holiness, so it is best and truest understood by the sons of the Spirit, who love God, and therefore know Him. *Gnosis ekaston di homoioteta ginetai*, 'every thing is best known by its own similitudes and analogies.'[34]

But I must take some other time to speak fully of these things. I have but one thing more to say, and then I shall make my applications of this doctrine, and so conclude.

(e) Lastly, there is a sort of God's dear servants who walk in perfectness, who 'perfect holiness in the fear of God;' and they have a degree of clarity and divine knowledge more than we can discourse of, and more certain than the demonstrations of geometry, brighter than the sun, and indeficient as the light of heaven. This is called by the apostle *the apaugasma tou theou*. Christ is this 'brightness of God,' manifested in the hearts of His dearest servants [...]. But I shall say no more of this at this time, for this is to be felt and not to be talked of; and they that never touched it with their finger, may secretly perhaps laugh at it in their heart, and be never the wiser. All that I shall now say of it is, that a good man is united unto God, *kentron kentro sunapsas*, as a flame touches a flame, and combines into splendour and to glory: so is the spirit of a man united unto Christ by the Spirit of God. These are the friends of God, and they best know God's mind, and they only that are so know how much such men do know. They have a special 'unction from above:'[35] so that now you are come to the top of all; this is the highest round of the ladder, and the angels stand upon it: they dwell in love and contemplation, they worship and obey, but dispute not: and our quarrels and impertinent wranglings about religion are nothing else but the want of the measures of this state. Our light is like a candle, every wind of vain doctrine blows it out, or spends the wax, and makes the light tremulous; but the lights of heaven are fixed and bright, and shine for ever.

III. But that we may speak not only things mysterious, but things intelligible; how does it come to pass, by what means and what economy is it effected, that a holy life is the best determination of all questions, and the surest way of knowledge [...] and is a temperate man always a better scholar than a drunkard? To this I answer, that in all things in which true wisdom consists, holiness, which is the best wisdom, is the surest way of understanding them. And this,

---

32 Rev 5:2.   33 Dan 4:8.   34 Aristotle, *Nicomachean Ethics*, LCL, vol. 19, p. 324.   35 1 Jn 2:20.

(a) Is effected by holiness as a proper and natural instrument: for naturally every thing is best discerned by its proper light and congenial instrument [...]. For as the eye sees visible objects, and the understanding perceives the intellectual; so does the spirit the things of the Spirit. 'The natural man,' saith St Paul, 'knows not the things of God for they are spiritually discerned:'[36] that is, they are discovered by a proper light, and concerning these things an unsanctified man discourses pitifully, with an imperfect idea, as a blind man does of light and colours which he never saw.

A good man though unlearned in secular notices is like the windows of the temple, narrow without and broad within: he sees not so much of what profits not abroad, but whatsoever is within, and concerns religion and the glorifications of God, that he sees with a broad inspection: but all human learning without God is but blindness and ignorant folly.

But when it is [...] 'righteousness dipped in the wells of truth,' it is like an eye of gold in a rich garment or, like the light of heaven, it shews itself by its own splendour. What learning is it to discourse of the philosophy of the sacrament, if you do not feel the virtue of it? And the man that can with eloquence and subtilty discourse of the instrumental efficacy of baptismal waters, talks ignorantly in respect of him who hath 'the answer of a good conscience'[37] within, and is cleansed by the purifications of the Spirit [...]; and how can an evil and unworthy communicant tell what it is to have received Christ by faith, to dwell with Him, to be united to Him, to receive Him in his heart? The good man only understands that: the one sees the colour, and the other feels the substance; the one discourses of the sacrament, and the other receives Christ; the one discourses for or against transubstantiation, but the good man feels himself to be changed, and so joined to Christ, that he only understands the true sense of transubstantiation, while He becomes to Christ bone of His bone, flesh of His flesh, and of the same Spirit with his Lord [...], and most of the questions of christendom are such which either are good for nothing, and therefore to be laid aside; or if they be complicated with action, and are ministries of practice, no man can judge them so well as the spiritual man. That which best pleases God [...], that which speaks honour of God and does Him honour, that only is truth.

(b) Holiness is not only an advantage to the learning all wisdom and holiness, but for the discerning that which is wise and holy from what is trifling and useless and contentious; and to one of these heads all questions will return: and therefore in all, from holiness we have the best instructions. And this brings me to the next particle of the general consideration. For that which we are taught by the holy Spirit of God, this new nature, this vital principle within us it is that which is worth our learning; not vain and empty, idle and insignificant notions, in which

---

[36] 1 Cor 2:14. [37] 1 Pet 3:21.

when you have laboured till your eyes are fixed in their orbs, and your flesh unfixed from its bones, you are no better and no wiser. If the Spirit of God be your teacher, He will teach you such truths as will make you know and love God, and become like to Him, and enjoy Him for ever, by passing from similitude to union and eternal fruition. But what are you the better if [...] you should study and find out what place Adam should for ever have lived in if he had not fallen? and what is any man the more learned if he hears the disputes, whether Adam should have multiplied children in the state of innocence, and what would have been the event of things if one child had been born before his father's sin?

Too many scholars have lived upon air and empty notions for many ages past, and troubled themselves with tying and untying knots, like hypochondriacs in a fit of melancholy, thinking of nothing, and troubling themselves with nothing, and falling out about nothings, and being very wise and very learned in things that are not and work not, and were never planted in Paradise by the finger of God. Men's notions are too often like the mules, begotten by equivocal and unnatural generations; but they make no species: they are begotten, but they can beget nothing; they are the effects of long study, but they can do no good when they are produced: they are not that which Solomon calls *via intelligentiae*,'[38] 'the way of understanding.' No, no; the man that is wise, he that is conducted by the Spirit of God, knows better in what Christ's kingdom does consist, than to throw away his time and interest, and peace and safety, - for what? for religion? no; for the body of religion? not so much; for the garment of the body of religion? no, not for so much; but for the fringes of the garment of the body of religion; for such and no better are the disputes that trouble our discontented brethren; they are things, or rather circumstances and manners of things, in which the soul and spirit is not at all concerned [...]. The old man that confuted the Arian priest by a plain recital of his creed, found a mighty power of God effecting His own work by a strange manner, and by a very plain instrument: it wrought a divine blessing just as sacraments use to do: and this lightning sometimes comes in a strange manner as a peculiar blessing to good men [...]. And St Paul, though he went very far to the knowledge of many great and excellent truths by the force of human learning, yet he was far short of perfective truth and true wisdom till he learned a new lesson in a new school, at the feet of one greater than his Gamaliel; his learning grew much greater, his notions brighter, his skill deeper, by the love of Christ, and his desires, his passionate desires after Jesus.

(c) The force and use of human learning, and of this divine learning I am now speaking of, are both well expressed by the prophet Isaiah, 'And the vision of all is

---

[38] Prov 9:6; 21:16.

become unto you as the words of a book that is sealed, which men deliver to one that is learned, saying, Read this, I pray thee: and he saith, I cannot, for it is sealed. And the book is delivered to him that is not learned, saying, Read this, I pray thee: and he saith, I am not learned.'[39] He that is no learned man, who is not bred up in the schools of the prophets, cannot read God's book for want of learning. For human learning is the gate and first entrance of divine vision; not the only one indeed, but the common gate. But beyond this, there must be another learning; for he that is learned, bring the book to him, and you are not much the better as to the secret part of it, if the book be sealed, if his eyes be closed, if his heart be not opened, if God does not speak to him in the secret way of discipline. Human learning is an excellent foundation; but the top-stone is laid by love and conformity to the will of God [...].

(d) When this is reduced to practice and experience, we find not only in things of practice, but even in deepest mysteries, not only the choicest and most eminent saints, but even every good man can best tell what is true, and best reprove an error.

He that goes about to speak of and to understand the mysterious Trinity, and does it by words and names of man's invention [...], if he only talks of essences and existences, *hypostases* and personalities, distinctions without difference, and priority in co-equalities, and unity in pluralities, and of superior predicates of no larger extent than the inferior subjects, he may amuse himself, and find his understanding will be like St Peter's upon the mount of Tabor at the transfiguration: he may build three tabernacles in his head, and talk something, but he knows not what. But the good man feels the 'power of the Father,' and he to whom the Son is become 'wisdom, righteousness, sanctification, and redemption;' he 'in whose heart the love of the Spirit of God is spread,' to whom God hath communicated the 'holy Ghost, the Comforter;' this man, though he understands nothing of that which is unintelligible, yet he only understands the mysteriousness of the holy Trinity. No man can be convinced well and wisely of the article of the holy, blessed, and undivided Trinity, but he that feels the mightiness of the Father begetting him to a new life, the wisdom of the Son building him up in a most holy faith, and the love of the Spirit of God making him to become like unto God.

He that hath passed from his childhood in grace under the spiritual generation of the Father, and is gone forward to be a 'young man' in Christ, strong and vigorous in holy actions and holy undertakings, and from thence is become an old disciple, and strong and grown old in religion, and the conversation of the Spirit; this man best understands the secret and undiscernible economy, he feels this unintelligible mystery, and sees with his heart what his tongue can never express, and his metaphysics can never prove [...], and when we communicate of the Spirit

---

39 Is 29:11.

of God, when we pray for Him, and have received Him, and entertained Him, and dwelt with Him, and warmed ourselves by His holy fires, then we know Him too. But there is no other satisfactory knowledge of the blessed Trinity but this; and therefore whatever thing is spoken of God metaphysically, there is no knowing of God theologically, and as He ought to be known, but by the measures of holiness, and the proper light of the Spirit of God. [...]

IV. And now to conclude, to you fathers and brethren, you who are or intend to be of the clergy: [...] It is not by reading multitudes of books, but by studying the truth of God: it is not by laborious commentaries of the doctors that you can finish your work, but by the expositions of the Spirit of God [...]. And let me tell you this; the great learning of the fathers was more owing to their piety than to their skill; more to God than to themselves: and to this purpose is that excellent ejaculation of St Chrysostom,[40] with which I will conclude; 'O blessed and happy men, whose names are in the book of life, from whom the devils fled, and heretics did fear them, who (by holiness) have stopped the mouths of them that spake perverse things! But I, like David, will cry out, Where are Thy loving-kindnesses which have been ever of old? where is the blessed quire of bishops and doctors, who shined like lights in the world, and contained the word of life? *Dulce est meminisse*, their very memory is pleasant. Where is that Evodius, the sweet savour of the church, the successor and imitator of the holy apostles? where is Ignatius, in whom God dwelt? where is St Dionysius the Areopagite, that bird of paradise, that celestial eagle? where is Hippolytus, that good man, *aner chrestos*, that gentle sweet person? where is great St Basil, a man almost equal to the apostles? where is Athanasius, rich in virtue? where is Gregory Nyssen, that great divine? and Ephrem the great Syrian, that stirred up the sluggish, and awakened the sleepers, and comforted the afflicted, and brought the young men to discipline [...]. These were the men that prevailed against error, because they lived according to truth: and whoever shall oppose you and the truth you walk by, may better be confuted by your lives than by your disputations. Let 'your adversaries have no evil thing to say of you,' and then you will best silence them [...]. But if ye become 'burning and shining lights;' [...] if ye 'walk in light' and 'live in the spirit;' your doctrines will be true, and that truth will prevail [...].

I pray God give you all grace to follow this wisdom, to study this learning, to labour for the understanding of godliness; so your time and your studies, your persons and your labours, will be holy and useful, sanctified and blessed, beneficial to men and pleasing to God through Him who is the 'Wisdom of the Father', 'who is made' to all that love Him 'wisdom, and righteousness, and sanctification, and redemption:' to whom with the Father &c.

40 Chrysostom, *The End of the Ages*, PG 63.938.

The Marriage Ring[1]

JEREMY TAYLOR

> This is a great mystery, but I speak concerning Christ and the church. Nevertheless, let every one of you in particular so love his wife even as himself, and the wife see that she reverence her husband. (Eph 5:32-33)

The first blessing God gave to man was society, and that society was a marriage, and that marriage was confederate by God himself, and hallowed by a blessing [...]. This was the consequent of the first blessing, 'Increase and multiply.' The next blessing was the promise of the Messias, and that also increased in men and women a wonderful desire of marriage: for as soon as God had chosen the family of Abraham to be the blessed line from whence the world's Redeemer should descend according to the flesh, every of his daughters hoped to have the honour to be His mother or His grandmother or something of His kindred: and to be childless in Israel was a sorrow to the Hebrew women great as the slavery of Egypt or their dishonours in the land of their captivity.

But when the Messias was come, and the doctrine was published, [...] it pleased God in this new creation to inspire into the hearts of His servants a disposition and strong desires to live a single life, lest the state of marriage should in that conjunction of things become an accidental impediment to the dissemination of the gospel, which called men from a confinement in their domestic charges to travel, and fight, and poverty, and difficulty, and martyrdom: upon this necessity the apostles and apostolical men published doctrines declaring the advantages of single life, not by any commandment of the Lord, but by the spirit of prudence, *dia ten enestosan anagken*, 'for the present and then incumbent necessities,'[2] and in order to the advantages, which did accrue to the public ministries and private piety [...].

But in this first interval, the public necessity and the private zeal mingling together did sometimes overact their love of single life, even to the disparagement of marriage, and to the scandal of religion: which was increased by the occasion of some pious persons renouncing their contract of marriage, not consummate, with unbelievers. For when Flavia Domitilla, being converted by Nereus and Achilleus, the eunuchs, refused to marry Aurelianus to whom she was contracted, if there were not some little envy and too sharp hostility in the eunuchs to a married state, yet Aurelianus thought himself an injured person, and caused St Clemens, who veiled her, and his spouse

---

[1] Sermon XVII, in J. Taylor, vol. 4, pp 207-33. [2] 1 Cor 7:26.

both, to die in the quarrel. St Thecla being converted by St Paul grew so in love with virginity, that she leaped back from the marriage of Tamyris where she was lately engaged. St Iphigenia denied to marry king Hyrtacus, and it is said to be done by the advice of St Matthew. And Susanna the niece of Dioclesian refused the love of Maximianus the emperor; and these all had been betrothed; and so did St Agnes, and St Felicula, and divers others then and afterwards: insomuch that it was reported among the gentiles, that the Christians did not only hate all that were not of their persuasion, but were enemies of the chaste laws of marriage; and indeed some that were called Christians were so, 'forbidding to marry, and commanding to abstain from meats.'[3] Upon this occasion it grew necessary for the apostle to state the question right, and to do honour to the holy rite of marriage, and to snatch the mystery from the hands of zeal and folly, and to place it in Christ's right hand, that all its beauties might appear, and a present convenience might not bring in a false doctrine and a perpetual sin and an intolerable mischief [...]. 'Marriage is honourable in all men;'[4] so is not single life; for in some it is a snare and a *purosis*, 'a trouble in the flesh,' a prison of unruly desires which is attempted daily to be broken [...]. Marriage was ordained by God, instituted in paradise, was the relief of a natural necessity and the first blessing from the Lord; He gave to man not a friend, but a wife, that is, a friend and a wife too; for a good woman is in her soul the same that a man is, and she is a woman only in her body; that she may have the excellency of the one, and the usefulness of the other, and become amiable in both. It is the seminary of the church, and daily brings forth sons and daughters unto God; it was ministered to by angels, and Raphael[5] waited upon a young man that he might have a blessed marriage, and that that marriage might repair two sad families, and bless all their relatives [...]. Marriage was in the world before sin, and is in all ages of the world the greatest and most effective antidote against sin, in which all the world had perished if God had not made a remedy: and although sin hath soured marriage, and stuck the man's head with cares, and the woman's bed with sorrows in the production of children; yet these are but throes of life and glory, and 'she shall be saved in child-bearing, if she be found in faith and righteousness.'[6] Marriage is a school and exercise of virtue; and though marriage hath cares, yet the single life hath desires which are more troublesome and more dangerous, and often end in sin, while the cares are but instances of duty and exercises of piety; and therefore if single life hath more privacy of devotion, yet marriage hath more necessities and more variety of it, and is an exercise of more graces.

In two virtues celibate or single life may have the advantage of degrees ordinarily and commonly, that is, in chastity and devotion; but as in some persons this may fail, and it does in very many, and a married man may spend as much time in

---

3 1 Tim 4:3.   4 Heb 13:4.   5 Tobit 5:1.   6 1 Tim 2-15.

devotion as any virgins or widows do; yet as in marriage even those virtues of chastity and devotion are exercised, so in other instances this state hath proper exercises and trials for those graces for which single life can never be crowned. Here is the proper scene of piety and patience, of the duty of parents and the charity of relatives; here kindness is spread abroad, and love is united and made firm as a centre: marriage is the nursery of heaven; the virgin sends prayers to God, but she carries but one soul to Him, but the state of marriage fills up the numbers of the elect, and hath in the labour of love, and the delicacies of friendship, the blessing of society, and the union of hands and hearts; it hath in it less of beauty, but more of safety, than the single life; it hath more care, but less danger; it is more merry, and more sad; is fuller of sorrows, and fuller of joys; it lies under more burdens, but it is supported by all the strengths of love and charity, and those burdens are delightful. Marriage is the mother of the world, and preserves kingdoms, and fills cities, and churches, and heaven itself. A celibate, like the fly in the heart of an apple, dwells in a perpetual sweetness, but sits alone, and is confined and dies in singularity; but marriage, like the useful bee, builds a house and gathers sweetness from every flower, and labours and unites into societies and republics, and sends out colonies, and feeds the world with delicacies, and obeys their king, and keeps order, and exercises many virtues, and promotes the interest of mankind, and is that state of good things to which God hath designed the present constitution of the world. [...]

Single life makes men in one instance to be like angels, but marriage in very many things makes the chaste pair to be like to Christ. 'This is a great mystery,' but it is the symbolical and sacramental representment of the greatest mysteries of our religion. Christ descended from His Father's bosom, and contracted His divinity with flesh and blood, and married our nature and we became a church, the spouse of the Bridegroom, which He cleansed with His blood, and gave her His holy spirit for a dowry, and heaven for a jointure, begetting children unto God by the gospel. This spouse He hath joined to Himself by an excellent charity. He feeds her at His own table, and lodges her nigh His own heart, provides for all her necessities, relieves her sorrows, determines her doubts, guides her wanderings; He is become her head, and she as a signet upon His right hand; He first indeed was betrothed to the synagogue and had many children by her, but she forsook His love. and then He married the church of the gentiles, and by her as by a second venter had a more numerous issue, *atque una domus est omnium filiorum ejus*, 'all the children dwell in the same house,' and are heirs of the same promises, entitled to the same inheritance. Here is the eternal conjunction, the indissoluble knot, the exceeding love of Christ, the obedience of the spouse, the communicating of goods, the uniting of interests, the fruit of marriage, a celestial generation, a new creature: *Sacramentum hoc magnum est*, 'this is the sacramental mystery' represented by the holy rite of marriage; so that marriage is divine in its institution, sacred in its union, holy in the mystery, sacramental in its signification, honourable in its appellative, religious in its employments; it is advantage to the societies of men, and it is 'holiness to the Lord.'

Dico autem in Christo et ecclesia, it must be 'in Christ and the church.' If this be not observed, marriage loses its mysteriousness; but because it is to effect much of that which it signifies, it concerns all that enter into those golden fetters to see that Christ and His church be in at every of its periods, and that it be entirely conducted and overruled by religion; for so the apostle passes from the sacramental rite to the real duty; 'Nevertheless,' that is, although the former discourse were wholly to explicate the conjunction of Christ and His church by this similitude, yet it hath in it this real duty, 'that the man love his wife, and the wife reverence her husband:' and this is the use we shall now make of it, the particulars of which precept I shall thus dispose; I shall propound,

> First, the duty as it generally relates to man and wife in conjunction;
> Secondly, the duty and power of the man;
> Thirdly, the rights and privileges and the duty of the wife.

I. *In Christo et ecclesia*; that begins all, and there is great need it should be so: for they that enter into the state of marriage cast a die of the greatest contingency, and yet of the greatest interest in the world, next to the last throw for eternity; [...]

(a) Life or death, felicity or a lasting sorrow, are in the power of marriage. A woman indeed ventures most, for she hath no sanctuary to retire to from an evil husband; she must dwell upon her sorrow, and hatch the eggs which her own folly or infelicity hath produced; and she is more under it, because her tormentor hath a warrant of prerogative, and the woman may complain to God as subjects do of tyrant princes, but otherwise she hath no appeal in the causes of unkindness. And though the man can run from many hours of his sadness, yet he must return to it again, and when he sits among his neighbours he remembers the objection that lies in his bosom, and he sighs deeply. *Ah tum te miserum, malique fati, / Quem, attractis pedibus, patente porta,/ Percurrent raphanique mugilesque.*7

The boys, and the pedlars, and the fruiterers, shall tell of this man, when he is carried to his grave, that he lived and died a poor wretched person. The stags in the Greek epigram whose knees were clogged with frozen snow upon the mountains came down to the brooks of the valleys, *chlienai noterois, namasin oku gonu*, 'hoping to thaw their joints with the waters of the stream,' but there the frost overtook them, and bound them fast in ice, till the young herdsmen took them in their stranger

---

7 Catullus, 15:17, LCL, p. 22.

snare. It is the unhappy chance of many men; finding many inconveniences upon the mountains of single life, they descend into the valleys of marriage to refresh their troubles, and there they enter into fetters, and are bound to sorrow by the cords of a man's or woman's peevishness: and the worst of the evil is, they are to thank their own follies, for they fell into the snare by entering an improper way; Christ and the church were no ingredients in their choice. But as the Indian women enter into folly for the price of an elephant, and think their crime warrantable; so do men and women change their liberty for a rich fortune, - like Eriphyle the Argive, *H chruson philou andros edexato timeenta,* 'she preferred gold before a good man,'[8] - and shew themselves to be less than money by overvaluing that to all the content and wise felicity of their lives; and when they have counted the money and their sorrows together, how willingly would they buy, with the loss of all that money, modesty, or sweet nature, to their relative![9] The odd thousand pound would gladly be allowed in good nature and fair manners. As very a fool is he that chooses for beauty principally; *cui sunt cruditi oculi, et stulta mens,* [10] as one said, 'whose eyes are witty, and their souls sensual:' it is an ill band of affections to tie two hearts together by a little thread of red and white; [...] they can love no longer but till the next ague comes; and they are fond of each other but at the chance of fancy, or the smallpox, or childbearing, or care, or time, or any thing that can destroy a pretty flower.[11] But it is the basest of all when lust is the paranymph, and solicits the suit, and makes the contract, and joined the hands; for this is commonly the effect of the former, according to the Greek proverb, [...] 'at first for his fair cheeks and comely beard the beast is taken for a lion, but at last he is turned to a dragon, or a leopard, or a swine:'[12] that which is at first beauty on the face, may prove lust in the manners; [...] they offer in their marital sacrifices nothing but the thigh, and that which the priests cut from the goats when they were laid to bleed upon the altars [...]; 'he or she that looks too curiously upon the beauty of the body, looks too low, and hath flesh and corruption in his heart, and is judged sensual and earthly in his affections and desires,' said St Clement.[13] Begin therefore with God; Christ is the president of marriage, and the Holy Ghost is the fountain of purities and chaste loves, and He joins the hearts; and therefore let our first suit be in the court of heaven, and with designs of piety, or safety, or charity; let no impure spirit defile the virgin purities and 'castifications of the soul,'[14] and let all such contracts begin with religious affections.

Conjugium petimus partumque uxoris, at illis / Notum qui pueri qualisve futura sit uxor; [15] 'we sometimes beg of God for a wife or a child; and He alone knows what the wife shall prove, and by what dispositions and manners, and into what

---

8 Homer, *Odyssey*, 11:326, LCL, vol. 1, p. 424.   9 Plautus, LCL, vol. 1., p. 56.   10 Juvenal, *Satires*, 6:143, CS, p. 37.   11 Ibid.   12 Homer, *Odyssey*, 4:456, LCL, vol. 1, p. 150.   13 Clement of Alexandria, *Stromata*, PG 9:29   14 1 Pet 1:22.

fortune that child shall enter:' but we shall not need to fear concerning the event of it, if religion, and fair intentions, and prudence, manage and conduct it all the way. The preservation of a family, the production of children, the avoiding fornication, the refreshment of our sorrows by the comforts of society; all these are fair ends of marriage and hallow the entrance: but in these there is a special order; society was the first designed, 'It is not good for man to be alone;' children was the next, 'Increase and multiply;' but the avoiding fornication came in by the superfetation of the evil accidents of the world. The first makes marriage delectable, the second necessary to the public, the third necessary to the particular. This is for safety, for life, and heaven itself, *Nam simul ac venas inflavit tetra libido, / Huc juvenes aequum est descendere;*[16] the other have in them joy and a portion of immortality. The first makes the man's heart glad; the second is the friend of kingdoms, and cities, and families; and the third is the enemy to hell, and an antidote to the chiefest inlet to damnation. But of all these the noblest end is the multiplying children: [...] 'it is religion to marry for children;' and Quintilian puts it into the definition of a wife [...]. And therefore St Ignatius,[18] when he had spoken of Elias, and Titus, and Clement, with an honourable mention of their virgin state, lest he might seem to have lessened the married apostles, at whose feet in Christ's kingdom he thought himself unworthy to sit, he gives this testimony; [...] that they might not be disparaged in their great names of holiness and severity, they were secured by 'not marrying to satisfy their lower appetites, but out of desire of children'[...].[19]

(b) Man and wife are equally concerned to avoid all offences of each other in the beginning of their conversation: every little thing can blast an infant blossom; and the breath of the south can shake the little rings of the vine when first they begin to curl like the locks of a new-weaned boy; but when by age and consolidation they stiffen into the hardness of a stem, and have by the warm embraces of the sun and the kisses of heaven brought forth their clusters, they can endure the storms of the north and the loud noises of a tempest, and yet never be broken: so are the early unions of an unfixed marriage; watchful and observant, jealous and busy, inquisitive and careful, and apt to take alarm at every unkind word [...]. Plutarch[20] compares a new marriage to a vessel before the hoops are on; [...] 'everything dissolves their tender compaginations;' [...] but [...] 'when the joints are stiffened and are tied by a firm compliance and proportioned bending, scarcely can it be dissolved without fire or the violence of iron.' After the hearts of the man and the wife are endeared and hardened by a mutual confidence, and an experience longer than artifice and pretence can last, there are a great many remembrances, and some things present,

---

15 Juvenal, *Satires*, 10:352, CS, p. 77. 16 Horace, *Satires*, 1:2:33, LCL, p. 20. 17 Macrobius, *Saturnalia*, 1:16. 18 Quintilian, 10:6:2, LCL, vol. 4, p.128. 19 Ignatius, *Letter to the Philadelphians*, 4 = FOTC I. 113-17. 20 Plutarch, *Moralia*, LCL, vol. 2, p. 298.

that dash all little unkindnesses in pieces. The little boy in the Greek epigram that was creeping down a precipice, was invited to his safety by the sight of his mother's pap when nothing else could entice him to return: and the bond of common children, and the sight of her that nurses what is most dear to him, and the endearments of each other in the course of a long society, and the same relation, in an excellent security to redintegrate and to call that love back which folly and trifling accidents would disturb [...].

(c) Let man and wife be careful to stifle little things,[21] that as fast as they spring they be cut down and trod upon; for if they be suffered to grow by numbers, they make the spirit peevish and the society troublesome, and the affections loose and easy by an habitual aversation. Some men are more vexed with a fly than with a wound; and when the gnats disturb our sleep, and the reason is disquieted but not perfectly awakened, it is often seen that he is fuller of trouble than if in the daylight of his reason he were to contest with a potent enemy. In the frequent little accidents of a family a man's reason cannot always be awake; and when his discourses are imperfect, and a trifling trouble makes him yet more restless, he is soon betrayed to the violence of passion. It is certain that the man or woman are in a state of weakness and folly then when they can be troubled with a trifling accident, and therefore it is not good to tempt their affections when they are in that state of danger. In this case the caution is to subtract fuel from the sudden flame; for stubble though it be quickly kindled, yet it is as soon extinguished if it be not blown by a pertinacious breath, or fed with new materials. Add no new provocations to the accident, and do not inflame this, and peace will soon return, and the discontent will pass away soon as the sparks from the collision of a flint: even remembering that discontents proceeding from daily little things do breed a secret undiscernible disease which is more dangerous than a fever proceeding from a discerned notorious surfeit.

(d) Let them be sure to abstain from all those things which by experience and observation they find to be contrary to each other [...]. The ancients in their marital hieroglyphics[22] used to depict Mercury standing by Venus, to signify that by fair language and sweet entreaties the minds of each other should be united; and hard by them *Suadam et Gratias descripserunt*, they would have all deliciousness of manners, compliance and mutual observance to abide.

(e) Let the husband and wife infinitely avoid a curious distinction of mine and thine, for this hath caused all the laws and all the suits and all the wars in the world; let them who have but one person have also but one interest [...]. And when either of them begins to impropriate, it is like a tumour in the flesh,[23] it draws more than its share, but what it feeds on turns to a bile. And therefore the

21 Juvenal, *Satires*, 6:184, CS, p. 39.   22 Plutarch, *Moralia*, LCL, vol. 2, p. 298.   23 Juvenal, *Satires*, 6:178, CS, p. 38.

Romans forbad any donations to be made between man and wife, because neither of them could transfer a new right of those things which already they had in common; [...] so are the riches of a family; they are a woman's as well as a man's: they are hers for need, and hers for ornament and hers for modest delight, and for the uses of religion and prudent charity [...]. Macarius[24] in his thirty-second homily, speaks fully in this particular; a woman betrothed to a man bears all her portion, and with a mighty love pours it into the hands of her husband, and says, *emon, ouden echo*, 'I have nothing of my own;' my goods, my portion, my body and my mind, is yours[...]; 'all that a woman hath is reckoned to the right of her husband; not her wealth and her person only, but her reputation and her praise:'[25] so Lucian. But as the earth, the mother of all creatures here below, sends up all its vapours and proper emissions at the command of the sun, and yet requires them again to refresh her own needs, and they are deposited between them both in the bosom of a cloud, as a common receptacle, that they may cool his flames, and yet descend to make her fruitful: so are the proprieties of a wife to be disposed of by her lord; and yet all are for her provisions, it being a part of his seed to refresh and supply hers, and it serves the interest of both while it serves the necessities of either.

These are the duties of them both, which have common regards and equal necessities and obligations. And indeed there is scarce any matter of duty but it concerns them both alike, and is only distinguished by names, and hath its variety by circumstances and little accidents: and what in one is called 'love,' in the other is called 'reverence;' and what in the wife is 'obedience,' the same in the man is 'duty:' he provides, and she dispenses; he gives commandments, and she rules by them; he rules her by authority, and she rules him by love; she ought by all means to please him, and he must by no means displease her. For as the heart is set in the midst of the body, and though it strikes to one side by the prerogative of nature, yet those throbs and constant motions are felt on the other side also, and the influence is equal to both: so it is in conjugal duties; some motions are to the one side more than to the other, but the interest is on both, and the duty is equal in the several instances. If it be otherwise, the man enjoys a wife as Periander[26] did his dead Melissa, by an unnatural union, neither pleasing nor holy, useless to all the purposes of society, and dead to content.

II. The next enquiry is more particular, and considers the power and duty of the man. 'Let every one of you so love his wife even as himself;' she is as himself, the man hath power over her as over himself, and must love her equally.

(a) A husband's power over his wife is paternal and friendly, not magisterial and despotic. The wife is in *perpetua tutela*, 'under conduct and counsel;' for the

---

24 Macarius the Egyptian, 9 = PG 34, 405-822. 25 Lucian, LCL, vol. 8, p. 147. 26 Herodotus, cf. Baldry, *Greek Literature for the Modern Reader*, Cambridge, 1951, pp 188-213.

power a man hath is founded in the understanding, not in the will or force; it is not a power of coercion, but a power of advice; [...] 'husbands should rather be fathers than lords,' said Valerius in Livy,[27] and Homer[28] adds more soft appellatives to the character of a husband's duty; [...] thou art to be 'a father and a mother to her, and a brother:' and great reason, unless the state of marriage, should be no better than the condition of an orphan; for she that is bound to leave father and mother and brother for thee, either is miserable like a poor fatherless child, or else ought to find all these, and more, in thee. Medea in Euripides[29] had cause to complain when she found it otherwise, [...] which St Ambrose well translates, 'It is sad when virgins are with their own money sold to slavery; and that services are in better state than marriages; for they receive wages, but these buy their fetters, and pay dear for their loss of liberty.'[30] [...] It was rarely observed of Philo, [...][31] when Adam made that fond excuse for his folly in eating the forbidden fruit, he said, 'The woman Thou gavest to be *with* me, she gave me.' He says not, 'The woman which Thou gavest *to* me,' no such thing: she is none of his goods, none of his possessions, not to be reckoned amongst his servants; God did not give her to him so; but, 'The woman Thou gavest to be *with* me,' that is, to be my partner, the companion of my joys and sorrows, Thou gavest her for use, not for dominion. The dominion of a man over his wife is no other than as the soul rules the body; for which it takes a mighty care, and uses it with a delicate tenderness, and cares for it in all contingencies, and watches to keep it from all evils, and studies to make for it fair provisions; [...] the soul governs, [...] but the government is no other than provision [...]. And yet even the very government itself is divided, for man and wife in the family are as the sun and moon in the firmament of heaven [...]. But else there is no difference [...]. So many differences can be in the appellative's of *dominus* and *domina*, governor and governess, lord and lady, master and mistress, the same difference there is in the authority of man and woman, and no more; *si tu caius, ego caia*,[32] was publicly proclaimed upon the threshold of the young man's house, when the bride entered into his hands and power; and the title of *domina* in the sense of the civil law was among the Romans given to wives. *Hi dominam Ditis thalamo deducere adorti*,[33] said Virgil: where though Servius says it was spoken after the manner of the Greeks, who called the wife *despoinan*, 'lady', or 'mistress,' yet it was so amongst both the nations.

(b) 'Let him love his wife even as himself:' that's his duty, and the measure of it too; which is so plain, that if he understands how he treats himself, there needs nothing be added concerning his demeanour towards her, [...] they have the same

---

27 Livy, 34:7, LCL, vol. 9, p. 435.   28 Homer, *Iliad*, 6:429, LCL, vol. 1, p. 292.   29 Euripides, *Medea*, 230, LCL, vol. 4, p. 302.   30 Ambrose, *Exhortatio Virginibus*, 4:23 = PL 16:343.   31 Philo, *Allegorical Interpretations*, 3:56, LCL, vol. 1. p. 337.   32 Plutarch, *Moralia*, LCL, vol. 4, p. 16.   33 Virgil, *Aeneid*, 6:397, SCBO, p. 239.

fortune, the same family, the same children, the same religion, the same interest, 'the same flesh,' *erunt duo in carnem unam*; and therefore this the apostle urges for his *me pikrainete*, 'no man hateth his own flesh, but nourisheth and cherisheth it;'and he certainly is strangely sacrilegious and a violator of the rights of hospitality and sanctuary, who uses her rudely, who is fled for protection, not only to his house, but also to his heart and bosom [...].

The marital love is infinitely removed from all possibility of such rudeness: it is a thing pure as light, sacred as a temple, lasting as the world; *Amicitia quae desinere potuit nunquam vera fuit*, said one; 'that love that can cease was never true:' it is *omilia*, so Moses called it,[34]; it is *eunoia*, so St Paul;[35] it is *philotes*,[36] so Homer; it is *philophrosune*,[37] so Plutarch; that is, it contains in it all sweetness, and all society, and all felicity, and all prudence, and all wisdom. For there is nothing can please a man without love; and if a man be weary of the wise discourses of the apostles, and of the innocency of an even and a private fortune, or hates peace or a fruitful year, he hath reaped thorns and thistles from the choicest flowers of paradise; 'for nothing can sweeten felicity itself, but love;' but when a man dwells in love, then the breasts of his wife are pleasant as the droppings upon the hill of Hermon, her eyes are fair as the light of heaven, she is a fountain sealed, and he can quench his thirst, and ease his cares, and lay his sorrows down upon her lap, and can retire home as to his sanctuary and refectory, and his gardens of sweetness and chaste refreshments. No man can tell but he that loves his children, how many delicious accents make a man's heart dance in the pretty conversation of those dear pledges; their childishness, their stammering, their little angers, their innocence, their imperfections, their necessities, are so many little emanations of joy and comfort to him that delights in their persons and society; but he that loves not his wife and children feeds a lioness at home, and broods a nest of sorrows; and blessing itself cannot make him happy; so that all the commandments of God enjoining a man to love his wife, are nothing but so many necessities and capacities of joy. 'She that is loved is safe, and he that loves is joyful.'[38]

(c) Above all the instances of love let him preserve towards her an inviolable faith, and an unspotted chastity; for this is the marriage-ring; it ties two hearts by an eternal band; it is like the cherubim's flaming sword set for the guard of paradise; he that passes into that garden now that it is immured by Christ and the church, enters into the shades of death. No man must touch the forbidden tree, that in the midst of the garden, which is the tree of knowledge and life. Chastity is the security of love, and preserves all the mysteriousness like the secrets of a temple. Under this lock is deposited security of families, the union of affections, the repairer of accidental breaches [...]. This is a grace that is shut up and secured by all arts of heaven, and the

---

[34] Ex 21: 10 [35] 1 Cor 7:3. [36] Homer, *Iliad*, 14:209 *et passim*. [37] Plutarch, *Moralia*, LCL, vol. 2, p. 298. [38] Horace, *Odes*, 1:1 3:17.

defence of laws, the locks and bars of modesty, by honour and reputation, by fear and shame, by interest and high regards; and that contract that is intended to be for ever, is yet dissolved and broken by the violation of this; nothing but death can do so much evil to the holy rites of marriage, as unchastity and breach of faith can [...]. Now in this grace it is fit that the wisdom and severity of the man should hold forth a pure taper, that his wife may, by seeing the beauties and transparency of that crystal, dress her mind and her body by the light of so pure reflections; it is certain he will expect it from the modesty and retirement, from the passive nature and colder temper, from the humility and fear, from the honour and love, of his wife, that she be pure as the eye of heaven: and therefore it is but reason that the wisdom and nobleness, the love and confidence, the strength and severity of the man, should be as holy and certain in this grace, as he is a severe exactor of it at her hands, who can more easily be tempted by another, and less by herself.

These are the little lines of a man's duty, which, like threads of light from the body of the sun, do clearly describe all the regions of his proper obligations.

III. Now concerning the woman's duty, although it consists in doing whatsoever her husband commands, and so receives measures from the rules of his government, yet there are also some lines of life depicted upon her hands by which she may read and know how to proportion out her duty to her husband.

(a) The first is obedience; which because it is no where enjoined that the man should exact of her, but often commanded to her to pay, gives demonstration that it is a voluntary cession that is required; such a cession as must be without coercion and violence on his part, but upon fair inducements, and reasonableness in the thing, and out of love and honour on her part. When God commands us to love Him, He means we should obey Him; 'This is love, that ye keep My commandments;' and 'if he love Me,' said our Lord, 'keep My commandments:' now as Christ is to the church, so is man to the wife [...]. The man's authority is love, and the woman's love is obedience; and it was not rightly observed of him that said, when woman fell, 'God made her timorous, that she might be ruled,' apt and easy to obey; for this obedience is no way founded in fear, but in love and reverence; *receptae reverentiae est si mulier viro subsit*, said the law. Unless also that we will add, that it is an effect of that modesty which like rubies adorns the necks and cheeks of women; [...] 'it is modesty to advance and highly to honour them, who have honoured us by making us to be the companions'[39] of their dearest excellencies, said the maiden in the comedy. For the woman that went before the man in the way of death, is commanded to follow him in the way of love; and that makes the society to be perfect, and the union profitable, and the harmony complete [...]. 'Male and female created He them, and called their name Adam,' saith the holy scripture [...].[40]

39 Plautus, LCL, vol. 5, p. 13. 40 Gen 5.2.

(b) The next line of the woman's duty is compliance, which St Peter calls 'the hidden man of the heart, the ornament of a meek and a quiet spirit,'[41] and to it he opposes the outward and pompous ornament of the body; concerning which as there can be no particular measure set down to all persons, but the proportions are to be measured by the customs of wise people, the quality of the woman, and the desires of the man; yet it is to be limited by christian modesty, and the usages of the more excellent and severe matrons.[42] Menander in the comedy brings in a man turning his wife from his house because she stained her hair yellow, which was then the beauty [...]. A studious gallantry in clothes cannot make a wise man love his wife the better: *eis tous tragodous chresim, ouk eis ton bion,*[43] said the comedy; 'Such gaieties are fit for tragedies, but not for the uses of life:' *decor occultus ... et tecta venustas,*[44] that's the christian woman's fineness; 'the hidden man of the heart,' [...] 'to partake secretly and in her heart of all his joys and sorrows;' to believe him comely and fair though the sun hath drawn a cypress over him; for as marriages are not to be contracted by the hands and eye, but with reason and the hearts, so are these judgments to be made by the mind, not by the sight; and diamonds cannot make the woman virtuous, nor him to value her who sees her put them off then, when charity and modesty are her brightest ornaments [...]. And indeed those husbands that are pleased with undecent gaieties of their wives, are like fishes taken with ointments and intoxicating baits, apt and easy for sport and mockery, but useless for food; and when Circe had turned Ulysses' companions[45] into hogs and monkeys by pleasures and the enchantments of her bravery and luxury, they were no longer useful to her, she knew not what to do with them; but on wise Ulysses she was continually enamoured. Indeed the outward ornament is fit to take fools, but they are not worth the taking; but she that hath a wise husband must entice him to an eternal dearness by the veil of modesty and the grave robes of chastity, the ornament of meekness and the jewels of faith and charity; she must have no *fucus* but blushings, her brightness must be purity, and she must shine round about with sweetnesses and friendship, and she shall be pleasant while she lives, and desired when she dies. If not, [...] her grave shall be full of rottenness and dishonour, and her memory shall be worse after she is dead. After she is dead; for that will be the end of all merry meetings; and I choose this to be the last advice to both,

c) 'Remember the days of darkness, for they are many;' the joys of the bridal-chambers are quickly past, and the remaining portion of the state is a dull progress, without variety of joys, but not without the change of sorrows; but that portion that

---

[41] 1 Pet 3:4. [42] Clement of Alexandria, *Paidagogos*, 3 = FOTC 23, pp. 199-278. [43] Propertius, *Elegies*,1:2:1 LCL, p. 4. [44] Clement of Alexandria, *Paidagogos*, 3 = FOTC 23, pp 93-198. [45] Homer, *Odyssey*, 10:237, LCL, vol. 1. p. 374.

shall enter into the grave must be eternal.[46] It is fit that I should infuse a bunch of myrrh into the festival goblet, and after the Egyptian manner serve up a dead man's bones at a feast; I will only shew it and take it away again; it will make the wine bitter, but wholesome. But those married pairs that live as remembering that they must part again, and give an account how they treat themselves and each other, shall at the day of their death be admitted to glorious espousals, and when they shall live again be married to their Lord, and partake of His glories, with Abraham and Joseph, St Peter and St Paul, and all the married saints: *Thneta ta ton thneton, kaipanta parercheti hemas / hen de me, all hemeis auta parerchometha,* 'all those things that now please us shall pass from us, or we from them;'[47] but those things that concern the other life are permanent as the numbers of eternity: and although at the resurrection there shall be no relation of husband and wife, and no marriage shall be celebrated but the marriage of the Lamb; yet then shall be remembered how men and women passed through this state which is a type of that, and from this sacramental union all holy pairs shall pass to the spiritual and eternal, where love shall be their portion, and joys shall crown their heads, and they shall lie in the bosom of Jesus and in the heart of God to eternal ages. Amen.

---

46 Pliny, *Natural History*, 14:15, LCL vol. 4, p. 248; Martial, *Epigrams*, 14:113, LCL, vol. 3, p. 268.
47 Lucilius, 43. cf. Duff, *Literary History of Rome: Golden Age*, pp 172-6.

CHAPTER 3

Biblical and Liturgical

INTRODUCTION

Uppingham in 1638 as rector, with the earl of Northampton as patron; Golden Grove in 1645 as chaplain with Lord Carbery as patron; Portmore in 1658 as a sort of scholar-bishop-in-waiting, with Lord Conway as patron – these were 'the manifestations of that tender providence that shrouded him under her wings'[1] and, in their own ways, patron and place left their mark on his life and work. Born about 1611 and dying in 1667 he spanned the Caroline or first half of the 17th century, which is of such significance for Reformation studies in England. Then the spirit of the Renaissance breathed over the circle of friends at the Mermaid Tavern in Cheapside, with Shakespeare, Marlow, Jonson, Fletcher and a host of others. Music and poetry blossomed in this period between the Armada and the Civil War. It was the era of the Globe Theatre with William Byrd, Orlando Gibbons and the many other composers in that age of madrigals. But it was also the age of religious and political controversy, and the attempt to force all Englishmen inside the doors of a state-church continued unabated.

At Uppingham, the young Laudian, platonic in his philosophy and poetic in his prose, was biblical in the depths of his prophetic being. A cursory glance at *the Great Exemplar*, published in 1648 at Golden Grove and overladen with *Meditations, Discourses* and *Prayers*, reveals its origins at Uppingham, where he must have preached continuously on the mysteries of Christ in the church year, in spite of the Reformation attitude to liturgical time. Underlying this volume of a thousand pages is the narrative of *The History of the Life and Death of the Holy Jesus*, rivalling in length the heroic novels at that time being introduced from France. 'Bulk and prolixity were no disadvantage in that age of the Commonwealth, when Puritan asceticism had sealed up the sources of genial enjoyment [...]. The only entertainment left was literature,' and people could not have it too elaborately prolonged.'[2] Taylor was never again so inordinately lengthy, but in the continuous narrative, as can be seen in the *Selected Works*, the text of the King James is made to live and dance with the ease and grace of Taylor's style and imagination. In this sense and only at Uppingham is Taylor's

1 E. Gosse, *Jeremy Taylor, English Men of Letters*, London, 1904, p. 62.   2 Ibid., pp. 58-9.

preaching biblical and liturgical. Otherwise he is in the medieval tradition of the *schema* and the *exemplum;* more correctly, he is a preacher and a prophet, in the true spirit of the Renaissance and the Reformation. But at Uppingham he is already the holyman he will be at Golden Grove and the mystic he will become at Portmore:[3]

> The first beginners in religion are employed in the mastering of their first appetites, casting out their devils, exterminating all evil customs, lessening the proclivity of habits, and countermanding the too great forwardness of vicious inclinations; and this, which divines call the purgative way, is wholly spent in repentance, mortification. and self-denial [...].
>
> After our first step is taken, and the punitive part of repentance is resolved on, and begun, and put forward into good degrees of progress ... into the illuminative way, the soul passes to affections of intimate and more immediate love – the love God requires of us – an operative, material, and communicative love, 'If ye love Me, keep My commandments:' so that still a good life is the effect of the sublimest meditation [...].
>
> Beyond this I have described, there is a degree of meditation so exalted, that it changes the very name, and is called contemplation; and it is in the unitive way of religion, that is, it consists in unions and adherences to God; it is a prayer of quietness and silence, and a meditation extraordinary; a discourse without variety, a vision and intuition of divine excellencies, an immediate entry into an orb of light, and a resolution of all our faculties into sweetness, affections, and starings upon the divine beauty; and is carried on to ecstasies, raptures, suspensions, elevations, abstractions and apprehensions beatifical [...].
>
> But this is a thing not to be discoursed of, but felt: and although in other sciences the terms must first be known, and then the rules and conclusions scientifical; here it is otherwise: for first, the whole experience of this must be obtained before we can so much as know what it is; and the end must be acquired first, the conclusion before the premises. They that pretend to these heights call them the secrets of the kingdom; but they are such which no man can describe; such which God hath not revealed in the publication of the gospel; such for the acquiring of which there are no means prescribed.[4]

Such secrets and the heart that holds them are the stuff that preachers and poets are made of, and Taylor had them both: 'God's secrets are to Himself,' he

---

3 M. Gest, op. cit., p. 115.   4 Ibid., p. 113.

says, 'and to the sons of His house;'[5] in the *Great Exemplar* he speaks of the secrets of spiritual benediction 'which are understood only by them to whom they are conveyed, even by the children of the house;' elsewhere he refers to the secret of the spirit, or the meaning of the meaning, which is deep down and heartfelt by any disciple, who is grown old in religion and conversation of the Spirit: 'This man best understands the secret [...] and feels this unintelligible mystery, and sees with his heart what his tongue can never express and his metaphysics can never prove.' This vision of the heart – 'what heart heard of, ghost guessed' – and which not even the poet's tongue can express 'nor mouth had, no, nor mind, expressed' – is God-given. God opens the heart and creates a new one, and without this new creation, this new principle of life, we may hear the sound of God's word but never feel its meaning.

> Although the scriptures themselves are written by the Spirit of God, yet they are written within and without; and besides the light that shines on the face of them, unless there be a light shining within our hearts, unfolding the leaves and interpreting the mysterious sense of the Spirit, convincing our consciences and preaching to our hearts, to look for Christ in the leaves of the gospel is to look for the living among the dead. There is a life in them, but unless the Spirit of God be the *promo-condus*, we shall never draw it forth.[6]

This biblical and poetic mode of perception and expression, begun at Uppingham, was continued and developed at Golden Grove in the following decade, when the liturgy of the *Prayer Book* was forbidden and replaced by the *Directory* for worship. In the absence of the Church's liturgy, but in the peace and quiet of this golden grove, Taylor found the leisure and the audience he needed to develop his oratorical powers, and to produce the poetical prose on which his literary fame rests. In his own words, when the storm had finally 'dashed the vessel of the Church all in pieces,' he 'was cast upon the coast of Wales;' here too, in the words of the scriptures, 'the speaker learned to speak in words that seem to come from God' (1 Pet 4:10). From the *Prefaces* of his works published at this time he claimed the first countess of Carbery, who died in 1650, as the inspiration of his most artistic works, the *Holy Living* and *Holy Dying*, and at her obsequies he spoke the most touching of his best funeral sermons. Through the opportunity afforded by her request for a manual of devotions he had the incentive to imitate and create the elegance of classical style in the harmonious, lucid and beautiful prose which distinguishes the Sunday Sermons.

The two sermons considered in this chapter are found at the beginning of each half-year collection: the one on Advent Sunday, *Christ's Advent to Judgment*, introduces

---

5 Ibid., p. 115. 6 J. Taylor, vol. 8, p. 379.

the Winter Collection of Twenty-Five Sermons, published in 1651, and the other on Whitsunday, *Of the Spirit of Grace*, introduces the Summer Collection of Twenty-Seven Sermons, published in 1653. Both Collections are now included in the one volume, *Eniautos* or 'A Course of Sermons for All the Sundays of the Year.' In this collection of rich rhythms, there is an abundance of literary and historical allusion and a wealth of figurative ornament acknowledged by the scholars: 'if the ornate style of these sermons reflects the beauty of the surroundings and the tranquility of Taylor's life there, it also indicates, according to the rules of classical decorum with which both Taylor and his patron were familiar, that they were addressed to persons whose learning and refinement demanded an embellished prose.'[7]

In these sermons on Advent and Whitsun there is no awareness of the liturgical seasons introduced by them; neither is there any association between the other fifty sermons of the *Eniautos* and the liturgical time of their occurrence. But the collection of themes and topics is nonetheless interesting in itself and has much to tell about the nature and place of the sermon in 17th-century England. Then the sermon was looked upon as the English counterpart of the classical oration, and the conscious attempt of the Renaissance to link the sermon with the masterpieces of the past not only raised the standards of preaching, but also led to a revival of the whole oratorical tradition. Indeed, by virtue of its position at the apex of school rhetoric, which set the standards of literary taste, the sermon of Taylor's century serves as an index to the history of oratorical prose; it shows that the rhythmic periods of classical and Christian oratory are all interwoven into the fabric of English prose.

In an age of intense religious zeal, like that of Taylor's day, the recovery of the classical concept of rhetoric as the art of persuasion was much welcomed, as was every other resource of the ancient orator: 'it exercised the five rhetorical skills in the collection and arrangement of the materials, in the adornment of the composition with tropes and figures, in the memorization, and in the delivery. Its three divisions – exordium, body and peroration – were a modified form of the exordium, statement of facts, confirmation, and peroration of Greek and Roman days.' To accomplish its three functions of teaching, pleasing and persuading, the sermon took over the classical purpose of each part of the oration; in the exordium it won the good will of the congregation and gave them a clear statement of the plan; in the body it secured conviction by proof and refutation; in the peroration it clinched the issue with a summary and an appeal to the emotions. Such was the underlying scheme or *schema* of Taylor's sermons, which had its origins in the rhetoric of the ancients but was perfected by the Friars, Dominican and Franciscan, in the schools of Europe.

---

[7] G. Worley, *Jeremy Taylor. A Sketch of His Life and Times, with a popular exposition of his Works*, London, 1904, pp. 150-69.

These two sermons on Advent and Whitsun, like all Reformation preaching, are no more biblical, in the strict sense of the term, than they are liturgical. They have the structure and embellishments of the medieval *schema* and *exemplum* more than the exegetical, liturgical and prophetic dimensions of the earlier Greek homilies and Latin sermons, which continued to do and to say what was said and done in the synagogue at Nazareth (Lk 4: 16-30) with the presence of the Word that was there. In fact in Taylor's time, as in our own, there was little awareness of this distinction of homily and sermon and its significance for preaching in its more general form. For John Donne *homily* was first used by Origen (+253) to describe his form of preaching, and *sermon* by his contemporary, Gregory of Neocaesarea: 'so words multiplied – Conciones and lectures, Enarrationes for Augustine, Orations for Cyril and Damascen, Dictiones or Speeches, and nay one exercise of Caesareus, conveied in the forrne of a Dialogue, and all were sermons.'[8]

The Advent sermon, divided into three distinct sermons in the Winter Collection, like all Reformation preaching, is a prophetic exposition of a well-chosen scripture text and developed according to the *schema* or structure of the classical oration. The text creates its own context and provides the new material for the old form as can be easily seen in Taylor's choice of Paul's words to the Corinthians: 'For we must all appear before the judgment-seat of Christ, that every one may receive the things done in his body, according to that he hath done, whether it be good or bad' (2 Cor 5:10).

> This is what the apostle in the next verse calls 'the terror of the Lord.' It is His terror, because Himself shall appear in his dress of majesty and robes of justice; formidable in itself; fearful to us I shall so present it that we may be afraid of sin [...]. First we will consider the persons that are to be judged – 'we must all appear;' secondly, the Judge and His judgment-seat – 'before the judgment-seat of Christ; thirdly, the sentence they are to receive – 'the things due to the body, good or bad;' according as we now please, but then cannot alter. Every of these are dressed with circumstances of affliction and affright-ment to those to whom such terrors shall appertain as a portion of their inheritance.[9]

The Whitsun sermon, or the two sermons *Of the Spirit of Grace* that introduce the Summer Collection, or second part of the *Eniautos*, is again a structured exposition of spiritual reality with a text of Taylor's special choice : 'But ye are not in the flesh, but in the Spirit, if so be that the Spirit of God dwell in you. Now if any

---

8 P.G. Stanwood, *John Donne and the Theology of Language*, Columbia, Ohio 1986, pp 336-9.   9 J. Taylor, vol. 4, p. 7; *Advent Sunday* or *Christ's Advent to Judgment*.

man have not the Spirit of Christ, he is none of His. And if Christ be in you, the body is dead because of sin, but the Spirit is life because of righteousness' (Rom 8:9-10). In this world of the Spirit, grace was for Taylor as for Newman, *glory in exile*, and he was, at one and the same time, at home in the one and on his way to the other: *exemplum* or adornment is the only dress for this *schema* or structure:

> In the law, God gave His spirit in small proportions like the dew upon Gideon's fleece; a little portion was wet sometimes with the dew of heaven when all the earth besides was dry [...]. Jews called it *filiam vocis* or *daughter of a voice*, still, small and seldom and that by secret whispers, sometimes inarticulate; and God spake by the prophets, transmitting the sound as through an organ pipe. But in the gospel the Spirit is given without measure falling like tears of balsam upon the lowest of the people; now not the *daughter of a voice*, but the mother of many voices, of divided tongues and united hearts [...] so that maidens and boys, priest and people [...] are full of the Spirit if they belong to God. Moses' wish is fulfilled, and all the Lord's people are prophets in some sense or other.[10]

Advent Sunday: Christ's Advent to Judgment[1]

JEREMY TAYLOR

> For we must all appear before the judgment-seat of Christ, that every one may receive the things done in his body, according to that he hath done, whether it be good or bad.
> (2 Cor 5:10)

Virtue and vice are so essentially distinguished, and the distinction is so necessary to be observed in order to the wellbeing of men in private and in societies, that to divide them in themselves, and to separate them by sufficient notices, and to distinguish them by rewards, hath been designed by all laws, by the sayings of wise men, by the order of things, by their proportions to good or evil; and the expectations of men have been framed accordingly: that virtue may have a proper seat in the will and in the affections, and may become amiable by its own excellency and its appendent blessing; and that vice may be as natural an enemy to a man as a wolf to the lamb, and as darkness to light; destructive of its being, and a contradiction of its nature.

---

[10] Ibid., vol. 4, p. 336; *Whit Sunday, Of the Spirit of Grace*. [1] Sermons I, II, III in J. Taylor, vol. 4, pp 7-46.

But it is not enough, that all the world hath armed itself against vice, and by all that is wise and sober among men hath taken the part of virtue, adorning it with glorious appellatives, encouraging it by rewards, entertaining it with sweetness, and commanding it by edicts [...] all this is short of man's necessity: for this will in all modest men secure their actions in theatres and highways, in markets and churches, before the eye of judges and in the society of witnesses; but the actions of closets and chambers, the designs and thoughts of men, their discourses in dark places, and the actions of retirements and of the night, are left indifferent to virtue or to vice; and of these as man can take no cognizance, so he can make no coercitive, and therefore above one half of human actions is by the laws of man left unregarded and unprovided for.

And besides this [...] there are some sins so popular and universal that to punish them is either impossible or intolerable; and to question such would betray the weakness of the public rods and axes, and represent the sinner to be stronger than the power that is appointed to be his bridle. And after all this we find sinners so prosperous that they escape, so potent that they fear not; and sin is made safe when it grows great; and innocence is oppressed, and the poor cries, and he hath no helper; and he is oppressed, and he wants a patron [...]. It must follow from hence that it is but reasonable, for the interest of virtue and the necessities of the world, that the private should be judged, and virtue should be tied upon the spirit, and the poor should be relieved, and the oppressed should appeal, and the noise of widows should be heard, and the saints should stand upright, and the cause that was ill judged should be judged over again, and tyrants should be called to account, and our thoughts should be examined, and our secret actions viewed on all sides, and the infinite number of sins which escape here should not escape finally. And therefore God hath so ordained it that there shall be a day of doom, wherein all that are let alone by men shall be questioned by God, and every word and every action shall receive its just recompense of reward; 'for we must all appear before the judgment-seat of Christ, that every one may receive the things done in his body, according to that he hath done, whether it be good or bad' [...].

This is that which the apostle calls 'the terror of the Lord.' It is His terror, because Himself shall appear in His dress of majesty and robes of justice; and it is His terror, because it is of all things in the world the most formidable in itself, and it is most fearful to us: where shall be acted the interest and final sentence of eternity; and because it is so intended, I shall all the way represent it as 'the Lord's terror,' that we may be afraid of sin, for the destruction of which this terror is intended. First therefore we will consider the persons that are to be judged, with the circumstances of our advantages or our sorrows: 'we must all appear;' secondly, the Judge and His judgment-seat: 'before the judgment-seat of Christ;' thirdly, the sentence that they are to receive: 'the things due to the body, good or bad;' according as we now please, but then cannot alter. Every of these are dressed with circumstances of affliction and affrightment to those to whom such terrors shall appertain as a portion of their inheritance.

I. The persons who are to be judged; even you, and I, and all the world; kings and priests, nobles and learned, the crafty and the easy, the wise and the foolish, the rich and the poor, the prevailing tyrant and the oppressed party, shall all appear to receive their symbol; and this is so far from abating any thing of its terror and our dear concernment, that it much increases it: for, although concerning precepts and discourses we are apt to neglect in particular what is recommended in general, and in incidences of mortality and sad events the singularity of the chance heightens the apprehension of the evil [...], yet in final and extreme events the multitude of sufferers does not lessen but increase the sufferings; and when the first day of judgment happened, that of the universal deluge of waters upon the old world, the calamity swelled like the flood, and every man saw his friend perish, and the neighbours of his dwelling, and the relatives of his house, and the shares of his joys, and yesterday's bride, and the new-born heir, the priest of the family, and the honour of the kindred, all dying or dead, drenched in water and the divine vengeance; and then they had no place to flee unto, no man cared for their souls; they had none to go unto for counsel, no sanctuary high enough to keep them from the vengeance that rained down from heaven; and so it shall be at the day of judgment, when that world and this, and all that shall be born hereafter, shall pass through the same Red sea, and be all baptized with the same fire, and be involved in the same cloud, in which shall be thunderings and terrors infinite; every man's fear shall be increased by his neighbour's shrieks, and the amazement that all the world shall be in shall unite as the sparks of a raging furnace into a globe of fire, and roll upon its own principle, and increase by direct appearances and intolerable reflections. He that stands in a churchyard in the time of a great plague, and hears the passing-bell perpetually telling the sad stories of death, and sees crowds of infected bodies pressing to their graves, and others sick and tremulous, and death dressed up in all the images of sorrow round about him, is not supported in his spirit by the variety of his sorrow: and at doomsday when the terrors are universal, besides that it is in itself so much greater because it can affright the whole world, it is also made greater by communication and a sorrowful influence; grief being then strongly infectious when there is no variety of state, but an entire kingdom of fear, and amazement is the king of all our passions, and all the world its subjects: and that shriek must needs be terrible when millions of men and women at the same instant shall fearfully cry out, and the noise shall mingle with the trumpet of the archangel, with the thunders of the dying and groaning heavens and the crack of the dissolving world, when the whole fabric of nature shall shake into dissolution and eternal ashes [...].

In this great multitude we shall meet all those who by their example and their holy precepts have, like tapers enkindled with a beam of the Sun of righteousness, enlightened us and taught us to walk in the paths of justice. There we shall see all those good men whom God sent to preach to us, and recall us from human follies and inhuman practices: and when we espy the good man that chid us for our last drunkenness or adulteries, it shall then also be remembered how we mocked at counsel, and were civilly modest at the reproof, but laughed when the man was gone, and accepted it for a religious compliment, and took our leaves, and went and did the same again. But then things shall put on another face; and that which we smiled at here and slighted fondly, shall then be the greatest terror in the world; men shall feel that they once laughed at their own destruction, and rejected health when it was offered by a man of God upon no other condition but that they would be wise, and not be in love with death. Then they shall perceive that if they had obeyed an easy and a sober counsel, they had been partners of the same felicity which they see so illustrious upon the heads of those preachers, 'whose work is with the Lord,'[2] and who by their life and doctrine endeavour to snatch the soul of their friend or relatives from an intolerable misery [...].

There in that great assembly shall be seen all those converts who upon easier terms, and fewer miracles, and a less experience, and a younger grace, and a seldomer preaching, and more unlikely circumstances, have suffered the work of God to prosper upon their spirits, and have been obedient to the heavenly calling. There shall stand the men of Nineveh. and 'they shall stand upright in judgment,'[3] for they, at the preaching of one man, in a less space than forty days returned unto the Lord their God; but we have heard Him call all our lives, and like the deaf adder stopped our ears against the voice of God's servants, 'charm they never so wisely.'[4] There shall appear the men of Capernaum, and the queen of the South, and the men of Berea, and the first-fruits of the christian church, and the holy martyrs, and shall proclaim to all the world that it was not impossible to do the work of grace in the midst of all our weaknesses and accidental disadvantages: and that 'the obedience of faith,' and the 'labour of love,' and the contentions of chastity, and the severities of temperance and self-denial, are not such insuperable mountains but that an honest and sober person may perform them in acceptable degrees, if he have but a ready ear, and a willing mind, and an honest heart [...].

But there is a worse sight than this yet, which in that great assembly shall distract our sight and amaze our spirits. There men shall meet the partners of their sins, and them that drank the round when they crowned their heads with folly and forgetfulness, and their cups with wine and noises. There shall ye see that poor perishing

---

[2] Cf. Is 49:4.   [3] Mt 12:4.   [4] Ps 58:5.

soul whom thou didst tempt to adultery and wantonness, to drunkenness or perjury, to rebellion or an evil interest, by power or craft, by witty discourses or deep dissembling, by scandal or a snare, by evil example or pernicious counsel, by malice or unwariness [...]. Thy lust betrayed and rifled her weak, unguarded innocence; thy example made thy servant confident to lie, or to be perjured; thy society brought a third into intemperance and the disguises of a beast: and when thou seest that soul with whom thou didst sin dragged into hell, well mayest thou fear to drink the dregs of thy intolerable potion. And most certainly it is the greatest of evils to destroy a soul for whom the Lord Jesus died, and to undo that grace which our Lord purchased with so much sweat and blood, pains and a mighty charity [...].

Of all the considerations that concern this part of the horrors of doomsday, nothing can be more formidable than this, to such whom it does concern: and truly it concerns so many, and amongst so many perhaps some persons are so tender, that it might affright their hopes, and discompose their industries and spriteful labours of repentance; but that our most merciful Lord hath, in the midst of all the fearful circumstances of His second coming, interwoven this one comfort relating to this which to my sense seems the most fearful and killing circumstance, 'Two shall be grinding at one mill, the one shall be taken and the other left; two shall be in a bed, the one shall be taken and the other left:' that is, those who are confederate in the same fortunes and interests and actions, may yet have a different sentence: for an early and an active repentance will wash off this account, and put it upon the tables of the cross; and though it ought to make us diligent and careful, charitable and penitent, hugely penitent, even so long as we live, yet when we shall appear together, there is a mercy that shall there separate us, who sometimes had blended each other in a common crime. Blessed be the mercies of God, who hath so carefully provided a fruitful shower of grace, to refresh the miseries and dangers of the greatest part of mankind [...].

The sum is this, all that are born of Adam shall appear before God and His Christ, and all the innumerable companies of angels and devils shall be there: and the wicked shall be affrighted with every thing they see; and there they shall see those good men that taught them the ways of life, and all those evil persons whom themselves have tempted into the ways of death, and those who were converted upon easier terms; and some of these shall shame the wicked, and some shall curse them, and some shall upbraid them, and all shall amaze them; and yet this is but the *arche odinon*, the beginning of those evils which shall never end till eternity hath a period; but concerning this they must first be judged; and that's the second general consideration, 'we must appear before the judgment-seat of Christ,' and that's a new state of terrors and affrightments. Christ, who is our Saviour and is our advocate, shall then be our judge: and that will strangely change our confidences and all the face of things.

II. That's then the place and state of our appearance, 'before the judgment-seat of Christ:' for Christ shall rise from the right hand of His Father; He shall descend towards us, and ride upon a cloud, and shall make Himself illustrious by a glorious majesty, and an innumerable retinue, and circumstances of terror and a mighty power: and this is that which Origen[5] affirms to be the sign of the Son of man [...]. All the Greek and Latin Fathers do unanimously affirm that the representment of the cross is the sign of the Son of man spoken of by Matthew;[6] and indeed they affirm it very generally, but Origen after his manner is singular [...]; I list not to spin this curious cobweb; but Origen's opinion seems to me more reasonable; and it is more agreeable to the majesty and power of Christ to signify Himself with proportions of His glory rather than of His humility, with effects of His being exalted into heaven rather than of His poverty and sorrows upon earth [...], and he disparages the beauty of the sun who enquires for a rule to know when the sun shines, or the light breaks forth from its chambers of the east; and the Son of man shall need no other signification but His infinite retinue, and all the angels of God worshipping Him, and sitting upon a cloud, and leading the heavenly host, and bringing His elect with Him, and being clothed with the robes of majesty, and trampling upon devils, and confounding the wicked, and destroying death: but all these great things shall be invested with such strange circumstances and annexes of mightiness and divinity, that all the world shall confess the glories of the Lord. And this is sufficiently signified by St Paul, 'We shall all be set before the throne or place of Christ's judicature; for it is written, As I live, saith the Lord, every knee shall bow to Me, and every tongue shall confess to God:' that is, at the day of judgment when we are placed ready to receive our sentence, all knees shall bow to the holy Jesus, and confess Him to be God the Lord; meaning, that our Lord's presence should be such as to force obeisance from angels and man and devils, and His address to judgment shall sufficiently declare His person and His office and His proper glories. This is the greatest scene of majesty that shall be in that day, till the sentence be pronounced; but there goes much before this, which prepares all the world to the expectation and consequent reception of this mighty Judge of men and angels.

1. The majesty of the Judge, and the terrors of the judgment, shall be spoken aloud by the immediate forerunning accidents, which shall be so great violences to the old constitutions of nature, that it shall break her very bones, and disorder her till she be destroyed. St Hierome relates out of the Jews' books, that their doctors used to account fifteen days of prodigy immediately before Christ's coming, and to every day assign a wonder, any one of which if we should chance to see in the days of our flesh,

---

5 Origen, *Commentary on St Matthew*, 24:30 = ANF, vol.4, pp 409-512. 6 Mt 24-50.

it would affright us into the like thoughts which the old world had when they saw the countries round about them covered with water and the divine vengeance; or as those poor people near Adria and the Mediterranean sea, when their houses and cities are entering into graves, and the bowels of the earth rent with convulsions and horrid tremblings. The sea, they say, shall rise fifteen cubits above the highest mountains, and thence descend into hollowness and a prodigious drought; and when they are reduced again to their usual proportions, then all the beasts and creeping things, the monsters and the usual inhabitants of the sea, shall be gathered together, and make fearful noises to distract mankind: the birds shall mourn and change their songs into threnes and sad accents: rivers of fire shall rise from the east to west, and the stars shall be rent into threads of light, and scatter like the beards of comets; then shall be fearful earthquakes, and the rocks shall rend in pieces, the trees shall distil blood, and the mountains and fairest structures shall return unto their primitive dust; the wild beasts shall leave their dens, and come into the companies of men, so that you shall hardly tell how to call them, herds of men, or congregations of beasts; then shall the graves open and give up their dead, and those which are alive in nature and dead in fear, shall be forced from the rocks whither they went to hide them, and from caverns of the earth where they would fain have been concealed; because their retirements are dismantled. and their rocks are broken into wider ruptures, and admit a strange light into their secret bowels; and the men being forced abroad into the theatre of mighty horrors, shall run up and down distracted and at their wits' end; and then some shall die, and some shall be changed, and by this time the elect shall be gathered together from the four quarters of the world, and Christ shall come along with them to judgment.

These signs although the Jewish doctors reckon them by order and a method, concerning which they had no other revelation, nor sufficiently credible tradition, yet for the main parts of the things themselves the holy scripture records Christ's own words, and concerning the most terrible of them; the sum of which, as Christ related them and His apostles recorded and explicated, is this, 'the earth shall tremble, and the powers of the heavens shall be shaken, the sun shall be turned into darkness, and the moon into blood,' that is, there shall be strange eclipses of the sun, and fearful aspects in the moon, who when she is troubled looks red like blood; 'the rocks shall rend, and the elements shall melt with fervent heat; the heavens shall be rolled up like a parchment, the earth shall be burned with fire, the hills shall be like wax, for there shall go a fire before Him, and a mighty tempest shall be stirred round about Him:'

The trumpet of God shall sound, and the voice of the archangel, that is, of him who is the prince of all that great army of spirits which shall then attend their Lord and wait upon and illustrate His glory; and this also is part of that which is called the sign of the Son of man; for the fulfilling of all these predictions, and the preaching of the gospel to all nations, and the conversion of the Jews, and these prodigies, and the address of majesty, make up that sign. The notice of which things some way or other came to the very heathen themselves, who were alarmed into caution and sobriety by these dead remembrances [...].

Which things when they are come to pass, it will be no wonder if men's hearts shall fail them for fear, and their wits be lost with guilt, and their fond hopes destroyed by prodigy and amazement; but it will be an extreme wonder if the consideration and certain expectation of these things shall not awake our sleeping spirits, and raise us from the death of sin, and the baseness of vice and dishonourable actions, to live soberly and temperately, chastely and justly, humbly and obediently, that is, like persons that believe all this; and such who are not madmen or fools will order their actions according to these notices. For if they do not believe these things, where is their faith? If they do believe them and sin on, and do as if there were no such thing to come to pass, where is their prudence, and what is their hopes, and where their charity? how do they differ from beasts, save that they are more foolish, for beasts go on and consider not, because they cannot, but we can consider and will not; we know that strange terrors shall affright us all, and strange deaths and torments shall seize upon the wicked, and that we cannot escape, and the rocks themselves will not be able to hide us from the fears of those prodigies which shall come before the day of judgment: and that the mountains, though when they are broken in pieces we call upon them to fall upon us, shall not be able to secure us one minute from the present vengeance; and yet we proceed with confidence or carelessness, and consider not that there is no greater folly in the world than for a man to neglect his greatest interest, and to die for trifles and little regards, and to become miserable for such interests which are not excusable in a child. He that is youngest hath not long to live: he that is thirty, forty, or fifty years old, hath spent most of his life, and his dream is almost done, and in a very few months he must be cast into his eternal portion; that is, he must be in an unalterable condition; his final sentence shall pass according as he shall then be found: and that will be an intolerable condition when he shall have reason to cry out in the bitterness of his soul, 'Eternal woe is to me, who refused to consider when I might have been saved and secured from this intolerable calamity.' – But I must descend to consider the particulars and circumstances of the great consideration, 'Christ shall be our Judge at doomsday.'

2. If we consider (further) the person of the Judge, we first perceive that He is interested in the injury of the crimes He is to sentence: *Videbunt quem crucifixerunt*, 'they shall look on Him whom they pierced.' It was for their sins that the Judge did suffer such unspeakable pains as were enough to reconcile all the world to God; the sum and spirit of which pains could not be better understood than by the

consequence of His own words,' 'My God, My God, why hast Thou forsaken Me?' meaning that He felt such horrible pure unmingled sorrows, that although His human nature was personally united to the Godhead, yet at that instant He felt no comfortable emanations by sensible perception from the Divinity, but He was so drenched in sorrow that the Godhead seemed to have forsaken Him [...]. But this is half of the consideration [...]. For after that Christ had done all this by the direct actions of His priestly office of sacrificing Himself for us, He hath also done very many things for us, which are also the fruits of His first love and prosecutions of our redemption. I will not instance in the strange arts of mercy that our Lord uses to bring us to live holy lives; but I consider that things are so ordered and so great a value set upon our souls, since they are the images of God and redeemed by the blood of the holy Lamb, that the salvation of our souls is reckoned as a part of Christ's reward, a part of the glorification of His humanity [...]. For all that Christ did or suffered, and all that He now does as a priest in heaven, is to glorify His Father by bringing souls to God: for this it was that He was born and died, and that He descended from heaven to earth, from life to death, from the cross to the grave; this was the purpose of His resurrection and ascension, of the end and design of all the miracles and graces of God manifested to all the world by Him [...].

But in all these annexes of the great Judge, that which I shall now remark, is that indeed which hath terror in it, and that is the severity of our Lord. For then is the day of vengeance and recompenses, and no mercy at all shall be shewed but to them that are the sons of mercy; for the other, their portion is such as can be expected from these premises –

(a) If we remember the instances of God's severity in this life, in the days of mercy and repentance, in those days when judgment waits upon mercy and receives laws by the rules and measures of pardon, and that for all the rare streams of loving-kindness issuing out of paradise and refreshing all our fields with a moisture more fruitful than the floods of Nilus, still there are mingled some storms and violences, some fearful instances of the divine justice; we may more readily expect it will be worse, infinitely worse, at that day when judgment shall ride in triumph, and mercy shall be the accuser of the wicked. But so we read and are commanded to remember, because they are written for our example, that God destroyed at once five cities of the plain and all the country; and Sodom and her sisters are set forth for an example suffering the vengeance of eternal fire. Fearful it was when God destroyed at once twenty-three thousand for fornication, and an exterminating angel in one night killed one hundred and eighty-five thousand of the Assyrians, and the first-born of all the families of Egypt, and for the sin of David in numbering the people, threescore and ten thousand of the people died, and God sent ten tribes into captivity and eternal oblivion and indistinction from a common people for their idolatry. Did not God strike Corah and his company with fire from heaven? and the earth opened and swallowed up the congregation of Abiram? and is not evil come upon all the world for one sin of Adam? did not the anger of God break the nation of the Jews all in pieces with judgments so great that no nation ever suffered the like, because none ever sinned so? and at once it was done that God in anger destroyed all the world and eight persons only escaped the angry baptism of water. And yet this world is the time of mercy; God hath opened here His magazines, and sent His only Son as the great fountain of it too: here He delights in mercy, and in judgment loves to remember it, and it triumphs over all his works, and God contrives instruments and accidents, chances and designs, occasions and opportunities, for mercy: if therefore now the anger of God make such terrible eruptions upon the wicked people that delight in sin, how great may we suppose that anger to be, how severe that judgment, how terrible that vengeance, how intolerable those inflictions, which God reserves for the full effusion of indignation on the great day of vengeance?

(b) We may also guess at it by this; if God upon all single instances, and in the midst of our sins before they are come to the full and sometimes in the beginning of an evil habit, be so fierce in His anger; what can we imagine it to be in that day when the wicked are to drink the dregs of that horrid potion, and count over all the particulars of their whole treasure of wrath? 'This is the day of wrath, and God shall reveal His righteous judgments'[7] [...]. For so did the Libyan lion that was brought up under discipline, and taught to endure blows, and eat the meat of order and regular provision, and to suffer gentle usages and familiarities of societies; but once he brake out into his own wildness [...] and killed two Roman boys; but those that forage in the Libyan mountains, tread down and devour all that they meet or master; and when they have fasted two days, lay up an anger great as is their appetite, and bring certain death to all that can be overcome. God is pleased to compare Himself to a lion; and though in this life He hath confined Himself with promises and gracious emanations of an infinite goodness, and limits Himself to be overcome by prayers, and Himself hath invented ways of atonement and expiation; yet when He is provoked by our unhandsome and unworthy actions, He makes sudden breaches, and tears some of us in pieces; and of others He breaks their bones or affrights their hopes and secular gaieties, and fills their house with mourning and cypress and groans and death: but when this Lion of the tribe of Judah shall appear upon His own mountain, the mountain of the Lord, in His natural dress of majesty, and that justice shall have her chain and golden fetters taken off, then justice shall strike, and mercy shall not hold her hands; she shall strike sore strokes, and pity shall not break the blow; and God

---

7 Rom 2:5.

shall account with us by minutes, and for words, and for thoughts: and then He shall be severe to mark what is done amiss; and that justice may reign entirely, God shall open the wicked man's treasure, and tell the sums and weigh grains and scruples [...].

III. It remains that we consider the sentence itself, 'We must receive according to what we have done in the body, whether it be good or bad' [...]. When the prophet Joel was describing the formidable accidents in the day of the Lord's judgment, and the fearful sentence of an angry Judge, he was not able to express it, but stammered like a child, or an amazed, imperfect person, *A, a, a, diei, quia prope est dies Domini*.[8] It is not sense at first; he was so amazed he knew not what to say, and the Spirit of God was pleased to let that sign remain; like Agamemnon's sorrow for the death of Iphigenia, nothing could describe it but a veil; it must be hidden and supposed; and the stammering tongue that is full of fear can best speak that terror which will make all the world to cry, and shriek, and speak fearful accents, and significations of an infinite sorrow and amazement.

But so it is, there are two great days in which the fate of all the world is transacted. This life is man's day, in which man does what he please, and God holds His peace. Man destroys his brother, and destroys himself [...], and all this while God is silent, save that He is loud and clamorous with His holy precepts, and over-rules the event; but leaves the desires of men to their own choice, and their course of life such as they generally choose. But then God shall have His day too; the day of the Lord shall come, in which He shall speak, and no man shall answer; He shall speak in the voice of thunder and fearful noises, and man shall do no more as he please, but must suffer as he hath deserved [...].

'What we have done in the body.' But certainly this is the greatest terror of all. The thunders and the fires, the earthquakes and the trumpets, the brightness of holy angels and the horror of accursed spirits, the voice of the archangel who is the prince of the heavenly host, and the majesty of the Judge in whose service all that army stands girt with holiness and obedience, all those strange circumstances which have been already reckoned, and all those others which we cannot understand, are but little preparatories and umbrages of this fearful circumstance. All this amazing majesty and formidable preparatories are for the passing of an eternal sentence upon us, according to what we have done in the body. Woe and alas! and God help us all. All mankind is an enemy to God, his nature is accursed and his manners are depraved. It is with the nature of man, and with all his manners, as Philemon said of the nature of foxes; 'every fox is crafty and mischievous, and if you gather a whole herd of them, there is not a good-natured

---

8 Joel 1:15.

beast amongst them all.' So it is with man; by nature he is the child of wrath, and by his manners he is the child of the devil; we call christian, and we dishonour our Lord; and we are brethren, but we oppress and murder one another; it is a great degree of sanctity nowadays not to be so wicked as the worst of men; and we live at the rate as if the best of men did design to themselves an easier condemnation, and as if the generality of men considered not concerning the degrees of death, but did believe that in hell no man shall perceive any ease or refreshment in being tormented with a slower fire. For consider what we do in the body; twelve or fourteen years pass before we choose good or bad; and of that which remains, above half is spent in sleep and the needs of nature; for the other half, it is divided as the stag was when the beasts went a hunding, the lion hath five parts of six. The business of the world takes so much of our remaining portion, that religion and the service of God have not much time left that can be spared; and of that which can, if we consider how much is allowed to crafty arts of cozenage, to oppression and ambition, to greedy desires and avaricious prosecutions, to the vanities of our youth and the proper sins of every age, to the mere idleness of man and doing nothing, to his fantastic imaginations of greatness and pleasures, of great and little devices, of impertinent lawsuits and uncharitable treatings of our brother; it will be intolerable when we consider that we are to stand or fall eternally according to what we have done in the body [...].

The sentence of that day shall be passed, not by the proportions of an angel, but by the measures of a man, [...] not by strange and secret propositions, or by the fancies of men, or by the subtilties of useless distinctions, or evil persuasions [...] but by the plain rules of justice, by the ten commandments, by the first apprehensions of conscience, by the plain rules of scripture, and the rules of an honest mind, and a certain justice [...]. We shall be judged as Christians rather than as men, that is, as persons to whom much is pardoned, and much is pitied, and many things are (not accidentally, but consequently) indulged, and great helps are ministered, and many remedies supplied, and some mercies extra-regularly conveyed, and their hopes enlarged upon the stock of an infinite mercy, that hath no bounds but our needs, our capacities, and our proportions to glory. The sentence is to be given by Him that once died for us, and does now pray for us, and perpetually intercedes; and upon souls that He loves, and in the salvation of which Himself hath a great interest and increase of joy. And now upon these premises we may dare to consider what the sentence itself shall be, that shall never be reversed, but shall last for ever and ever.

'Whether it be good or bad.' I cannot discourse now the greatness of the good or bad, so far I mean as is revealed to us; the considerations are too long to be crowded into the end of a sermon; only in general; if it be good [...], it is a day of recompenses, in which all our sorrows shall be turned into joys, our persecutions into a crown, the cross into a throne, poverty into the riches of God; loss, and affronts, and inconveniences, and death, into sceptres, and hymns, and rejoicings, and hallelujahs, and such great things which are fit for us to hope, but too great for us to discourse of, while we see as in a glass darkly and imperfectly. And he that chooses to do an evil rather than suffer one, shall find it but an ill exchange that he deferred his little to change for a great one. I remember that a servant in the old comedy did choose to venture the lash rather than to feel a present inconvenience [...] but this will be but an ill account when the rods shall for the delay be turned into scorpions, and from easy shall become intolerable. Better it is to suffer here, and to stay till the day of restitution for the good and the holy portion; for it will recompense both for the suffering and the stay.[9]

But how if the portion be bad? It shall be bad to the greatest part of mankind; that's a fearful consideration; the greatest part of men and women shall dwell in the portion of devils to eternal ages. So that these portions are like the prophet's figs in the vision; the good are the best that ever were, and the worst are so bad that worse cannot be imagined. For though in hell the accursed souls shall have no worse than they have deserved, and there are not there over-running measures as there are in heaven, and therefore that the joys of heaven are infinitely greater joys than the pains of hell are great pains, yet even these are a full measure to a full iniquity, pain above patience, sorrows without ease, amazement without consideration, despair without the intervals of a little hope, indignation without the possession of any good; there dwells envy and confusion, disorder and sad remembrances, perpetual woes and continual shriekings, uneasiness and all the evils of the soul [...]. But in those regions and days of sorrow, when the soul shall be no more depending upon the body, but the perfect principle of all its actions, the actions are quick and the perceptions brisk; the passions are extreme and the motions are spiritual; the pains are like the horrors of a devil and the groans of an evil spirit; not slow like the motions of a heavy foot, or a loaden arm, but quick as an angel's wing, active as lightning; and a grief then, is nothing like a grief now; and the words of a man's tongue which are fitted to the uses of this world, are as unfit to signify the evils of the next, as person, and nature, and hand, and motion, and passion, are to represent the effects of the divine attributes, actions, and subsistence [...].

It is certain that the torments of hell shall certainly last as long as the soul lasts; for 'eternal' and 'everlasting' can signify no less but to the end of that duration, to the perfect end of the period in which it signifies. So Sodom and Gomorrah, when God rained down hell from heaven upon the earth, as Salvian's expression is, they are said 'to suffer the vengeance of eternal fire:'[10] that is, of a fire that consumed them finally, and they never were restored [...]. But the generality of

---

9 *Plautus,* LCL, vol. 4, p. 220.   10 Salvian, *The Governance of God,* 1 = FOTC, vol. 2.

Christians have been taught to believe worse things yet concerning them;[11] and the words of our blessed Lord are *kolasis aionios*, 'eternal affliction' or 'smiting.' [...] And St John, who knew the mind of his Lord, saith, 'the smoke of their torment ascendeth up for ever and ever, and they have no rest day nor night:'[12] that is, their torment is continual, and it is eternal [...]. God will never admit man to favour; he shall be tormented beyond all the measure of human ages, and be destroyed for ever and ever.

Therefore it concerns us all who hear and believe these things to do as our blessed Lord will do before the day of His coming; He will call and convert the Jews and strangers: conversion to God is the best preparatory to doomsday: and it concerns all them who are in the neighbourhood and fringes of the flames of hell, that is, in the state of sin, quickly to arise from the danger, and shake the burning coals off our flesh, lest it consume the marrow and the bones [...]. 'No man is safe long, that is so near to danger;' for suddenly the change will come, in which the judge shall be called to judgment, and no man to plead for him, unless a good conscience be his advocate; and the rich shall be naked as a condemned criminal to execution; and there shall be no regard of princes or of nobles, and the differences of men's account shall be forgotten, and no distinction remaining but of good or bad, sheep and goats, blessed and accursed souls. Among the wonders of the day of judgment our blessed Saviour reckons it that men shall be marrying and giving in marriage, marrying and cross-marrying, that is, raising families and lasting greatness and huge estates; when the world is to end so quickly, and the gains of a rich purchase so very a trifle, but no trifling danger; a thing that can give no security to our souls, but much hazards and a great charge. More reasonable it is that we despise the world and lay up for heaven, that we heap up treasures by giving alms, than make friends of unrighteous mammon; but at no hand to enter into a state of life that is all the way a hazard to the main interest, and at the best an increase to the particular charge. Every degree of riches, every degree of greatness, every ambitious employment, every great fortune, every eminency above our brother, is a charge to the accounts of the last day. He that lives temperately and charitably, whose employment is religion, whose affections are fear and love, whose desires are after heaven, and do not dwell below; that man can long and pray for the hastening of the coming of the day of the Lord [...].

In the mean time wonder not that God, who loves mankind so well, should punish him so severely: for therefore the evil fall into an accursed portion, because they despised that which God most loves, His Son and His mercies, His graces, and His holy spirit: and they that do all this, have cause to complain of nothing but their own follies; and they shall feel the accursed consequents then, when they

---

[11] Jude 1:7 [12] Rev 14:11.

shall see the Judge sit above them, angry and severe, inexorable and terrible; under them an intolerable hell; within them, their consciences clamorous and diseased: without them, all the world on fire on the right hand, those men glorified whom they persecuted or despised: on the left hand, the devils accusing; for this is the day of the Lord's terror, and who is able to abide it?

Whitsunday: Of the Spirit of Grace[1]

JEREMY TAYLOR

> But we are not in the flesh, but in the Spirit, if so be that the Spirit of God dwell in you. Now if any man have not the Spirit of Christ he is none of His: and if Christ be in you, the body is dead because of sin, but the spirit is life because of righteousness.
> (Rom 8:9-10)

The day in which the church commemorates the descent of the Holy Ghost upon the apostles, was the first beginning of the gospel of Jesus Christ. This was the first day that the religion was professed; now the apostles first opened their commission, and read it to all the people. 'The Lord gave His spirit,' or, 'the Lord gave his word,' and 'great was the company of the preachers;'[2] for so I make bold to render that prophecy of David. Christ was the 'Word of God, *Verbum aeternum*; but the Spirit was the Word of God, *Verbum patefactum:* Christ was the Word manifested 'in' the flesh; the Spirit was the Word manifested 'to' flesh., and set in dominion over, and in hostility against, the flesh. The gospel and the Spirit are the same thing; not in substance; but 'the manifestation of the Spirit' is 'the gospel of Jesus Christ:' and because He was this day manifested, the gospel was this day first preached, and it became a law to us, called 'the law of the Spirit of life;' that is, a law taught us by the Spirit, leading us to life eternal.[3]

But the gospel is called 'the Spirit:'

1. Because it contains in it such glorious mysteries which were revealed by the immediate inspirations of the Spirit, not only in the matter itself, but also in the manner and powers to apprehend them. For what power of human understanding could have found out the incarnation of a God; that two natures, a finite and an infinite, could have been concentred into one *hypostasis* or person; that a

---

[1] Sermons I, II, in J. Taylor, vol. 4, pp 331-56.   [2] Ps 68: 11.   [3] Rom 8:2.

virgin should be a mother; that dead men should live again; that God should crown the imperfect endeavours of His saints with glory, and that a human act should be rewarded with an eternal inheritance; that the wicked for the transient pleasure of a few minutes should be tormented with an absolute eternity of pains; that the waters of baptism, when they are hallowed by the Spirit, shall purge the soul from sin; and that the spirit of a man should be nourished with the consecrated and mysterious elements, and that any such nourishment should bring a man up to heaven: and after all this, that all christian people, all that will be saved, must be 'partakers of the divine nature,' of the nature, the infinite nature, of God, and must dwell in Christ, and Christ must dwell in them, and they must be in the Spirit, and the Spirit must be for ever in them? These are articles of so mysterious a philosophy that we could have inferred them from no premises, discoursed them upon the stock of no natural or scientifical principles; nothing but God and God's spirit could have taught them to us: and therefore the gospel is *Spiritus patefactus*, 'the manifestation of the Spirit,' *ad aedificationem*, as the apostle calls it, 'for edification,' and building us up to be a holy temple to the Lord.[4]

2. But when we had been taught all these mysterious articles, we could not by any human power have understood them unless the Spirit of God had given us a new light, and created in us a new capacity, and made us to be a new creature, of another definition. *Animalis homo, psuchikos*, that is, as St Jude expounds the word, *pneuma me echon*;[5] 'the animal', or 'the natural man,' the man that 'hath not the Spirit', 'cannot discern the things of God, for they are spiritually discerned;'[6] that is, not to be understood but by the light proceeding from the Sun of righteousness, and by that eye whose bird is the holy Dove, whose candle is the gospel [...]. We find this true by a sad experience. How many times doth God speak to us by His servants the prophets, by His Son, by His apostles, by sermons, by spiritual books, by thousands of homilies, and arts of counsel and insinuation; and we sit as unconcerned as the pillars of a church, and hear the sermons as the Athenians did a story, or as we read a gazette? [...] The reason of this is, a sad condemnation to such persons; they have not yet entertained the Spirit of God, they are in darkness; they were washed in water, but never baptized with the Spirit; for these things 'are spiritually discerned.' They would think the preacher rude if he should say, they are not Christians, they are not within the covenant of the gospel; but it is certain that 'the Spirit of manifestation' is not yet upon them, and that is the first effect of the Spirit whereby we can be called sons of God or relatives of Christ. If we do not apprehend and greedily suck in the precepts of this holy discipline as aptly as merchants do discourse of gain or farmers of fair harvests, we have nothing but the name of Christians, but we are no more such really than mandrakes are men or sponges are living creatures.

4 1 Cor 12:7. 5 Jude 1:19. 6 1 Cor 2:14.

3. The gospel is called 'Spirit,' because it consists of spiritual promises and spiritual precepts, and makes all men that embrace it truly to be spiritual men; and therefore St. Paul adds an epithet beyond this, calling it 'a quickening Spirit,'[7] that is, it puts life into our spirits, which the law could not. The law bound us to punishment, but did not help us to obedience, because it gave not the promise of eternal life to its disciples. The Spirit, that is, the gospel, only does this; and this alone is it which comforts afflicted minds, which puts activeness into wearied spirits, which inflames our cold desires, and does *anazopurein*, blows up sparks into live coals, and coals up to flames, and flames to perpetual burnings [...].

4. But beyond this is the reason which is the consummation of all the faithful. The gospel is called the Spirit, because by and in the gospel God hath given to us not only 'the Spirit of manifestation' that is, of instruction and of catechism, of faith and confident assent, but the 'Spirit of confirmation,' or 'obsignation,' to all them that believe and obey the gospel of Christ: that is, the power of God is come upon our hearts, by which in an admirable manner we are made sure of a glorious inheritance; made sure, I say, in the nature of the thing; and our own persuasions also are confirmed with an excellent, a comfortable, a discerning, and a reasonable hope; in the strength of which, and by whose aid, as we do not doubt of the performance of the promise, so we vigorously pursue all the parts of the condition, and are enabled to work all the work of God, so as not to be affrighted with fear, or seduced by vanity, or oppressed by lust, or drawn off by evil example, or abused by riches, or imprisoned by ambition and secular designs. This the Spirit of God does work in all His servants; and is called 'the Spirit of obsignation,' or 'the confirming Spirit,' because it confirms our hope, and assures our title to life eternal [...]. And this is the sense of 'the Spirit' mentioned in the text; 'Ye are not in the flesh but in the Spirit, if so be that the Spirit of God dwell in you:' that is, if ye be made partakers of the gospel, or of 'the Spirit of manifestation;' if ye be truly entitled to God, and have received the promise of the Father, then are ye not carnal men; ye are 'spiritual,' ye are 'in the Spirit:' if ye have the Spirit in one sense to any purpose, ye have it also in another: if the Spirit be in you, you are in it; if it hath given you hope, it hath also enabled and ascertained your duty. For 'the Spirit of manifestation' will but upbraid you in the shame and horrors of a sad eternity if you have not 'the Spirit of obsignation:' if the Holy Ghost be not come upon you to great purposes of holiness, all other pretences are vain, ye are still in the flesh which shall never inherit the kingdom of God.

'In the Spirit:' that is, in the power of the Spirit. So the Greeks call him *entheon*, who is 'possessed by a spirit,' whom God hath filled with a celestial immission; he is said to be in God, when God is in him. And it is a similitude taken from persons

---

7 1 Cor 15:45.

encompassed with guards; they are *in custodia*, that is ,in their power, under their command, moved at their dispose; they rest in their time, and receive laws from their authority, and admit visitors whom they appoint, and must be employed as they shall suffer: so are men who are in the Spirit; that is, they believe as He teaches, they work as He enables, they choose what He calls good, they are friends of His friends, and they hate with His hatred: with this only difference, that persons in custody are forced to do what their keepers please, and nothing is free but their wills; but they that are under the command of the Spirit do all things which the Spirit commands, but they do them cheerfully; and their will is now the prisoner, but it is *in libera custodia*, the will is where it ought to be, and where it desires to be, and it cannot easily choose any thing else because it is extremely in love with this [...].

Such in our proportions is the liberty of the sons of God; it is a holy and amiable captivity to the Spirit: the will of man is in love with those chains which draw us to God, and loves the fetters that confine us to the pleasures and religion of the kingdom. And as no man will complain that his temples are restrained and his head is prisoner when it is encircled with a crown; so when the Son of God hath made us free, and hath only subjected us to the service and dominion of the Spirit, we are free as princes within the circles of their diadem, and our chains are bracelets. and the law is a law of liberty, and 'His service is perfect freedom;'[8] and the more we are subjects the more we shall 'reign as kings;' and the faster we run, the easier is our burden; and Christ's yoke is like feathers to a bird, not loads, but helps to motion; without them the body falls; and we do not pity birds when in summer we wish them unfeathered and callow, or bald as eggs, that they might be cooler and lighter. Such is the load and captivity of the soul when we do the work of God, and are His servants, and under the government of the Spirit [...] He that is in the Spirit is under tutors and governors until the time appointed of the Father, just as all great heirs are; only the first seizure the Spirit makes is upon the will. He that loves the yoke of Christ and the discipline of the gospel, he is in the Spirit, that is, in the Spirit's power.

Upon this foundation the apostle hath built these two propositions;

I. Whosoever hath not the Spirit of Christ, he is none of His; he does not belong to Christ at all; he is not partaker of His spirit, and therefore shall never be partaker of His glory.

II. Whosoever is in Christ is dead to sin, and lives to the Spirit of Christ: that is, lives a spiritual, a holy, and a sanctified life.

These are to be considered distinctly.

III. All that belong to Christ have the Spirit of Christ. Immediately before the ascension our blessed Savious bid His disciples 'tarry in Jerusalem till they should receive the promise of the Father:'[9] whosoever stay at Jerusalem, and are in the

---

8 1 Cor 4:8. 9 Lk 24:49.

actual communion of the church of God, shall certainly receive this promise; 'for it is made to you and to your children,' saith St Peter, 'and to as many as the Lord our God shall call.'[10] All shall receive the Spirit of Christ, the promise of the Father, because this was the great instrument of distinction between the law and the gospel. In the law, God gave His spirit, first, to some; secondly, to them extraregularly; thirdly, without solemnity; fourthly, in small proportions, like the dew upon Gideon's fleece; a little portion was wet sometimes with the dew of heaven when all the earth besides was dry. And the Jews called it *filiam vocis*, 'the daughter of a voice,' still, and small, and seldom, and that by secret whispers, and sometimes inarticulate, by way of enthusiasm rather than of instruction; and God spake by the prophets, transmitting the sound as through an organ pipe, things which themselves oftentimes understood not. But in the gospel the Spirit is given without measure:[11] first poured forth upon our Head, Christ Jesus; then descending upon the beard of Aaron, the fathers of the Church; and thence falling, like the tears of the balsam of Judea, upon the foot of the plant, upon the lowest of the people. And this is given regularly to all that ask it, to all that can receive it, and by a solemn ceremony, and conveyed by a sacrament; and is now not the 'daughter of a voice' but the mother of many voices, of divided tongues and united hearts, of the tongues of prophets and the duty of saints, of the sermons of apostles and the wisdom of governors; it is the parent of boldness and fortitude to martyrs, the fountain of learning to doctors, an ocean of all things excellent to all who are within the ship and bounds of the catholic church: so that old men and young men, maidens and boys, the scribe and the unlearned, the judge and the advocate, the priest and the people, are full of the Spirit if they belong to God. Moses' wish is fulfilled, and all the Lord's people are prophets in some sense or other.

In the wisdom of the ancient it was observed that there are four great cords which tie the heart of man to inconvenience and a prison, making it a servant of vanity and an heir of corruption: Pleasure, and Pain; Fear and Desire. These are they that exercise all the wisdom and resolutions of man, and all the powers that God hath given him [...]. These are those evil spirits that possess the heart of man, and mingle with all his actions; so that either men are tempted to lust, by pleasure; or secondly, to baser arts, by covetousness; or thirdly, to impatience, by sorrow; or fourthly, to dishonourable actions, by fear: and this is the state of man by nature, and under the law, and for ever, till the Spirit of God came, and by four special operations cured these four inconveniences, and restrained or sweetened these unwholesome waters.

(a) God gave us His spirit that we might be insensible of worldly pleasures, having our souls wholly filled with spiritual and heavenly relishes. For when God's

---

10 Acts 2:39.   11 Jn 3:34.

spirit hath entered into us, and possessed us as His temple or as His dwelling, instantly we begin to taste Manna, and to loathe the diet of Egypt; we begin to consider concerning heaven, and to prefer eternity before moments, and to love the pleasures of the soul above the sottish and beastly pleasures of the body [...]. Then we wonder that any man should venture his head to get a crown unjustly, or that for the hazard of a victory he should throw away all his hopes of heaven certainly.

A man that hath tasted of God's spirit can instantly discern the madness that is in rage, the folly and the disease that is in envy, the anguish and tediousness that is in lust, the dishonour that is in breaking our faith and telling a lie, and understands things truly as they are; that is, that charity is the greatest nobleness in the world; that religion hath in it the greatest pleasures; that temperance is the best security of health; that humility is the surest way to honour. And all these relishes are nothing but antepasts of heaven, where the quintessence of all these pleasures shall be swallowed for ever; where the chaste shall follow the Lamb, and the virgins sing there where the mother of God shall reign, and the zealous converters of souls and labourers in God's vineyard shall worship eternally; where St Peter and St Paul do wear their crowns of righteousness; and the patient persons shall be rewarded with Job, and the meek persons with Christ and Moses, and all with God: the very expectation of which, proceeding from a hope begotten in us by 'the Spirit of manifestation,' and bred up and strengthened by 'the Spirit of obsignation', is so delicious an entertainment of all our reasonable appetites, that a spiritual man can no more be removed or enticed from the love of God and of religion, than the moon from her orb, or a mother from loving the son of her joys and of her sorrows.

This was observed by St Peter: 'As new-born babes, desire the sincere milk of the word, that ye may grow thereby; if so be that ye have tasted that the Lord is gracious.'[12] When once we have tasted the grace of God, the sweetnesses of His spirit, then no food but 'the food of angels,'[13] no cup but 'the cup of salvation,'[14] the 'divining cup,'[15] in which we drink salvation to our God and call upon the name of the Lord with ravishment and thanksgiving. And there is no greater external testimony that we are in the Spirit and that the Spirit dwells in us, than if we find joy and delight and spiritual pleasures in the greatest mysteries of our religion; if we communicate often, and that with appetite, and a forward choice, and an unwearied devotion, and a heart truly fixed upon God and upon the offices of a holy worship. He that loathes good meat is sick at heart, or near it; and he that despises, or hath not a holy appetite to, the food of angels, the wine of elect souls, is fit to succeed the prodigal at his banquet of sin and husks, and to be partaker of the table of devils: but all they who have God's spirit love to feast at the supper of the Lamb, and have no appetites but what are of the Spirit or servants to the Spirit [...].

[12] 1 Pet 2:2.   [13] Ps 78:25.   [14] Ps 116:12.   [15] Gen 44:5.

And if it were given to any of us to see paradise or the third heaven, as it was to St Paul, could it be that ever we should love any thing but Christ, or follow any guide but the Spirit, or desire any thing but heaven, or understand any thing to be pleasant but what shall lead thither? Now what a vision can do, that the Spirit doth certainly to them that entertain Him. They that have Him really and not in pretence only, are certainly great despisers of the things of the world. The Spirit doth not create or enlarge our appetites of things below; spiritual men are not designed to reign upon earth, but to reign over their lusts and sottish appetites. The Spirit doth not inflame our thirst of wealth, but extinguishes it, and makes us to 'esteem all things as loss, and as dung, so that we may gain Christ;'[16] no gain then is pleasant but godliness, no ambition but longings after heaven, no revenge but against ourselves for sinning; nothing but God and Christ: *Deus meus, et omnia:* and, *date nobis animas, caetera vobis tollite*, as the king of Sodom said to Abraham: 'Secure but the souls to us, and take our goods.'[17] Indeed, this is a good sign that we have the Spirit.

(b) The Spirit of God is given to all who truly belong to Christ, as an antidote against sorrows, against impatience against the evil accidents of the world, and against the oppression and sinking of our spirits under the cross. There are in scripture noted two births besides the natural; to which also by analogy we may add a third. The first is, to be 'born of water and the Spirit.' It is *en dia duoin*, one thing signified by a divided appellative, by two substantives, 'water and the Spirit,'[18] that is, *Spiritus aqueus*, the 'Spirit moving upon the waters of baptism.' The second is, to be born of Spirit and fire; for so Christ was promised to 'baptize us with the Holy Ghost and with fire,' that *is, cum Spiritu igneo*, 'with a fiery Spirit,'[19] the Spirit as it descended in Pentecost in the shape of fiery tongues. And as the watery Spirit washed away the sins of the church, so the Spirit of fire enkindles charity and the love of God. *To pur kathairei, to udor agnizei*, says Plutarch;[20] the Spirit is the same under both the titles, and it enables the church with gifts and graces. And from these there is another operation of the new birth, but the same Spirit, the Spirit of rejoicing, or *spiritus exultans, spiritus laetitiae;* 'May the God of hope fill you with all 'joy' and peace in believing, that ye may abound in hope through the power of the Holy Ghost.'[21]

There is a certain joy and spiritual rejoicing that accompanies them in whom the Holy Ghost doth dwell; a joy in the midst of sorrow: a joy given to allay the sorrows of secular troubles, and to alleviate the burden of persecution. This St Paul notes to this purpose: 'And ye became followers of us, and of the Lord, having received the word in much affliction, with joy of the Holy Ghost.'[22] Worldly afflictions and spiritual joys may very well dwell together; and if God did not supply us out of His

---

16 Phil 3:8.   17 Gen 14:21.   18 Jn 3:5.   19 Mt 3:11.   20 Plutarch, *Moralia*, LCL, vol. 4, p. 6.
21 Rom 15:13.   22 1 Thess 1:6.

storehouses, the sorrows of this world would be more and unmixed, and the troubles of persecution would be too great for natural confidences. For who shall make him recompense that lost his life in a duel, fought about a draught of wine, or a cheaper woman? What arguments shall invite a man to suffer torments in testimony of a proposition of natural philosophy? And by what instruments shall we comfort a man who is sick and poor, and disgraced, and vicious, and lies cursing, and despairs of any thing hereafter? That man's condition proclaims what it is to want the Spirit of God, 'the Spirit of comfort.' Now this Spirit of comfort is the hope and confidence, the certain expectation, of partaking in the inheritance of Jesus; this is the faith and patience of the saints; this is the refreshment of all wearied travellers, the cordial of all languishing sinners, the support of the scrupulous, the guide of the doubtful, the anchor of timorous and fluctuating souls, the confidence and the staff of the penitent. He that is deprived of his whole estate for a good conscience, by the Spirit meets this comfort, that he shall find it again with advantage in the day of restitution: and this comfort was so manifest in the first days of christianity, that it was no infrequent thing to see holy persons court a martyrdom with a fondness as great as is our impatience and timorousness in every persecution.

Till the Spirit of God comes upon us, we are *oligopsuchoi,* we have 'little souls,' little faith, and as little patience; we fall at every stumbling-block, and sink under every temptation; and our hearts fail us, and we die for fear of death, and lose our souls to preserve our estates or our persons, till the Spirit of God 'fills us with joy in believing:' and a man that is in a great joy, cares not for any trouble that is less than his joy; and God hath taken so great care to secure this to us, that He hath turned it into a precept, 'Rejoice evermore;'[23] and, 'Rejoice in the Lord always, and again I say rejoice.'[24] But this rejoicing must be only in the hope that is laid up for us, *en elpidi chairontes* so the apostle, 'rejoicing in hope.'[25] For although God sometimes makes a cup of sensible comfort to overflow the spirit of a man, and thereby loves to refresh his sorrows; yet that is from a secret principle not regularly given, not to be waited for, not to be prayed for, and it may fail us if we think upon it: but the hope of life eternal can never fail us, and the joy of that, is great enough to make us suffer any thing, or to do any thing [...] as long as this anchor holds, we may suffer a storm, but cannot suffer shipwreck. And I desire you by the way to observe how good a God we serve, and how excellent a religion Christ taught, when one of His great precepts is that we should 'rejoice and be exceeding glad:'[26] and God hath given us the spirit of rejoicing, not a sullen melancholy spirit, not the spirit of bondage or of a slave, but the Spirit of His Son, consigning us by a holy conscience to 'joys unspeakable and full of glory.'[27] And from hence you may also infer that those who sink under a persecution, or are impatient in a sad accident, they put out their own fires which

23 1 Thess 5:16.   24 Phil 4:4.   25 Rom 12:12.   26 Mt 5:12.   27 1 Pet 1:8.

the Spirit of the Lord hath kindled, and lose those glories which stand behind the cloud.

(c) The Spirit of God is given us as an antidote against evil concupiscences and sinful desires, and is then called 'the Spirit of prayer and supplication.' For ever since the affections of the outward man prevailed upon the ruins of the soul, all our desires were sensual, and therefore hurtful: for ever after our body grew to be our enemy. In the loosenesses of nature, and amongst the ignorance or imperfection of gentle philosophy, men used to pray with their hands full of rapine, and their mouths of blood, and their hearts of malice; and they prayed accordingly for an opportunity to steal, for a fair body, for a prosperous revenge, for a prevailing malice, for the satisfaction of whatsoever they could be tempted to by any object, by any lust, by any devil whatsoever.

The Jews were better taught; for God was their teacher, and He gave the Spirit to them in single rays. But as the 'Spirit of obsignation' was given to them under a seal, and within a veil, so the 'Spirit of manifestation,' or 'patefaction,' was like the gem of a vine, or the bud of a rose, plain indices and significations of life, and principles of juice and sweetness, but yet scarce out of the doors of their causes: they had the infancy of knowledge, and revelations to them were given as catechism is taught to our children; which they read with the eye of a bird, and speak with the tongue of a bee, and understand with the heart of a child; that is, weakly and imperfectly. And they understood so little that, first, they thought God heard them not unless they spake their prayers, at least efforming their words within their lips; and secondly, their forms of prayer were so few and seldom, that to teach a form of prayer or to compose a collect was thought a work fit for a prophet or the founder of an institution. Add to this, thirdly, that, as their promises were temporal, so were their hopes; as were their hopes, so were their desires; and according to their desires, so were their prayers. And although the psalms of David was their great office, and the treasury of devotion to their nation. and very worthily; yet it was full of wishes for temporals, invocations of God the avenger, on God the Lord of hosts, on God the enemy of their enemies: and they desired their nation to be prospered, and themselves blessed and distinguished from all the world, by the effects of such desires. This was the state of prayer in their synagogues; save only that it had also this allay, fourthly, that their addresses to God were crass, material, typical, and full of shadows and imagery, patterns of things to come; and so in its very being and constitution was relative and imperfect.

But that we may see how great things the Lord hath done for us, God hath poured His spirit into our hearts, 'the Spirit of prayer and supplication;' and now, Christians 'pray in their spirit,'[28] with sighs and groans, and know that God who dwells within them can as clearly distinguish those secret accents, and read their

28 Eph 6:18.

meaning in the Spirit as plainly, as He knows the voice of His own thunder, or could discern the letter of the law written in the tables of stone by the finger of God.

Likewise 'the Spirit helpeth our infirmities; for we know not what we should pray for as we ought.'[29] That is, when God sends an affliction or persecution upon us, we are indeed extreme apt to lay our hand upon the wound, and never take it off but when we lift it up in prayer to be delivered from that sadness; and then we pray fervently to be cured of a sickness, to be delivered from a tyrant, to be snatched from the grave, not to perish in the danger. But the Spirit of God hath from all sad accidents drawn the veil of error and the cloud of intolerableness, and hath taught us that our happiness cannot consist in freedom or deliverances from persecutions, but in patience, resignation, and noble sufferance; and that we are not then so blessed when God hath turned our scourges into ease and delicacy, as when we convert our very scorpions into the exercise of virtues: so that now the Spirit having helped our infirmities, that is, comforted our weaknesses and afflictions, our sorrows and impatience, by this proposition, that 'all things work together for the good of them that fear God,'[30] He hath taught us to pray for grace, for patience under the cross, for charity to our persecutors, for rejoicing in tribulations, for perseverance and boldness in the faith, and for whatsoever will bring us safely to heaven [...].

Furthermore, the Spirit of God made our services to be spiritual, intellectual, holy, and effects of choice and religion, the consequents of a spiritual sacrifice and of a holy union with God. The prayer of a Christian is with the effects of the 'Spirit of sanctification;' and then we pray with the Spirit when we pray with holiness, which is the great fruit, the principal gift, of the Spirit. And this is by St James called 'the prayer of faith,'[31] and is said to be certain that it shall prevail: such a praying with the Spirit when our prayers are the voices of our spirits, and our spirits are first taught, then sanctified, by God's spirit, shall never fail of its effect; because then it is that 'the Spirit himself maketh intercession for us;'[32] that is, hath enabled us to do it upon His strengths; we speak His sense, we live His life, we breathe His accents, we desire in order to His purposes, and our persons are gracious by His holiness, and are accepted by His interpellation and intercession in the act and offices of Christ: this is 'praying with the Spirit.'[33] To which by way of explication I add [...] that prayer is charity, it is faith, it is a conformity to God's will, a desiring according to the desires of heaven, an imitation of Christ's intercession, and prayer must suppose all holiness, or else it is nothing; and therefore all that in which men need God's spirit, all that is in order to prayer. Baptism is but a prayer, and the holy sacrament of the Lord's supper is but a prayer; a prayer of sacrifice representative, and a prayer of oblation,

---

29 Rom 8:26.   30 Rom 8:28.   31 Jas 5:15.   32 Rom 8:26.   33 1 Cor 14:15.

and a prayer of intercession, and a prayer of thanksgiving. And obedience is a prayer, and begs and procures blessings: and if the Holy Ghost hath sanctified the whole man, then He hath sanctified the prayer of the man, and not till then [...].

II. Thus I have described the effluxes of the Holy Spirit upon us in His great channels. But the great effect of them is this: that as by the arts of the spirits of darkness and our own malice our souls are turned into flesh, not in the natural sense but in the moral and theological, and *animalis homo* is the same with *carnalis*, that is, his soul is a servant of the passions and desires of the flesh, and is flesh in its operations and ends, in its principles and actions: so on the other side by the grace of God, and 'the promise of the Father,'[34] and the influences of the Holy Ghost, our souls are not only recovered from the state of flesh and reduced back to the entireness of animal operations, but they are heightened into spirit and transformed into a new nature. And this is a new article, and now to be considered.

St Hierome tells of the custom of the empire, when a tyrant was overcome, they used to break the head of his statues, and upon the same trunk to set the head of the conqueror, and so it passed wholly for the new prince. So it is in the kingdom of grace: as soon as the tyrant sin is overcome, and a new heart is put into us, or that we serve under a new head, instantly we have a new name given us, and we are esteemed a new creation; and not only changed in manners, but we have a new nature within us, even a third part of an essential constitution. This may seem strange; and indeed it is so, and it is one of the great mysteriousnesses of the gospel. Every man naturally consists of soul and body; but every christian man that belongs to Christ, hath more, for he hath body, and soul, and spirit. My text is plain for it: 'If any man have not the Spirit of Christ, he is none of His.' And by 'spirit' is not meant only the graces of God, and His gifts enabling us to do holy things: there is more belongs to a good man than so. But as when God made man, He made him after His own image, and breathed into him the spirit of life, and he was made in *animam viventem*. 'into a living soul;'[35] then he was made a man: so in the new creation, Christ, 'by whom God made both the worlds,'[36] intends to conform us to His image, and He hath given us 'the Spirit of adoption,'[37] by which we are made sons of God; and by the spirit of a new life we are made new creatures, capable of a new state, entitled to another manner of duration, enabled to do new and greater actions in order to higher ends; we have new affections, new understandings, new wills: *vetera transierunt, et ecce omnia nova facta sunt*, 'all things are become new.'[38] And this is called 'the seed of God,'[39] when it relates to the principle and cause of this production; but the thing that is produced is a spirit, and that is as much in nature beyond a soul as a soul is beyond a body [...] and that hath taught us to distinguish the principle of a new life from the principle of the old, the celestial from the natural.

34 Acts 1:4.   35 Gen. 2:7.   36 Heb 1:2.   37 Rom. 8:15.   38 2 Cor 5:17.   39 1 Jn 3:9.

The spirit, as I now discourse of it, is a principle infused into us by God when we become His children, whereby we live the life of grace, and understand the secrets of the kingdom, and have passions and desires of things beyond and contrary to our natural appetites, enabling us not only to sobriety, which is the duty of the body; not only to justice, which is the rectitude of the soul; but to such a sanctity as makes us like to God; for so saith the Spirit of God, 'Be ye holy, as I am:' 'be pure, be perfect, as your heavenly Father is pure, as He is perfect:'[40] which because it cannot be a perfection of degrees, it must be *in similitudine naturae*, 'in the likeness of that nature'[41] which God hath given us in the new birth, that by it we might resemble His excellency and holiness. And this I conceive to be the meaning of St Peter, 'According to His divine power hath given us all things that pertain to life and godliness,'[42] that is, to this new life of godliness, 'through the knowledge of Him that hath called us to glory and virtue; whereby are given unto us exceeding great and precious promises, that by these you might be partakers of the divine nature:' so we read it: but it is something mistaken: it is not *tes theias phuseos*, 'the' divine nature; for God's nature is indivisible and incommunicable; but it is spoken *participative*, or *per analogiam*, 'partakers of a divine nature,' that is, of this new and godlike nature given to every person that serves God, whereby he is sanctified, and made the child of God, and framed into the likeness of Christ. The Greeks generally called this *charisma*, 'a gracious gift,' an extraordinary superaddition to nature; not a single gift in order to single purposes, but an universal principle; and it remains upon all good men during their lives, and after their death; and is that 'white stone' spoken of in the Revelation,[43] 'and in it a new name written, which no man knoweth but he that hath it:' and by this God's sheep at the day of judgment shall be discerned from goats; if their spirits be presented to God pure and unblamable, this great *charisma*, this talent which God hath given to all Christians to improve in the banks of grace and of religion, if they bring this to God increased and grown up to the fulness of the measure of Christ (for it is Christ's spirit, and as it is in us it is called 'the supply of the Spirit of Jesus Christ'),[44] then we shall be acknowledged for sons, and our adoption shall pass into an eternal inheritance in the portion of our elder brother [...].

In the mean time, if the fire be quenched, the fire of God's spirit, God will kindle another in His anger that shall never be quenched: but if we entertain God's spirit with our own purities, and employ it diligently, and serve it willingly (for God's spirit is a loving Spirit),[45] then we shall really be turned into spirits. Irenaeus had a proverbial saying, 'they that present three things right to God, they are perfect;' that is, a chaste body, a righteous soul, and a holy spirit.[46] And the event shall be this, which

---

40 Lev 11:44. 41 Mt 5:48. 42 2 Pet 1:3,4. 43 Rev 2:17. 44 Phil 1:19. 45 Wis 1:6. 46 Irenaeus, *Against Heresies*, PG 7:1136.

Maimonides expressed not amiss, though he did not at all understand the secret of this mystery; the soul of man in this life is *in potentia ad esse spiritum*, 'it is designed to be a spirit,' but in the world to come it shall be actually as very a spirit as an angel is. And this state is expressed by the apostle, calling it 'the earnest of the Spirit:'[47] that is, here it is begun, and given as an antepast of glory, and a principle of grace; but then we shall have it *in plenitudine*: here and there it is the same; but here we have the earnest, there the riches and the inheritance.

But then, if this be a new principle, and be given us in order to the actions of a holy life, we must take care that we 'receive not the Spirit of God in vain,'[48] but remember it is a new life [...]; indeed, he that hath the Spirit of God, doth acknowledge God for his Father and his Lord, he despises the world, and hath no violent appetites for secular pleasures, and is dead to the desires of this life, and his hopes are spiritual, and God is his joy, and Christ is his pattern and his support, and religion is his employment, and 'godliness' is his 'gain:'[49] and this man understands the things of God, and is ready to die for Christ, and fears nothing but to sin against God; and his will is filled with love, and it springs out in obedience to God and in charity to his brother. And of such a man we cannot make judgment by his fortune, or by his acquaintance; by his circumstances, or by his adherencies; for they are the appendages of a natural man: but 'the spiritual is judged of no man;'[50] that is, the rare excellencies that make him happy do not yet make him illustrious, unless we will reckon virtue to be a great fortune, and holiness to be great wisdom, and God to be the best friend, and Christ the best relative, and the Spirit the hugest advantage, and heaven the greatest reward. He that knows how to value these things, may sit down and reckon the felicities of him that hath the Spirit of God.

The purpose of this discourse is this; that since the Spirit of God is a new nature and a new life put into us, we are thereby taught and enabled to serve God by a constant course of holy living, without the frequent returns and intervening of such actions which men are pleased to call 'sins of infirmity.' Whosoever hath the Spirit of God lives the life of grace; the Spirit of God rules in him, and is strong according to its age and abode, and allows not of those often sins, which we think unavoidable, because we call them 'natural infirmities.'

'But if Christ be in you, the body is dead because of sin, but the spirit is life because of righteousness.'[51] The state of sin is a state of death. The state of man under the law was a state of bondage and infirmity, as St Paul largely describes him in the seventh chapter of the Romans: but he that hath the Spirit, is made alive, and free and strong, and a conqueror over all the powers and violences of sin. Such a man resists temptations, falls not under the assault of sin, returns not

---

[47] 1 Cor 1:22. [48] 2 Cor 6:1. [49] 1 Tim 6:6. [50] 1 Cor 2:15. [51] Rom 8:1 0.

to the sin which he last repented of, acts no more that error which brought him to shame and sorrow: but he that falls under a crime to which he still hath a strong and vigorous inclination, he that acts his sin, and then curses it, and then is tempted, and then sins again, and then weeps again, and calls himself miserable, but still the enchantment hath confined him to that circle; this man hath not the Spirit: 'for where the Spirit of God is, there is liberty;'[52] there is no such bondage, and a returning folly to the commands of sin [...].

The sum is this: an animal man, a man under the law, a carnal man (for as to this they are all one), is sold under sin, he is a servant of corruption, he falls frequently into the same sin to which he is tempted; he commends the law, he consents to it that it is good; he does not commend sin, he does some little things against it, but they are weak and imperfect, his lust is stronger, his passions violent and unmortified, his habits vicious, his customs sinful, and he lives in the regions of sin, and dies and enters into its portion. But a spiritual man, a man that is in the state of grace, who is born anew of the Spirit, that is regenerate by the Spirit of Christ, he is led by the Spirit, he lives in the Spirit, he does the works of God cheerfully, habitually, vigorously; and although he sometimes slips, yet it is but seldom, it is in small instances; his life is such as he cannot pretend to be justified by works and merit, but by mercy and the faith of Jesus Christ; yet he never sins great sins: if he does, he is for that present fallen from God's favour, and though possibly he may recover (and the smaller or seldomer the sin is, the sooner may be his restitution) yet for the present, I say, he is out of God's favour. But he that remains in the grace of God, sins not by any deliberate, consultive, knowing act: he is incident to such a surprise as may consist with the weakness and judgment of a good man; but whatsoever is or must be considered, if it cannot pass without consideration it cannot pass without sin, and therefore cannot enter upon him while he remains in that state. For 'he that is in Christ, in him the body is dead by reason of sin.'[53] And the gospel did not differ from the law, but that the gospel gives grace and strength to do whatsoever it commands, which the law did not; and the greatness of the promise of eternal life is such an argument to them that consider it, that it must needs be of force sufficient to persuade a man to use all his faculties and all his strength that he may obtain it. God exacted all upon this stock; God knew this could do every thing: *nihil non in hoc praesumpsit Deus*, said one. This will make a satyr chaste, and Silenus to be sober, and Dives to be charitable, and Simon Magus himself to despise reputation, and Saul to turn from a persecutor to an apostle. For since God hath given us reason to choose, and a promise to exchange for our temperance and faith and charity and justice, for these (I say) happiness, exceeding great happiness, that we shall be kings, that we shall reign with God, with Christ, with all the holy angels for ever, in felicity so great that

52 2 Cor 3:17.   53 Rom 8:10.

we have not now capacities to understand it, our heart is not big enough to think it; there cannot in the world be a greater inducement to engage us, a greater argument to oblige us, to do our duty. God hath not in heaven a bigger argument; it is not possible any thing in the world should be bigger; which because the Spirit of God hath revealed to us, if by this strength of His we walk in His ways, and be ingrafted into His stock, and bring forth His fruits, 'the fruits of the Spirit,' then 'we are in Christ,' and 'Christ in us;' then we 'walk in the Spirit,' and 'the Spirit dwells in us;' and our portion shall be there where 'Christ by the Spirit maketh intercession for us,' that is, at the right hand of His Father, for ever and ever. Amen.

CHAPTER 4

Moral and Doctrinal

INTRODUCTION

Titles, like those of these chapter-headings, are more useful for structuring material than accurate in their analysis for, certainly, such distinctions must be more notional than real. H.R. McAdoo, the late Church of Ireland archbishop of Dublin, and master and disciple of Jeremy Taylor, was ever ready to present the entire corpus of his work as *practical divinity* or religion in practice: 'here is how the mystery of the eucharist appears to one who is primarily a moral theologian, preacher, spiritual director, and practical theologian. Taylor wants us to be transformed into a new nature, and instrumental in this process is the Anglican spirituality of the five Ds, devotion, duty, discipline, detail and doctrine.'[1]

Elsewhere and earlier Dr McAdoo had commented on Taylor's unique approach to holy living and holy dying: 'there are throughout his work an interlocking of themes and underlying unity of thought, so that one must first see his eucharistic theology in the context of his general theology. We shall find throughout a vein of moral / ascetic theology and a vein of sacramental theology, which merge and undergird all that he writes. His methodology is that which has created and creates the Spirit of Anglicanism – the appeal to scripture, antiquity, and reason.'[2] In fact, the selection from Taylor's works, made for the volume in the Classics of Western Spirituality series, was structured and presented in its chapter divisions to illustrate in its theological unity the McAdoo thesis; hence, 1. Jesus Christ – The Great Exemplar; 2. The Heavenly Sacrifice and Earthly Sacraments; 3. Faith and Repentance; 4. Sermon, Discourse and Prayer; 5. Holy Living and Holy Dying.[3]

The fifty-two sermons of the *Eniautos* were probably preached to the select congregation of the Carbery household, where their magic of style, dramatic presentation and classical allusion were appreciated. Nevertheless, there is not one of them that does not lay stress on some homely duty or virtue and point out the practical path. Here are no idle flights of fancy or picturesque descriptions of an

---

[1] H.R. McAdoo, *The Mystery of the Eucharist in the Anglican Tradition*, Norwich, 1995, pp 52-3. [2] H.R. McAdoo, *The Eucharistic Theology of Jeremy Taylor Today*, Norwich, 1988, p. 14. [3] T.K. Carroll, *Jeremy Taylor, Selected Works*, Classics of Western Spirituality, New York, 1990.

unattainable sanctity. He is at all times, like Chrysostom, his prototype, driving home his point, for 'sermons', he said, 'are not like curious enquiries after new nothings, but pursuance of old truths.' These truths, moral and doctrinal, were the content that inspired the beauty of his style, for in the true artist there is no distinction between manner and meaning; indeed, the form in any work of art expresses the reaction of the artist to the subject, and cannot be separated from that totality of meaning that the work conveys to our senses and imagination. It is his possession of style in this true sense of poetry – the revelation of a unique vision in the music and magic of words – that makes him the renowned preacher: 'always there is his love of God, His essence, His wisdom and His power, reflected in the forces of nature and in the little creations of the earth as well as in the actions of a holy life, whereby God is pleased to glorify Himself.'[4]

This knowledge or awareness, moral and doctrinal, of Christian revelation and faith, is the reality or Word, personal and cosmic, of this speaker, 'who speaks in words that seem to come from God'(1 Pet 4:11). In Taylor, as in Milton, there was that blend of Word and words, or vision and language, that was before our present 'Age of the Vulgar' or the common description. Even the very titles of his sermons, unfortunately truncated in this chapter – 'Apples of Sodom' or the fruits of sin; 'The House of Feasting' or the Epicure's measures; 'The Good and Evil Tongue;' and 'The Deceitfulness of the Heart' were obviously chosen to arouse curiosity by partly revealing and partly concealing the content. Other titles like 'The Serpent and the Dove'; 'The Faith and Patience of the Saints'; 'The Flesh and the Spirit'; 'The Foolish Exchange' or 'Of Growth in Grace' and 'Of Growth in Sin' are less ambiguous, but each and every one is the exposition of a carefully and happily chosen biblical text. This combination of bible and poetry, of which Taylor was the great master in prose, is the dream world of Rahner's *primordial* words as *priest calls to poet*, and *poet calls to priest*, but it has lost its footing in the philosophy and language of our brave new world for it does not speak the scientific truth.[5]

The critic Logan Pearsall Smith calls Taylor's *magic of style* a combination of sound and image, 'which enchants the ear and fascinates the eye.' His mastery of verbal music, 'the felicity of sound and rhythm,' is frequently noted in the sermons when he expresses the same idea in a less and then a more perfect form. In one passage he compares the death of virtuous men to 'the descending of ripe and wholesome fruits from a pleasant and florid tree,' but in another 'to ripe and pleasant fruit falling from a fair tree, and gathered into baskets for the planter's use.' Here, with just a slight change of cadence, a new arrangement of epithets,

---

[4] M. Gest, *The House of Understanding: Selections from the writings of Jeremy Taylor*, Philadelphia, 1954, p. 17. [5] J. Taylor, vol. 8, *Eniautos*, 'A Course of Sermons for All the Sundays of the Year.'

the crystallization takes place, the miracle happens and the phrase becomes one of enchantment. This felicity of sound and rhythm is often enhanced by his use of the unexpected and sometimes archaic adjective, which, being out of context, insinuates a remoter meaning, like the receding tide deserting 'the *unfaithful* dwelling of the sand.'[6]

In addition to this mastery of verbal music, Taylor possessed an extraordinarily rich and wonderful visual imagination as he personifies abstractions and turns them into living creatures. For example, he speaks of sin, 'that will look prettily, and talk flattering words, and entice thee with softnesses and easy fallacies;' again, he speaks to grief as to a person; 'if you stay but till tomorrow you will be weary, and will lie down to rest.' But in this constant creation of simile and metaphor he presents visual images, which convey, as only figured diction can, his religious ideas and transcendental experience. His sermons, consequently, are full of poetic images, flashing out in brief similes, as when he speaks of wealth 'that flies away like a bird from the hand of a child,' or compares the charity and humility of the Virgin to 'the pure leaves of the whitest lily,' or describe her grief at the crucifixtion as being 'deep as the waters of the abyss, but smooth as the face of a pool.'[7]

Renaissance in words and Reformation in Word were the *fons et origo* of the Catholic and Caroline renewal in which people like Hooker, Herbert, Andrewes and Laud were baptized and confirmed. Educated at Perse Free Grammar School at Cambridge he had to master Lilly's Grammar, the prescribed text, as a preparation for the 'reading of the good authors who had withstood the test of the ages.' Among these authors was Cicero whose rhetorical style was the recognised ideal. In the fifth grade came the letters of Seneca, and in the upper grades the orations of Isocrates and Demosthenes. Afterwards at Gonville and Caius in Cambridge were advanced courses in rhetoric, logic, theology, oriental languages and science. After his first outing at St Paul's in London he was acclaimed a worthy successor to John Donne, and became the protégé of Laud and a fellow at All Souls, Oxford, where the future leaders were being trained. Under Laud's tutelage he mastered the art of Christian oratory and formed the habit of relying on the early Greek and Latin Fathers for moral precepts and the ornamental devices that now at last scholars of rhetoric are noticing in the sermons.[8]

In the preaching manuals of the seventeenth century, in addition to the emphasis on the classical principles of rhetoric, there is a new stress on the nature and needs of the audience and on the preacher's need for a broad cultural background as well as his moral integrity. In their interpretation of rhetorical ideals as applied to the

---

[6] L.P. Smith, *Jeremy Taylor: Selected Passages*, Oxford, 1930, p. xxxiii.   [7] Carroll, op. cit., pp 68-9.
[8] M.S. Antoine, 'The Rhetoric of Jeremy Taylor's Prose: Ornament of the Sunday Sermons' dissertation, CUA, Washington, 1946, pp 1-21.

sermon, the manuals reflect, on the one hand, the Puritan preference for methodical preaching in keeping with the *schema* of tradition, and, on the other hand, the Anglican taste for a more finished pulpit style by a cultivated use of the *exemplum*, as a classical or literary embellishment of the scripture text and its development. This required not only the collection of suitable materials and their appropriate arrangement according to the principles of the manuals, but more importantly, a wise choice and a judicious use of the tropes and figures defined and exemplified in the rhetorics. In the preaching of the medieval Church, as has been seen, the *exempla* or anecdotes of the jovial friar were frequently, in practice, the corruption of the gospel; in the new world of the Renaissance the sermon achieved literary merit when the *exempla* were in harmony with the text and at the service of the Word.

In great measure Jeremy Taylor was the creator in English of pulpit oratory in its written form, and is recognised as such for the most part. In his published sermons of the *Golden Grove* period he achieved the desired blend of matter and form that is literary art, but his command of literary ornament is seldom seen as the explanation of his success. Yet rhetorical terms are scattered throughout his every work, as is clear from the manner in which he used these terms to explain biblical texts and Anglican doctrines; for example, sacraments are for him 'allegorical admonitions of Christian mortification and give grace by a *metonymy* and sacramental manner of speaking, which is also a *synecdoche* of the whole:' furthermore, he states that 'a metaphorical or mystical expression may be the veil of a mysterious truth, but cannot pass into a sign and signification of it, and that there is a *catachresis* in the phrase naturally engendered of the offspring of Adam.'[9] These are the words of the trade and Jeremy Taylor was a master craftsman.

Simile and metaphor were for Aristotle the most significant elements in style, and Taylor loved them both. According to one definition, known in the seventeenth century, 'the essence of metaphor is the friendly borrowing of a word to express a thing with more light and better note, though not so directly and properly as the natural name of the things meant would signify.'[10] Many of the similes, found in the sermons, are drawn from the sun and moon for he delighted in the phenomena of light as he also did in the mystery and magic of water: 'repentance is like the sun, which enlightens not only the tops of the Eastern hills, or warms the wall-fruits of Italy; it makes the little Balsam tree to weep precious tears with staring upon its beauties; it produces rich spices in Arabia, and warms the cold hermit in his grot.'[11] More often these sermons are decorated with images of the highest poetic beauty, clothed in a soft radiance of words, which can speak of death in one of the most beautiful similes of the English language:

9 Ibid., p. 20 at fn. 88.   10 Ibid., p. 24.   11 Smith, op cit., p. xliii.

> But so have I seen a Rose newly springing from the clefts of its hood, and at first it was fair as the Morning, and full with the dew of Heaven, as a Lamb's fleece; but when a ruder breath hath forced open its virgin modesty, and dismantled its too youthful and unripe retirements, it began to put on darkness, and to decline to softness, and the symptoms of a sickly age; it bowed the head, and broke its stalk, and at night having lost some of its leaves, and all its beauty, it fell into the portion of weeds and outworn faces.[12]

As when he writes on death so too when he speaks on prayer as 'the peace of our spirit, the stillness of our thoughts, the evenness of recollection [...], the seat of meditation [...], the rest of our cares, the calm of our tempest, the issue of a quiet mind and of untroubled thoughts:'

> For so have I seen a lark rising from his bed of grass and soaring upwards sings as he rises and hopes to get to heaven, and climb above the clouds but the poor bird was beaten back with the loud sighings of an Eastern wind [...] till the little creature was forced to sit down and pant, and stay till the storm was over [...] and then did rise and sing as if it had learned music from an Angel as he passed sometimes through the air about his ministries here below.[13]

In seventeenth-century rhetorical theory the use of the *exemplum* as an ornament of style rather than a means of instruction, as in medieval theory and practice, is seen at its best in Taylor's sermons. In theory the *exemplum* is a unit of a sentence or two, complete in itself, which may be inserted into the text or removed from it, without any loss of meaning on either side. In medieval times, as in contemporary practice, the *exemplum* or story was and, unfortunately is again, an intrusion of more than a few sentences introduced into the sermon as extraneous matter in the name of relevance: on this supposition that the words of the preacher will succeed where the Word of God has failed, all becomes grist at the preacher's mill for grinding out the Word of God. Renaissance taste then, and hopefully will again, demanded better, and the wisdom of the ages, Christian and classical, was made the measure of the preacher's words. In the sermons there are references to most of the great masters with more than a hundred to the *Opera Moralia*, or essays of Plutarch on his times and their problems. But in itself the classical quotation is merely a summary remark, and is not, like the seventeenth-century *exemplum* was, an adornment of style:[14]

---

12 Ibid., p. xxxix.   13 Ibid., p. lv.   14 M.C. Albrecht, 'The Exemplum in the Sermons of Taylor,' dissertation, CUA, Washington, 1947, pp 1-16.

Philomusus was a wild young fellow in Domitian's time and he was hard put to it to make a large pension to maintain his lust and luxury, and he was every month put to beggarly arts to feed his crime. But when his Father died and left him all, he disinherited himself; he spent it all though he knew he was to suffer that trouble always, which vexed his lustful soul in the frequent periods of his violent want. Now this is a state of slavery that persons that are sensible ought to complain ... there is a lord within that rules and rages – *intus in pecore aegro pascuntur dominia* – sin dwells there, and makes a man a miserable servant.[15]

Such is the adornment of the classical *exemplum*, and biblical and patristic sources are no less resourceful:

He that had seen the Vandals besiege the city of Hippo, and had known the barbarousness of that unchristianed people, and had observed that St Austin with all his prayers and vows could not obtain peace in his own days, not so much as a reprieve for the persecution, and then had observed St Austin die with grief that very night, would have perceived his calamity more visible than the reward of his piety and holy religion.[16]

Such *exempla*, unlike the classical references, are few in number in the sermons with never more than one or two in any of them and none at all in some of them. For Taylor his poetic words, Christian and classical in their inspiration, were always at the service of the Word, moral and doctrinal, as the prophet in him speaks with the authority of Another and 'in words that seem to come from God' (1 Pet 4:11).

Apples of Sodom; or The Fruits of Sin[1]

JEREMY TAYLOR

What fruit had ye then in those things whereof ye are now ashamed? for the end of those things is death. (Rom 6:21)

The son of Sirach did prudently advise concerning making judgments of the felicity or infelicity of men, 'judge none blessed before his death, for a man shall

---

15 Ibid., p. 56.   16 Ibid., p. 63.   1 Sermons XIX, XX, XXI, in J. Taylor, vol. 4, 233-72.

be known in his children.'[2] Some men raise their fortunes from a cottage to the chairs of princes, from a sheep-cote to a throne, and dwell in the circles of the sun and in the lap of prosperity; their wishes and success dwell under the same roof, and Providence brings all events into their design, and ties both ends together with prosperous successes; and even the little conspersions and intertextures of evil accidents in their lives are but like a feigned note in music, by an artificial discord making the ear covetous, and then pleased with the harmony into which the appetite was enticed by passion and a pretty restraint; and variety does but adorn prosperity, and make it of a sweeter relish and of more advantages; and some of these men descend into their graves without a change of fortune – *eripitur persona manet res*.[3] Indeed they cannot longer dwell upon the estate, but that remains unrifled and descends upon the heir, and all is well till the next generation: but if the evil of his death, and the change of his present prosperity for an intolerable danger of an uncertain eternity, does not sour his full chalice; yet if his children prove vicious or degenerous, cursed or unprosperous, we account the man miserable, and his grave to be strewed with sorrows and dishonours. The wise and valiant Chabrias grew miserable by the folly of his son Ctesippus;[4] and the reputation of brave Germanicus began to be ashamed when the base Caligula entered upon his scene of dishonourable crimes. Commodus, the wanton and feminine son of wise Antoninus, gave a check to the great name of his father; and when the son of Hortensius Corbia[5] was prostitute, and the heir of Q. Fabius Maximus[6] was disinherited by the sentence of the city praetor as being unworthy to enter into the fields of his glorious father, and young Scipio[7] the son of Africanus was a fool and a prodigal; posterity did weep afresh over the monuments of their brave progenitors, and found that infelicity can pursue a man and overtake him in his grave.

    This is a great calamity when it falls upon innocent persons: and that Moses died upon Mount Nebo in the sight of Canaan, was not so great an evil as that his sons Eliezer and Gerson were unworthy to succeed him; but that priesthood was devolved to his brother, and the principality to his servant: and to Samuel, that his sons proved corrupt and were exauthorated for their unworthiness, was an allay to his honour and his joys, and such as proclaims to all the world that the measures of our felicity are not to be taken by the lines of our own person, but of our relations too; and he that is cursed in his children, cannot be reckoned among the fortunate.

    This which I have discoursed concerning families in general is most remarkable in the retinue and family of sin; for it keeps a good house, and is full of company and servants, it is served by the possessions of the world, it is courted by the unhappy, flattered by fools, taken into the bosom by the effeminate, made the end of human

---

2 Eccles 11:28.   3 Lucretius, *De Rerum Natura*, 3:58, LCL, p. 352.   4 Suetonius, *Lives of the Caesars*, Caligula, 11.   5 Valerius Maximus, 3:5.   6 Ibid.   7 Ibid.

designs, and feasted all the way of its progress: wars are made for its interest, and men give or venture their lives that their sin may be prosperous; all the outward senses are its handmaids, and the inward senses are of its privy-chamber; the understanding is its counsellor, the will its friend, riches are its ministers, nature holds up its train, and art is its emissary to promote its interest and affairs abroad; and upon this account, all the world is enrolled in its taxing-tables, and are subjects or friends of its kingdom, or are so kind to it as to make too often visits, and to lodge in its borders; because all men stare upon its pleasures, and are enticed to taste of its wanton delicacies. But then if we look what are the children of this splendid family, and see what issue sin produces – *esti gar tekna kai tode* – it may help to untie the charm. Sin and concupiscence marry together, and riot and feast it high, but their fruits, the children and production of their filthy union, are ugly and deformed, foolish and ill-natured; and the apostle calls them by their names, 'shame,' and 'death.' These are the fruits of sin, 'the apples of Sodom,' fair outsides, but if you touch them they turn to ashes and a stink; and if you will nurse these children, and give them whatsoever is dear to you, then you may be admitted into the house of feasting, and chambers of riot where sin dwells; but if you will have the mother, you must have the daughters; the tree and the fruits go together; and there is none of you all that ever entered into this house of pleasure, but he left the skirts of his garment in the hands of shame, and had his name rolled in the chambers of death. 'What fruit had ye then?' That's the question. In answer to which question we are to consider,

First, what is the sum total of the pleasure of sin?

Secondly, what fruits and relishes it leaves behind by its natural efficiency?

Thirdly, what are its consequents by its demerit, and the infliction of the superadded wrath of God which it hath deserved?

Of the first St Paul gives no account; but by way of upbraiding asks, 'what they had?' that is, nothing that they dare own, nothing that remains: and where is it? shew it; what's become of it?

Of the second he gives the sum total: all its natural effects are 'shame' and its appendages.

The third, or the superinduced evils by the just wrath of God, he calls 'death,' the worst name in itself and the greatest of evils that can happen.

I. Let us consider what pleasures there are in sin [...]. Sin is of so little relish and gust, so trifling a pleasure, that it is always greater in expectation than it is in the possession. But if men did beforehand see what the utmost is which sin ministers to please the beastly part of man, it were impossible it should be pursued with so much earnestness and disadvantages. It is necessary it should promise more than it can give; men could not otherwise be cozened. And if it be enquired why men should sin again after they had experience of the little and great deception, it is to be confessed it is a wonder they should: but then we may remember that men sin again though their sin did afflict them; they will be drunk again though they were sick; they will again commit folly though they be surprised in their shame, though they have needed an hospital; and therefore there is something else that moves them, and not the pleasure; for they do it without and against its interest; but either they still proceed, hoping to supply by numbers what they find not in proper measures; or God permits them to proceed as an instrument of punishment; or their understandings and reasonings grow cheaper; or they grow in love with it, and take it upon any terms; or contract new appetites, and are pleased with the baser and the lower rewards of sin: but whatsoever can be the cause of it, it is certain by the experience of all the world that the fancy is higher, the desires more sharp, and the reflection more brisk, at the door and entrance of the entertainment, than in all the little and shorter periods of its possession: for then it is but limited by the natural measures, and abated by distemper, and loathed by enjoying, and disturbed by partners, and dishonoured by shame and evil accidents; so that as men coming to the river Lucius, – *echei men leukotaton udaton kai rei dieidestata*,[8] – and seeing waters pure as the tears of the spring or the pearls of the morning, expect that in such a fair promising bosom the inmates should be fair and pleasant; *tiktei de ichthus melanas ischuros*, but find the fishes black, filthy, and unwholesome: so it is in sin, its face is fair and beauteous, softer than sleep or the dreams of wine, tenderer than the curds of milk; but when you come to handle it, it is filthy, rough as the porcupine, black as the shadows of the night, and having promised a fish it gives a scorpion, and a stone instead of bread […].

The fruits of its present possession, the pleasures of its taste, are less pleasant, because no sober person, no man that can discourse, does like it long; but he approves it in the height of passion and in the disguises of a temptation, but at all other times he finds it ugly and unreasonable, and the very remembrances must at all times abate its pleasures and sour its delicacies. In the most parts of man's life he wonders at his own folly and prodigious madness, that it should be ever possible for him to be deluded by such trifles; and he sighs next morning, and knows it over-night; and is it not therefore certain that he leans upon a thorn, which he knows will smart, and he dreads the event of to-morrow? But so have I known a bold trooper fight in the confusion of a battle, and being warm with heat and rage, received from the swords of his enemy wounds open like a grave; but he felt them not, and when by the streams of blood he found himself marked for pain, he refused to consider then what he was to feel to-morrow: but when his rage had cooled into the temper of a man, and a clammy moisture had checked

---

8 Aelian, *On the Nature of Animals*, 10:38, LCL, vol. 2, p. 334.

the fiery emission of spirits, he wonders at his own boldness, and blames his fate, and needs a mighty patience to bear his great calamity. So is the bold and merry sinner; when he is warm with wine and lust, wounded and bleeding with the strokes of hell, he twists with the fatal arm that strikes him, and cares not; but yet it must abate his gaiety, because he remembers that when his wounds are cold and considered, he must roar or perish, repent or do worse, that is, be miserable or undone. The Greeks call this 'the felicity of condemned slaves feasted high in sport;' [...] they make him a king for three days, and clothe him with royal robes, and minister to him all the pleasures he can choose,' and all the while he knows he is to die a sacrifice to mirth and folly. But then let it be remembered what checks and allays of mirth the poor man starts at, when he remembers the axe and the altar where he must shortly bleed; and by this we may understand what that pleasure is, in the midst of which the man sighs deeply when he considers what opinion he had of this sin in the days of counsel and sober thoughts; and what reason against it he shall feel to-morrow when he must weep or die. [...]

II. We have already opened this dunghill covered with snow, which was indeed on the outside white as the spots of leprosy, but it was no better; and if the very colours and instruments of deception, if the *fucus* and ceruse be so spotted and sullied, what can we suppose to be under the wrinkled skin, what in the corrupted liver, and in the sinks of the body of sin? That we are next to consider [...]; we are to consider into what an evil condition sin puts us, for which we are not only disgraced and disparaged here, marked with disgraceful punishments, despised by good men, our follies derided, our company avoided, and hooted at by boys, talked of in fairs and markets, pointed at and described by appellatives of scorn, and every body can chide us, and we die unpitied, and lie in our graves eaten up by worms and a foul dishonour; but after all this at the day of judgment we shall be called from our charnel-houses, where our disgrace could not sleep, and shall, in the face of God, in the presence of angels and devils, before all good men and all the evil, see and feel the shame of all our sins written upon our foreheads. Here in this state of misery and folly we make nothing of it; and though we dread to be discovered to men, yet to God we confess our sins without a trouble or a blush, but tell an even story, because we find some forms of confession prescribed in our prayer-books; and, that it may appear how indifferent and unconcerned we seem to be, we read and say all, and confess the sins we never did with as much sorrow and regret as those that we have acted a thousand times. But in that strange day of recompenses, we shall find the devil to upbraid the criminal, Christ to disown them, the angels to drive them from the seat of mercy, and shame to be their smart, the consigning them to damnation; they shall then find that they cannot dwell where virtue is rewarded, and where honour and glory hath a throne; there is no veil but what is rent, no excuse to any but to them that are declared as innocent: no circumstances concerning the wicked to be considered, but them that aggravate; then the disgrace is not confined to the talk of a village or a province, but is scattered to all the world: not only in one age shall the shame abide, but the men of all generations shall see and wonder at the vastness of that evil that is spread upon the souls of sinners for ever and ever [...]. No night shall then hide it; for in those regions of darkness where the dishonoured man shall dwell for ever, there is nothing visible but the shame; there is light enough for that, but darkness for all things else; and then he shall reap the full harvest of his shame: all that for which wise men scorned him, and all that for which God hated him; all that in which he was a fool, and all that in which he was malicious; that which was public, and that which was private; that which fools applauded, and that which himself durst not own; the 'secrets of his lust, and the criminal contrivances of his thoughts; the base and odious circumstances, and the frequency of the action, and the partner of his sin; all that which troubles his conscience, and all that he willingly forgets, shall be proclaimed by the trumpet of God, by the voice of an archangel, in the great congregation of spirits and just men.

III. There is one great circumstance more of the shame of sin, which extremely enlarges the evil of a sinful state, but that is not consequent to sin by a natural emanation, but is superinduced by the just wrath of God [...] as in nature, so in divinity too, there are sympathies and antipathies, effects which we feel by experience, and are forewarned of by revelation, which no natural reason can judge, nor any providence can prevent but by living innocently and complying with the commandments of God. The rod of God, which 'cometh not into the lot of the righteous,'[9] strikes the sinning man with sore strokes of vengeance [...] and this therefore is to be considered in the third part, which is next to be handled.

(a) The first that I shall note is, that which I called the aggravation of the shame of sin; and that is, an impossibility of being concealed in most cases of heinous crimes [...]. 'Let no man suppose that he shall for ever hide his sin.'[10] [...] The ancients, especially the scholars of Epicurus, believed that no man could be secured or quiet in his spirit from being discovered; 'they are not secure, even when they are safe;'[11] but are afflicted with perpetual jealousies; and every whisper is concerning them, and all new noises are arrests to their spirits; and the day is too light, and the night is too horrid, and both are the most opportune for their discovery [...].

But there are so many ways of discovery, and amongst so many some one does so certainly happen, that they are well summed up by Sophocles by saying that 'Time hears all, and tells all.'[12] A cloud may be its roof and cover till it passes over,

---

9 Ps 125:3. 10 *Isocrates*, LCL, vol. 1, p. 12. 11 Seneca, *Tragedies*, LCL, vol. 1, p. 330. 12 Clement of Alexandria, *Stromata*, 2:2, PG 8:933.

but when it is driven by a fierce wind or runs fondly after the sun, it lays open a deformity, which, like an ulcer, had a skin over it and a pain within, and drew to it a heap of sorrows big enough to run over all its enclosures. Many persons have betrayed themselves by their own fears, and knowing themselves never to be secure enough, have gone to purge themselves of what nobody suspected them; offered an apology when they had no accuser but one within, which, like a thorn in the flesh, or like 'a word in a fool's heart,'[13] was uneasy till it came out. *Non amo se nimium purgitantes*;[14] when men are over busy in justifying themselves, it is a sign themselves think they need it. Plutarch[15] tells of a young gentleman that destroyed a swallow's nest, pretending to them that reproved him for doing the thing which in their superstition the Greeks esteemed so ominous, that the little bird accused him for killing his father. And to this purpose it was that Solomon gave counsel, 'curse not the king, no, not in thy thought, nor the rich in thy bedchamber; for a bird of the air shall carry the voice, and that that hath wings shall tell the matter.'[16] [...]

(b) A second superinduced consequent of sin brought upon it by the wrath of God, is sin; when God punishes sin with sin He is extremely angry; for then the punishment is not medicinal, but final and exterminating; God in that case takes no care concerning him, though he dies, and dies eternally [...]. It was a sad calamity when God punished David's adultery by permitting him to fall to murder, and Solomon's wanton and inordinate love with the crime of idolatry, and Ananias his sacrilege with lying against the Holy Ghost, and Judas his covetousness with betraying his Lord, and that betraying with despair, and that despair with self-murder [...].

(c) Sin brings in its retinue fearful plagues and evil angels, messengers of the displeasure of God, concerning which 'there are enough of dead;'[17] I mean, the experience is so great, and the notion so common, and the examples so frequent, and the instances so sad, that there is scarce any thing new in this particular to be noted; but something is remarkable, and that is this; that God, even when He forgives the sin, does reserve such 'remains of punishment,'[18] and those not only to the less perfect but to the best persons, that it makes demonstration that every sinner is in a worse condition than he dreams of. For consider; can it be imagined that any one of us should escape better than David did? We have reason to tremble when we remember what he suffered even when God had sealed his pardon. Did not God punish Zedekiah with suffering his eyes to be put out in the house of bondage? Was not God so angry with Valentinian, that He gave him into his enemy's hand to be flayed alive? Have not many persons been struck suddenly in the very act of sin, and some been seized upon by the devil and carried away alive? These are fearful contingencies: but God hath been more

---

[13] Eccles 19:12 [14] *Plautus*, LCL, vol. 1, p. 312. [15] Plutarch, *Moralia*, LCL, vol. 7, p. 556. [16] Eccles 10:20. [17] *Euripides*, LCL, vol. 1, p. 270. [18] Col 1:24.

angry yet; rebellion was punished in Korah and his company by the gaping of the earth, and the men were buried alive [...].

[In conclusion,] it is God's appellative to be 'a giver of excellent rewards to just and innocent persons, but to assign to evil men fury, wrath, and sorrow, for their portion.' If I should launch further into this Dead sea, I should find nothing but horrid shriekings, and the skulls of dead men utterly undone. Fearful it is to consider that sin does not only drive us into calamity, but it makes us also impatient, and imbitters our spirit in the sufferance: it cries loud for vengeance, and so torments men before the time even with such fearful outcries and horrid alarms that their hell begins before the fire is kindled. It hinders our prayers, and consequently makes us hopeless and helpless. It perpetually affrights the conscience, unless by its frequent stripes it brings a callousness and an insensible damnation upon it. It makes us to lose all that which Christ purchased for us, all the blessings of His providence, the comforts of His spirit, the aids of His grace, the light of His countenance, the hopes of His glory; it makes us enemies to God, and to be hated by Him more than He hates a dog: and with a dog shall be his portion to eternal ages; with this only difference, that they shall both be equally excluded from heaven, but the dog shall not, and the sinner shall, descend into hell; and which is the confirmation of all evil, for a transient sin God shall inflict an eternal death. Well might it be said in the words of God by the prophet,[19] *Ponam Babylonem in possessionem erinacei,* – 'Babylon shall be the possession of a hedgehog;' that's a sinner's dwelling, encompassed round with thorns and sharp prickles, afflictions and uneasiness all over. So that he that wishes his sin big and prosperous, wishes his bee as big as a bull, and his hedgehog like an elephant; the pleasure of the honey would not cure the mighty sting, and nothing make recompense or be a good equal to the evil of an eternal ruin. But of this there is no end. I sum up all with the saying of Publius Mimus – *Tolerabilior est qui mori jubet, quam qui male vivere,* 'he is more to be endured that puts a man to death than he that betrays him into sin;' for the end of this is 'death eternal.'

---

[19] Is 14:23.

The House of Feasting; or The Epicure's Measures [1]

JEREMY TAYLOR

Let us eat and drink, for to-morrow we die. (1 Cor 15:32)

This is the epicure's proverb, begun upon a weak mistake, started by chance from the discourse of drink, and thought witty by the undiscerning company; and prevailed infinitely, because it struck their fancy luckily, and maintained the merry meeting; but as it happens commonly to such discourses, so this also, when it comes to be examined by the consultations of the morning and the sober hours of the day, it seems the most witless and the most unreasonable in the world. When Seneca describes[2] the spare diet of Epicurus and Metrodorus, he uses this expression, *Liberaliora sunt alimenta carceris; sepositos ad capitale supplicium non tam anguste qui occisurus est pascit,* 'The prison keeps a better table, and he that is to kill the criminal tomorrow morning, gives him a better supper overnight.' By this he intended to represent his meal to be very short; for as dying persons have but little stomach to feast high, so they that mean to cut their throat will think it a vain expense to please it with delicacies which, after the first alteration, must be poured upon the ground, and looked upon as the worst part of the accursed thing. And there is also the same proportion of unreasonableness, that because men shall 'die to-morrow,' and by the sentence and unalterable decree of God they are now descending to their graves, that therefore they should first destroy their reason, and then force dull time to run faster, that they may die sottish as beasts, and speedily as a fly: but they thought there was no life after this; or if there were, it was without pleasure, and every soul thrust into a hole, and a dorter of a span's length allowed for his rest, and for his walk; and in the shades below no numbering of healths by the numeral letters of Philenium's name, no fat mullets, no oysters of Lucrinus, no Lesbian or Chian wines [...]. Therefore now enjoy the delicacies of nature, and feel the descending wines distilled through the limbeck of thy tongue and larynx, and suck the delicious juices of fishes, the marrow of the laborious ox, and the tender lard of Apulian swine, and the condited bellies of the *scarus;* but lose no time, for the sun drives hard, and the shadow is long, and 'the days of mourning are at hand,' but the number of the days of darkness and the grave cannot be told.

Thus they thought they discoursed wisely, and their wisdom was turned into folly; for all their arts of providence, and witty securities of pleasure, were nothing but unmanly prologues to death, fear, and folly, sensuality and beastly pleasures.

---

1 Sermons XV, XVI, in J. Taylor, vol. 4, pp 180-206.   2 Seneca, *Epistulae Morales*, LCL, vol. 1, p. 116.

But they are to be excused rather than we. They placed themselves in the order of beasts and birds, and esteemed their bodies nothing but receptacles of flesh and wine, larders and pantries, and their souls the fine instrument of pleasure and brisk perception of relishes and gusts, reflexions and duplications of delight; and therefore they treated themselves accordingly. But then, why we should do the same things, who are led by other principles, and a more severe institution, and better notices of immortality, who understand what shall happen to a soul hereafter, and know that this time is but a passage to eternity, this body but a servant to the soul, this soul a minister to the spirit, and the whole man in order to God and to felicity; this, I say, is more unreasonable than to eat *aconita* to preserve our health, and to enter into the flood that we may die a dry death; this is a perfect contradiction to the state of good things whither we are designed, and to all the principles of a wise philosophy whereby we are instructed that we may become 'wise unto salvation.' That I may therefore do some assistances towards the curing the miseries of mankind, and reprove the follies and improper motions towards felicity, I shall endeavour to represent to you,

1. That plenty and the pleasures of the world are no proper instruments of felicity.
2. That intemperance is a certain enemy to it; making life unpleasant, and death troublesome and intolerable.
3. I shall add the rules and measures of temperance in eating and drinking, that nature and grace may join to the constitution of man's felicity.

I. Plenty and the pleasures of the world are no proper instruments of felicity. It is necessary that a man have some violence done to himself, before he can receive them: for nature's bounds are, *non esurire, non sitire, non algere,* 'to be quit from hunger, and thirst, and cold,' that is, to have nothing upon us that puts us to pain; against which she hath made provisions by the fleece of the sheep and the skins of beasts, by the waters of the fountain and the herbs of the field, and of these no good man is destitute for that share that he can need to fill those appetites and necessities he cannot otherwise avoid; *ton arkounton oudeis penes esti.*[3] For it is unimaginable that nature should be a mother natural and indulgent to the beasts of the forest and the spawn of fishes, to every plant and fungus, to cats and owls, to moles and bats, making her storehouses always to stand open to them; and that for the lord of all these, even to the noblest of her productions, she should have made no provisions, and only produced in us appetites sharp as the stomach of wolves, troublesome as the tiger's hunger, and then run away, leaving art and chance, violence and study, to feed us and

---

3 Plutarch, *Moralia*, LCL, vol. 7, p.5.

to clothe us. This is so far from truth, that we are certainly more provided for by nature than all the world besides; for every thing can minister to us, and we can pass into none of nature's cabinets but we can find our table spread; so that what David said to God, 'Whither shall I go from Thy presence? If I go to heaven, Thou art there; if I descend to the deep, Thou art there also; if I take the wings of the morning, and flee into the uttermost parts of the wilderness, even there Thou wilt find me out, and Thy right hand shall uphold me,'[4] we may say it concerning our table and our wardrobe; if we go into the fields, we find them tilled by the mercies of heaven, and watered with showers from God, to feed us, and to clothe us; if we go down into the deep, there God hath multiplied our stores, and filled a magazine which no hunger can exhaust; the air drops down delicacies, and the wilderness can sustain us, and all that is in nature, that which feeds lions and that which the ox eats, that which the fishes live upon and that which is the provision for the birds, all that can keep us alive; and if we consider that of the beasts and birds, for whom nature hath provided but one dish, it may be flesh or fish, or herbs or flies, and these also we secure with guards from them, and drive away birds and beasts from that provision which nature made for them, yet seldom can we find that any of these perish with hunger: much rather shall we find that we are secured by the securities proper for the more noble creatures, by that providence that disposes all things, by that mercy that gives us all things which to other creatures are ministered singly, by that labour that can procure what we need, by that wisdom that can consider concerning future necessities, by that power that can force it from inferior creatures, and by that temperance which can fit our meat to our necessities. For if we go beyond that is needful, as we find sometimes more than was promised, and very often more than we need, so we disorder the certainty of our felicity, by putting that to a hazard which nature hath secured. For it is not certain that if we desire to have the wealth of Susa, or garments stained with the blood of the Tyrian fish, that if we desire to feed like Philoxenus, or to have tables loaden like the boards of Vitellius, that we shall never want. It is not nature that desires these things, but lust and violence; and by a disease we entered into the passion and the necessity, and in that state of trouble it is likely we may dwell for ever, unless we reduce our appetites to nature's measures [...] And therefore it is, that plenty and pleasures are not the proper instruments of felicity: because felicity is not a jewel that can be locked in one man's cabinet; God intended that all men should be made happy, and He that gave to all men the same natural desires, and to all men provision of satisfactions by the same meats and drinks, intended that it should not go beyond that measure of good things which corresponds to those desires which all men naturally have [...].

4 Ps 139:7ff.

If men did but know what felicity dwells in the cottage of a virtuous poor man, how sound his sleeps, how quiet his breast, how composed his mind, how free from care, how easy his provision, how healthful his morning, how sober his night, how moist his mouth, how joyful his heart, they would never admire the noises and the diseases, the throng of passions and the violence of unnatural appetites, that fill the houses of the luxurious and the heart of the ambitious. *Nam neque divitibus contingunt gaudia solis*;[5] these which you call pleasures are but the imagery and fantastic appearances, and such appearances even poor men may have. It is like felicity that the king of Persia should come to Babylon in the winter, and to Susa in the summer; and be attended with all the servants of a hundred and twenty-seven provinces, and with all the princes of Asia.[6] It is like this, that Diogenes went to Corinth in the time of vintage, and to Athens when winter came; and instead of courts, visited the temples and the schools, and was pleased in the society of scholars and learned men, and conversed with the students of all Asia and Europe. If a man loves privacy, the poor fortune can have that when princes cannot; if he loves noises, he can go to markets and to courts, and may glut himself with strange faces, and strange voices, and stranger manners, and the wild designs of all the world: and when that day comes in which we shall die, nothing of the eating and drinking remains, nothing of the pomp and luxury, but the sorrow to part with it, and shame to have dwelt there where wisdom and virtue seldom comes, unless it be to call men to sober counsels, to a plain, and a severe, and more natural way of living; and when Lucian[7] derides the dead princes and generals [...], he intended to represent that in the shades below and in the state of the grave the princes and voluptuous have a being different from their present plenty [...].

II. Intemperance in eating and drinking is the most contrary course to the epicure's design in the world, and the voluptuous man hath the least of pleasure; and upon this proposition the consideration is more material and more immediately reducible to practice, because in eating and drinking men please themselves so much, and have the necessities of nature to usher in the inordination of gluttony and drunkenness, and our need leads in vice by the hand, that we know not how to distinguish our friend from our enemy; and St Austin is sad upon this point; 'Thou, O Lord, hast taught me that I should take my meat as I take my physic;'[8] but while I pass from the trouble of hunger to the quietness of satisfaction, in the very passage I am ensnared by the cords of my own concupiscence. Necessity bids me pass, but I have no way to pass from hunger to fulness, but over the bridge of pleasure; and although health and life be the cause of eating and drinking, yet pleasure, a dangerous pleasure, thrusts herself into attendance, and sometimes endeavours to be

---

5 Horace, *Epigrams*, 1:17:9.   6 Plutarch, *Moralia*, LCL, vol. 6, p.18.   7 Lucian, cf. Baldry, *Greek Literature for the Modern Reader*, pp 284-5.   8 Augustine, *Confessions*, 10:3, PL 32:797.

the principal, and I do that for pleasure's sake which I would only do for health. And yet they have distinct measures whereby they can be separated, and that which is enough for health is too little for delight, and that which is for my delight destroys my health, and still it is uncertain for what end I do indeed desire; and the worst of the evil is this, that the soul is glad because it is uncertain, and that an excuse is ready, that under the pretence of health *obumbret negotium voluptatis*, 'the design of pleasure may be advanced and protected.' [...] If we remember that the epicure's design is pleasure principally, we may the better reprove his folly by considering that intemperance is a plain destruction to all that which can give real and true pleasure [...].

First, it is an enemy to health, without which it is impossible to feel any thing of corporal pleasure; secondly, a constant full table hath in it less pleasure than the temperate provisions of the hermit or the labourer, or the philosophical table of scholars, and the just pleasures of the virtuous; thirdly, intemperance is an impure fountain of vice, and a direct nurse of uncleanness; fourthly, it is a destruction of wisdom; fifthly, it is a dishonour and disreputation to the person and the nature of the man [...].

Intemperance is indeed a perfect destruction of wisdom; 'a full-gorged belly never produced a sprightly mind:' and therefore these kind of men are called *gasteres argai*, 'slow bellies,'[9] so St Paul concerning the intemperate Cretians out of their own poet: they are like the tigers of Brazil, which when they are empty are bold and swift and full of sagacity; but being full, sneak away from the barking of a village dog. So are these men, wise in the morning, quick and fit for business; but when the sun gives the sign to spread the tables, and intemperance brings in the messes, and drunkenness fills the bowls, then the man falls away, and leaves a beast in his room; nay worse, *nekuas mesauchenas*, they are dead all but their throat and belly, so Aristophanes hath fitted them with a character, 'carcasses above half way.' Plotinus[10] descends one step lower yet, affirming such persons *apodendrothenai* they are made trees, whose whole employment and life is nothing but to feed and suck juices from the bowels of their nurse and mother; and indeed commonly they talk as trees in a wind and tempest; the noise is great and querulous, but it signifies nothing but trouble and disturbance. A full meal is like Sisera's[11] banquet, at the end of which there is a nail struck into a man's head; 'it knocks a man down, and nails his soul to the sensual mixtures of the body,' so Porphyry. For what wisdom can be expected from them whose soul dwells in clouds of meat, and floats up and down in wine, like the spilled cups which fell from their hands when they could lift them to their heads no longer?[...] It is a perfect shipwreck of a man, the pilot is drunk, and the helm dashed in pieces, and the ship first reels, and by swallowing too much is itself swallowed up at last. And therefore the *Navis Agrigentina*, the madness of the young

9 Tit 1:12   10 Plotinus, *Enneads*, 4:2, LCL, vol. 3, p.144.   11 Judg 4:21.

fellows of Agrigentum, who, being drunk, fancied themselves in a storm, and the house the ship, was more than the wild fancy of their cups; it was really so, they were all cast away, they were broken in pieces by the foul disorder of the storm [...].

So have I seen the eye of the world looking upon a fenny bottom, and drinking up too free draughts of moisture, gathered them into a cloud, and that cloud crept about his face, and made him first look red, and then covered him with darkness and an artificial night: so is our reason at a feast; the clouds gather about the head, and according to the method and period of the children and productions of darkness, it first grows red, and that redness turns into an obscurity and a thick mist, and reason is lost to all use and profitableness of wise and sober discourses; 'a cloud of folly and distraction darkens the soul,'[12] and makes it crass and material, polluted and heavy, clogged and loaden like the body; and there cannot be anything said worse; reason turns into folly, wine and flesh into a knot of clouds, 'the soul itself into a body,' and the spirit into corrupted meat; there is nothing left but the rewards and portions of a fool to be reaped and enjoyed there where flesh and corruption shall dwell to eternal ages. And therefore in scripture such men are called *barukardioi*[13] – their heads are gross, their souls are immerged in matter, and drowned in the moistures of an unwholesome cloud; they are dull of hearing, slow in apprehension, and to action they are as unable as the hands of a child who too hastily hath broken the enclosures of his first dwelling. [...]

III. And now that I have told you the foulness of the epicure's feasts and principles, it will be fit that I describe the measures of our eating and drinking, that the needs of nature may neither become the cover to an intemperate dish, nor the freer refreshment of our persons be changed into scruples, that neither our virtue nor our conscience fall into an evil snare.

(a) The first measure of our eating and drinking, is our natural needs [...]. Hunger and thirst and cold are the natural diseases of the body; and food and raiment are their remedies, and therefore are the measures [...]. But, this hunger must be natural, not artificial and provoked; for many men make necessities to themselves, and then think they are bound to provide for them. It is necessary to some men to have garments made of the Calabrian fleece, stained with the blood of the murex, and to get money to buy pearls round and orient; but it is the man's luxury that made it so; and by the same principle it is that in meats what is abundant to nature is defective and beggarly to art; and when nature willingly rises from table, when the first course of flesh plain and natural is done, then art, and sophistry, and adulterate dishes, invite him to taste and die [...].

(b) Reason is the second measure, or rather the rule whereby we judge of intemperance; for whatsoever loads of meat and drink make the reason useless or

---

12 Clement of Alexandria, *Paidagogos*, 2:2 = FOTC, vol. 23, pp 93-198. 13 Ps 4:2, LXX.

troubled are effects of this deformity. Not that reason is the adequate measure, for a man may be intemperate upon other causes, though he do not force his understanding, and trouble his head; some are strong to drink, and can eat like a wolf, and love to do so, as fire to destroy the stubble;[14] these persons are to take their accounts from the measures of religion and the Spirit: though they can talk still or transact the affairs of the world, yet if they be not fitted for the things of the Spirit, they are too full of flesh or wine, and cannot or care not to attend to the things of God. But reason is the limit beyond which temperance never wanders; and in every degree in which our discourse is troubled, and our soul is lifted from its wheels, in the same degree the sin prevails [...].

(c) Though reason be so strictly to be preserved at our tables as well as at our prayers, and we can never have leave to do any violence to it; yet the measures of nature may be enlarged beyond the bounds of prime and common necessity. For besides hunger and thirst, there are some labours of the body, and others of the mind, and there are sorrows and loads upon the spirit by its communications with the indispositions of the body; and as the labouring man may be supplied with bigger quantities, so the student and contemplative man with more delicious and spriteful nutriment: for as the tender and more delicate easily digested meats will not help to carry burdens upon the neck, and hold the plough in society and yokes of the laborious oxen; so neither will the pulse and the leeks, Lavinian sausages, and the Cisalpine suckets or gobbets of condited bull's-flesh, minister such delicate spirits to the thinking man; but his notion will be as flat as the noise of the Arcadian porter, and thick as the first juice of his country lard, unless he makes his body a fit servant to the soul, and both fitted for the employment. But in these cases necessity and prudence and experience are to make the measures and the rule [...].

To sum up this particular; there are, as you perceive, many cautions to make our pleasure safe, but any thing can make it inordinate, and then scarce any thing can keep it from becoming dangerous, and the pleasure of the honey will not pay for the smart of the sting; [...]. for this is the law of our nature and fatal necessity; life is always poured forth from two goblets [...].[15]

That which I deplore is, that some men prefer a cause before their life, and yet prefer wine before that cause, and by one drunken meeting set it more backward in its hopes and blessings than it can be set forward by the counsels and arms of a whole year [...]. Much safer it is to go to the severities of a watchful and a sober life; for all that time of life is lost, when wine, and rage, and pleasure, and folly, steal away the heart of a man, and make him go singing to his grave.

I end with the saying of a wise man, 'He is fit to sit at the table of the Lord, and to feast with saints, who moderately uses the creatures which God hath given

14 Is 5:22. 15 Synesius of Cyrene, Hymns, 663ff. = PG 66, 1587-1616.

him; but he that despises even lawful pleasures, shall not only sit and feast with God, but reign together with Him, and partake of His glorious kingdom.'[16]

The Good and Evil Tongue[1]

JEREMY TAYLOR

Let no corrupt communication proceed out of your mouth, but that which is good to the use of edifying, that it may minister grace unto the hearers. (Eph 4:29)

He that had an ill memory did wisely comfort himself by reckoning the advantages he had by his forgetfulness. For by this means he was hugely secured against malice, and ambition: for his anger went off with the short notice and observation of the injury; and he saw himself unfit for the businesses of other men, or to make records in his head, and undertake to conduct the intrigues of affairs of a multitude, who was apt to forget the little accounts of his own seldom reading [...]. Besides these, it brought him to tell truth for fear of shame, and in mere necessity made his speech little and his discourses short; because the web drawn from his brain was soon spun out, and his fountain grew quickly dry, and left running through forgetfulness.

   He that is not eloquent and fair-spoken hath some of these comforts to plead in excuse of his ill fortune or defective nature. For if he can but hold his peace, he shall be sure not to be troublesome to his company, not marked for lying, or become tedious with multiplicity of idle talk; he shall be presumed wise, and oftentimes is so; he shall not feel the wounds of contention, nor be put to excuse an ill-taken saying, nor sigh for the folly of an irrecoverable word; if his fault be that he hath not spoken, that can at any time be mended, but if he sinned in speaking, it cannot be unspoken again. Thus he escapes the dishonour of not being believed, and the trouble of being suspected: he shall never fear the sentence of judges nor the decrees of courts, high reproaches, or the angry words of the proud, the contradiction of the disputing man, or the thirst of talkers. By these and many other advantages he that holds his peace, and he that cannot speak, may please themselves; and he may at least have the rewards and effects of solitariness, if he misses some of the pleasures of society. But by the use of the tongue God hath distinguished us from beasts, and by the well or

---

16 *Epictetus*, LCL, vol. 2, p. 498. 1 Sermons XXII, XXIII, XXIV, XXV, in J. Taylor, vol. 4, pp 273–320.

ill using it we are distinguished from one another; and therefore though silence be innocent as death, harmless as a rose's breath to a distant passenger, yet it is rather the state of death than life; and therefore when the Egyptians sacrificed to Harpocrates, their god of silence, in the midst of their rites they cried out, *glossa daimon*, 'the tongue is an angel,'[2] good or bad, that's as it happens; silence was to them a god, but the tongue is greater; it is the band of human intercourse, and makes men apt to unite in societies and republics. And I remember what one of the ancients said;[3] that we are better in the company of a known dog, than of a man whose speech is not known; ut *externus alieno non sit hominis vice* 'a stranger to a stranger in his language is not as a man to a man;'[4] for by voices and homilies, by questions and answers, by narratives and invectives, by counsel and reproof, by praises and hymns, by prayers and glorifications, we serve God's glory, and the necessities of men; and by the tongue our tables are made to differ from mangers, our cities from deserts, our churches from herds of beasts and flocks of sheep. 'Faith comes by hearing, and hearing by the word of God'[5] spoken by the tongues of men and angels; and the blessed spirits in heaven cease not from saying night and day their *Trisagion*, their song of glory 'to Him that sitteth on the throne, and to the Lamb, for ever and ever;'[6] and then our employment shall be glorious as our state, when our tongues shall to eternal ages sing hallelujahs to their Maker and Redeemer. And therefore since nature hath taught us to speak, and God requires it, and our thankfulness obliges us, and our necessities engage us, and charity sometimes calls for it, and innocence is to be defended, and we are to speak in the cause of the oppressed, and open our mouths in the cause of God, and it is always a seasonable prayer that God would open our lips, that our mouth may do the work of heaven, and declare His praises, and shew forth His glory, it concerns us to take care that nature be changed into grace, necessity into choice, that while we speak the greatness of God, and minister to the needs of our neighbour, and do the works of life and religion, of society and prudence, we may be fitted to bear a part in the songs of angels when they shall rejoice at the feast of the marriage-supper of the Lamb. But the tongue is a fountain both of bitter waters and of pleasant; it sends forth blessing and cursing; it praises God and rails at men; it is sometimes set on fire, and then it puts whole cities in combustion; it is unruly, and no more to be restrained than the breath of a tempest; it is volatile and fugitive: reason should go before it, and when it does not, repentance comes after it; it was intended for an organ of the divine praises, but the devil often plays upon it, and then it sounds like the screech-owl or the groans of death; sorrow and shame, folly and repentance, are the notes and formidable accents of that discord. We all are naturally *logophiloi*, 'lovers of speech,' more or less; and God

2 Plutarch, *Moralia*, LCL, vol. 5, p. 6.   3 Augustine, *The City of God*, 19,7 = FOTC 8.   4 Pliny, *Natural History*, 7:1, LCL, vol. 2, p. 506.   5 Rom 10:17.   6 Rev 5:13.

reproves it not, provided that we be also *philologoi*, wise and material, useful and prudent, in our discourses. For since speech is for conversation, let it be also charitable and profitable, let it be without sin, but not without profit and grace to the hearers, and then it is as God would have it; and this is the precept of the text, first telling us what we should avoid, and then telling us what we should pursue; what our discourse ought not to be, and secondly what it ought to be. There being no more variety in the structure of the words, I shall discourse,

First, of the vices of the tongue;

Secondly, of its duty and proper employment.

I. 'Let no corrupt communication proceed out of your mouth;' *pas sapros logos*, 'corrupt' or 'filthy communication;' so we read it [...]; but the word which the apostle uses means more than this [...]; it signifies 'musty, rotten, and out-worn with age;' [...] language proceeding from our old iniquity, evil habits, or unworthy customs, called in the style of scripture 'the remains of the old man,' and by the Greeks, 'doting' or 'talking fondly;' 'the boy talks like an old dotard.' Secondly, *sapros* signifies 'wicked or reproachful;' 'any thing that is in its own nature criminal and disgraceful, any language that ministers to mischief.' But thirdly, it is worse than all this: it is a 'deletery,' and 'extinction' of all good; it is 'a destruction, an entire corruption,' of all morality; and to this sense is that of Menander, quoted by St Paul, 'evil words corrupt good manners.' And therefore under this word is comprised, all the evil of the tongue, that wicked instrument of the unclean spirit, in the capacity of all the appellatives; –

(a) Here is forbidden the useless, vain, and trifling conversation, the *Beelzeboul*, 'the god of flies,' so is the devil's name; he rules by these little things, by trifles and vanity, by idle and useless words, by the entercourse of a vain conversation.

(b) The devil is *diabolos*, 'an accuser of the brethren,' and the calumniating, slandering, undervaluing, detracting tongue does his work; that's *logos aischros*, the second that I named; for it is 'slander, hatred, and calumny.'

(c) But the third is *apolluon*, the devil's most appellative, 'the destroyer', the dissolute, wanton, tempting, destroying conversation; and its worst instance of all is flattery, that malicious, cozening devil, that strengthens our friend in sin, and ruins him from whom we have received, and from whom we expect good. Of these in order:

(a) The first part of this inordination is *multiloquium*, 'talking too much;' [...] and indeed there are some persons so full of nothings, that like the straight sea of Pontus they perpetually empty themselves by their mouth, making every company or single person they fasten on to be their Propontis; such a one as was Anaximenes, he was 'an ocean of words, but a drop of understanding' [...]. But this thing is considerable to further issues; for though no man can say, that much speaking is a sin, yet the scripture says, *In multiloquio peccatum non deerit*,[7] sin goes along with it, and is an ingredient in the whole composition [...]. Some talk themselves into anger, and some furnish out their dialogues with the lives of others; either they detract, or censure, or they flatter themselves, and tell their own stories with friendly circumstances, and pride creeps up the sides of the discourse; and the man entertains his friend with his own panegyric; or the discourse looks one way and rows another, and more minds the design than its own truth; and most commonly will be so ordered that it shall please the company, and that truth or honest plainness seldom does [...]. Like soothsayers, men speak fine words to serve ends, and then they are not believed, or at last are found liars, and such discourses are built up to serve the ministries or pleasures of the company, but nothing else. Pride and flattery, malice and spite, self-love and vanity, these usually wait upon much speaking; and the reward of it is, that the persons grow contemptible and troublesome, they engage in quarrels, and are troubled to answer exceptions; some will mistake them and some will not believe them, and it will be impossible that the mind should be perpetually present to a perpetual talker, but they will forget truth and themselves, and their own relations [...].

(b) Let no calumny, no slandering, detracting communication proceed out of your mouth [...]. This crime is a conjugation of evils, and is productive of infinite mischiefs; it undermines peace, and saps the foundation of friendship; it destroys families, and rends in pieces the very heart and vital parts of chairty; it makes an evil man party, and witness, and judge, and executioner of the innocent, who is hurt though he deserved it not; and no man's interest nor reputation, no man's peace or safety can abide, where this nurse of jealousy and parent of contention, like the earwig, creeps in at the ear, and makes a diseased noise and scandalous murmur.

But such tongues as these, where they dare and where they can safely, love to speak louder, and then it is 'detraction;' when men under the colour of friendship will certainly wound the reputation of a man, while by speaking some things of him fairly he shall without suspicion be believed when he speaks evil of him; such was he that Horace[8] speaks of, 'Capitolinus is my friend, and we have long lived together, and obliged each other by mutual endearments, and I am glad he is acquitted by the criminal judges; yet I confess I wonder how he should escape; but I'll say no more, because he is my friend.' 'This is a new way of accusation, to destroy a man by praises,' says Polybius.[9] These men strike obliquely, like a wild swine, or 'like bulls in a yoke, they have horns upon their necks,' and do you a mischief when they plough your ground; and, as Joab slew Abner, he took him by the beard and kissed him, and smote him under the fifth rib that he died; so

---

[7] Prov 10:19.   [8] Horace, *Satires*, 1:4:96.   [9] Polybius, 4:87, LCL, vol. 2, p. 506.

doth the detracting tongue, like the smooth-tongued lightning, it will break your bones when it kisses the flesh; so Syphax[10] did secretly wound Masinissa, and made Scipio watchful and implacable against Sophonisba, only by commending her beauty and her wit, her constance and unalterable love to her country, and by telling how much himself was forced to break his faith by the tyranny of her prevailing charms. This is that which the apostle calls *ponerian*, a crafty and deceitful way of hurting, and renders a man's tongue venomous as the tongue of a serpent that bites even though he be charmed [...]. This is the direct murder of the tongue, for 'Life and death are in the hand of the tongue,' said the Hebrew proverb [...].[11]

(c) I am now to instance in the third sort of filthy communication, that in which the devil does the most mischief; by which he undoes souls; by which he is worse than *diabolos*, 'an accuser:' for though he accuses maliciously, and instances spitefully, and heaps objections diligently, and aggravates bitterly, and with all his powers endeavours to represent the separate souls to God as polluted and unfit to come into His presence, yet this malice is ineffective, because the scenes are acted before the wise Judge of men and angels who cannot be abused; before our Father and our Lord, who knows whereof we be made, and remembereth that we are but dust; before our Saviour and our elder brother, who hath felt our infirmities, and knows how to pity, to excuse, and to answer for us: but though this accusation of us cannot hurt them who will not hurt themselves, yet this malice is prevailing when the spirit of flattery is let forth upon us. This is the *apolluon*, 'the destroyer,' and is the most contrary thing to charity in the whole world: and St Paul noted it in his character of charity,[12] 'charity vaunteth not itself;' so we translate it, but certainly not exactly, for it signifieth 'easiness,' 'complying foolishly,' and 'flattering;' 'charity flattereth not;' 'it signifies any thing that serves rather for ornament than for use, for pleasure than for profit,' saith Suidas, out of St Basil [...].[13]

Some flatter by giving great names and propounding great examples; and thus the Egyptian villains hung a tumbler's rope upon their prince, and a piper's whistle, because they called their Ptolemy by the name of Apollo, their god of music [...]. Others flatter by imitation [...]; the flattering man doing the vice of his lord takes off the wonder, and the fear of being stared at; and so encourages it by making it popular and common. Plutarch[14] tells of one that divorced himself from his wife because his friend did so, that the other might be hardened in the mischief; and when Plato[15] saw his scholars stoop in the shoulders, and Aristotle observed his to stammer, they began to be less troubled with those imperfections which they thought common to themselves and others [...].

I only add this advice; that since self-love is the serpent's milk that feeds this viper, flattery, we should do well to choke it with its mother's milk; I mean, learn

---

10 Livy, 30:13, LCL, vol. 8, p. 410. 11 Prov 18:21. 12 1 Cor 13:4. 13 Basil, *Regulae brevis tractatae* (Short Rules) = PG 31:1080-1305. 14 Plutarch, *Moralia*. 15 Ibid.

to love ourselves more, for then we should never endure to be flattered. For he that because he loves himself loves to be flattered, does because he loves himself love to entertain a man to abuse him, to mock him, and to destroy him finally. But he that loves himself truly, will suffer fire, will endure to be burnt, so he may be purified; put to pain, so he may be restored to health; for 'of all sauces,' said Evenus, sharpness, severity, and 'fire, is the best.'[16] [...]

II. 'Men teach us to speak, and God teaches us to hold our tongue;'[17] the first we are taught by the lectures of our schools, the latter by the mysteries of the temple. But now in the new institution we have also a great master of speaking; and though silence is one of the great paths of innocence, yet holy speaking is the instrument of spiritual charity, and is a glorification of God; and therefore this kind of speaking is a degree of perfection beyond the wisdom and severity of silence; [...] the first goes to a good school, but the second is proceeded towards greater perfection; [...] and going to heaven by religion and charity, by serving God and converting souls, is better than going to heaven by prayers and secret thoughts. So it is with silence and religious communication; that does not offend God, this glorifies Him: that prevents sin, this sets forward the interests of religion. And therefore Plutarch[18] said well, 'to be taught first to be silent, then to speak well and handsomely, is education for a prince;' and that is St Paul's method here: first we were taught how to restrain our tongues in the foregoing instances, and now we are called to employ them in religion.

We must speak, 'that which is good': so our text [...]. And here the measures of God are especially by the proportions of our neighbour: and therefore though speaking honourable things of God be an employment that does honour to our tongues and voices, yet we must tune and compose even these notes so as may best profit our neighbour; for so it must be 'good speech', such as is 'for the edification of necessity:'[...] that is, that we so order our communication that it be apt to instruct the ignorant, to strengthen the weak, to recall the wandered, to restrain the vicious, to comfort the disconsolate, so speak a word in season to every man's necessity, 'that it may minister grace;' something that may please and profit them according as they shall need. All which I shall reduce to these three heads; –

(a) To instruct. (b) To comfort. (c) To reprove

(a) Our conversation must be *didaktitos*, 'apt to teach' [...]. Here therefore we must remember that it is the duty of us all in our several measures and proportions to instruct those that need it, and whose necessity is made ready for our ministration; and let us tremble to think what will be the sad account which we shall make when even our families are not taught in the fundamentals of religion: for how can it be possible for those who could not account concerning the stories of Christ's life and death, the ministries of their redemption, the foundation of all their hopes, the great

---

16 Ibid.   17 Plutarch, *Moralia*, LCL, vol. 6.   18 Plutarch, *Moralia*.

argument of all their obediences; how can it be expected that they should ride in triumph over all the evils which the devil, and the world, and their own follies, daily present to them in the course of every day's conversation? And it will be an ill return to say that God will require no more of them than He hath given them; for suppose that be true in your own sense, yet He will require it of thee, because thou gavest them no more; and however, it is a formidable danger, and a trifling hope, for any man to put all the hopes of his being saved upon the only stock of ignorance; for if his ignorance should never be accounted for, yet it may leave him in that state in which his evils shall grow great, and his sins may be irremediable.

(b) Our conversation must be *parakletos*, 'apt to comfort' the disconsolate: and than this men in present can feel no greater charity: for since half the duty of a Christian in this life consists in the exercise of passive graces, and the infinite variety of providence, and the perpetual adversity of chances, and the dissatisfaction and emptiness that is in things themselves, and the weariness and anguish of our spirit, does call us to the trial and exercise of patience even in the days of sunshine, and much more in the violent storms that shake our dwellings and make our hearts tremble; God hath sent some angels into the world whose office it is to refresh the sorrows of the poor and to lighten the eyes of the disconsolate; He hath made some creatures whose powers are chiefly ordained to comfort; wine, and oil, and society, cordials, and variety; and time itself is checkered with black and white; stay but till to-morrow, and your present sorrow will be weary and will lie down to rest. But this is not all: the third person of the holy Trinity is known to us by the name and dignity of the 'Holy Ghost, the Comforter;' and God glories in the appellative that He is 'the Father of mercies, and the God of all comfort;' and therefore to minister in the office is to become like God, and to imitate the charities of heaven.

And God hath fitted mankind for it: he most needs it, and he feels his brother's wants by his own experience; and God hath given us speech, and the endearments of society, and pleasantness of conversation, and powers of seasonable discourse, arguments to allay the sorrow by abating our apprehensions and taking out the sting or telling the periods of comfort, or exciting hope, or urging a precept, and reconciling our affections, and reciting promises, or telling stories of the divine mercy, or changing it into duty, or making the burden less by comparing it with greater, or by proving it to be less than we deserve, and that it is so intended, and may become the instrument of virtue. And certain it is that as nothing can better do it, so there is nothing greater for which God made our tongues, next to reciting His praises, than to minister comfort to a weary soul. And what greater measure can we have than that we should bring joy to our brother, who with his dreary eyes looks to heaven and round about, and cannot find so much rest as to lay his eyelids close together; than that thy tongue should be tuned with heavenly accents, and make the weary soul to listen for light and ease, and when he perceives that there is such a thing in the world and in the order of things as comfort and joy, to begin to break out from the prison of his sorrows at the door of sighs and tears, and by little and little melt into showers and refreshment?

This is glory to thy voice, and employment fit for the brightest angel. But so have I seen the sun kiss the frozen earth which was bound up with the images of death and the colder breath of the north; and then the waters break from their enclosures, and melt with joy, and run in useful channels; and the flies do rise again from their little graves in walls, and dance awhile in the air to tell that there is joy within, and that the great mother of creatures will open the stock of her new refreshment, become useful to mankind, and sing praises to her Redeemer: so is the heart of a sorrowful man under the discourses of a wise comforter; he breaks from the despairs of the grave and the fetters and chains of sorrow; he blesses God, and he blesses thee, and he feels his life returning; for to be miserable is death, but nothing is life but to be comforted; and God is pleased with no music from below so much as in the thanksgiving songs of relieved widows, of supported orphans, of rejoicing, and comforted, and thankful persons.

This part of communication does the work of God and of our neighbours, and bears us to heaven in streams of joy made by the overflowings of our brother's comfort. It is a fearful thing to see a man despairing; none knows the sorrow and the intolerable anguish but themselves, and they that are damned; and so are all the loads of a wounded spirit when the staff of a man's broken fortune bows his head to the ground, and sinks like an osier under the violence of a mighty tempest: but therefore in proportion to this I may tell the excellency of the employment, and the duty of that charity, which bears the dying and languishing soul from the fringes of hell to the seat of the brightest stars, where God's face shines and reflects comforts for ever and ever. And though God hath for this especially intrusted His ministers and servants of the church, and hath put into their hearts and notices great magazines of promises, and arguments of hope, and arts of the Spirit, yet God does not always send angels on these embassies, but sends a man, *ut sit homo homini deus,* 'that every good man in his season may be to his brother in the place of God,' to comfort and restore him; and that it may appear how much it is the duty of us all to minister comfort to our brother, we may remember, that the same words and the same arguments do oftentimes more prevail upon our spirits when they are applied by the hand of another, than when they dwell in us and come from our own discoursings. This is indeed *logos chrestos and agathos,* it is *eis oikodomen tes chreias,* 'to edification of our needs,' and the greatest and most holy charity.

(c) Our communication must in its just season be *elegktikos,* we must 'reprove' our sinning brother; for 'the wounds of a friend are better than the kisses of an enemy,' saith Solomon:[19] we imitate the office of the great 'Shepherd and Bishop of

---

[19] Prov 27:6.

souls,' if we go 'to seek and save that which was lost;' and it is a fearful thing to see a friend go to hell undisturbed, when the arresting him in his horrid progress may possibly make him to return; this is a course that will change our vile itch of judging and censuring others into an act of charity; it will alter slander into piety, detraction into counsel, revenge into friendly and most useful offices, that the viper's flesh may become Mithridate, and the devil be defeated in his malicious employment of our language. He is a miserable man whom none dares to tell of his faults so plainly that he may understand his danger; and he that is uncapable and impatient of reproof can never become a good friend to any man. For besides that himself would never admonish his friend when he sins, he is also 'proud, and scorner is his name;'[20] he thinks himself exempt from the condition and failings of men; or if he does not, he had rather go to hell than be called to his way by an angry sermon, or driven back by the sword of an angel, or endure one blushing for all his hopes and interest of heaven. It is no shame to be reproved, but to deserve it; but he that deserves it and will do so still, shall increase his shame into confusion, and bring upon himself a sorrow bigger than the calamities of war, and plagues, and hospitals, and poverty. He only is truly wise and will be certainly happy, that so understands himself and hates his sin, that he will not nurse it, but get to himself a reprover on purpose, whose warrant shall be liberty, whose thanks shall be amendment, whose entertainment shall be obedience; for a flattering word is like a bright sunshine to a sore eye, it increases the trouble, and lessens the sight; 'the severe word of the reproving man is wise and healthful'[21] [...].

I end this with the saying of a wise person, advising to every one concerning the use of the tongue; if they speak, let them minister to the good of souls; if they speak not, let them minister to sobriety; in the first, they serve the end of charity; in the other, of humility.

The Deceitfulness of the Heart[1]

JEREMY TAYLOR

> The heart is deceitful above all things, and desperately wicked; who can know it? (Jer 17:19)

Folly and subtility divide the greatest part of mankind, and there is no other difference but this, that some are crafty enough to deceive, others foolish enough

---

20 Prov 21:24.   21 Last line of a supposed epitaph on Lucan.   1 Sermons VII, VIII, in J. Taylor, vol. 4, 408-30.

to be cozened and abused; and yet the scales also turn, for they that are the most crafty to cozen others are the veriest fools, and most of all abused themselves. They rob their neighbour of his money, and lose their own innocency; they disturb his rest, and vex their own conscience; they throw him into prison, and themselves into hell; they make poverty to be their brother's portion, and damnation to be their own. Man entered into the world first alone; but as soon as he met with one companion, he met with three to cozen him: the serpent, and Eve, and himself, all joined, first to make him a fool and to deceive him, and then to make him miserable. But he first cozened himself, giving himself up to believe a lie; and being desirous to listen to the whispers of a tempting spirit, he sinned before he fell; that is, he had within him a false understanding, and a depraved will: and these were the parents of his disobedience, and this was the parent of his infelicity, and a great occasion of ours. And then it was that he entered, for himself and his posterity, into the condition of an ignorant, credulous, easy, wilful, passionate, and impotent person; apt to be abused, and so loving to have it so that if nobody else will abuse him he will be sure to abuse himself; by ignorance and evil principles being open to an enemy, and by wilfulness and sensuality doing to himself the most unpardonable injuries in the whole world. So that the condition of man in the rudenesses and first lines of its visage seems very miserable, deformed, and accursed [...].

What shall this poor helpless thing do? trust in God? Him he hath offended, and he fears Him as an enemy; and God knows if we look only on ourselves and on our own demerits, we have too much reason so to do [...]. Who then shall we trust in? in our friend? Poor man! he may help thee in one thing, and need thee in ten; he may pull thee out of the ditch, and his foot may slip and fall into it himself; [...] like a person void of all understanding, he is willing enough to preserve thy interest, and is very careless of his own; for he does highly despise to betray or to be false to thee, and in the mean time is not his own friend, and is false to God [...]. But what then? [...] We seek life of a physician that dies, and go to him for health who cannot cure his own health or gout; and so become vain in our imaginations, abused in our hopes, restless in our passions, impatient in our calamity, unsupported in our need, exposed to enemies, wandering and wild, without counsel, and without remedy. At last, after the infatuating and deceiving all our confidences without, we have nothing left us but to return home, and dwell within ourselves [...]. Alas, and God help us! [...], we are partial in our own questions, deceived in our sentences, careless of our interests, and the most false, perfidious creatures to ourselves in the whole world: even the 'heart of a man,' a man's own heart, 'is deceitful above all things, and desperately wicked; who can know it?' and who can choose but know it?

And there is no greater argument of the deceitfulness of our hearts than this, that no man can know it all; it cozens us in the very number of its cozenage. But yet we can reduce it all to two heads. We say concerning a false man, Trust him not, for he will deceive you; and we say concerning a weak and broken staff, Lean not upon it, for that will also deceive you. The man deceives because he is false, and the staff because it is weak; and the heart, because it is both, so that it is 'deceitful above all things;' that is, failing and disabled to support us in many things, but in other things where it can, it is false and 'desperately wicked.'

The first sort of deceitfulness is its calamity, and the second is its iniquity; and that is the worse calamity of the two.

I. The heart is deceitful in its strength; [...] it hath not strength enough to think one good thought of itself; it cannot command its own attention to a prayer of ten lines long, but before its end it shall wander after something that is to no purpose; and no wonder then that it grows weary of a holy religion, which consists of so many parts as make the business of a whole life. And there is no greater argument in the world of our spiritual weakness, and falseness of our hearts in the matters of religion, than the backwardness which most men have always, and all men have sometimes, to say their prayers; so weary of their length, so glad when they are done, so witty to excuse and frustrate an opportunity: and yet there is no manner of trouble in the duty, no weariness of bones, no violent labours; nothing but begging a blessing, and receiving it; nothing but doing, ourselves the greatest honour of speaking to the greatest person and greatest King of the world: and that we should be unwilling to do this, so unable to continue in it, so backward to return to it, so without gust and relish in the doing it, can have no visible reason in the nature of the thing but something within us, a strange sickness in the heart, a spiritual nauseating or loathing of Manna, something that hath no name; but we are sure it comes from a weak, a faint, and false heart.

And yet this weak heart is strong in passions, violent in desires, unresistable in its appetites, impatient in its lust, furious in anger: here are strengths enough, one should think. But so have I seen a man in a fever, sick and distempered, unable to walk, less able to speak sense or to do an act of counsel; and yet when his fever hath boiled up to a delirium, he was strong enough to beat his nursekeeper and his doctor too, and to resist the loving violence of all his friends, who would fain bind him down to reason and his bed; and yet we still say, he is weak, and sick to death; for these strengths of madness are not health, but furiousness and disease; 'it is weakness another way:'[2] and so are the strengths of a man's heart; they are fetters and manacles; strong, but they are the cordage of imprisonment; so strong that the heart is not able

---

[2] Arrian, *Epictetus*, 2:15. Arrian was a prose writer of the second century, who preserved for us the teachings of Epictetus of Hierapolis.

to stir. And yet it cannot but be a huge sadness that the heart shall pursue a temporal interest with wit and diligence and an unwearied industry, and shall not have strength enough, in a matter that concerns its eternal interest, to answer one objection, to resist one assault, to defeat one art of the devil; but shall certainly and infallibly fall whenever it is tempted to a pleasure [...].

Again [...] the heart of man is deceitful in making judgment concerning its own acts. It does not know when it is pleased or displeased; it is peevish and trifling; it would, and it would not; and it is in many cases impossible to know whether a man's heart desires such a thing or not [...]. Now suppose a man that hath spent his younger years in vanity and folly, and is by the grace of God apprehensive of it, and thinks of returning to sober counsels; this man will find his heart so false, so subtle and fugitive, so secret and undiscernible, that it will be very hard to discern whether he repents or no. For if he considers that he hates sin, and therefore repents; alas! he so hates it that he dares not, if he be wise, tempt himself with an opportunity to act it; for in the midst of that which he calls hatred he hath so much love left for it that if the sin comes again and speaks him fair, he is lost again, he kisses the fire, and dies in its embraces. And why else should it be necessary for us to pray that 'we be not led into temptation,' but because we hate the sin, and yet love it too well; we curse it, and yet follow it; we are angry at ourselves, and yet cannot be without it; we know it undoes us, but we think it pleasant. And when we are to execute the fierce anger of the Lord upon our sins, yet we are kind-hearted, and spare the Agag, the reigning sin, the splendid temptation; we have some kindnesses left towards it [...].

Finally [...] the heart is deceitful in its own resolutions and purposes; for many times men make their resolutions only in their understanding, not in their wills; they resolve it fitting to be done, not decree that they will do it; and instead of beginning to be reconciled to God by the renewed and hearty purposes of holy living, they are advanced so far only as to be convinced and apt to be condemned by their own sentence.

But suppose our resolutions advanced further, and that our will and choices also are determined; see how our hearts deceive us still [...]. I will not be drunk in the streets; but I may sleep till I be recovered, and then come forth sober; or if I be overtaken, it shall be in civil and genteel company. Or it may be not so much; I will leave my intemperance and my lust too, but I will remember it with pleasure; I will revolve the past action in my mind, and entertain my fancy with a morose delectation in it, and by a fiction of imagination will represent it present, and so be satisfied with a little effeminacy or fantastic pleasure. Beloved, suffer not your hearts so to cozen you; as if any man can be faithful in much, that is faithless in a little. He certainly is very much in love with sin, and parts with it very unwillingly, that keeps its picture, and wears its favour, and delights in the fancy of it [...].

There is so much falseness and iniquity in man's heart that it defiles all the members; it makes the eyes lustful, and the tongue slanderous; it fills the head with mischief, and the feet with blood, and the hands with injury, and the present condition of man with folly, and makes his future state apt to inherit eternal misery. But this is but the beginning of those throes and damnable impieties which proceed out of the heart of man, and defile the whole constitution: I have yet told but the 'weaknesses' of the heart; I shall the next time tell you the 'iniquities,' those inherent devils which pollute and defile it to the ground, and make it 'desperately wicked,' that is, wicked beyond all expression.

II. 'It is the beginning of wisdom to know a man's own weaknesses and failings in things of greatest necessity,' said Cicero;[3] and we have here so many objects to furnish out this knowledge, that we find it with the longest and latest, before it be obtained. A man does not begin to know himself till he be old, and then he is well stricken in death. A man's heart at first being like a plain table; unspotted, indeed, but then there is nothing legible in it: as soon as ever we ripen towards the imperfect uses of our reason, we write upon this table such crooked characters, such imperfect configurations, so many fooleries, and stain it with so many blots and vicious inspersions, that there is nothing worth the reading in our hearts for a great while: and when education and ripeness, reason and experience, christian philosophy and the grace of God, hath made fair impressions, and written the law in our hearts with the finger of God's holy spirit, we blot out this hand-writing of God's ordinances, or mingle it with false principles and interlinings of our own; we disorder the method of God, or deface the truth of God; either we make the rule uneven, we bribe or abuse our guide, that we may wander with an excuse; or if nothing else will do it, we turn head and profess to go against the laws of God. Our hearts are (a) blind, or our hearts are (b) hardened; for these are two great arguments of the wickedness of our hearts; they do not see, or they will not see, the ways of God; or if they do, they make use of their seeing that they may avoid them.

(a) Our hearts are blind, wilfully blind [...]. God hath opened all the windows of heaven, and sent the Sun of righteousness with glorious apparition, and hath discovered the abysses of His own wisdom, made the second Person in the Trinity to be the doctor and preacher of His sentences and secrets, and the third Person to be His amanuensis or scribe, and our hearts to be the book in which the doctrine is written, and miracles and prophecies to be its arguments, and all the world to be the verification of it: and those leaves contain within their folds all that excellent morality which right reason picked up after the shipwreck of nature, and all those wise sayings which singly made so many men famous for preaching some one of them; all them Christ gathered, and added some more out of the immediate book of revelation. So

---

3 Ibid., 2:11.

that now the wisdom of God hath made every man's heart to be the true Veronica, in which He hath imprinted His own lineaments so perfectly, that we may dress ourselves like God, and have the air and features of Christ our elder brother; that we may be pure as God is, perfect as our Father, meek and humble as the Son, and may have the Holy Ghost within us, in gifts and graces, in wisdom and holiness. This hath God done for us; and see what we do for Him. We stand in our own light, and quench God's; we love darkness more than light, and entertain ourselves accordingly. For how many of us are there that understand nothing of the ways of God; that know no more of the laws of Jesus Christ than is remaining upon them since they learned the children's catechism?[...] and if you talk to them of growth in grace, or the Spirit of obsignation, or the melancholy lectures of the cross, and imitation of, and conformity to, Christ's sufferings, or adherences to God, or rejoicing in Him, or not quenching the Spirit; you are too deep learned for them [...].

The effect of all is this, that we are ignorant of the things of God. We make religion to be the work of a few hours in the whole year; we are without fancy or affection to the severities of holy living; we reduce religion to the believing of a few articles, and doing nothing that is considerable; we pray seldom, and then but very coldly and indifferently, we communicate not so often as the sun salutes both the tropics [...]. All the mischiefs that you can suppose to happen to a furious inconsiderate person, running after the wild-fires of the night, over rivers, and rocks, and precipices, without sun or star, or angel or man, to guide him; all that, and ten thousand times worse, may you suppose to be the certain lot of him who gives himself up to the conduct of a passionate, blind heart, whom no fire can warm, and no sun enlighten; who hates light, and loves to dwell in the regions of darkness. That's the first general mischief of the heart, it is possessed with blindness wilful and voluntary.

(b) But the heart is hard too. Not only 'folly,' but mischief also, 'is bound up in the heart'[4] of man. If God strives to soften it with sorrow and sad accidents, it is like an ox, it grows callous and hard. Such a heart was Pharaoh's. When God makes the clouds to gather round about us, we wrap our heads in the clouds, and, like the malcontents in Galba's time, 'we seem sad and troubled, but it is doggedness and murmur.'[5] Or else if our fears be pregnant, and the heart yielding, it sinks low into pusillanimity and superstition; and our hearts are so childish, so timorous, or so impatient, in a sadness, that God is weary of striking us, and we are glad of it. And yet when the sun shines upon us, our hearts are hardened with that too; and God seems to be at a loss, as if He knew not what to do to us. War undoes us, and makes us violent; peace undoes us, and makes us wanton; prosperity makes us proud; adversity renders us impatient; plenty dissolves us, and makes us tyrants; want makes us greedy, liars, and rapacious, – 'no fortune

[4] Prov 22:15.   [5] Tacitus, *Annals*, 1:24, SCBO, p. 15.

can save that city to whom neither peace nor war can do advantage.'⁶ And what is there left for God to mollify our hearts whose temper is like both to wax and dirt; whom fire hardens, and cold hardens; and contradictory accidents produce no change, save that the heart grows worse and more obdurate for every change of providence? But here [...] we must confess our ignorance; and say that 'the heart of man is desperately wicked;' and that is the truth in general, but we cannot fathom it by particular comprehension [...].

But besides that now the wells of a deeper iniquity are discovered, we see by too sad experience that there are some sins proceeding from the heart of man which have nothing but simple and unmingled malice; actions of mere spite, doing evil because it is evil, sinning without sensual pleasures, sinning with sensual pain, with hazard of our lives, with actual torment, and sudden deaths, and certain and present damnation; sins against the Holy Ghost, open hostilities, and professed enmities against God and all virtue. I can go no further, because there is not in the world or in the nature of things a greater evil. And that is the nature and folly of the devil; he tempts men to ruin, and hates God, and only hurts himself, and those he tempts, and does himself no pleasure, and some say he increases his own accidental torment.

Although I can say nothing greater, yet I had many more things to say, if the time would have permitted me, to represent the falseness and baseness of the heart. We are false ourselves, and dare not trust God; we love to be deceived, and are angry if we be told so; we love to seem virtuous, and yet hate to be so; [...] we fear to die, and yet use all means we can to make death terrible and dangerous; we are busy in the faults of others, and negligent of our own; we live the life of spies, striving to know others, and to be unknown ourselves; we worship and flatter some men and some things, because we fear them, not because we love them; we are ambitious of greatness, and covetous of wealth, and all that we get by it is that we are more beautifully tempted; and a troop of clients run to us as to a pool, whom first they trouble, and then draw dry; we make ourselves unsafe by committing wickedness, and then we add more wickedness, to make us safe and beyond punishment; we are more servile for one courtesy that we hope for, than for twenty that we have received; we entertain slanderers, and without choice spread their calumnies; and we hug flatterers, and know they abuse us. And if I should gather the abuses and impieties and deceptions of the heart, as Chrysippus did the oracular lies of Apollo, into a table, I fear they would seem remediless, and beyond the cure of watchfulness and religion. Indeed they are great and many; but the grace of God is greater; and 'if iniquity abounds,' then 'doth grace superabound:'⁷ and that's our comfort and our medicine.

---

6 Aristophanes, cfr. Baldry, *Greek Literature for the Modern Reader*, pp. 188-213.   7 Rom 5:20.

CHAPTER 5

Preacher and Panegyric

INTRODUCTION

Taylor's mastery of the rhetorical tradition can be seen at its best in the funeral oration which is one of the most elaborate of Christian literary forms. It represents an attempt to adapt to Christian usage an ancient pagan form which in itself is only one example of the literary genre known as the Encomium. This genre developed out of the praise of those that had fallen in battle. The famous funeral speech of Pericles as presented by Thucydides (*c*.450 BC)[1] is probably the earliest extant example of this *epitaphios logos*, 'epitaph' for the dead, whose schema or basic structure may be presented as follows: (1) Exordium or Introduction; (2) Encomium or Laudation proper, combined with lament and developed under the following headings – family, birth, upbringing, education, natural gifts, moral qualities, achievements, fortune, and especially comparison with the great and famous; (3) Final Exhortation and Prayer. In the Greek schools of rhetoric this form was much cultivated, especially in the second half of the fourth century AD, when it was taught in theory and in practice at Constantinople, Athens and Antioch. Libanius, the most famous rhetorician of his age, was undoubtedly one of the principal teachers of Gregory Nazianzus in rhetoric as he was also of Julian the Apostate. It is not surprising, then, to find the influence of the pagan Encomium so marked in the first great Christian funeral orations, of which Gregory is the great exponent.[2]

The Greek treatise on grief or consolation was a closely related genre and had a profound influence on the development and content of the funeral oration. Although many of the great Greek philosophers, including Plato and Aristotle, dealt with the problem of death and the possibility of consolation, the first treatise on grief as such was written in the fourth century BC by a certain Crantor. Throughout antiquity this work was regarded as the most comprehensive and model of its kind. His treatise was cast in the form of a letter to a certain Hippocles on the death of his children, and, both in form and in content, it exercised a great influence on all later works on the consolation theme.[3]

[1] T.K. Carroll, *Preaching the Word*, MFOC, vol. 11, Wilmington, Del., 1984. For a fuller treatment cf. M. Maguire, *Gregory Nazianzen and Ambrose*, FOTC, Funeral Orations, vol. 22, Washington, D.C., 1953. [2] Ibid., p. 65. [3] Ibid.

Gregory's funeral orations reflect both these dimensions, laudation and consolation, but, at the same time, also exhibit modifications and new elements which give them their specific Christian character with their emphasis on the resurrection of the body and life everlasting in Christ. The commonplaces of the Greek funeral oration, even when influenced by consolation literature, were, on the whole, little more than a litany of platitudes. On the other hand, Christians in their divine scriptures possessed a consolation literature of unique power and beauty; one that enjoyed unique authority as the Word of God and gave new life to the old forms. In this field of adaptation, Gregory Nazianzus was a pioneer and there are extant four of his orations: (1) On his brother, Caesarius; (2) On his sister, Gorgonia; (3) On his father, Gregory the Elder, bishop of Nazianzus; and (4) On his friend, Basil the Great, bishop of Caesarea – the masterpiece of Christian Greek funeral orations.[4]

The *Oration on Caesarius* follows the classical structure of Exordium, Encomium and Conclusion. In the Exordium or introduction, he introduces the notion of grief and consolation. Then follows the extended Encomium in praise of ancestry and parentage; physical endowments; upbringing and education; occupation and achievements; his struggles against Julian, the apostate emperor, and other enemies of the Church. In the Encomium nothing worthy of praise is forgotten: even the performance of Caesarius, the student, in his public debate with the young Emperor Julian in the school of Alexandria, 'a workshop of all kinds of learning,' is remembered and magnified. In conclusion Gregory contrasts 'the vanity of the flesh' with 'the worth of the soul' and addresses the deceased Caesarius. The consolation motif then appears with the light of Christian faith dispelling the darkness of the pagan commonplace, and the oration ends with a prayer which reflects the authentic liturgical spirit of that age with its recognition and praise of the creative Word.[5]

In the Christian funeral orations of the Greek Fathers can be seen the interaction of Christianity and paganism that took place in the fourth century as the schools of rhetoric informed the eloquence of the Fathers, and the Fathers transformed the eloquence of the schools. Like the Greek encomium the Latin *laudatio funebris* was also influenced by Latin consolation literature whose commonplaces were no different from those of the Greek. Once again the loss of wealth, health, friendship, beauty, vigour and power was softened by vision and insight. Men were reminded of the transience of the living and the repose of the dead. Grief was tempered by reason, and emotion controlled accordingly. Time alone was the great solace, for it cured all ills and healed all things.[6]

To such commonplaces of consolation Christianity added the incomparably superior means of consolation furnished by the Christian faith with its emphasis on the central doctrines of the Christian religion. Furthermore, in the Psalms and

---

4 PG, 35:756.   5 Carroll, op. cit., pp. 66-9.   6 Ibid., p. 144.

Prophets of the Old Testament Christians possessed a literature of grief and consolation with unique power and beauty which also enjoyed unique authority as the Word of God Himself.[7]

The three funeral orations of Ambrose on Valentinian the emperor, on Theodosius, and on Satyrus, his brother, are the only known examples of this genre in ancient Christian Latin literature. In these Ambrose, for the most part, followed the classical rhetorical structure of Exordium and Lament, Encomium and Consolation, Exhortation and Prayer, canonized in a sense by Gregory Nazianzus; but already in contrast with the orations of the Greeks there can be detected in those of Ambrose the conciseness and brevity of the Latin language, and a new humanism which is the fruit of Christian faith. The oration on Satyrus illustrates the point. In the exordium and lament we read: 'We have here [...], beloved brethren, my sacrifice in the person of my lord and brother Satyrus, an untainted victim and one acceptable to God [...]. I have considered nothing, dear brethren, in human relationships more priceless than such a brother, nothing worthier of my affection, nothing more dear.'[8]

The grief of the exordium is extended into the encomium by way of a prolonged lamentation in which he grieves for his personal loss but is consoled by the sympathy of his people: 'Naturally, I am deeply grateful to you, beloved brethren, my holy people, that you participate in our sorrow as your own sorrow, that you think that our bereavement has fallen upon yourselves, and that with this new and wonderful demonstration of affection you are offering the tears of the whole city, of every order and age.'[9]

In the encomium he sings the praises of his brother and extols his virtues. The loss of such a soul is then lamented, but the notion of Christian consolation is dominant. Thus Christian faith and human sorrow are both acknowledged: they dwell together in the heart of the pilgrim Christian for belief and grief are fellow travellers in the Christian odyssey: 'But why am I tarrying, brother? Why am I waiting for my address to die with you and, as it were, be buried with you? Even though the sight and form of your lifeless body give solace, and your abiding grace and beauty comfort my eyes, I will delay no longer. I repeat; let us proceed to the tomb. But first, before all of the people, I bid you the last farewell. I give you peace, and I pay the last kiss. Precede us to that common abode to which we must all go, and for which I long beyond all else. Prepare for us a common place and just as here we had all things in common, there let us also have all things in common. Then follows the conclusion and final prayer: 'Almighty God, I now commend to you an innocent soul, a true oblation. Accept favourably a brother's

---

7 Ibid.   8 CSEL, 73 Text: 7:209.   9 Carroll, op. cit., p. 146.

gift, the sacrifice of Thy priest. I am coming to you with my brother as a surety, not with a pledge of money but of a life. Do not make me remain in debt for so great a sum too long. I can bear the burden if I can pay quickly.'[10]

Jeremy Taylor, biblical preacher and renaissance rhetor, was a complete master of these ancient forms, Greek and Latin, classical and Christian. But, in his pulpit, he reversed the order of their presentations, and dealt in the first place with the biblical text, chosen for the occasion, and afterwards with the person and life of the deceased, as an embodiment of that text. What could be better, for instance, and less likely to have occurred to the average preacher, than the text for the countess of Carbery's funeral sermon: 'For we must needs die, and are as water spilt on the ground, which cannot be gathered up again: neither doth God respect any person; yet doth He devise means, that His banished be not expelled from Him' (2 Sam 14:14);[11] or that for the funeral of the lord primate of Ireland: 'Every man in his own order: Christ the first fruits; afterwards they that are Christ's at His coming' (1 Cor 15:23):[12] and again at the funeral of a certain Sir George Dalstone on the text: 'If in this life only we have hope in Christ, we are of all men most miserable' (l Cor 15:19).[13]

In the Spring and Fall of Anno Domini 1653, Taylor – at Golden Grove like Hopkins and Keats after him – had every reason to *grieve* and *live* with the deaths of Frances Carbery and Phoebe, his wife: 'My lord [the earl of Carbery], it is a great art to die well, and to be learnt by men in health, by them that can discourse and consider, by those whose understanding and acts of reason are not abated with fear or pains; [...] he that prepares not for death before his last sickness is like him that begins to study philosophy when he is going to dispute publicly in the faculty.'[14] The funeral sermon at the obsequies of the countess was a model of its kind, and marked an advance upon the conventional type of elegy in prose and verse: it offers no preposterous panegyric of the deceased, but rather a reasonable and thoughtful enumeration of her qualities, what Taylor himself called 'a drawing in water colours:'[15]

> She was [...] of a temperate, plain and natural diet, without curiosity or an intemperate palate. She spent less time in dressing than many servants. Her recreations were little and seldom, her prayers often, her reading much. She was of a most noble and charitable soul; a great lover of honourable actions, and as great a despiser of base things. Hugely loving to oblige others, she was very unwilling to be in arrear to any upon the stock of courtesies and liberality. So free in all acts of favour, that she would not stay to hear herself thanked [...]. She was an excellent friend, and hugely dear to very many, especially to the best and most discerning persons; to all that conversed with her, and could understand her great

---

10 Ibid., pp 147-9.　11 Taylor, vol. 8, p. 429.　12 Ibid., p. 395.　13 Ibid., p. 543.　14 Ibid., p. 427.　15 Ibid.

worth and sweetness. She was of an honourable, nice and tender reputation; and of the pleasures of the world, which were laid before her in heaps, she took a very small share.[16]

In this chapter on 'Preacher and Panegyric' there are two of Taylor's three funeral sermons, which are in this genre of consolation literature in English as unique in their being and essence as the four homilies of Gregory Nazianzus in Greek and the three orations of Ambrose in Latin. It should, however, be emphasised that Ambrose was not as closely bound by his pagan models as were his Greek contemporaries. Furthermore, his funeral orations are more thoroughly permeated with Christian thought and with scriptural quotation, phraseology and imagery and as a whole are more marked by personal tone and warmth of feeling. But in the funeral sermons of Jeremy Taylor his whole perception of reality, of nature as of history, is much more biblical than homeric, coming as he did in the time of Milton and after the age of Shakespeare that Aquinas, Dante and the Gothic had ordered, composed and clarified. Taylor's emphasis on the Word filled his passing words with the Glory of God:[17]

> Upon this account it is that the day of judgment is a day of recompense. So said our blessed Lord himself, 'Thou shalt be recompensed at the resurrection of the just.'[18] And this is the day in which all things shall be restored; for 'the heavens must receive Jesus till the time of restitution of all things;' and till then the reward is said to be 'laid up.'[19] So St Paul, 'Henceforth is laid up for me a crown of righteousness, which the righteous Judge shall give me in that day:' and that you may know he means the resurrection and the day of judgment, he adds, 'and not to me only, but to all them that love His coming,'[20] of whom it is certain many shall be alive at that day, and therefore cannot before that day receive the crown of righteousness: and then also, and not till then, shall be his appearing; but till then it is a depositum. – The sum is this; in the world we walk and live by faith; in the state of separation we live by hope; and in the resurrection we shall live by an eternal charity. Here we see God as in a glass darkly; in the separation we shall behold Him, but it is afar off; and after the resurrection we shall see Him face to face, in the everlasting comprehensions of an intuitive beatitude. In this life we are warriors, in the separation we are conquerors, but we shall not triumph till after the resurrection.
>
> And in proportion to this is also the state of devils and damned spirits. 'Art Thou come to torment us before the time,' said the devils to our blessed Saviour;[21] there is for them also an appointed time, and when that is, we learn

---

16 Ibid., p. 449.   17 What follows is an excerpt from Taylor's sermon at the funeral of Sir George Dalstone.
18 Ibid., p. 559; cf. Lk 14:14.   19 Ibid., cf. Acts 3:21.   20 Ibid., cf. 2 Tim 4:8.   21 Ibid., cf. Mt 8:29.

from St Jude, they 'are reserved in chains under darkness unto the judgment of the great day.'[22] Well therefore did St James affirm that 'the devils believe and tremble;'[23] and so do the damned souls, with an insupportable amazement, fearing the revelation of that day. They know that day will come, and they know they shall find an intolerable sentence on that day; and they fear infinitely, and are in amazement and confusion, feeling the worm of conscience, and are in the state of devils, who fear God and hate Him; they tremble, but they love Him not: and yet they die because they would not love Him, because they would not with their powers and strengths keep His commandments.

The Countess of Carbery's Funeral Sermon[1]

JEREMY TAYLOR

For we must needs die, and are as water spilt on the ground, which cannot begathered up again; neither doth God respect any person; yet doth He devise means that His banished be not expelled from Him. (2 Sam 14:14)

When our blessed Saviour and His disciples viewed the temple, some one amongst them cried out, *Magister aspice, quales lapides*, 'Master, behold what fair, what great stones are here.'[2] Christ made no reply but foretold their dissolution, and a world of sadness and sorrow which should bury that whole nation, when the teeming cloud of God's displeasure should produce a storm which was the daughter of the biggest anger, and the mother of the greatest calamity which ever crushed any of the sons of Adam: 'The time shall come that there shall not be left one stone upon another.' The whole temple and the religion, the ceremonies ordained by God, and the nation beloved by God, and the fabric erected for the service of God, shall run to their own period, and lie down in their several graves. Whatsoever had a beginning can also have an ending, and it shall die, unless it be daily watered with the purles flowing from the fountain of life, and refreshed with the dew of heaven, and the wells of God. And therefore God had provided a tree in paradise to have supported Adam in his artificial immortality: immortality was not in his nature, but in the hands and arts, in the favour and superadditions of God. Man was always the same mixture of heat and cold, of dryness and moisture; ever the same weak thing, apt to feel rebellion in the humours, and to suffer the evils of a civil war in his body natural: and

22 Ibid., cf. Jude 1:6.   23 Ibid., cf. Jas 2:19.   1 Sermon VIII, in J. Taylor, vol. 8, pp 425-50.   2 Mk 13:1.

therefore health and life was to descend upon him from heaven, and he was to suck life from a tree of earth; himself being but ingrafted into a tree of life, and adopted into the condition of an immortal nature: but he that in the best of his days was but a scion of this tree of life, by his sin was cut off from thence quickly, and planted upon thorns, and his portion was for ever after among the flowers, which to-day spring and look like health and beauty, and in the evening they are sick, and at night are dead, and the oven is their grave. And as before, even from our first spring from the dust on earth, we might have died if we had not been preserved by the continual flux of a rare providence; so now that we are reduced to the laws of our own nature, 'we must needs die.' It is natural, and therefore necessary: it is become a punishment to us, and therefore it is unavoidable; and God hath bound the evil upon us by bands of natural and inseparable propriety, and by a supervening unalterable decree of heaven; and we are fallen from our privilege, and are returned to the condition of beasts, and buildings, and common things. And we see temples defiled unto the ground, and they die by sacrilege; and great empires die by their own plenty and ease, full humours, and factious subjects; and huge buildings fall by their own weight, and the violence of many winters eating and consuming the cement, which is the marrow of their bones; and princes die like the meanest of their servants; and every thing finds a grave and a tomb; and the very tomb dies by the bigness of its pompousness and luxury,

> [...] *Phario nutantia pondera saxo*
> *Quae cineri vanus dat ruitura labor,*[3]

and becomes as friable and uncombined dust as the ashes of the sinner or the saint that lay under it, and is now forgotten in his bed of darkness. And to this catalogue of mortality man is enrolled with a *statutum est*, 'it is appointed for all men once to die, and after death comes judgment.' And if a man can be stronger than nature, or can wrestle with a decree of heaven, or can escape from a divine punishment by his own arts, so that neither the power nor the providence of God, nor the laws of nature, nor the bands of eternal predestination can hold him, then he may live beyond the fate and period of flesh, and last longer than a flower: if all these can hold us and tie us to conditions, then we must lay our heads down upon a turf, and entertain creeping things in the cells and little chambers of our eyes, and dwell with worms till time and death shall be no more. 'We must needs die,' that's our sentence: but that's not all; – 'We are as water spilt on the ground, which cannot be gathered up again.' Stay,

1. We are as water, weak, and of no consistence, always descending, abiding in no certain place, unless where we are detained with violence; and every little breath of wind makes us rough and tempestuous, and troubles our faces; every

---

3 Martial, *Epigrams*, 1:80, LCL, vol. 1, p. 102.

trifling accident discomposes us; and as the face of the waters wafting in a storm so wrinkles itself that it makes upon its forehead furrows deep and hollow like a grave; so do our great and little cares and trifles first make the wrinkles of old age, and then they dig a grave for us: and there is in nature nothing so contemptible, but it may meet with us in such circumstances, that it may be too hard for us in our weaknesses; and the sting of a bee is a weapon sharp enough to pierce the finger of a child or the lip of a man; and those creatures which nature hath left without weapons, yet they are armed sufficiently to vex those parts of men which are left defenceless and obnoxious to a sunbeam, to the roughness of a sour grape, to the unevenness of a gravelstone, to the dust of a wheel, or the unwholesome breath of a star looking awry upon a sinner.

2. But besides the weaknesses and natural decaying of our bodies, if chances and contingencies be innumerable, then no man can reckon our dangers, and the preternatural causes of our death: so that he is a vain person whose hopes of life are too confidently increased by reason of his health: and he is too unreasonably timorous, who thinks his hopes at an end when he dwells in sickness. For men die without rule, and with and without occasions; and no man suspecting or foreseeing any of death's addresses, and no man in his whole condition is weaker than another. A man in a long consumption is fallen under one of the solemnities and preparations to death: but at the same instant the most healthful person is as near death, upon a more fatal and a more sudden, but a less discerned cause. There are but few persons upon whose foreheads every man can read the sentence of death written in the lines of a lingering sickness, but they (sometimes) hear the passing-bell ring for stronger men, even long before their own knell calls at the house of their mother to open her womb, and make a bed for them. No man is surer of to-morrow than the weakest of his brethern [...]. There is no age of man but it hath proper to itself some posterns and outlets for death, besides those infinite and open ports out of which myriads of men and women every day pass into the dark, and the land of forgetfulness. Infancy hath life but in effigy, or like a spark dwelling in a pile of wood: the candle is so newly lighted, that every little shaking of the taper, and every ruder breath of air puts it out, and it dies. Childhood is so tender, and yet so unwary; so soft to all the impressions of chance, and yet so forward to run into them, that God knew there could be no security without the care and vigilance of an angel-keeper [...] for [...] infancy is as liable to death as old age, and equally exposed to danger, and equally uncapable of a remedy: with this only difference, that old age hath diseases incurable by nature, and the diseases of childhood are incurable by art: and both the states are the next heirs of death.

3. But all the middle way the case is altered: nature is strong, and art is apt to give ease and remedy, but still there is no security; and there the case is not altered.

For ... very many principles in the art of physic are so uncertain, that after they have been believed seven or eight ages, and that upon them much of the practice hath been established, they come to be considered by a witty man, and others established in their stead; by which men must practise, and by which three or four generations of men more (as happens) must live or die [...] so that we may well be likened to water; our nature is no stronger, our abode no more certain; if the sluices be opened, 'it falls away and runneth apace;'[4] if its current be stopped, it swells and grows troublesome, and spills over with a great diffusion; if it be made to stand still, it putrifies: and all this we do. For,

4. In all the process of our health we are running to our grave: we open our own sluices by viciousness and unworthy actions; [...] nay, we kill one another's souls and bodies with violence and folly, with the effects of pride and uncharitableness; we live and die like fools, and bring a new mortality upon ourselves; wars and vexatious cares, and private duels and public disorders, and every thing that is unreasonable, and every thing that is violent: so that now we may add this fourth gate to the grave: besides nature, – and chance, – and the mistakes of art, – men die with their own sins, and then enter into the grave in haste and passion, and pull the heavy stone of the monument upon their own heads. And thus we make ourselves like water spilt on the ground; [...] we let our years slip through our fingers like water; and nothing is to be seen, but like a shower of tears upon a spot of ground; there is a grave digged, and a solemn mourning, and a great talk in the neighbourhood, and when the days are finished, they shall be, and they shall be remembered, no more: and that's like water too, when it is spilt, 'it cannot be gathered up again.'

There is no redemption from the grave. Men live in their course and by turns; their light burns a while, and then it burns blue arid faint, and men go to converse with spirits, and then they reach the taper to another; and as the hours of yesterday can never return again, so neither can the man whose hours they were, and who lived them over once; he shall never come to live them again, and live them better. When Lazarus, and the widow's son of Naim, and Tabitha, and the saints that appeared in Jerusalem at the resurrection of our blessed Lord arose, they came into this world, some as strangers only to make a visit, and all of them to manifest a glory: but none came upon the stock of a new life, or entered upon the stage as at first, or to perform the course of a new nature: and therefore it is observable that we never read of any wicked person that was raised from the dead [...]. We never read that a wicked person felt such a miracle, or was raised from the grave to try the second time for a crown; but where he fell, there he lay down dead, and saw the light no more.

This consideration I intend to you as a severe monitor and an advice of carefulness, that you order your affairs so that you may be partakers of the first resurrection; that

4 Ps 58:6.

is, from sin to grace, from the death of vicious habits to the vigour, life, and efficacy of an habitual righteousness. For [...] you only that serve God in a holy life; you who are not dead in trespasses and sins; you who serve God with an early diligence and an unwearied industry, and a holy religion, you and you only shall come to life eternal, you only shall be called from death to life; the rest of mankind shall never live again, but pass from death to death; from one death to another, to a worse; from the death of the body to the eternal death of body and soul. And therefore in the apostles' creed there is no mention made of the resurrection of wicked persons, but of 'the resurrection of the body to everlasting life.' The wicked indeed shall be hailed forth from their graves, from their everlasting prisons, where in chains of darkness they are kept unto the judgment of the great day: but this therefore cannot be called *in sensu favoris* 'a resurrection,' but the solemnities of the eternal death; it is nothing but a new capacity of dying again; such a dying as cannot signify rest; but where death means nothing but an intolerable and never-ceasing calamity; and therefore these words of my text are otherwise to be understood of the wicked, otherwise of the godly: the wicked are spilt like water and shall never be gathered up again; no, not in the gatherings of eternity; they shall be put into vessels of wrath and set upon the flames of hell; but that is not a gathering, but a scattering from the face and presence of God. But the godly also come under the sense of these words: they descend into their graves, and shall no more be reckoned among the living; they have no concernment in all that is done under the sun [...]. What is it to me that Rome was taken by the Gauls? and what is it now to Camillus if different religions be tolerated amongst us? These things that now happen concern the living, and they are made the scenes of our duty or danger respectively: and when our wives are dead and sleep in charnel-houses, they are not troubled when we laugh loudly at the songs sung at the next marriage-feast; nor do they envy when another snatches away the gleanings of their husbands' passion.

It is true, they envy not, and they lie in a bosom where there can be no murmur; and they that are consigned to kingdoms, and to the feast of the marriage-supper of the Lamb, the glorious and eternal Bridegroom of holy souls, they cannot think our marriages here, our lighter laughings and vain rejoicings, considerable as to them. And yet there is a relation continued still: Aristotle said that to affirm the dead take no thought for the good of the living, is a disparagement to the laws of that friendship which in their state of separation they cannot be tempted to rescind.[5]

And the church hath taught in general that they pray for us, they recommend to God the state of all their relatives, in the union of the intercession that our blessed Lord makes for them and us; and St Ambrose gave some things in charge to his dying brother Satyrus, that he should do for him in the other world: he gave it him, I say, when he was dying, not when he was dead. And certain it is

---

[5] Aristotle, *Nicomachean Ethics*, LCL, vol. 19, p. 56.

that though our dead friends' affection to us is not to be estimated according to our low conceptions, yet it is not less, but much more than ever it was; it is greater in degree, and of another kind.

But then we should do well also to remember that in this world we are something besides flesh and blood; that we may not without violent necessities run into new relations, but preserve the affections we bore to our dead when they were alive. We must not so live as if they were perished, but so as pressing forward to the most intimate participation of the communion of saints. And we also have some ways to express this relation, and to bear a part on this communion, by actions of intercourse with them, and yet proper to our state: such as are, strictly performing the will of the dead, providing for, and tenderly and wisely educating their children, paying their debts, imitating their good example, preserving their memories privately, and publicly keeping their memorials, and desiring of God with hearty and constant prayer [...] that 'God would shew them mercy in that day,'[6] that fearful and yet much to be desired day, in which the most righteous person hath need of much mercy and pity, and shall find it. Now these instances of duty shew that the relation remains still; and though the relict of a man or woman hath liberty to contract new relations, yet I do not find they have liberty to cast off the old, as if there were no such thing as immortality of souls. Remember that we shall converse together again; [...] in the mean time, God watcheth concerning all their interest, and He will in His time both discover and recompense. For though, as to us, they are like water spilt; yet to God they are as water fallen into the sea, safe and united in His comprehension and inclosures.

But we are not yet past the consideration of the sentence. This descending to the grave is the lot of all men, 'neither doth God respect the person of any man;' the rich is not protected for favour, nor the poor for pity, the old man is not reverenced for his age, nor the infant regarded for his tenderness; youth and beauty, learning and prudence, wit and strength, lie down equally in the dishonours of the grave [...]. For so have I seen the pillars of a building assisted with artificial props bending under the pressure of a roof, and pertinaciously resisting the infallible and prepared ruin ... till the determined day comes, and then the burden sunk upon the pillars, and disordered the aids and auxiliary rafters into a common ruin and a ruder grave: so are the desires and weak arts of man; with little aids and assistances of care and physic we strive to support our decaying bodies, and to put off the evil day; but quickly that day will come, and then neither angels nor men can rescue us from our grave; but the roof sinks down upon the walls, and the walls descend to the foundation; and the beauty of the face, and the dishonours of the belly, the discerning head and the servile feet, the

6 2 Tim 1:18.

thinking heart and the working hand, the eyes and the guts together shall be crushed into the confusion of a heap, and dwell with creatures of an equivocal production, with worms and serpents, the sons and daughters of our own bones, in a house of dirt and darkness.

Let not us think to be excepted or deferred: if beauty, or wit, or youth, or nobleness, or wealth, or virtue could have been a defence, and an excuse from the grave, we had not met here to-day to mourn upon the hearse of an excellent lady: and God only knows for which of us next the mourners shall 'go about the streets'[7] or weep in houses [...]. We have lived so many years; and every day and every minute we make an escape from those thousands of dangers and deaths that encompass us round about, and such escapings we must reckon to be an extraordinary fortune, and that cannot last long [...]. Therefore let no vain confidence make you hope for long life: if you have lived but little, and are still in youth, remember that now you are in your biggest throng of dangers both of body and soul; and the proper sins of youth, to which they rush infinitely and without consideration, are also the proper and immediate instruments of death. But if you be old you have escaped long and wonderfully, and the time of your escaping is out: you must not for ever think to live upon wonders, or that God will work miracles to satisfy your longing follies, and unreasonable desires of living longer to sin and to the world. Go home and think to die, and what you would choose to be doing when you die, that do daily: for you will all come to that pass to rejoice that you did so, or wish that you had: that will be the condition of every one of us; for 'God regardeth no man's person.'[8]

Well; but all this you will think is but a sad story. What? we must die, and go to darkness and dishonour; and we must die quickly, and we must quit all our delights, and all our sins, or do worse, infinitely worse; and this is the condition of us all, from which none can be excepted; every man shall be spilt and fall into the ground, and 'be gathered up no more.' Is there no comfort after all this? Shall we 'go from hence and be no more seen,'[9] and have no recompense? [...] And is there no allay to this huge calamity? Yes, there is: there is a 'yet' in the text, – For all this, 'yet doth God devise means that His banished be not expelled from Him.' [...] Holy scripture instructs our faith and entertains our hope in these words, 'God is still the God of Abraham, Isaac, and Jacob, [...] for all do live to Him:' and the souls of saints are with Christ; 'I desire to be dissolved,' saith St Paul, 'and to be with Christ, for that is much better'; and, 'Blessed are the dead which die in the Lord; they rest from their labours, and their works follow them:' 'For we know, that if our earthly house of this tabernacle were dissolved, we have a building of God, a house not made with hands, eternal in the heavens:' and this state of separation St Paul calls 'a being absent from

7 Eccles 12:5. 8 Gal 2:6. 9 Ps 39:15.

the body, and being present with the Lord:' this is one of God's means which He hath devised, that although our dead are like persons banished from this world, yet they are not expelled from God: they are 'in the hands of Christ;' they are 'in His presence;' they are, or shall be 'clothed with a house of God's making;' 'they rest from all their labours;' 'all tears are wiped from their eyes,' and all discontents from their spirits; and in the state of separation, before the soul be re-invested with her new house, the spirits of all persons are with God, so secured, and so blessed, and so scaled up for glory, that this state of interval and imperfection is, in respect of its certain event and end, infinitely more desirable than all the riches, and all the pleasures, and all the vanities, and all the kingdoms of this world.

I will not venture to determine what are the circumstances of the abode of holy souls in their separate dwellings; and yet possibly that might be easier than to tell what or how the soul is and works in this world, where it is in the body *tanquam in aliena domo*, as in a prison, in fetters and restraints; for here the soul is discomposed and hindered; it is not as it shall be, as it ought to be, as it was intended to be; it is not permitted to its own freedom and proper operation; so that all that we can understand of it here, is that it is so incommodated with a troubled and abated instrument, that the object we are to consider cannot be offered to us in a right line, in just and equal propositions; or if it could, yet because we are to understand the soul by the soul, it becomes not only a troubled and abused object, but a crooked instrument; and we here can consider it just as a weak eye can behold a staff thrust into the waters of a troubled river; the very water makes a refraction, and the storm doubles the refraction, and the water of the eye doubles the species, and there is nothing right in the thing; the object is out of its just place, and the *medium* is troubled, and the organ is impotent. *At cum exierit et in liberum coelum quasi in domum suam venerit*, 'when the soul is entered into her own house, into the free regions of the rest, and the neighbour-hood of heavenly joys,' then its operations are more spiritual, proper, and proportioned to its being; and though we cannot see at such a distance, yet the object is more fitted, if we had a capable understanding; it is in itself in a more excellent and free condition.

Certain it is that the body does hinder many actions of the soul: it is an imperfect body, and a diseased brain, or a violent passion, that makes fools; no man hath a foolish soul; and the reasonings of men have infinite difference and degrees, by reason of the body's constitution. Among beasts, which have no reason, there is a greater likeness than between men, who have: and as by faces it is easier to know a man from a man, than a sparrow from a sparrow, or a squirrel from a squirrel; so the difference is very great in our souls; which difference because it is not original in the soul it must needs derive wholly from the body, from its accidents and circumstances. From whence it follows, that because the body casts fetters and restraints, hindrances and impediments upon the soul, the soul is much freer in the state of separation; and if it hath any act of life, it is much more noble and expedite.

That the soul is alive after our death, St Paul affirms: 'Christ died for us, that whether we wake or sleep, we should live together with Him.'[10] Now it were strange that we should be alive, and live with Christ and yet do no act of life [...]. As nutrition, generation, eating and drinking are actions proper to the body and its state; so ecstasies, visions, raptures, intuitive knowledge, and consideration of its self, acts of volition, and reflex acts of understanding, are proper to the soul. And therefore it is observable, that St Paul said that 'he knew not whether his visions and raptures were in or out of the body' [...].[11]

If in the state of blessedness there are some actions of the soul which do not pass through the body, such as contemplation of God, and conversing with spirits [...], it follows that the necessity of the body's ministry is but during the state of this life [...]. And therefore when the body shall be re-united, it shall be so ordered that then the body shall confess it gives not any thing, but receives all its being and operation, its manner and abode from the soul; and that then it comes not to serve a necessity, but to partake a glory. For as the operations of the soul in this life begin in the body, and by it the object is transmitted to the soul; so then they shall begin in the soul, and pass to the body: and as the operations of the soul by reason of its dependence on the body are animal, natural, and material; so in the resurrection the body shall be spiritual by reason of the pre-eminence, influence, and prime operation of the soul. Now between these two states stands the state of separation, in which the operations of the soul are of a middle nature, that is, not so spiritual as in the resurrection, and not so animal and natural as in the state of conjunction.

To all which I add this consideration, that our souls have the same condition that Christ's soul had in the state of separation, because He took on Him all our nature, and all our condition; and it is certain Christ's soul in the three days of His separation did exercise acts of life, of joy and triumph, and did not sleep, but visited the souls of the fathers, trampled upon the pride of devils, and satisfied those longing souls which were 'prisoners of hope:'[12] and from all this we may conclude that the souls of all the servants of Christ are alive, and therefore do the actions of life, and proper to their state; and therefore it is highly probable that the soul works clearer, and understands brighter, and discourses wiser, and rejoices louder, and loves noblier, and desires purer, and hopes stronger than it can do here.

But if these arguments should fail, yet the felicity of God's saints cannot fail, for [...] God 'devises' other 'means that His banished be not expelled from Him.' [...] God will restore the soul to the body, and raise the body to such a perfection that it

10 1 Thess 5:10.   11 2 Cor 12:2f.   12 Zech 9:12.

shall be an organ fit to praise Him upon; it shall be made spiritual to minister to the soul, when the soul is turned into a spirit ... as soon as ever God shall but tune our instrument, and draw the curtains, and but light up the candle of immortality [...] then we shall be made fit to converse with God after the manner of spirits, we shall be like to angels.

In the mean time, although upon the persuasion of the former discourse it be highly probable that the souls of God's servants do live in a state of present blessedness, and in the exceeding joys of a certain expectation of the revelation of the day of the Lord and the coming of Jesus; yet it will concern us only to secure our state by holy living, and leave the event to God, that whether present or absent, whether sleeping or waking, whether perceiving or perceiving not, we may be accepted of Him; that when we are banished from this world, and from the light of the sun, we may not be expelled from God, and from the light of His countenance, but that from our beds of sorrows our souls may pass into the bosom of Christ, and from thence to His right hand in the day of sentence. 'For we must all appear before the judgment-seat of Christ,'[13] and then if we have done well in the body, we shall never be expelled from the beatifical presence of God, but be domestics of His family, and heirs of His kingdom, and partakers of His glory. Amen.

I have done with my text, but yet am to make you another sermon. I have told you the necessity and the state of death, it may be, too largely for such a sad story; I shall therefore now with a better compendium teach you how to live, by telling you a plain narrative of a life, which if you imitate, and write after the copy, it will make that death shall not be an evil, but a thing to be desired, and to be reckoned amongst the purchases and advantages of your fortune. When Martha and Mary went to weep over the grave of their brother, Christ met them there, and preached a funeral sermon, discoursing of the resurrection, and applying to the purposes of faith, and confession of Christ, and glorification of God. We have no other, we can have no better precedent to follow: and now that we are come to weep over the grave of our dear sister, this rare personage, we cannot choose but have many virtues to learn, many to imitate, and some to exercise.

1. I chose, not to declare her extraction and genealogy; it was indeed fair and honourable; but having the blessing to be descended from worthy and honoured ancestors, and herself to be adopted and ingraffed into a more noble family; yet she felt such outward appendages to be none of hers [...] but the purchase of the virtues of others [...]. It is fit for us all to honour the nobleness of a family: but it is also

[13] Rom 14:10.

fit for them that are noble to despise it, and to establish their honour upon the foundation of doing excellent things, and suffering in good causes, and despising dishonourable actions, and in communicating good things to others. For this is the rule in nature; those creatures are most honourable which have the greatest power, and do the greatest good: and accordingly myself have been a witness of it, how this excellent lady would by an act of humility and christian abstraction strip herself of all that fair appendage and exterior honour which decked her person and her fortune, and desired to be owned by nothing but what was her own, that she might only be esteemed honourable according to that which is the honour of a Christian and a wise person.

2. She had a strict and severe education, and it was one of God's graces and favours to her: for being the heiress of a great fortune, and living amongst the throng of persons in the sight of vanities and empty temptations, that is, in that part of the kingdom where greatness is too often expressed in great follies and great vices, God had provided a severe and angry education to chastise the forwardnesses of a young spirit and a fair fortune, that she might for ever be so far distant from a vice, that she might only see it and lothe it, but never taste of it, so much as to be put to her choice whether she be virtuous or no. God, intending to secure this soul to Himself, would not suffer the follies of the world to seize upon her by way of too near a trial or busy temptation.

3. She was married young; and besides her businesses of religion, seemed to be ordained in the providence of God to bring to this honourable family a part of a fair fortune, and to leave behind her a fairer issue, worth ten thousand times her portion: and as if this had been all the public business of her life, when she had so far served God's ends, God in mercy would also serve hers, and take her to an early blessedness.

4. In passing through which line of providence, she had the art to secure her eternal interest, by turning her condition into duty, and expressing her duty in the greatest eminency of a virtuous, prudent, and rare affection, that hath been known in any example. I will not give her so low a testimony, as to say only that she was chaste; she was a person of that severity, modesty, and close religion, as to that particular, that she was not capable of uncivil temptation; and you might as well have suspected the sun to smell of the poppy that he looks on, as that she could have been a person apt to be sullied by the breath of a foul question.

5. But that which I shall note in her, is that which I would have exemplar to all ladies, and to all women: she had a love so great for her lord, so entirely given up to a dear affection, that she thought the same things, and loved the same loves, and hated according to the same enmities [...]. And although this was a great enamel to the beauty of her soul, yet it might in some degrees be also a reward to the virtue of her lord: for [...] she would delight to say, that he called her to her devotion, he

encouraged her good inclinations, he directed her piety, he invited her with good books [...]. So God usually brings us to Him by instruments of nature and affections, and then incorporates us into His inheritance by the more immediate relishes of heaven, and the secret things of the Spirit. He only was (under God) the light of her eyes, and the cordial of her spirits, and the guide of her actions, and the measure of her affections, till her affections swelled up into a religion, and then it could go no higher, but was confederate with those other duties which made her dear to God: which rare combination of duty and religion I choose to express in the words of Solomon, 'She forsook not the guide of her youth, nor brake the covenant of her God.'[14]

6. As she was a rare wife, so she was an excellent mother: for in so tender a constitution of spirit as hers was, and in so great a kindness towards her children, there hath seldom been seen a stricter and more curious care of their persons, their deportment, their nature, their disposition, their learning, and their customs: and if ever kindness and care did contest, and make parties in her, yet her care and her severity was ever victorious; and she knew not how to do an ill turn to their severer part, by her more tender and forward kindness [...]. And her prudence in managing her children was so singular and rare, that whenever you mean to bless this family, and pray a hearty and a profitable prayer for it, beg of God that the children may have those excellent things which she designed to them, and provided for them in her heart and wishes, that they may live by her purposes, and may grow thither whither she would fain have brought them. All these were great parts of an excellent religion, as they concerned her greatest temporal relations.

7. But if we examine how she demeaned herself towards God, there also you will find her not of a common, but of an exemplar piety. She was a great reader of scripture, confining herself to a great portion every day; which she read not to the purposes of vanity and impertinent curiosities, not to seem knowing or to become talking, not to expound and rule; but to teach her all her duty, to instruct her in the knowledge and love of God and of her neighbours; to make her more humble, and to teach her to despise the world and all its gilded vanities; and that she might entertain passions wholly in design and order to heaven. I have seen a female religion that wholly dwelt upon the face and tongue; that like a wanton and an undressed tree spends all its juice in suckers and irregular branches, in leaves and gum, and after all such goodly outsides you should never eat an apple, or be delighted with the beauties or the perfumes of a hopeful blossom. But the religion of this excellent lady was of another constitution; it took root downward in humility, and brought forth fruit upward in the substantial graces of a Christian, in charity and justice, in chastity and modesty, in fair friendships and

[14] Prov 2:17.

sweetness of society. She had not very much of the forms and outsides of godliness, but she was hugely careful for the power of it, for the moral, essential, and useful parts; such which would make her be, not seem to be, religious.

8. She was a very constant person at her prayers, and spent all her time which nature did permit to her choice, in her devotions, and reading and meditating, and the necessary offices of household government; every one of which is an action of religion, some by nature, some by adoption. To these also God gave her a very great love to hear the word of God preached; in which because I had sometimes the honour to minister to her, I can give this certain testimony, that she was a diligent, watchful, and attentive hearer: and to this had so excellent a judgment, that if ever I saw a woman whose judgment was to be revered, it was hers alone: and I have sometimes thought that the eminency of her discerning faculties did reward a pious discourse, and placed it in the regions of honour and usefulness, and gathered it up from the ground, where commonly such homilies are spilt, or scattered in neglect and inconsideration. But her appetite was not soon satisfied with what was useful to her soul: she was also a constant reader of sermons, and seldom missed to read one every day; and that she might be full of instruction and holy principles, she had lately designed to have a large book, in which she purposed to have a stock of religion transcribed in such assistances as she would choose, that she might be 'readily furnished and instructed to every good work.' But God prevented that, and hath filled her desires, not out of cisterns and little aqueducts, but hath carried her to the fountain, where she 'drinks of the pleasures of the river,' and is full of God.

9. She always lived a life of much innocence, free from the violences of great sins: her person, her breeding, her modesty, her honour, her religion, her early marriage, the guide of her soul, and the guide of her youth, were so many fountains of restraining grace to her, to keep her from the dishonours of a crime. *Bonum est portare jugum ab adolescentia,*[15] 'it is good to bear the yoke of the Lord from our youth;' and though she did so, being guarded by a mighty providence, and a great favour and grace of God from staining her fair soul with the spots of hell, yet she had strange fears and early cares upon her, but these were not only for herself, but in order to others, to her nearest relatives. For she was so great a lover of this honourable family of which now she was a mother, that she desired to become a channel of great blessings to it unto future ages, and was extremely jealous lest any thing should be done, or lest any thing had been done, though an age or two since, which should entail a curse upon the innocent posterity [...] and because she knew the sins of parents descent upon children, she endeavoured by justice and religion, by charity and honour to secure that her channel should convey nothing but health, and a fair example and a blessing.

15 Lam 3:27.

10. And though her accounts to God was made up of nothing but small parcels, little passions, and angry words, and trifling discontents, which are the allays of the piety of the most holy persons; yet she was early at her repentance; and toward the latter end of her days, grew so fast in religion, as if she had had a revelation of her approaching end, and therefore that she must go a great way in a little time: her discourses more full of religion, her prayers more frequent, her charity increasing, her forgiveness more forward, her friendships more communicative, her passion more under discipline; and so she trimmed her lamp, not thinking her night was so near, but that it might shine also in the daytime, in the temple, and before the altar of incense.

But in this course of hers, there were some circumstances, and some appendages of substance, which were highly remarkable.

1. In all her religion, and in all her actions of relation towards God, she had a strange evenness and untroubled passage, sliding toward her ocean of God and of infinity with a certain and silent motion. So have I seen a river deep and smooth passing with a still foot and a sober face, and paying to the *fiscus*, the great exchequer of the sea, the prince of all the watery bodies, a tribute large and full: and hard by it a little brook skipping and making a noise upon its unequal and neighbour bottom: and after all its talking and bragged motion, it payed to its common audit no more than the revenues of a little cloud, or a contemptible vessel. So have I sometimes compared the issues of her religion to the solemnities and famed outsides of another's piety; it dwelt upon her spirit, and was incorporated with the periodical work of every day; she did not believe that religion was intended to minister to fame and reputation, but to pardon of sins, to the pleasure of God, and the salvation of souls. For religion is like the breath of heaven; if it goes abroad into the open air, it scatters and dissolves like camphire: but if it enters into a secret hollowness, into a close conveyance, it is strong and mighty, and comes forth with vigour and great effect at the other end, at the other side of this life, in the days of death and judgment.

2. The other appendage of her religion, which also was a great ornament to all the parts of her life, was a rare modesty and humility of spirit, a confident despising and undervaluing of herself. For though she had the greatest judgment, and the greatest experience of things and persons that I ever yet knew in a person of her youth, and sex, and circumstances; yet as if she knew nothing of it, she had the meanest opinion of herself; and like a fair taper, when she shined to all the room, yet round about her own station she had cast a shadow and a cloud, and she shined to every body but herself. But the perfectness of her prudence and excellent parts could not be hid; and all her humility and arts of concealment, made the virtues more amiable and illustrious. For as pride sullies the beauty of the fairest virtues, and makes our understanding but like the craft and learning of

a devil: so humility is the greatest eminency and art of publication in the whole world; and she in all her arts of secrecy and hiding her worthy things, was but 'like one that hideth the wind, and covers the ointment of her right hand.'[16]

I know not by what instrument it happened; but when death drew near, before it made any show upon her body, or revealed itself by a natural signification, it was conveyed to her spirit: she had a strange secret persuasion that the bringing this child should be her last scene of life: and we have known, that the soul when she is about to disrobe herself of her outer garment, sometimes speaks rarely, *Magnifica verba mors prope admota excutit*;[17] sometimes it is prophetical; sometimes God by a superinduced persuasion wrought by instruments or accidents of His own, serves the ends of His own providence and the salvation of the soul. But so it was, that the thought of death dwelt long with her, and grew from the first steps of fancy and fear, to a consent, from thence to a strange credulity and expectation of it; and without the violence of sickness she died, as if she had done it voluntarily, and by design, and for fear her expectation should have been deceived, or that she should seem to have had an unreasonable fear, or apprehension; or rather (as one said of Cato), 'she died, as if she had been glad of the opportunity.'[18]

And in this I cannot but adore the providence, and admire the wisdom and infinite mercies of God. For having a tender and soft, a delicate and fine constitution and breeding, she was tender to pain, and apprehensive of it, as a child's shoulder is of a load and burden. *Grave est tenerae cervici jugum*: and in her often discourses of death which she would renew willingly and frequently, she would tell, that she feared not death, but she feared the sharp pains of death. *Emori nolo, me esse mortuam non curo*; the being dead, and being freed from the troubles and dangers of this world, she hoped would be for her advantage, and therefore that was no part of her fear: but she believing the pangs of death were great, and the use and aids of reason little, had reason to fear lest they should do violence to her spirit and the decency of her resolution. But God, that knew her fears and her jealousy concerning herself, fitted her with a death so easy, so harmless, so painless, that it did not put her patience to a severe trial. It was not (in all appearance) of so much trouble as two fits of a common ague; so careful was God to remonstrate to all that stood in that sad attendance that this soul was dear to Him: and that since she had done so much of her duty towards it, He that began would also finish her redemption, by an act of a rare providence, and a singular mercy. Blessed be that goodness of God, who does so careful actions of mercy for the ease and security of His servants. But this one instance was a great demonstration that the apprehension of death is worse than the pains of death; and that God loves to reprove the unreasonableness of our fears, by the mightiness and by the arts of His mercy.

16 Prov 27:16.   17 Seneca, *Tragedies*, LCL, vol. I, p.172.   18 Cicero, *Tusculan Disputations*, 1:30, LCL, p.84.

She had in her sickness (if I may so call it, or rather in the solemnities and graver preparations towards death) some curious and well-becoming fears, concerning the final state of her soul: but from thence she passed into a *deliquium*, or a kind of trance, and as soon as she came forth of it, as if it had been a vision, or that she had conversed with an angel, and from his hand had received a label or scroll of the book of life, and there seen her name enrolled, she cried out aloud, 'Glory be to God on high; now I am sure I shall be saved.' Concerning which manner of discoursing we are wholly ignorant what judgment can be made: but certainly there are strange things in the other world; and so there are in all the immediate preparations to it; and a little glimpse of heaven, a minute's conversing with an angel, any ray of God, and communication extraordinary from the Spirit of comfort, which God gives to His servants in strange and unknown manners, are infinitely far from illusions; and they shall then be understood by us, when we feel them, and when our new and strange needs shall be refreshed by such unusual visitations.

But I must be forced to use summaries and arts of abbreviature in the enumerating those things in which this rare personage was dear to God and to all her relatives.

If we consider her person, she was in the flower of her age; [...] and of the pleasures of this world, which were laid before her in heaps, she took a very small and inconsiderable share, as not loving to glut herself with vanity, or take her portion of good things here below.

If we look on her as a wife, she was chaste and loving, fruitful and discreet, humble and pleasant, witty and compliant, rich and fair; and wanted nothing to the making her a principal and precedent to the best wives of the world, but a long life, and a full age.

If we remember her as a mother, she was kind and severe, careful and prudent, very tender, and not at all fond, a greater lover of her children's souls than of their bodies, and one that would value them more by the strict rules of honour and proper worth, than by their relation to herself.

Her servants found her prudent, and fit to govern, and yet openhanded, and apt to reward; a just exactor of their duty, and a great rewarder of their diligence.

She was in her house a comfort to her dearest lord, a guide to her children, a rule to her servants, an example to all.

But as she related to God in the offices of religion, she was even and constant, silent and devout, prudent and material; she loved what she now enjoys, and she feared what she never felt, and God did for her what she never did expect: her fears went beyond all her evil; and yet the good which she hath received was, and is, and ever shall be beyond all her hopes.

She lived as we all should live, and she died as I fain would die; I pray God I may feel those mercies on my death-bed that she felt, and that I may feel the same effect of my repentance which she feels of the many degrees of her innocence. Such was her death, that she did not die too soon; and her life was so useful and so excellent, that she could not have lived too long. *Nemo parum diu vixit qui virtutis perfectae perfecto functus est munere.*[19] And as now in the grave it shall not be enquired concerning her, how long she lived, but how well; so to us who live after her, to suffer a longer calamity, it may be some ease to our sorrows, and some guide to our lives, and some security to our conditions, to consider that God hath brought the piety of a young lady to the early rewards of a never ceasing and never dying eternity of glory. And we also, if we live as she did, shall partake of the same glories; not only having the honour of a good name, and a dear and honoured memory, but the glories of these glories, the end of all excellent labours, and all prudent counsels, and all holy religion, even the salvation of our souls in that day when all the saints, and amongst them this excellent woman, shall be shewn to all the world to have done more, and more excellent things than we know of or can describe. *Mors illos consecrat, quorum exitum et qui timent, laudant,*[20] death consecrates and makes sacred that person whose excellency was such, that they that are not displeased at the death, cannot dispraise the life; but they that mourn sadly, think they can never commend sufficiently.

Preached at the Funeral of the Lord Primate of Ireland[1]

JEREMY TAYLOR

But every man in his own order: Christ the first-fruits; afterward they that are Christ's at His coming. (1 Cor 15:23)

The condition of man in this world is so limited and depressed, so relative and imperfect, that the best things he does he does weakly, and the best things he hath are imperfections in their very constitution. I need not tell how little it is that we know; the greatest indication of this is, that we can never tell how many things we know not: and we may soon span our own knowledge, but our ignorance we can never fathom. Our very will, in which mankind pretends to be most noble and imperial, is a direct state of imperfection; and our very liberty of choosing good and evil is permitted to us, not to make us proud, but to make us humble; for it supposes weakness of reason and weakness of love. For if we understood all the degrees of amability in the service of God, or if we had such love to God as He deserves,

---

19 Seneca, *Moral Essays*, LCL, vol. 1, p.6.   20 Ibid.   1 Sermon VII, in J. Taylor, vol. 8, pp 395-423.

and so perfect a conviction as were fit for His services, we could no more deliberate: for liberty of will is like the motion of a magnetic needle toward the north, full of trembling and uncertainty till it were fixed in the beloved point; it wavers as long as it is free, and is at rest when it can choose no more. And truly what is the hope of man? It is indeed the resurrection of the soul in this world from sorrow and her saddest pressures, like the twilight to the day, and the harbinger of joy; but still it is but a conjugation of infirmities, and proclaims our present calamity, only because it is uneasy here; it thrusts us forward toward the light and glories of the resurrection.

For as a worm creeping with her belly on the ground, with her portion and share of Adam's curse, lifts up its head to partake a little of the blessings of the air, and opens the junctures of her imperfect body, and curls her little rings into knots and combinations, drawing up her tail to a neighbourhood of the head's pleasure and motion; but still it must return to abide the fate of its own nature, and dwell and sleep upon the dust: so are the hopes of a mortal man; he opens his eyes and looks upon fine things at distance, and shuts them again with weakness, because they are too glorious to behold; and the man rejoices because he hopes fine things are staying for him; but his heart aches, because he knows there are a thousand ways to fail and miss of those glories; and though he hopes, yet he enjoys not; he longs, but he possesses not, and must be content with his portion of dust; and being 'a worm and no man'[2] must lie down in this portion, before he can receive the end of his hopes, the salvation of his soul in the resurrection of the dead. For as death is the end of our lives, so is the resurrection the end of our hopes; and as we 'die daily,'[3] so we daily hope: but death which is the end of our life, is the enlargement of our spirits from hope to certainty, from uncertain fears to certain expectations, from the death of the body to the life of the soul; that is, to partake of the light and life of Christ, to rise to life as He did; for His resurrection is the beginning of ours: He died for us alone, not for Himself; but He rose again for Himself and us too. So that if He did rise, so shall we; the resurrection shall be universal; good and bad, all shall rise: but not altogether; first Christ, then we that are Christ's. And yet there is a third resurrection, though not spoken of here; but this it shall be: 'The dead of Christ shall rise first,'[4] that is, next to Christ; and after them the wicked shall rise to condemnation.

Here is the sum of affairs treated of in my text: the enquiry here is, whether we are to be Christians or no? […] whether it is permitted to us to live with lust or covetousness acted with all the daughters of rapine and ambition? whether there be any such thing as sin, any judicatory for consciences, any rewards of piety, any difference of good and bad, any rewards after this life? This is the design of these

---

2 Ps 12:6.   3 1 Cor 15:31.   4 Cf 1 Thess 4:16.

words by proper interpretation: for if men shall die like dogs and sheep, they will certainly live like wolves and foxes: but he that believes the article of the resurrection, hath entertained the greatest demonstration in the world, that nothing can make us happy but the knowledge of God, and conformity to the life and death of the holy Jesus.

Here therefore are the great hinges of all religion: 1) Christ is already risen from the dead. 2) We also shall rise in God's time and our order. Christ is the first-fruits: but there shall be a full harvest of the resurrection, and all shall rise. My text speaks only of the resurrection of the just, of them that belong to Christ; explicitly I say of these, and therefore directly of resurrection to life eternal. But because he also says there shall be an order for every man, and yet every man does not belong to Christ; therefore indirectly also he implies the more universal resurrection unto judgment. But this shall be the last thing that shall be done; for according to the proverb of the Jews, 'Michael flies but with one wing, and Gabriel with two;' God is quick in sending angels of peace, and they fly apace; but the messengers of wrath come slowly: God is more hasty to glorify His servants than to condemn the wicked. And therefore in the story of Dives and Lazarus[5] we find that the beggar died first; the good man Lazarus was first taken away from his misery to his comfort, and afterwards the rich man died: and as the good, many times, die first, so all of them rise first, as if it were a matter of haste: and as the mother's breasts swell and shoot and long to give food to her babe, so God's bowels did yearn over His banished children, and He longs to cause them to eat and drink in His kingdom. And at last the wicked shall rise unto condemnation, for that must be done too; every man in his own order: first Christ, then Christ's servants, and at last Christ's enemies. The first of these is the great ground of our faith, the second is the consummation of all our hopes: the first is the foundation of God that stands sure, the second is that superstructure that shall never perish: by the first we believe in God unto righteousness, by the second we live in God unto salvation. But the third, for that also is true and must be considered, is the great affrightment of all them that live ungodly. But in the whole, Christ's resurrection and ours is the *Alpha* and *Omega* of a Christian; that as 'Jesus Christ' is 'the same yesterday and to-day, and the same for ever',[6] so may we in Christ become in the morrow of the resurrection, the same or better than yesterday in our natural life; the same body and the same soul tied together in the same essential union, with this only difference, that not nature but grace and glory with an hermetic seal give us a new signature, whereby we shall no more be changed, but like unto Christ our head we shall become the same for ever. Of these I shall discourse in order.

5 Lk 16:22.   6 Heb 13:8.

I. That Christ who is the first-fruits, is the first in this order: He is already risen from the dead.

II. We shall all take our turns, we shall all die, and as sure as death we shall all rise again; and,

III. This very order is effective of the thing itself. That Christ is first risen, is the demonstration and certainty of ours, for because there is an order in this economy, the first in the kind is the measure of the rest. If Christ be the first-fruits, we are the whole vintage, and we shall all die in the order of nature, and shall rise again in the order of Christ: they that are Christ's, and are found so at His coming shall partake of His resurrection: but Christ first, then they that are Christ's: that's the order.

I. Christ is the first-fruits; He is already risen from the dead; He alone 'could not be held by death;'[7] 'free among the dead,'[8] [...] death was sin's eldest daughter, and the grave clothes were her first mantle; but Christ was conqueror over both, and came to take that away, and to disarm this. This was a glory fit for the head of mankind, but it was too great and too good to be easily believed by incredulous and weak-hearted man. It was at first doubted by all that were concerned; but they that saw it had no reason to doubt any longer. But what's that to us who saw it not? Yes, very much, *Valde dubitatum est ab illis, ne dubitaretur a nobis*, saith St Augustine, 'they doubted very much, that by their confirmation we might be established and doubt no more. Mary Magdalene saw Him first, and she ran with joy and said 'she had seen the Lord, and that He was risen from the dead; but they believed her not: after that divers women together saw Him,' and they told it, but had no thanks for their pains, and obtained no credit among the disciples. The two disciples that went to Emmaus saw Him, talked with Him, ate with Him, and they ran and told it: they told true, but nobody believed them. Then St Peter saw Him, but he was not yet got into the chair of the catholic church; they did not think him infallible, and so they believed him not at all. Five times in one day He appeared; for after all this He appeared to the eleven; they were indeed transported with joy and wonder, but they would scarce believe their own eyes, and though they saw Him they doubted. Well, all this was not enough; He was seen also of James, and suffered Thomas to trust his hand into His side, and appeared to St Paul, and was seen by 'five hundred brethren at once.' So that there is no capacity of mankind, no time, no place, but had an ocular demonstration of His resurrection. He appeared to men and women, to the clergy and the laity, to sinners of both sexes; to weak men and to criminals, to doubters and deniers, at home and abroad, in public and in private, in their houses and their journeys, unexpected and by appointment, betimes in the morning and late at night, to

7 Acts 2:24. 8 Ps 88:5.

them in conjunction, and to them in dispersion, when they did look for Him and when they did not; He appeared upon earth to many, and to St Paul and St Stephen from heaven. So that we can require no greater testimony than all these are able to give us; and they saw for themselves and for us too, that the faith and certainty of the resurrection of Jesus might be conveyed to all that shall die and follow Christ in their own order.

Now [...] if this be not sufficient credibility in a matter of fact as this was, then we can have no story credibly transmitted to us, no records kept, no acts of courts, no narratives of the days of old, no traditions of our fathers, no memorials of them in the third generation. Nay, if from these we have not sufficient causes and arguments of faith, how shall we be able to know the will of heaven upon earth, unless God do not only tell it once, but always; and not only always to some men, but always to all men? For if some men must believe others, they can never do it in any thing more reasonably than in this; and if we may not trust them in this, then without a perpetual miracle no man could have faith: for faith could never come by hearing, by nothing but by seeing. But if there be any use of history, any faith in men, any honesty in manners, any truth in human intercourse; if there be any use of apostles or teachers, of ambassadors or letters, of ears or hearing; if there be any such thing as the grace of faith, that is less than demonstration or intuition, then we may be as sure that Christ the first-fruits is already risen, as all these credibilities can make us [...].

But [...] presently it came to pass that the religion of the despised Jesus did infinitely prevail ... a religion that would change the face of things, and the hearts of men, and break vile habits into gentleness and counsel; that such a religion, in such a time, by the sermons and conduct of fishermen, should so speedily triumph over the philosophy of the world, and the arguments of the subtle, and the sermons of the eloquent [...], that is, against wit and power, superstition and wilfulness, fame and money, nature and empire, which are all the causes in this world that can make a thing impossible; this, this is to be ascribed to the power of God, and is the great demonstration of the resurrection of Jesus. Everything was an argument for it, and improved it; no objection could hinder it, no enemies destroy it [...], and quickly it was that the world became disciple to the glorious Nazarene, and men could no longer doubt of the resurrection of Jesus, when it became so demonstrated by the certainty of them that saw it, and the courage of them that died for it, and the multitude of them that believed it; who by their sermons and their actions [...] by their living in the obedience of Jesus, and dying for the testimony of Jesus, have greatly advanced His kingdom, and His power, and His glory, into which He entered after His resurrection from the dead. For He is the first-fruits; and if we hope to rise through Him, we must confess that Himself is first risen from the dead. That's the first particular.

II. There is an order for us also: we also shall rise again [...]. If it was done once, it may be done again; for since it could never have been done but by a power that is infinite, that infinite must also be eternal and indeficient. By the almighty power which restored life to the dead body of our living Lord, we may all be restored to a new life in the resurrection of the dead.

When man was not, what power, what causes made him to be? Whatsoever it was, it did then as great a work as to raise his body to the same being again; and because we know not the method of nature's secret changes, and how we can be fashioned beneath *in secreto terrae*[9] [...], must our ignorance in philosophy be put in balance against the articles of religion, the hopes of mankind, the faith of nations and the truth of God? [...] For God, knowing that the great hope of man [...] does wholly derive from the article of the Resurrection, was pleased not only to make it credible, but easy and familiar to us; and we so converse every night with the image of death, that every morning we find an argument of the resurrection. Sleep and death have but one mother, and they have one name in common: charnel-houses are but *koimeteria*, cemeteries or sleeping-places, and they that die are fallen asleep, and the resurrection is but an awakening and standing up from sleep: but in sleep our senses are as fast bound by nature as our joints are by the grave-clothes; and unless an angel of God awaken us every morning, we must confess ourselves as unable to converse with men, as we now are afraid to die and to converse with spirits. But however, death itself is no more; it is but darkness and a shadow, a rest and a forgetfulness. What is there more in death? what is there less in sleep? For do we not see by experience that nothing of equal loudness does awaken us sooner than a man's voice, especially if he be called by name? and thus also it shall be in the resurrection: we shall be awakened by the voice of a man, and He that called Lazarus by name from his grave shall also call us: for although St Paul affirms that 'the trumpet shall sound, and there shall be the voice of an archangel;' yet this is not a word of nature, but of office and ministry. Christ himself is that archangel, and He shall 'descend with a mighty shout,' saith the apostle,[10] 'and all that are in the grave shall hear His voice,' saith St John.[11] So that we shall be awakened by the voice of a man, because we are only fallen asleep by the decree of God; and when the cock and the lark call us up to prayer and labour, the first thing we see is an argument of our resurrection from the dead [...].

Night and day, the sun returning to the same point of east, every change of species in the same matter, generation and corruption, the eagle renewing her youth, and the snake her skin, the silk-work and the swallows, the care of posterity and the care of an immortal name, winter and summer, the fall and spring, the Old testament and

---

9 Ps 139:15.   10 1 Thess 4:16.   11 Jn 5:28.

the New, the words of Job,[12] and the visions of the prophets, the prayer of Ezekiel for the resurrection of the men of Ephraim,[13] and the return of Jonas from the whale's belly, the histories of the Jews and the narrative of Christians, the faith of believers and the philosophy of the reasonable; all join in the verification of this mystery [...]. And it is remarkable what St Augustine observes, that when the world saw the righteous Abel destroyed, and that the murderer outlived his crime and built up a numerous family, and grew mighty upon earth, they neglected the service of God upon that account, till God in pity of their prejudice and foolish arguings took Enoch up to heaven to recover them from their impieties by shewing them that their bodies and souls should be rewarded for ever in an eternal union. But Christ the first-fruits is gone before, and Himself did promise that when Himself was lifted up He would draw all men after Him. 'Every man in His own order; first Christ, then they that are Christ's at His coming.' – And so I have done with the second particular, not Christ only, but we also shall rise in God's time and our order.

III. First Christ, and then we: and we therefore because Christ is already risen [...]. For we must know that God hath sent Christ into the world to be a great example and demonstration of the economy and dispensation of eternal life. As God brought Christ to glory, so He will bring us, but by no other method. He first obeyed the will of God, and patiently suffered the will of God; He died and rose again, and entered into glory; and so must we. Thus Christ is made *via, veritas, et vita*, 'the way, the truth, and the life;' that is, the true way to eternal life. He first trod this wine-press, and we must insist in the same steps, or we shall never partake of this blessed resurrection. He was made the Son of God in a most glorious manner, and we by Him, by His merit, by His grace and by His example; but other than this there is no way of salvation for us. That's the first and great effect of this glorious order.

But there is one thing more in it yet, 'Every man in his own order; first Christ, and then they that are Christ's;' but what shall become of them that are not Christ's? Why there is an order for them too: first, 'they that are Christ's;' and then 'they that are not His.' 'Blessed and holy is he that hath his part in the first resurrection:'[14] there is a first and a second resurrection even after this life; 'The dead in Christ shall rise first:'[15] now blessed are they that have their portion here, for upon these the second death shall have no power. As for the recalling the wicked from their graves, it is no otherwise in the sense of the Spirit to be called a resurrection, than taking a criminal from the prison to the bar is a giving of liberty; [...] they shall receive their souls, that they may be a portion for devils; they shall receive their bodies that they may feel the everlasting burning: they shall see Christ, that they may 'look on Him whom they have pierced:'[16] and they shall hear the voice of God passing upon them the intolerable sentence; they shall come from their graves that they may go into hell;

12 Job 19:26f.   13 Ezek 37.   14 Rev 20:6.   15 1 Thess 4:16.   16 Zech 12:10.

and live again, that they may die for ever. So have we seen a poor condemned criminal, the weight of whose sorrows sitting heavily upon his soul, hath benumbed him into a deep sleep, till he hath forgotten his groans, and laid aside his deep sighings; but on a sudden comes the messenger of death, and unbinds the poppy garland, scatters the heavy cloud that encircled his miserable head, and makes him return to acts of life, that he may quickly descend into death and be no more. So is every sinner that lies down in shame, and makes his grave with the wicked; he shall indeed rise again, and be called upon by the voice of the archangel; but then he shall descend into sorrows greater than the reason and the patience of a man, weeping and shrieking louder than the groans of the miserable children in the valley of Hinnom.

These indeed are sad stories, but true as the voice of God, and the sermons of the holy Jesus. They are God's words, and God's decrees; and I wish that all who profess the belief of these, would consider sadly what they mean [...], for if it be so hard to believe a resurrection from one death, let us not be dead in trespasses and sins; for a resurrection from two deaths will be harder to be believed, and harder to be effected. But if any of you have lost the life of grace, and so forfeited all your title to a life of glory, betake yourselves to an early and an entire piety, that when by this first resurrection you have made this way plain before your face, you may with confidence expect a happy resurrection from your graves. For if it be possible that the spirit, when it is dead in sin, can arise to a life of righteousness; much more it is easy to suppose that the body after death is capable of being restored again [...]. The first resurrection is certainly the greater miracle: but he that hath risen once, may rise again; and this is as sure as that he that dies once may die again, and die for ever. But he who partakes of the death of Christ by mortification, and of His resurrection by holiness of life and a holy faith, shall, according to the expression of the prophet Isaiah, 'enter into his chamber of death;'[17] when nature and God's decree 'shall shut the doors upon him, and there he shall be hidden for a little moment:' but then shall 'they that dwell in dust awake and sing, with Christ's dead body shall they arise;' all shall rise, 'but every man in his own order; Christ the first-fruits, then they that are Christ's, at His coming.' Amen.

I have now done with my meditation of the resurrection; but we have a new and a sadder subject to consider [...]. After great Cyrus had ruled long in a mighty empire, yet there came a message from heaven, not so sad it may be, yet as decretory as the hand-writing on the wall that arrested his successor Darius: 'prepare thyself, O Cyrus, and then go unto the gods;'[18] he laid aside his tire and his beauteous diadem, and covered his face with a cloth, and in a single linen laid his honoured head in a poor humble grave. And none of us all can avoid this sentence; for if wit and

---

17 Is 26:20. 18 Xenophon, *Cyrovaedia*, 8:7, LCL, vol. 2, p.422.

learning, great fame and great experience; if wise notices of things, and an honourable fortune; if courage and skill, if prelacy and an honourable age, if any thing that could give greatness and immunity to a wise and prudent man, could have been put in bar against a sad day, and have gone for good plea, this sad scene of sorrows had not been the entertainment of this assembly [...].

When Dorcas died,[19] the apostle came to see the dead corpse, and the friends of the deceased expressed their grief and their love by shewing the coats that she, whilst she lived, wrought with her own hands [...] and the apostle himself was not displeased with their little sermons, and that *euphemismos* which the woman made upon that sad interview. But if we may have the same liberty to record the worthy things of this our most venerable father and brother, and if there remains no more of that envy which usually obscures the splendour of living heroes; if you can behold the great gifts of God with which He adorned this great prelate, and not object the failings of humanity to the participation of the graces of the Spirit, or think that God's gifts are the less because they are born in earthen vessels, for all men bear mortality about them, and the cabinet is not so beauteous as the diamond that shines within its bosom; then we may without interruption pay this duty to piety and friendship and thankfulness, and deplore our sad loss by telling a true and sad story of this great man, whom God hath lately taken from our eyes.

He was bred in Cambridge, in Sidney college, under Mr Hulet, a grave and a worthy man; and [...] having passed the course of his studies in the university, and done his exercise with that applause which is usually the reward of pregnant wits and hard study, he was removed into Yorkshire, where first in the city of York he was an assiduous preacher [...].

But while he lived there he was like a diamond in the dust or Lucius Quinctius at the plough, his low fortune covered a most valuable person, till he became observed by Sir Thomas Wentworth, lord president of York, whom we all knew for his great excellencies and his great but glorious misfortunes. This rare person espied the great abilities of Doctor Bramhall, and made him his chaplain, and brought him into Ireland, as one whom he believed would prove the most fit instrument to serve in that design, which for two years before his arrival here he had greatly meditated and resolved, the reformation of religion, and the reparation of the broken fortunes of the church: the complaints were many, the abuses great, the causes of the church vastly numerous; but as fast as they were brought in, so fast they were by the lord deputy referred back to Dr Bramhall, who by his indefatigable pains, great sagacity, perpetual watchfulness, daily and hourly consultations, reduced things to a more tolerable condition than they had been left in by the schismatical principles of some, and the

---

19 Acts 9:39.

unjust prepossessions of others, for many years before [...]; and the first specimen of his abilities and diligence in recovery of some lost tithes being represented to his late majesty of blessed and glorious memory, it pleased his majesty upon the death of bishop Downham to advance the doctor to the bishopric of Derry [...].

At first indeed, as his blessed Master the most holy Jesus had, so he also had his *annum acceptabilem*.[20] At first the product was nothing but great admiration at his stupendious parts, and wonder at his mighty diligence, and observation of his unusual zeal in so good and great things; but this quickly passed into the natural daughters of envy, suspicion and detraction, the spirit of obloquy and slander. His zeal for recovery of the church revenues was called oppression and rapine, covetousness and injustice; his care of reducing religion to wise and justifiable principles was called popery and Arminianism, and I know not what names, which signify what the authors are pleased to mean, and the people to construe and to hate [...]. But because every man's cause is right in his own eyes, it was hard for him so to acquit himself, that in the intrigues of law and difficult cases some of his enemies should not seem to speak reason against him. But see the greatness of truth and prudence, and how greatly God stood with him. When the numerous armies of vexed people heaped up catalogues of accusations, when the parliament of Ireland imitating the violent procedures of the then disordered English, when his glorious patron was taken from his head, and he was disrobed of his great defences; when petitions were invited and accusations furnished, and calumny was rewarded and managed with art and power, when there were above two hundred petitions put in against him, and himself denied leave to answer by word of mouth; when he was long imprisoned, and treated so that a guilty man would have been broken into affrightment and pitiful and low considerations; yet then he himself standing almost alone, like Callimachus at Marathon, invested with enemies and covered with arrows, defended himself beyond all the powers of guiltiness, even with the defences of truth and the bravery of innocence, and answered the petitions in writing, sometimes twenty in a day, with so much clearness, evidence of truth, reality of fact and testimony of law, that his very enemies were ashamed and convinced; they found they had done like Aesop's viper, they licked the file till their tongues bled; but himself was wholly invulnerable. They were therefore forced to leave their muster-rolls and decline the particulars, and fall to their *en mega*, to accuse him for going about to subvert the fundamental laws; the way by which great Strafford and Canterbury fell; which was a device, when all reasons failed, to oppress the enemy by the bold affirmation of a conclusion they could not prove [...], so necessary it was for them who intended to do mischief to the public, to take away the strongest pillars of the house.

This thing I remark to acquit this great man from the tongue of slander, which had so boldly spoken, that it was certain something would stick; yet was so impotent

---

20 Is 61:2.

and unarmed, that it could not kill that great fame which his greater worthiness had procured him. It was said of Hippasus the Pythagorean, that being asked how and what he had done, he answered, 'I have done nothing yet, for no man envies me.' He that does great things cannot avoid the tongues and teeth of envy; but if calumnies must pass for evidences, the bravest heroes must always be the most reproached persons in the world [...]. But God, who takes care of reputations as He does of lives, by the orders of His providence confutes the slander, 'that the memory of the righteous man might be embalmed with honour:' and so it happened to this great man; for [...] he was restored *in integrum* to that fame where his great labours and just procedures had first estate him; which though it was but justice, yet it was also such honour, that it is greater than the virulence of tongues which his worthiness and their envy had armed against him [...].

But God having still resolved to afflict us, the good man was forced into the fortune of the patriarchs, to leave his country and his charges, and seek for safety and bread in a strange land; for so the prophets were used to do, wandering up and down in sheep's-clothing; but poor as they were, the world was not worthy of them: and this worthy man, despising the shame, took up his cross and followed his Master. He was not ashamed to suffer where the cause was honourable and glorious; but so God provided for the needs of his banished, and sent a man who could minister comfort to the afflicted, and courage to the persecuted, and resolutions to the tempted, and strength to that religion for which they all suffered.

And here this great man was indeed triumphant; this was one of the last and best scenes of his life: 'the last days are the best witnesses of a man.'[21] But so it was, that he stood up in public and brave defence for the doctrine and discipline of the church of England: first, by his sufferings and great example, for 'to talk well and not to do bravely, is for a comedian, not a divine;' but this great man did both; he suffered his own calamity with great courage, and by his wise discourses strengthened the hearts of others [...].

He wrote no apologies for himself, though it were much to be wished that, as Junius wrote his own life, or Moses his own story, so we might have understood from himself how great things God had done for him and by him; but all that he permitted to God, and was silent in his own defences. But when the honour and conscience of his king, and the interest of a true religion was at stake, the fire burned within him, and at last he spake with his tongue; he cried out like the son of Croesus, 'take heed and meddle not with the king;' his person is too sacred, and religion too dear to him to be assaulted by vulgar hands. In short, he acquitted himself in this affair with so much truth and piety, learning and judgment, that in those papers his memory will last unto very late succeeding generations.

21 Cf. *Pindar*, LCL, vol. 1, p. 52.

But this most reverend prelate found a nobler adversary, and a braver scene for his contention. He found that the Roman priests, being wearied and baffled by the wise discourses and pungent arguments of the English divines, had studiously declined any more to dispute the particular questions against us, but fell at last upon a general charge, imputing to the church of England the great crime of schism [...]; but now it was that *dignum nactus argumentum*, 'having an argument fit' to employ his great abilities, the bishop now undertook the question, and in a full discourse proves the church of Rome not only to be guilty of the schism, by making it necessary to depart from them; but they did actuate the schisms, and themselves made the first separation in the great point of the pope's supremacy, which was the *palladium* for which they principally contended [...]. The old bishop of Chalcedon, known to many of us, replied to this excellent book; but was so answered by a rejoinder made by the lord bishop of Derry, that the pleasures of reading the book would be the greatest, if the profit to the church of God were not greater. For so Samson's riddle[22] was again expounded, 'Out of the strong came meat, and out of the eater came sweetness.' [...] And whenever men will desire to be satisfied in those great questions, the bishop of Derry's book shall be his oracle [...].

He thus having served God and the king abroad, God was pleased to return to the king and to us all, as in the 'days of old,' and we 'sung the song of David,'[23] *in convertendo captivitatem Sion*. When king David and all his servants returned to Jerusalem, this great person having trode in the wine-press was called to drink of the wine, and as an honorary reward of his great services and abilities was chosen primate of this national church: in which time we are to look upon him, as the king and the king's great vicegerent did, as a person concerning whose abilities the world had too great testimony ever to make a doubt. It is true he was in the declension of his age and health; but his very ruins were goodly; and they who saw the broken heaps of Pompey's theatre, and the crushed obelisks, and the old face of beauteous Philenium, could not but admire the disordered glories of such magnificent structures, which were venerable in their very dust.

He ever was used to overcome all difficulties, only mortality was too hard for him [...]. And still he was indefatigable, and was not willing that God should take him unemployed: but, good man that he was, he felt his tabernacle ready to fall in pieces, and could go no further, for God would have no more work done by that hand; he therefore espying this, put his house in order, and had lately visited his diocese, and done what he then could to put his charge in order: for he had a good while since received the sentence of death within himself, and knew he was shortly to render an account of his stewardship. But God, who is the great *choragus* and master of the

---

22 Judg 14:14.

scenes of life and death, was not pleased then to draw the curtains; there was an epilogue to his life yet to be acted and spoken. He returned to actions [...] but though his spirit was willing, yet his flesh was weak; and as the apostles in the vespers of Christ's passion, so he in the eve of his own dissolution was heavy, not to sleep, but heavy unto death, and looked for the last warning, which seized on him in the midst of business; and though it was sudden, yet it could not be unexpected, or unprovided by surprise, and therefore could be no other than that *euthanasia* which Augustus[24] used to wish unto himself, a civil and well-natured death, without the amazement of troublesome circumstances, or the great cracks of a falling house, or the convulsions of impatience [...]. It happened so to this excellent man [...] his active graces had been abundantly demonstrated by the great and good things he did, and therefore his last scene was not so laborious, but God called him away something after the manner of Moses, which the Jews express by *osculum oris Dei*, 'the kiss of God's mouth;' that is, a death indeed fore-signified, but gentle and serene, and without temptation.

To sum up all; he was a wise prelate, a learned doctor, a just man, a true friend, a great benefactor to others, a thankful beneficiary where he was obliged himself [...]. The practice of his religion was not so much in forms and exterior ministeries, though he was a great observer of all the public rites and ministeries of the church, as it was in doing good for others. He was like Myson, whom the Scythian Anacharsis so greatly praised, he 'governed his family well,' he gave to all their due of maintenance and duty; he did great benefit to mankind [...]. He was an excellent scholar, and rarely well accomplished; first instructed to great excellency by natural parts, and then consummated by study and experience. Melancthon was used to say, that himself was a logician, Pomeranus a grammarian, Justus Jonas an orator, but that Luther was all these. It was greatly true of him, that the single perfections which make many men eminent, were united in this primate, and made him illustrious [...]. For in him was visible the great lines of Hooker's judiciousness, of Jewel's learning, of the acuteness of bishop Andrewes. He was skilled in more great things than one; and as one said of Phidias, he could not only make excellent statues of ivory, but he could work in stone and brass; he shewed his equanimity in poverty, and his justice in riches; he was useful in his country, and profitable in his banishment; for as Paraeus was at Anvilla, Luther at Wittenberg, St Athanasius and St Chrysostom in their banishment, St Hierome in his retirement at Bethlehem, they were oracles to them that needed it; so was he in Holland and France, where he was abroad; and beside the particular endearments which his friends received from him, for he did do relief to his brethern that wanted, and supplied the soldiers out of his store in Yorkshire, when himself could but ill spare it; but he received public thanks from the

23 Ps 126:1.　24 Suetonius, *Lives of the Caesars*, Augustus, 99.

convocation of which he was president, and public justification from the parliament where he was speaker; so that although, as one said, *miraculi instar vitae iter, si longum, sine offensione percurrere*, yet no man had greater enemies, and no man had greater justifications.

But God hath taken our Elijah from our heads this day: I pray God that at least his mantle may be left behind, and that his spirit may be doubled upon his successor; and that we may all meet together with him at the right hand of the Lamb, where every man shall receive according to his deeds, whether they be good or whether they be evil. I conclude with the words of Caius Plinius, *Equidem beatos puto quibus deorum munere datum est aut facere scribenda, aut scribere legenda*:[25] he wrote many things fit to be read, and did very many things worthy to be written; which if we wisely imitate, we may hope to meet him in the resurrection of the just, and feast with him in the eternal supper of the Lamb, there to sing perpetual anthems to the honour of God the Father, Son and holy Ghost: to whom be all honour, &c.

---

25 Pliny, *Letters*, 6:16, LCL, vol. 1, p.424.

EPILOGUE

Panegyric and Preacher

On 13 August 1667, in his fifty-fifth year, Jeremy Taylor, bishop of Down and Connor, died at Lisburn, and his last words were 'Bury me at Dromore.' At Dromore where he had been the administrator of the diocese but never its bishop, he had restored the cathedral and at his own expense rebuilt the chancel; ironically and symbolically he was laid to rest here in a church beyond his church, so to speak, for as bishop he never found rest in his Presbyterian diocese. From the historical perspective it is difficult to understand the rejection of the most distinguished churchman in England and Ireland at the time of the Restoration in 1660. In fact there is something pathetic about his final request to Sheldon, a lesser light than Taylor in the days of darkness, but afterwards at Canterbury his wick was no longer tremulous nor hidden under a bushel:

> I humbly desire that Your Grace will not wholly lay me aside, and cast off all thoughts of removing me. For no man shall with a greater diligence, humility and observance, endeavour to make up his other disabilities than I shall. The case is so that the country does not agree with my health as it hath done formerly, till the last Michaelmas; and if Your Grace be not willing I should die immaturely, I shall still hope you will bring me to or near yourself once more. But to God and to Your Grace I humbly submit the whole affair, humbly desiring a kind return to this letter and the comfort of a little hope.[1]

The 'immature' death of Taylor in 1667 after the compromises of the Restoration, and the *Via Media* of the Church, more or less concluded this formative period of Anglicanism that began around 1595 with Richard Hooker and was distinguished by such names as Lancelot Andrewes and William Laud in England, Arnold Ussher and John Bramhall in Ireland, and a host of others generally known as the Caroline Divines. These Carolines, Catholic in a new culture and language, were theologians in the tradition of John the Theologian or the Divine as the apostle and evangelist was earlier known; by fitting their Elizabethan words to the Sword of God, and moulding them for worship and prayer, they gave a new quality to the English

---

1 Gosse, op.cit., p. 203.

language, making it as apt as Hebrew, Greek and Latin had been made through liturgical usage to express the realities of grace and the sanctuary. Like Chrysostom in Greek and Augustine in Latin, Taylor in English is of the same sacramental tradition in word and symbol, recognising the real presence of the transcendent in true theological discourse, and the sheer emptiness of mere intellectual debate:

> He that desires to enter furthest into the secrets of this mystery of the Eucharist and to understand more than others, can better learn by love more than by enquiry [...] If he will pass through the mystety with great devotion and purest simplicity, and converse the purities of the sacrament frequently and with intention, this man shall understand more by his experience than the greatest clerks can by their subtilities, the commentaries of the doctors and the glosses of inquisitive men. 'The love of the Lord', saith the wise man, 'passeth all for illumination.'[2]

In the mysterious ways of God, as indeed in the devious ways of man, Taylor was left to the bitter end to continue in his place of torment, as one firmly established in institutional, if not in outer, darkness. The death of Bramhall in Armagh brought him to the pulpit for the sermon, but not to the cathedral for the Primacy; nor was this Castle and Trinity bishop transferred to Dublin when Archbishop Margetson was elevated to Armagh. But his reward was elsewhere on the harvest day of his death, and like manys the other literary man he left behind an unfinished work, or 'Discourse on the Beatitudes', which death would bring to a suitable conclusion in the presence of Him who spoke them. He was survived by Joanna, his second wife, and three daughters for whom there was little of the world's goods to share, for he had spent whatever he had on almsgiving and church building. There is no record of the marriage of his daughter, Phoebe, but Mary married Frances March, the archbishop of Dublin, and Joanna married Edward Harrison, a member of Parliament for Lisburn. His six sons he buried, and Charles, his seventh and only surviving son, was buried at St Margaret's, Westminster, at the age of twenty-four, on the octave day of Taylor's own death:

> When a good man dies, one that had lived innocently, or made joy in heaven at his effective repentance, and in whose behalf the Holy Jesus hath interceded prosperously, and for whose interest the Spirit makes interpolations with groans and sighs unutterable, and in whose defence the Angels drive away the devils on his death-bed, because his sins are pardoned, and because he resisted the devil in his life-time, and fought

2 J. Taylor, vol. 8, p. 47.

successfully, and persevered unto the end, then joy breaks forth through the cloud of sickness, and the conscience stands upright, and confesses the glories of God, and owns so much integrity that it can hope for pardon, and obtain it too; then the sorrows of the sickness, and the flames of the fever or the faintness of the consumption, do but untie the soul from its chain, and let it go forth, first into liberty and then to glory.[3]

George Rust, dean of Connor and afterwards bishop of Dromore, preached the panegyric in Dromore cathedral on 21 August 1667 and repeated it two weeks later at a special memorial service at St Patrick's cathedral in Dublin, where a few years earlier Taylor had preached at his own and the consecration of those others appointed as bishops after the Restoration. Rust was the friend of Taylor's youth at Cambridge, and the companion of his ministry in Down and Connor, for he was one of those clergymen invited in from England to fill the parishes Taylor had declared vacant. Our most intimate glimpses of Jeremy Taylor as a man are derived from this panegyric, preached by his friend, and as it is the source of every Taylor biography it is given here in full, making every allowance for the partiality of friendship, and the exaggerations of the funeral discourse.

Rust followed the *schema* or structure of the classical and Christian panegyric and courageously imitated the adaptation that Taylor had developed of meditation first on a well chosen scripture text, and afterwards the biographical details as an expression of the Word of God in the life of His servant. He was entirely successful; the composition, beautiful in itself and appropriately eloquent, is the invaluable contribution that made friendly every biography of Taylor. The text (1 John 3:2) – *It doth not yet appear what we shall be* – was surprisingly simple, but when revealed in its every word, was as full as the assurance of our faith and the substance of our hope;

> Glorious things are spoken in scripture concerning the future reward of the righteous; and all the words that are wont to signify what is of greatest price and value, or can represent the most enravishing of our desires, are made use of by the Holy Ghost to recommend this transcendent state of blessedness unto us. Such are these 'rivers of pleasures,' a 'fountain of living water,' a 'treasure that can never be wasted, nor never taken from us,' an 'inheritance in light,' an 'incorruptible crown,' a 'Kingdom' of God, of Christ and of Glory. The 'crown of glory and life; righteousness and immortality.' The vision of God, 'being filled with the fulness of God;' an 'exceeding and eternal weight of glory' – *kath uperbolen eis uperbolen aionion Bapos doxes* – words strangely emphatical, they cannot be put into

---
[3] Ibid., vol. 3, p. 307.

English; and if they could, they would not be able to convey to our minds the notion that they design: for it is too big for any expressions; and after all that can be said we must resolve with our apostle, – 'It doth not yet appear what we shall be.'[4]

This opening is according to the *schema* of the Fathers, Greek and Latin, whose scriptures gave new vision or faith to the wisdom and words of the ancients, just as the James Bible of the Reformation did for the Renaissance. Nor does he hesitate to attempt the *exemplum* with the taste of Taylor, the master of simile and metaphor, although he lacks the fancy and flight of his imagination, his magic of sound or verbal music, and the mystical word or phrase or 'resolution of all our faculties into sweetnesses, affections and starings upon the divine beauty – a thing not to be discoursed of, but felt:'[5]

> It is not for any mortal creature to make a map of that Canaan that lies above; it is to all of us that live here on the hither-side of death, an unknown country and an undiscovered land. It may be, some heavenly pilgrim, that with his holy thoughts and ardent desires is continually travelling thitherward arrives, sometimes near the borders of the promised land, and the suburbs of the new Jerusalem, and gets upon the tops of Pisgah, and has there an imperfect prospect of a brave country, that lies a far way off; but he cannot tell how to describe it, and all that he hath to say to satisfy the curious enquirer is only this, – if he would know the glories of it he he must go and see it.[6]

Then there follows the *exemplum* in the typical style of Taylor:

> It was believed of old that those places that lie under the line were burnt up under the continual heat of the sun, and were not habitable either by man or beast: but later discoveries tell us that these are the most pleasant countries that the earth can shew; insomuch that some have placed paradise itself in that climate [...] under the direct beams of the Sun of righteousness, where there is an eternal day and an eternal spring; where is that tree of life that beareth twelve manner of fruits, and yieldeth her fruit every month. Thus we may use figures, metaphors and allegories to tell of fruitful meads, and winding rivers [...] this is but to frame little comparisons to please our childish fancies; and just such discourses as a blind man would make concerning colours, so do we talk of those things we never saw, and disparage the state,

---

4 Ibid., vol. 1, p. cccxi.   5 Gest, op. cit., p. 110 = Taylor, vol. 2, pp 136-40.   6 Taylor, vol. 1, pp cccxi – cccxii.

> while we would recommend it. It requires some angel to discourse and yet that would not do neither; they might speak [...] yet we should want ears to hear.7

Then the eulogy follows in the most typical way of Taylor:

> I have as yet done but with the half of my text: and I have another text yet to preach upon, and a very large and copious one; the great person whose obsequies we here come to celebrate. His fame is so great [...] he stands in no need of an enconium; and yet his worth is much greater than his fame. It is impossible not to speak great things of him, and yet it is impossible to speak what he deserves and our meanness in word will but sully the brightness of his excellencies: but custom requires that something be said and it is a duty and a debt that we owe only unto his memory: and I hope his great soul, if it hath any knowledge of what is done here below, will not be offended at the smallness of our offering.8

In the course of the eulogy Rust does not hide the truth of his ministry in his Presbyterian diocese; 'He was,' he says. 'one of the brave philosophers that Laertius speaks of, that did not addict themselves to any particular sect, but ingeniously sought for truth among all the wrangling schools, and they found her miserably torn, and rent to pieces, and parcelled into rags by the several contending parties, and so disfigured and misshapen, that it was hard to know her; but they made a shift to gather up her scattered limbs, which, as soon as they came together, by a strange sympathy and connaturalness, presently united into a lovely and beautiful body. Such was the spirit of this great man; he weighed men's reasons and not their names [...] he did contend for Truth and not for Victory.'9

There are echoes here of Taylor's opening words in his most mystical sermon on the *Via Intelligentiae*: 'The ancients, in their mythological learning, tell us, that when Jupiter espied the men of the world striving for Truth, and pulling her in pieces to secure her to themselves, he sent Mercury down among them; and he with his usual arts dressed Error up in the image of Truth, and trust her into the crowd, and so left them to contend still; and though then, by contention, men were sure to get but little truth, yet they were as earnest as ever, and lost peace too, in their importune contentions for the very image of truth. And this, indeed, is no wonder; but when truth and peace are brought into the world together, and bound up in the same bundle of life; when we are taught a religion by the Prince of peace, who is the truth itself; to see men contending for this truth, to the breach of that peace; and when

7 Ibid. 8 Ibid., vol. 1, p. cccxxi. 9 Ibid., vol. 1, p. cccxxiv.

men fall out, to see that they should make Christianity their theme, that is one of the greatest wonders of the world.'[10] These are prophetic words spoken in the North of Ireland over three hundred years ago and centuries before the age of ecumenism.

The celebrated inscription – *si monumentum reguiris, circumspice* – might well have been applied to Taylor up and until 1827. No memorial other than the elegant words of Rust was erected to his memory until a white marble tablet with an elaborate epitaph was placed in Lisburn cathedral by the bishop of Down and Connor nearly two hundred years after his death. In the questionable taste of the time and recording his virtues and genius, it is in sharp contrast to anything that Taylor might have said and done; in fact in life he had expressed himself quite clearly to the contrary, when he wrote his own epitaph: 'Nor do I desire a stately sepulchre, a beautiful urn or that my name and actions should be engraven in marble.'[11] In Dromore cathedral, where he was buried under the altar, a brass to his memory was fixed in the choir in 1866 in commemoration of his death and burial. In the church of St Thomas in New York the pulpit rests on the shoulders of four carved figures or masters of the English language, Chaucer, Shakespeare, Taylor, Keble. But the episcopal chair in Dromore is the perfect monument:

In Piam Memoriam

JEREMY TAYLOR S.T.D.

eruditi Theologi,

diserti Oratoris

fidelis Pastoris

hujus diocesi Episcopi.

A.D. 1661-1667

---

10 Ibid., vol. 8, p. 336.   11 G. Worley, *Jeremy Taylor*, op. cit., p. 209.

Funeral Sermon[1]

preached at the obsequies of the Right Reverend Father in God, Jeremy, Lord Bishop of Down and Connor, who deceased at Lisburn, 13 August, 1667, by

GEORGE RUST, D.D.
Lord Bishop of Dromore

It doth not yet appear what we shall be. (1 Jn 3:2)

Glorious things are spoken in scripture concerning the future reward of the righteous; and all the words that are wont to signify what is of greatest price and value, or can represent the most enravishing objects of our desires, are made use of by the holy Ghost to recommend unto us this transcendent state of blessedness. Such are these 'river of pleasures,' a 'fountain of living water,' a 'treasure that can never be wasted, nor never taken from us:' an 'inheritance in light,' an 'incorruptible crown,' a 'kingdom,' the 'kingdom of God,' and 'the kingdom of Christ:' the 'kingdom of glory,' a 'crown of glory and life;' and 'righteousness,' and 'immortality;' the 'vision of God;' being 'filled with all the fulness of God'; an 'exceeding and eternal weight of glory,' *kath uperbolen eis uperbolen aionion Baros doxes*, words strangely emphatical, they cannot be put into English; and if they could, they would not be able to convey to our minds the notion that they design: for it is too big for any expressions; and after all that can be said, we must resolve with our apostle, 'It does not yet appear what we shall be.'

At this distance we cannot make any likely guesses or conjectures at the glory of that future state. Men make very imperfect descriptions of countries or cities, that never were there themselves, nor saw the places with their own eyes. It is not for any mortal creature to make a map of that Canaan that lies above: it is to all us that live here on the hither-side of death, an unknown country and an undiscovered land. It may be, some heavenly pilgrim, that with his holy thoughts and ardent desires is continually travelling thitherward, arrives sometimes near the borders of the promised land, and the suburbs of the new Jerusalem, and gets upon the top of Pisgah, and there he has an imperfect prospect of a brave country, that lies a far way off, but he

---

1 J. Taylor, vol. 1, pp cccix-cccxxvii.

cannot tell how to describe it, and all that he hath to say to satisfy the curious enquirer is only this: if he would know the glories of it, he must go and see it. It was believed of old that those places that lie under the line were burnt up by the continual heat of the sun, and were not habitable either by man or beast: but later discoveries tell us that there are the most pleasant countries that the earth can shew; insomuch that some have placed paradise itself in that climate. Sure I am, of all the regions of the intellectual world, and the several lands that are peopled either with men or angels, the most pleasant countries they lie under the line, under the direct beams of the Sun of righteousness, where there is an eternal day and an eternal spring; where is that tree of life that beareth twelve manner of fruits, and yieldeth her fruit every month. Thus we may use figures, and metaphor, and allegories, and tell you of fruitful meads, and spacious fields, and winding rivers, and purling brooks, and chanting birds, and shady groves, and pleasant gardens, and lovely bowers, and noble seats, and stately palaces, and goodly people, and excellent laws, and sweet societies; but this is but to frame little comparisons to please our childish fancies; and just such discourses as a blind man would make concerning colours; so do we talk of those things we never saw, and disparage the state while we would recommend it. Indeed it requires some saint or angel from heaven to discourse upon the subject; and yet that would not do neither: for though they might be able to speak something of it, yet we should want ears to hear it. Neither can those things be declared but in the language of heaven, which would be little understood by us, the poor inhabitants of this lower world; they are indeed things too great to be brought within the compass of words. St Paul[2] when he had been rapt up into the third heaven, he saw *remata arreta,* 'things unlawful, or unpossible, to be uttered;' and 'eye hath not seen, nor ear heard, nor can it enter into the heart of man to conceive, what God hath prepared for them that love Him;' and 'It does not yet appear what we shall be,' said that beloved disciple that lay in the bosom of our Saviour.

You will not now expect that I should give you a relation of that which 'cannot be uttered,' nor so much as 'conceived;' or declare unto you what our eagle-sighted evangelist tells us 'does not yet appear.' But that you may understand that that which sets this state of happiness so beyond the reach of all imagination, is only its transcendent excellency, I shall tell you something of what does already appear of it, and may be known concerning it.

1. First of all, we are assured that we shall then be freed from all the evils and miseries that we now labour under. Vanity and misery, they are two words that speak the whole of this present world; the enjoyments of it are dreams, and fancies, and shadows, and appearances; and, if any thing be, it is only evil and misery that is real and substantial.

2 2 Cor 12:4; 1 Cor 2:9.

Vanity and folly, labour and pains, cares and fears, crosses and disappointments, sickness and diseases, they make up the whole of our portion here. This life it is begun in a cry, and it ends in a groan; and he that lives most happily, his life is chequered with black and white, and his days are not all sunshine, but some are cloudy and gloomy, and there is a worm at the root of all his joy, that soon eats out the sap and heart of it; and the gourd in whose shade he now so much pleases himself, by tomorrow will be withered and gone. But heaven is not subject to these mixtures and uncertainties; it is a region of calmness and serenity, and the soul is there gotten above the clouds, and is not annoyed with those storms and tempests that are here below. All tears shall then be wiped from our eyes; and though sorrow may endure for the night of this world, yet joy will spring up in the morning of eternity.

2. We are sure we shall be freed from this earthly, and clothed with an heavenly and glorified body. These bodies of ours, they are the graves and sepulchres, the prisons and dungeons of our heaven-born souls; and though we deck and adorn them, and pride ourselves in their beauty and comeliness; yet when all is done [...] they expose us to many pains and diseases, and incline us to many lusts and passions, and the more we pamper them, the greater burden they are unto our minds; they impose upon our reasons, and by their steams and vapours cast a mist before our understandings; they clog our affections, and like a heavy weight depress us unto this earth, and keep us from soaring aloft among the winged inhabitants of the upper regions. But those robes of light and glory which we shall be clothed withal at the resurrection of the just, and those heavenly bodies which the gospel hath then assured unto us, they are not subject unto any of these mischiefs and inconveniences, but are fit and accommodate instruments for the soul in its highest exaltations. And this is an argument that the gospel[3] does dwell much upon, viz., the redemption of our bodies, that 'He shall change our vile bodies, that they may be like unto His glorious body' and we are taught to look upon it as one great piece of our reward, that we shall be 'clothed upon with our house which is from heaven;' that 'this corruptible shall put on incorruption, and this mortal immortality;' that 'as we have borne the image of the earthly, so we must bear the image of the heavenly' Adam: who was *ex ouranou epouranios,* 'of heaven heavenly,' as the first man was *ekges shoikos,* 'of the earth earthly,' [...] and if it be so, then the purer and more defecate the body is, the better will the soul be appointed for the exercise of its noblest operations; and it will be no mean piece of our reward hereafter, that that which is sown *soma psuchikon,* an 'animal', shall be raised a 'heavenly body.'

3. We are sure that we shall then be free from sin, and all those foolish lusts and passions that we are now enslaved unto. The life of a Christian, it is a continual

---

3 Phil 3:21; 2 Cor 5:2; 1 Cor 15:47.

warfare; and he endures many sore conflicts, and makes many sad complaints, and often bemoans himself after such a manner as this, 'Woe is me, that I am forced to dwell in Meshech, and to have my habitation in the tents of Kedar; that there should be so many Goliahs within me, that defy the host of Israel; so many sons of Anak that hinder my entrance into the 'land of promise' and the rest of God; that I should toil and labour among the bricks, and live in bondage unto these worse than Egyptian taskmasters.' Thus does he sit down by the rivers of Babylon, and weep over those ruins and desolations that these worse than Assyrian armies have made in the city and house of his God. And many a time does he cry out in the bitterness of his soul, 'Wretched creature that I am! Who shall deliver me from this body of death?' And though through his faith and courage and constancy, he be daily getting ground of his spiritual enemies; yet it is but by inches, and every step he takes he must fight for it; and living as he does in an enemy's country, he is forced always to be upon his guard; and if he slumber never so little, presently he is surprised by a watchful adversary. This is our portion here, and our lot is this; but when we arrive unto those regions of bliss and glory that are above, we shall then stand safely upon the shore, and see all our enemies, Pharaoh and all his host, drowned and destroyed in the Red sea, and being delivered from the world, and the flesh, and the devil – death, and sin, and hell – we shall sing the song of Moses and of the Lamb, an *epinicion* and song of eternal triumph unto the God of our salvation.

    4. We shall be sure to meet with the best company that earth or heaven affords. Good company it is the great pleasure of the life of man; and we shall then come 'to the innumerable company of angels, and the general assembly of the church of the firstborn, and to the spirits of just men made perfect, and to Jesus the mediator of the new covenant.'[4] The oracle tells Amelius, enquiring what was become of Plotinus's soul, that he was gone to Pythagoras, and Socrates, and Plato, and as many as had borne a part in the quire of heavenly love. And I may say to every good man, that he shall go to the company of Abraham, Isaac, and Jacob; Moses, David, and Samuel; all the prophets and apostles, and all the holy men of God that have been in all the ages of the world. All those brave and excellent persons that have been scattered at the greatest distance of time and place, and in their several generations have been the salt of the earth to preserve mankind from utter degeneracy and corruption; these shall be all gathered together, and meet in one constellation in that firmament of glory. *O praeclarum diem, eum ad illud divinum animorum concilium coetumque proficiscar, atque ex hac turba et colluvione discedam!*, 'that blessed day, when we shall make our escape from this medley confused riot, and shall arrive to that great council and general rendezvous of divine and god-like spirits!'[5] which is more than all, we shall

---

4 Heb 12:22.   5 Cicero, *De senectute*, ad fin.

then meet our Lord Jesus Christ, the head of our recovery, whose story is now so delightful unto us, as reporting nothing of Him but the greatest sweetness and innocence, and meekness and patience, and mercy and tenderness, lovely or amiable; and who out of His dear love and deep compassion unto mankind, gave up Himself unto the death for us men and for our salvation […]; and I cannot but believe a great part of heaven to be the blest society that is there; their enravishing beauty, that is to say, their inward life and perfection, flowering forth and raying itself through their glorified bodies; the rare discourses wherewith they entertain one another; the pure and chaste and spotless, and yet most ardent love, wherewith they embrace each other; the ecstatic devotions wherein they join together: and certainly every pious and devout soul will readily acknowledge with me, that it must needs be matter of unspeakable pleasure, to be taken into the quire of angels and seraphims, and the glorious company of the apostles, and the goodly fellowship of the prophets, and the noble army of martyrs; and to join with them in singing praises, and hallelujahs, and songs of joy, and triumph unto our great Creator and Redeemer, the Father of the spirits, and the Lover of souls, unto Him that sits upon the throne, and unto the Lamb for ever and ever.

5. We are sure we shall then have our capacities filled, and all our desires answered; 'They hunger no more, neither thirst any more; for the Lamb which is in the midst of the throne shall feed them, and shall lead them unto living fountains of waters.'[6] What vast degrees of perfection and happiness the nature of man is capable of, we may best understand by viewing it in the person of Christ, taken into the nearest union with divinity, and made God's vicegerent in the world, and the head and governor of the whole creation. In this our narrow and contracted state we are apt to think too meanly of ourselves, and do not understand the dignity of our own natures, what we were made for, and what we are capable of: but, as Plotinus somewhere observes, we are like children, from our birth brought up in ignorance of, and at a great distance from our parents and relations; and have forgot the nobleness of our extraction, and rank ourselves and our fortunes among the lot of beggars, and mean and ordinary persons; though we are the offspring of a great prince, and were born to a kingdom. It does indeed become creatures to think modestly of themselves; yet if we consider it aright, it will be found very hard to set any bounds or limits to our own happiness, and say, hitherto it shall arise and no further. For that wherein the happiness of man consists, viz., truth and goodness, the communication of the divine nature, and the illapses of divine love, it does not cloy, or glot, or satiate; but every participation of them does widen and enlarge our souls, and fits us for further and further receptions: the more we have, the more we are capable of, the

---

6 Rev 7:16.

more we are tilled, the more room is made in our spirits; and thus it is still and still, even till we arrive unto such degrees as we can assign no measures unto.

6. We shall then be made like unto God [...]. Men usually have very strange notions concerning God, and the enjoyment of Him; or rather, these are words to which there is no correspondent conception in their minds: but if we would understand God aright, we must look upon Him as infinite wisdom, righteousness, love, goodness, and whatever speaks any thing of beauty and perfection; and if we pretend to worship Him, it must be by loving and adoring His transcendent excellencies; and if we hope to enjoy Him, it must be by conformity unto Him, and participation of His nature. The frame and constitution of things is such, that it is impossible that man should arrive to happiness any other way. And if the sovereignty of God should dispense with our obedience the nature of the thing would not permit us to be happy without it. If we live only the animal life, we may indeed be happy, as beasts are happy; but the happiness that belongs to a rational and intellectual being can never be attained but in a way of holiness and conformity unto the divine will: for such a temper and disposition of mind is necessary unto happiness not by virtue of any arbitrarious constitution of heaven, but the eternal laws of righteousness, and immutable respects of things, do require and exact it. Yea, I may truly say, that God and Christ, without us, cannot make us happy: for we are not conscious to ourselves of any thing, but only the operations of our own minds; and it is not the person of God and Christ, but their life and nature, wherein consists our formal happiness: for what is the happiness of God himself, but only that pleasure and satisfaction that results from a sense of His infinite perfections? And how is it possible for a creature to be more happy than by partaking of that, in its measure and proportion, which is the happiness of God himself?

7. The soul being thus prepared shall live in the presence of God, and lie under the influences and illapses of divine love and goodness; 'Father, I will that they whom Thou hast given Me be with Me where I am, that they may behold My glory!' They that fight manfully under the banners of heaven, and overcome their spiritual enemies, 'They shall eat of the hidden manna, and become pillars in the temple of God, and shall go no more out:' 'They shall stand before the throne of God continually, and serve Him day and night in His temple, and He that sitteth on the throne shall dwell amongst them.'[7] God shall put under them His everlasting arms, and carry them in His bosom, and they shall suck the full breats of eternal goodness. For now there is nothing can hinder the most near and intimate conjunction of the soul with God; for things that are alike do easily mingle with

---

7 Jn 17:24.

one another; but the mixture that is betwixt bodies, be they never so homogeneal, comes but to an external touch; for their parts can never run up into one another. But there is no such *antitupia* or 'resistance' mongst spiritual beings; and we are estranged from God 'not by distance of place, but by difference and diversity of nature,' and when that is removed, He becomes present to us, and we to Him [...]. This therefore is the soul's progress from that state of 'purgation' to 'illumination' and so to 'union.'[8] There are several faculties in the soul of man, that are conformed to several kinds of objects; and according to that life a man is awaked into, so these faculties do exert themselves: and though whilst we live barely an animal life, we converse with little more than this outward world, and the objects of our senses; yet there are faculties within us that are receptive of God, and when we arrive once unto a due measure of purity of spirit, the rays of heavenly light will as certainly shine into our minds, as the beams of the sun, when it arises above the horizon, do illuminate the clear and pellucid air: and from this sight and illumination the soul proceeds to an intimate union with God, and to a 'taste' and 'touch' of Him. This is that 'silent touch,' with God, that fills the soul with unexpressible joy and triumph. For if the objects of this outward world that strike upon our senses do so hugely please and delight us; what infinite pleasure then must there needs be in those touches and impresses that the divine love and goodness shall make upon our souls? But these are things that we may talk of, as we would do of a sixth sense, or something we have no distinct notion or idea of, but the perfect understanding of them belongs only to the future state of 'comprehension.'

8. Lastly, we shall have our knowledge, and our love, which are the most perfect and beatifying acts of our minds, employed about their noblest objects in their most exalted measures [...]. When we come to heaven – I will not say we shall see all things in the mirror of divinity, for that it may be is an extravagancy of the schools; nor that any one true proposition through the concatentation of truth, will then multiply itself into the explicit knowledge of all conclusions whatsoever, for I believe that a fancy too; - but our knowledge shall be strangely enlarged, and, for aught I can determine, be for ever receiving new additions, and fresh accruments. The clue of divine providence will be unravelled, and all those difficulties which now perplex us will be easily assoiled, and we shall then perceive that the wisdom and goodness of God is a vast and comprehensive thing, and moves in a far larger sphere than we are aware of in this state of narrowness and imperfection. But there is something greater and beyond all this; and St John[9] has a strange expression, that 'we shall then see God even as He is' and God, we know, is the wellspring of perfection and happiness, the fountain and original of all beauty; He is infinitely glorious, and lovely, and excellent;

8 Rev 3:12; 8:15.   9 1 Jn 3:2

and if we see Him as He is, all His glory must descend into us and become ours: for we can no otherways see God (as I said before) but by becoming deiform, by being changed into the same glory. But love, that is it which makes us most happy, and by that we are most intimately conjoined unto God, 'For he that dwelleth in love, dwelleth in God, and God in him:'[10] and how pleasant beyond all imagination must it needs be, to have the soul melted into a flame of love, and that fire fed and nourished by the enjoyment of its beloved; to be transported into ecstasies and raptures of love; to be swallowed up in the embraces of eternal sweetness; to be lost in the source and fountain of happiness and bliss, like a spark in the fire, or a beam in the sun, or drop in the ocean.

It may be you will tell me I have been all this while confuting my text, and giving you a relation of that which St John tells us 'does not yet appear what it is:' but my design has been the same with the holy evangelist's; and that is, to represent unto you how transcendently great that state of happiness must needs be; when as, by what way we are able to apprehend of it, it is infinitely the object of our desires; and yet we are assured by those that are best able to tell, that the best and greatest part of the country is yet undiscovered, and that we cannot so much as guess at the pleasure of it, till we come to enjoy it. And indeed it is impossible it should be otherwise; for happiness being a matter of sense, all the words in the world cannot convey the notion of it into our minds, and it is only to be understood by them that feel it.

But though it does not yet appear what we shall be; yet so much already appears of it, that it cannot but seem the most worthy object of our endeavours and desires; and by some few clusters that have been shewn us of this good land, we may guess what pleasant and delightful fruit it bears. And if we have but any reverence of ourselves, and will but consider the dignity of our natures, and the vastness of that happiness we are capable of, methinks we should be always travelling towards that heavenly country, though our way lies through a wilderness: and be striving for this great prize and immortal crown; this vision of God; shaking off all fond passions, and dirty desires, and breathing forth our souls in such aspirations as these [...]. The heathen are come into Thine inheritance; Thy holy temple have they defiled: help us, O God of our salvation, and deliver us, and purge away our sins from us, for Thy name's sake! Oh that the Lord whom we seek would come to His own house, and give peace there, and fill it with His glory! Come and cleanse Thine own temple, for we have made it a den of thieves, which should have been a house of prayer! Oh that we might never give sleep to our eyes, nor slumber to our eye-lids, till we have prepared a house for the Lord, and a tabernacle for the God of Jacob!

The curse of Cain is fallen upon us, and we are as vagabonds in the earth, and wander from one creature to another. Oh that our souls might come at last to

---

10 1 Jn 4:16

dwell in God, our fixed and eternal habitation! We, like silly doves, fly up and down the earth, but can find no rest for the sole of our feet; Oh that, after all our weariness and our wanderings, we might return into the ark; and that God would put forth His hand and take us, and pull us in unto Himself!

We have too long lived upon vanity and emptiness, the wind and the whirlwind; oh that we may now begin to feed upon substance, and delight ourselves in marrow and fatness! Oh that God would strike our rocky hearts, that there might spring up a fountain in the wilderness, and pools in the desert; that we might drink of that water, whereof whosoever drinks shall never thirst more! that God would give us that portion of goods that falleth to us, not to waste it with riotous living, but therewith to feed our languishing souls, lest they be weary and faint by the way! We ask not the children's bread, but the crumbs that fall from Thy table; that our baskets may be filled with Thy fragments: for they will be better than wine, and sweeter than the honey and the honeycomb, and more pleasant to us than a feast of fat things.

We have wandered too long in a barren and howling desert, where wild beasts and doleful creatures, owls and bats, satyrs and dragons, keep their haunts; Oh that we might be fed in green pastures, and led by the still waters; that the winter might be past, and the rain over and gone; that the flowers may appear on the earth, and the time of the singing of birds may come, and the voice of the turtle may be heard in our land!

We have lived too long in Sodom, which is the place that God at last will destroy: Oh that we might arise and be gone; and while we are lingering, that the angels of God would lay hold upon our hands, and be merciful unto us, and bring us forth, and set us without the city; and that we may never look back any more, but may escape unto the mountain, and dwell safe in the Rock of ages! Wisdom hath killed her beasts, she hath mingled her wine, and furnished her table; Oh that we might eat of her meat, and drink of her wine which she hath mingled! God knocks at the doors of our hearts; Oh let us open unto Him those everlasting gates, that He may sup with us, and we with Him; for He will bring His cheer along with Him, and will feast us with manna and angels' food. Oh that the Sun of righteousness might arise and melt the iciness of our hearts; that God would send forth His spirit, and with His warmth and heat dissolve our frozen souls; that God would breathe into our minds those still and gentle gales of divine inspirations, that may blow up and increase in us the flames of heavenly love; that we may be a whole burnt-offering, and all the substance of our souls be consumed by fire sparks, we might be always mounting upward, till we return again into our proper elements; that, like so many particular rivulets, we may be continually making toward the sea, and never rest till we lose ourselves in that ocean of goodness, from whence we first came; that we may open our mouths wide, that God may satisfy them; that we may so perfectly discharge ourselves of all strange desires and passions, that our souls may be nothing else but a deep emptiness and vast capacity to be filled with 'all the fulness of God'!

Let but these be the breathings of our spirits, and this divine magnetism will most certainly draw down God into our souls, and we shall have some prelibations of that happiness; some small glimpses and little discoveries whereof, is all that belongs to this state of mortality.

I have as yet done but the half of my text: and I have another text yet to preach upon, and a very large and copious one; the great person whose obsequies we here come to celebrate. His fame is so great throughout the world, that he stands in no need of an encomium; and yet his worth is much greater than his fame. It is impossible not to speak great things of him, and yet it is impossible to speak what he deserves; and the meanness of an oration will but sully the brightness of his excellencies: but custom requires that something should be said, and it is a duty and a debt that we owe only unto his memory: and I hope his great soul, if it hath any knowledge of what is done here below, will not be offended at the smallness of our offering.

He was born at Cambridge, and brought up in the free-school there, and was ripe for the university before custom would allow of his admittance; but by that time he was thirteen years old he was entered into Caius college; and as soon as he was graduate he was chosen fellow. Had he lived amongst the ancient pagans he had been ushered into the world with a miracle, and swans must have danced and sung at his birth; and he must have been a great hero, and no less than the son of Apollo, the god of wisdom and eloquence.

He was a man long before he was of age: and knew little more of the state of childhood than its innocency and pleasantness. From the university, by that time he was master of arts, he removed to London, and became public lecturer in the church of St Paul's; where he preached to the admiration and astonishment of his auditory; and by his florid and youthful beauty, and sweet and pleasant air, and sublime and raised discourses, he made his hearers take him for some young angel, newly descended from the visions of glory. The fame of this new star, that out-shone all the rest of the firmament, quickly came to the notice of the great archbishop of Canterbury, who would needs have him preach before him; which he performed not less to his wonder than satisfaction; his discourse was beyond exception, and beyond imitation: yet the wise prelate thought him too young; but the great youth humbly begged his grace 'to pardon that fault' and promised 'if he lived he would mend it.' However, the grand patron of learning and ingenuity thought it for the advantage of the world, that such mighty parts should be afforded better opportunities of study and improvement than a course of constant preaching would allow of; and to that purpose he placed him in his own college of All Souls in Oxford, where love and admiration still waited upon him: which so long as there is any spark of ingenuity in the breasts of men, must needs be the inseparable attendants of so extraordinary a worth and sweetness. He had not been long here, afore my lord of Canterbury bestowed upon him the rectory of Uphingham in Rutlandshire, and soon after preferred him to be chaplain to King Charles the martyr of blessed and immortal memory. Thus were preferments heaped upon him, but still less than his deserts; and that not through the fault of his great masters, but because the amplest honours and rewards were poor and inconsiderable, compared with the greatness of his worth and merit.

This great man had no sooner launched into the world, but a fearful tempest arose, and a barbarous and unnatural war disturbed a long and uninterrupted peace and tranquility, and brought all things into disorder and confusion; but his religion taught him to be loyal, and engaged him on his prince's side, whose cause and quarrel he always owned and maintained with a great courage and constancy, till at last he and his little fortune were shipwrecked in that great hurricane that overturned both church and state: this fatal storm cast him ashore in a private corner of the world, and a tender providence shrouded him under her wings, and the prophet was fed in the wilderness; and his great worthiness procured him friends, that supplied him with bread and necessaries. In this solitude he began to write those excellent discourses, which are enough of themselves to furnish a library, and will be famous to all succeeding generations, for their greatness of wit, and profoundness of judgment, and richness of fancy, and clearness of expression, and copiousness of invention, and general usefulness to all the purposes of a Christian: and by these he soon got a great reputation among all persons of judgment and indifferency, and his name will grow greater still as the world grows better and wiser.

When he had spent some years in this retirement, it pleased God to visit his family with sickness, and to take to Himself the dear pledges of His favour, three sons of great hopes and expectations, within the space of two or three months: and though he had learned a quiet submission unto the divine will, yet the affliction touched him so sensibly that it made him desirous to leave the country; and going to London, he there met my lord Conway, a person of great honour and generosity; who making him a kind proffer, the good man embraced it, and that brought him over into Ireland, and settled him at Portmore, a place made for study and contemplation, which he therefore dearly loved; and here he wrote his 'Cases of Conscience', a book that is able alone to give its author immortality.

By this time the wheel of providence brought about the king's happy restoration, and there began a new world, and the Spirit of God moved upon the face of the waters, and out of a confused chaos brought forth beauty and order, and all the three nations were inspired with a new life, and became drunk with an excess of joy: among the rest, this loyal subject went over to congratulate the prince and people's happiness, and bear a part in the universal triumph.

It was not long ere his sacred majesty began the settlement of the church, and the great doctor Jeremy Taylor was resolved upon for the bishopric of Down and Connor; and not long after, Dromore was added to it: and it was but reasonable that the king and church should consider their champion, and reward the pains and sufferings he underwent in the defence of their cause and honour. With what care and faithfulness he discharged his office, we are all his witnesses; what good rules and directions he gave his clergy, and how he taught us the practice of them by his own example. Upon his coming over bishop, he was made a privy-councillor; and the university of Dublin gave him their testimony, by recommending him for their vice-chancellor: which honourable office he kept to his dying day.

During his being in this see he wrote several excellent discourses, particularly his 'Dissuasive from Popery,' which was received by a general approbation; and a vindication of it (now in the press) from some impertinent cavillers, that pretend to answer books, when there is nothing towards it more than the very title-page.

This great prelate improved his talent with a mighty industry, and managed his stewardship rarely well; and his Master, when He called for his accounts, found him busy and at his work, and employed upon an excellent subject, a 'Discourse upon the Beatitudes;' which if finished would have been of great use to the world, and solved most of the cases of conscience that occur to a Christian in all the varieties of states and conditions. But the all-wise God hath ordained it otherwise, and hath called home His good servant, to give him a portion in that blessedness that Jesus Christ hath promised to all His faithful disciples and followers.

Thus having given you a brief account of his life, I know you will now expect a character of his person; but I foresee it will befall him, as it does all glorious subjects that are but disparaged by a commendation. One thing I am secure of, that I shall not be thought to speak hyperboles; for the subject can hardly be reached by any expressions: for he was none of God's ordinary works, but his endowments were so many, and so great, as really made him a miracle.

Nature had befriended him much in his constitution; for he was a person of a most sweet and obliging humour, of great candour and ingenuity; and there was so much of salt and fineness of wit, and prettiness of address, in his familiar discourses, as made his conversation have all the pleasantness of a comedy, and all the usefulness of a sermon. His soul was made up of harmony, and he never spake but he charmed his hearer, not only with the clearness of his reason, but all his words, and his very tone and cadencies, were strangely musical.

But that which did most of all captivate and enravish was the gaiety and richness of fancy; for he had much in him of that natural enthusiasm that inspires all great poets and orators; and there was a generous ferment in his blood and spirits that set his fancy bravely a-work, and made it swell, and teem, and become pregnant to such degrees of luxuriancy, as nothing but the greatness of his wit and judgment could have kept it within due bounds and measures.

And indeed it was a rare mixture, and a single instance, hardly to be found in an age: for the great trier of wits has told us, that there is a peculiar and several complexion required for wit, and judgment, and fancy; and yet you might have found all these in this great personage, in their eminency and perfection. But that which made his wit and judgment so considerable, was the largeness and freedom of his spirit, for truth is plain and easy to a mind disintangled from superstition and prejudice; he was one of the *eklektikoi,* a sort of brave philosophers that Laertius speaks of, that did not addict themselves to any particular sect, but ingeniously sought for truth among all the wrangling schools; and they found her miserably torn and rent to pieces, and parcelled into rags, by the several contending parties, and so disfigured and misshapen that it was hard to know her; but they made a shift to gather up her scattered limbs, which, as soon as they came together, by a strange sympathy and connaturalness presently united into a lovely and beautiful body. This was the spirit of this great man; he weighed men's reasons, and not their names, and was not scared with the ugly visors men usually put upon persons they hate, and opinions they dislike; not afflighted with the anathemas and execrations of an infallible chair, which he looked upon only as bug-bears to terrify weak and childish minds. He considered, that it is not likely any one party should wholly engross truth to themselves; that obedience is the only way to true knowledge (which is an argument that he has managed rarely well in that excellent sermon of his which he calls *Via intelligentiae);* that God always, and only, teaches docible and ingenuous minds, that are willing to hear, and ready to obey according to their light; that it is impossible a pure, humble, resigned, godlike soul, should be kept out of heaven, whatever mistakes it might be subject to in this state of mortality; that the design of heaven is not to fill men's heads, and feed their curiosities, but to better their hearts, and mend their lives. Such considerations as these made him impartial in his disquisitions, and give a due allowance to the reasons of his adversary, and contend for truth and not for victory.

And now you will easily believe that an ordinary diligence would be able to make great improvements upon such a stock of parts and endowments; but to these advantages of nature, and excellency of his spirit, he added an indefatigable industry, and God gave a plentiful benediction: for there were very few kinds of learning but he was a *mystes* and a great master in them. He was a rare humanist, and hugely versed in all the polite parts of learning; and had thoroughly concocted all the ancient moralists, Greek and Roman, poets and orators; and was not unacquainted with the refined wits of the later ages, whether French or Italian.

But he had not only the accomplishments of a gentleman, but so universal were his parts that they were proportioned to every thing; and though his spirit and humour were made up of smoothness and gentleness, yet he could bear with the harshness and roughness of the schools; and was not unseen in their subtilties and spinosities, and upon occasion could make them serve his purpose; and yet I believe he thought many of them very near akin to the famous knight of the Mancha, and would make sport sometimes with the romantic sophistry and fantastic adventures of school-errantry. His skill was great, both in the civil and canon law, and casuistical divinity; and he was a rare conductor of souls, and knew how to counsel and to advise; to solve difficulties, and determine cases, and quiet consciences. And he was no novice in Mr I.S.[11] new science of controversy; but could manage an argument and repartees with a strange dexterity; he understood what the several parties in christendom have to say for themselves, and could plead their cause to better advantage than any advocate of their tribe: and when he had done, he could confute them too; and shew that better arguments than ever they could produce for themselves, would afford no sufficient ground for their fond opinions.

It would be too great a task to pursue his accomplishments through the various kinds of literature: I shall content myself to add only his great acquaintance with the fathers and ecclesiastical writers, and the doctors of the first and purest ages both of the Greek and Latin church; which he has made use of against the Romanist, to vindicate the church of England from the challenge of innovation, and prove her to be truly ancient, catholic and apostolical.

But religion and virtue is the crown of all other accomplishments; and it was the glory of this great man to be thought a Christian, and whatever you added to it, he looked upon as a term of diminution: and yet he was a zealous son of the church of England, but that was because he judged her (and with great reason) a church the most purely christian of any in the world. In his younger years he met with some assaults from popery, and the high pretensions of their religious orders were very accommodate to his devotional temper: but he was always so much master of himself that he would never be governed by any thing but reason, and the evidence of truth, which engaged him in the study of those controversies; and to how good purpose, the world is by this time a sufficient witness: but the longer and the more he considered, the worse he liked the Roman cause, and became at last to censure them with some severity; but I confess I have so great an opinion of his judgment, and the charitableness of his spirit, that I am afraid he did not think worse of them than they deserve.

11 Cf. J. Taylor, vol. 8, p. lxxii.

But religion is not a matter of theory and orthodox notions; and it is not enough to believe aright, but we must practise accordingly; and to master our passions, and to make a right use of that *antexousion* and power that God has given us over our own actions, is a greater glory than all other accomplishments that can adorn the mind of man; and therefore I shall close my character of this great personage with a touch upon some of those virtues for which his memory will be precious to all posterity. He was a person of great humility; and notwithstanding his stupendous parts, and learning, and eminency of place, he had nothing in him of pride and humour, but was courteous and affable, and of easy access, and would lend a ready ear to the complaints, yea to the impertinencies, of the meanest persons. His humility was coupled with an extraordinary piety, and I believe he spent the greatest part of his time in heaven; his solemn hours of prayer took up a considerable portion of his life; and we are not to doubt but he had learned of St Paul to pray continually, and that occasional ejaculations, and frequent aspirations and emigrations of his soul after God, made up the best part of his devotions. But he was not only a good man God-ward, but he was come to the top of St Peter's gradation, and to all his other virtues added a large and diffusive charity: and whoever compares his plentiful incomes with the inconsiderable estate he left at his death, will be easily convinced that charity was steward for a great proportion of his revenue. But the hungry that he fed, and the naked that he clothed, and the distressed that he supplied, and the fatherless that he provided for; the poor children that he put to apprentice, and brought up at school, and maintained at the university; will now sound a trumpet to that charity which he dispersed with his right hand, but would not suffer his left hand to have any knowledge of it.

To sum up all in a few words – This great prelate he had the good humour of a gentleman, the eloquence of an orator, the fancy of a poet, the acuteness of a schoolman, the profoundness of a philosopher, the wisdom of a counsellor, the sagacity of a prophet, the reason of an angel, and the piety of a saint. He had devotion enough for a cloister, learning enough for an university, and wit enough for a college of *virtuosi;* and had his parts and endowments been parcelled out among his poor clergy that he left behind him, it would perhaps have made one of the best dioceses in the world. But alas, 'Our father, our father, the horses of our Israel, and the chariot thereof!' he is gone, and has carried his mantle and his spirit along with him up to heaven; and the sons of the prophets have lost all their beauty and lustre which they enjoyed only from the reflexion of his excellencies, which were bright and radiant enough to cast a glory upon a whole order of men. But the sun of this our world, after many attempts to break through the crust of an earthly body, is at last swallowed up in the great *vortex* of eternity, and there all his *maculae* are scattered and dissolved, and he is fixed in an orb of glory, and shines among his brethern-stars, that in their several ages gave light to the world, and turned many souls unto righteousness; and we that are left behind, though we can never reach his perfections, must study to imitate his virtues, that we may at last come to sit at his feet in the mansions of glory; which God grant for His infinite mercies in Jesus Christ: to whom, with the Father, through the eternal Spirit, he ascribed all honour and glory, worship and thanksgiving, love and obedience, now and for evermore. Amen.

Two Prayers

BEFORE AND AFTER SERMON

PRAYER BEFORE SERMON[1]

O Eternal God, Father of our Lord Jesus Christ, Lord and Sovereign of all the creatures, we, though most unworthy by reason of our great and innumerable transgressions, yet invited by Thy essential goodness and commandment, do with all reverence and humble confidence approach to the throne of grace, begging of thee, for the passion of our dearest Lord, to remove our sins as far as the east from the west, and to remember them no more, lest Thou smite us in Thy jealousy, and consume us in Thy wrath and indignation, which we, by heaps and conjugations of sin, most sadly have deserved to feel, and sink under to eternal ages.

For we confess, O God, to Thy glory, who so long hast spared us, and to our own shame, who so long have resisted and despised so glorious a mercy, that we are the vilest of sinners, and the worst of men, lovers of the world, and neglecters of religion, and undervalue its interests, being passionate for trifles, and indifferent for eternal treasures; weak to serve Thee in our natural powers, and not careful to employ and to improve the aids of the Spirit. We are proud and envious, lustful and intemperate, prodigal of our time, and covetous of money, greedy of sin, but loathing manna, the bread that came down from heaven. Willing we are to suffer any thing, or to do any thing to please our senses, and to satisfy ambition, or to purchase the world, but are neither willing to do or suffer any contradiction for the cause of God. In prosperity, we are impudent and proud; in adversity, pusillanimous and cowardly: ready to promise any thing in the day of our calamity, but when Thou bringest us to comfort, we forget our duty, and do just nothing. We are full of inconsideration and carelessness, desirous to be accounted holy by men, but careless of being approved so to Thee our God. In all our conversation we are uneven, soon disturbed, quickly angry, not quickly appeased; petulant, and peevish, and disordered by a whole body of sin, and evil is our portion; we are heirs of wrath, infirmity, and folly; shame and death are our inheritance.

But, O God, Thou are our Father, gracious and merciful; Thou knowest whereof we are made, and rememberest that we are but dust. Be not wroth very sore, O

[1] J. Taylor, vol. 1, pp. 64-6.

Lord, neither remember our iniquities for ever; for we are ashamed of the sins we have desired, and are confounded for the pleasures we have chosen. O make us penitent and obedient, careful as the watches of the night, that we may never return to the folly whereof we are now ashamed; but that in holiness and righteousness we may serve and please Thee all our days, working out our salvation with fear and trembling.

O Lord, Father and governor of our whole life, leave us not to the sinful counsels of our own heart, and let us not any more fall by them. Set scourges over our thoughts, and the discipline of wisdom over our hearts, lest our ignorances increase, and our sins abound to our destruction. Let our repentance be speedy and perfect, bringing forth the fruits of holy conversation. Give unto us a faith that shall never be reproved, a hope that shall never make us ashamed, a charity that shall never cease, a confidence in Thee that shall never be discomposed, a patience that shall never faint, a noble christian courage that shall enable us, in despite of all opposition, to confess Thy faith, to publish Thy laws, and to submit to Thy dispensations, to glorify Thy name by holy living and dying, that in all changes and accidents we may be Thy servants, and Thou mayest take delight to pardon us, to sanctify us, and to save us, that we may rejoice in the mercies of God, in the day of recompenses, at the glorious appearance of our Lord Jesus.

Bless, O Lord, Thy holy catholic church, with all blessings and assistances of Thy Spirit and providence. Let the daily sacrifice of prayer and eucharist never cease, but for ever be presented unto Thee, united to the intercession of our Lord, and for ever prevail for the obtaining to all her sons and daughters grace and blessing, pardon and holiness, perseverance and glory.

In particular, we humbly recommend to Thy care and providence Thy afflicted handmaid the church of England. Thou hast humbled us for our pride, and chastised us for our want of discipline. O forgive us all our sins, which have provoked Thee to arm Thyself against us. Blessed God, smite us not with a final and exterminating judgment. Call not the watchmen off from their guards, nor the angels from their charges; let us not die by a famine of Thy word and sacraments; if Thou smitest us with the rod of a man, Thou canst sanctify every stroke, and bring good out of that evil: but nothing can make recompence to us if Thou hatest us, and sufferest our souls to perish. Unite our hearts and tongues: take the spirit of error and division from us, and so order all the accidents of Thy providence, that religion may increase, and our devotion may be great and popular, that truth may be encouraged and promoted, and Thy name glorified, and Thy servants instructed and comforted, that the Spirit may rule, and all interests may stoop and obey, publish and advance the interest of the Lord Jesus.

In order to which end, we pray Thee to look down in mercy upon Thy servants, and where Thou has placed the right and supreme authority over this nation, give the supreme and choicest of Thy blessings, health and peace, strength and victory a long and a prosperous government, a portion in the kingdom of grace here and glory hereafter, through Jesus Christ our Lord.

Give a double portion of Thy spirit to the ministers of the church, the dispensers and stewards of the holy things of God; grant that by a holy life, and a true belief, by well doing and patient suffering, by diligent and sincere preaching, and assiduous prayers and ministries, they may glorify Thee, the great lover of souls, and after a plentiful conversion of sinners from the errors of their way, they may shine like the stars in glory.

Give unto the ministers of justice the spirit of government and zeal, courage and prudence: to the nobility, wisdom, valour, and religious magnanimity: to old men, piety, prudence, and liberality: to young men, obedience, temperance, health, and diligence: to merchants, justice and faithfulness: to mechanics and artizans, truth and honesty: to all married pairs, faith and holiness, charity and sweet compliances: to all christian women, the ornament of a meek and a quiet spirit, chastity and charity, patience and obedience, a zeal of duty and religion: to all that are sick and afflicted, distressed in conscience or persecuted for it, give patience and comfort, a perfect repentance, and a perfect resignation, a love of God, and a perseverance in duty, proportionable comfort in this life and an eternal weight of glory in the great day of our Lord Jesus. Give to all schools of learning and nurseries of religion, peace and quietness, powerful and bountiful patrons, the blessings of God and of religion; to the whole land fair seasons of the year, good government, health, and plenty, an excellent religion, undivided, undisturbed, through Jesus Christ our Lord.

Give unto us Thy servants the assistance of Thy holy spirit; grant to me to speak Thy word piously, prudently, and with holy intention; to these thy servants, to hear it reverently, obediently, and without prejudice, with hearts ready to conform to Thy holy will and pleasure, that we, living in Thy love and fear, may die in Thy favour, and rest in hope, and rise in glory to the participation of the blessings of a blissful immortality, through the mercies of God in our Lord Jesus Christ, our dearest Saviour and ever glorious and most mighty Redeemer, in whose name let us pray in the words which Himself commanded:

Our Father, which art in heaven, etc.

PRAYER AFTER SERMON[2]

Almighty God, our glory and our hope, our Lord and master, the Father of mercy and God of all comfort, we present to Thee the sacrifice of a thankful spirit, in humble and joyful acknowledgment of those infinite favours by which Thou has supported our state, enriched our spirit, comforted our sorrows, relieved our necessities, blessed and defended our persons, instructed our ignorances, and promoted our eternal interests.

We praise Thy name for that portion of Thy holy word of which Thou hast made us partakers this day. Grant that it may bring forth fruit unto Thee, and unto holiness in our whole life, to the glory of Thy holy name, to the edification of our brethren, and the eternal comfort of our souls in the day of our Lord Jesus.

Have mercy on all that desire, and all that need, our prayers. Visit them with Thy mercy and salvation. Ease the pains of the sick, support the spirits of the disconsolate, restore to their rights all that are oppressed. Remember them that are appointed to die. Give them comfort, perfect and accept their repentance, give them pardon for Jesus Christ's sake, that in the glories of eternity they may magnify Thy mercy for ever and ever.

Hear the cries of the orphans and widows in their calamity; let all their sorrow be sanctified and end in peace and holiness, in the glorification of Thy name, and the salvation of their souls.

Lord, pity and pardon, direct and bless, sanctify and save us all. Give repentance to all that live in sin, and perseverance to all Thy sons and servants, for His sake who is Thy beloved, and the foundation of all our hopes, our blessed Lord and Saviour Jesus, to whom, with the Father and the holy Spirit, be all honour and glory, praise and adoration, now and for evermore.

The peace of God, which passeth all understanding, keep your hearts and minds in the knowledge and love of God, and of His Son Jesus Christ our Lord: and the blessing of God almighty, the Father, the Son, and the holy Ghost, be amongst you, and remain with you always!

2 Ibid., p. 67.

Select Bibliography

PRIMARY SOURCES

The Whole Works of the Right Reverend Jeremy Taylor, DD, with a *Life of the Author*, edited by Reginald Heber in 15 volumes, London, 1822 and 1828, known as the Heber Edition.

The Whole Works of the Right Reverend Jeremy Taylor, DD, with a *Life of the Author*, edited by Reginald Heber, revised and corrected by Charles Eden Page in 10 volumes, London, 1847-52, commonly known as the Heber-Eden Edition.

DISSERTATIONS

Antoine, Mary S., 'The Rhetoric of Jeremy Taylor's Prose, or Ornament of the Sunday Sermons,' PhD diss., Catholic University of America, Washington, DC, 1946.

Albrecht, de Ricci M., 'The Exemplum in the Sermons of Jeremy Taylor', MA diss., English Department, Catholic University of America, Washington, DC, 1947.

Carroll, Thomas K., 'Jeremy Taylor: Liturgist and Ecumenist. A study of Taylor's sacramental theology and its ecumenical implications', DD diss., Angelicum University, Rome, 1970.

—, 'Jeremy Taylor and the Anglican-Puritan Crisis in Worship, 1640-1660: A theological liturgical and ecumenical text in context', DSLit diss., Pont. Lit. Institute, Rome 1973.

Follo, K., 'Hofmannsthal and Wittgenstein', MA diss., Washington and Lee University, Lexington, VA, 1993.

Herndon, S., 'Jeremy Taylor's Use of the Bible', PhD diss., New York University, New York, 1949.

Jackson, R.K., 'The Meditative Life of Christ — a study in the background and structure of Taylor's *The Great Exemplar*', PhD diss., University of Michigan, Ann Arbor, 1959.

Peterson, R. A., 'The Theology of Jeremy Taylor, 'the temper of Caroline Anglicanism', PhD diss., Union Theological Seminary, New York, 1961.

MONOGRAPHS

Addleshaw, G., *The High Church Tradition: A Study in the Liturgical Thought of the Seventeenth Century*, London, 1941.
Armstrong, M., *Jeremy Taylor: A Selection from His Works*, London, 1923.
Askew, Reg., *Muskets and Altars: Jeremy Taylor and the Last of the Anglicans*, London, 1997.
Bolton, F.R., *The Caroline Tradition of the Church of Ireland with particular reference to Jeremy Taylor*, London, 1958.
Boone-Porter, H., *Jeremy Taylor, Liturgist*, London, 1979.
Brinkley, R.F. (ed.), *Coleridge on the Seventeenth Century*, Durham NC, 1955.
Brown, W., *Jeremy Taylor*, London, 1925.
Bush, Douglas, *English Literature in the Earlier 17th Century*, Oxford, 1945.
Carroll, T.K., *Jeremy Taylor Selected Works*, Classics of Western Spirituality Series, New York, 1990.
—, *Preaching the Word*, Message of the Fathers Series, Wilmington, Del., 1984.
—, *Liturgical Practice in the Fathers*, Message of the Fathers Series, Wilmington, Del., 1988.
Cropper, M., *Flame Touches Flame. Six Anglican Saints of the 17th Century*, London, 1949.
Cross, Frank, *The Oxford Movement and the Seventeenth Century*, London, 1933
Cuming, G., *A History of Anglican Liturgy*, London, 1969.
Davies, Horton, *The Worship of the English Puritan*, London, 1948.
Donne, John, *Sermons, Prayers, Devotions, Poems*, ed. J. Booty, Classics of Western Spirituality Series, New York, 1990.
Downey, James, *The Eighteenth Century Pulpit a study of the sermons of Butler, Berkeley, Whitefield and Wesley*, Oxford, 1969.
Frere, W. (ed.), *A Devotionarie Book of John Evelyn of Wotton*, London, 1936.
Frye, Northrop, *The Great Code. The Bible and Literature*, New York, 1982.
Gathorne-Hardy, R., *Words with Power. Being a Second Study*, New York, 1990
—, *The Double Vision. Language and Meaning in Religion*, Toronto, 1991.
Gest, Margaret, *The House of Understanding*, Philadelphia, 1954.
Gosse, Edmond, *Jeremy Taylor*, London, 1904.
A Bibliography of the Writings of Jeremy Taylor to 1700, Northern Illinois University, Dekalb, IL., 1971.
Hughes, H.T., *The Piety of Jeremy Taylor*, London, 1960.
Huntly, F.L., *Jeremy Taylor and the Great Rebellion. A Study of his Mind and Temper in Controversy*, Ann Arbor, 1970.
Janelle, Pierre, *English Devotional Literature in the 16th & 17th Centuries*, London, 1956.
McAdoo, H.R., *The Structure of Caroline Moral Theology*, London, 1949.

—, *The Spirit of Anglicanism*, London, 1965.
—, *The Eucharistic Theology of Jeremy Taylor Today*, Norwich, 1988.
—, *Anglican Heritage. Spirituality & Theology*, Norwich, 1991.
—, *First of Its Kind. Jeremy Taylor's 'Life of Christ,'* Norwich, 1994.
Miller, Perry, *The New England Mind: The Seventeenth Century*, New York, 1939.
Mitchell, W.F., *English Pulpit Oratory from Andrewes to Tillotson*, London, 1932.
Mueller, W.R., *John Donne: Preacher*, Princeton, NJ, 1962.
Pickstock, C., *After Writing: On the Liturgical Consummation of Philosophy*, Oxford, 1998.
Richardson, C.F., *English Preachers and Preaching 1640-1670*, London, 1928.
Smith, L.P., *The Golden Grove Selections from Jeremy Taylor*, Oxford, 1930.
—, *Donne's Sermons. Selected Passages*, Oxford, 1919.
Smyth, Charles H., *The Art of Preaching. A Practical Survey of Preaching in the Church of England, 747-1939*, London, 1940.
Stranks, C.J., *The Life and Writings of Jeremy Taylor*, London, 1952.
—, *Anglican Devotion*, London, 1961.
Sykes, Norman, *Old Priest and New Presbyter*, Cambridge, 1956
—, *Man as Churchman*, Cambridge, 1961.
Steiner, George, *Real Presences.* The Leslie Stephen Memorial, Cambridge, 1986.
Tuve, Rosemund, *Real Presences: A Secondary City; Broken Contract; Presences*, Chicago, 1989.
—, *Elizabethan and Metaphysical Imagery*, Chicago, 1961.
Walton, Isaak, *The Lives of John Donne, Sir Henry Wotton, Richard Hooker, George Herbert, and Robert Sanderson*, Oxford, 1927.
Watkin, Edward, *Poets and Mystics*, London, 1953.
Wedgewood, Cicely, *Seventeenth Century English Literature*, London, 1961.
White, Helen, *English Devotional Literature 1600-1640*, Madison, Wisconsin, 1931.
Willey, Basil, *The Seventeenth Century Background*, London, 1934.
Williamson, Ross, *Jeremy Taylor*, London, 1952.

Index of Biblical Citations

Page numbers are given in bold.

Genesis, **34**
1:1-4, **42**
2:7, **175**
5:2, **143**
14:21, **171**
18:17, **126**
18:19, **126**
44:6, **170**

Exodus
18:19, **102**
21:10, **142**

Leviticus
4:35, **104**
11:14, **176**
19:2, **59**

Numbers
12:6, **101**
15:25, **104**
16:3, **101**
16:9, **102**

Deuteronomy
6:4, **57**

Judges
4:21, **197**
14:14, **247**

1 Samuel
3:9, **124**

2 Samuel
14:14, **220**

Tobit
5:1, **134**

Job
19:26, **242**
Psalms
1:1, **103**
2:7, **108**
4:2, **198**
8:4, **27**
12:6, **237**
19:4, **100**
34:15, **107**
39:15, **226**
50:16, **103**
57:7, **124**
58:5, **71**, **115**, **154**
58:6, **223**
68:11, **165**
78:25, **170**
88:5, **239**
97:1, **62**
111:10, **120**
116:12, **170**
119:19, **120**
125:3, **190**
126:1, **248**
139:7, **195**
139:15, **241**
144:3, **27**

Proverbs
2:17, **231**
9:6, **130**
10:19, **203**
15:8, **105**
18:21, **204**
21:16, **130**
21:24, **208**
22:15, **213**
27:6, **207**
27:16, **234**

Ecclesiastes
6:2, **112**
10:20, **191**
11:28, **186**
12:5, **224**
19:12, **190**

Wisdom
1:6, **176**

Isaiah
5:22, **199**
6:3, **61**
11:1-10, **64**
14:23, **192**
25:7-9, **23**
26:20, **243**
29:11, **131**
53:3-7, **22**
54:13, **125**
55:10-11, **58**
61:2, **245**

Jeremiah
1:6, **61**
5:21, **122**
24:7, **61**

Lamentations
3:27, **232**

Ezekiel
3:7, **242**
8:10-12, **61**
11:16, **61**
12:2, **122**

Daniel
4:8, **128**
12:10, **126**

INDEX OF BIBLICAL CITATIONS

Joel
1:15, 161
2:28, 101

Amos
3:8, 57
17:15, 60

Zechariah
9:12, 228
12:10, 242

Malachi
1:11, 62

Matthew
3:11, 100, 171
5:12, 172
5:13, 106
5:20, 107
5:48, 59, 176
12:4, 154
24:50, 156
26:46, 63

Luke
4:16-30, 150
14, 34, 106
16:22, 238
22:20, 64
22:32, 104
24:49, 168

John
1:1-4, 42
1:3, 9
1:10-13, 42
1:11, 9
1:12-14, 10
2:4, 63
3:34, 169
3:5, 171
5:28, 241
6:45, 125
7:17, 118, 124
7:30, 63
10:16, 107
13:34, 64
17:1-19, 10, 63
17:24, 261
18:2, 10

Acts of the Apostles
1:4, 175
2:24, 239
2:39, 169
6:4, 64
9:39, 244
13: 26, 64
13:48, 100
14:3, 64
18:5, 64
24:25, 123

Romans
2:5, 160
5:20, 214
6:21, 185
8:2, 165
8:10, 178
8:15, 175
8:26, 174
8:28, 174
8:9-10, 165
10:17, 64, 201
12:12, 172
14:10, 229
14:25-6, 64
15:13, 171

1 Corinthians
1:18, 64
1:17, 31
1:22, 31, 177
2:14, 129, 166
2:15, 101, 177
2:9, 257
3:1, 101
4:1, 102
4:8, 168
7:26, 133
7:3, 142
8:1, 126
9:13, 105
11:5, 101
12:7, 166
13:4, 204
14:15, 174
15:23, 236
15:31, 237
15:32, 193
15:47, 258

2 Corinthians
2:10, 101
3:14, 122
5:10, 150, 151
5:19, 102
5:19, 64
5:2, 258
5:7, 175
6:1, 177
6:7, 64
7:1, 126
11:8, 105
12:2, 228
12:4, 257

Galatians
2:6, 226
6:1, 101

Ephesians
1:13, 64
4:29, 200
5:14, 127
5:27, 58
5:32-33, 133
6:18, 173

Colossians
1:24, 191

1 Thessalonians
1:6, 171
4:6, 242
4:9, 125
4:16, 237, 241
5:10, 228
5:16, 172

1 Timothy
2:1, 104
2:15, 134
4:3, 134
4:6, 105
6:5, 105
6:6, 177

2 Timothy
1:18, 225
2:9, 12

Titus
1:12, **197**
2:14, **100**, **105**
2:7-8, **99**
3:5, **108**

Philemon
1:19, **176**
2:16, **64**
3:21, **258**
3:8, **171**
4:4, **172**

Hebrews
1:2, **175**
4:12, **64**
12:22, **259**
13:4, **134**
13:8, **238**

James
5:14, **105**
5:15, **174**

1 Peter
1:8, **172**
1:22, **137**
1:23, **64**
2:2, **170**
2:9, **102**
3:4, **144**
3:21, **129**
4:11, **181**, **185**

2 Peter
1:3, **125**
1:3-4, **176**
1:5, **125**
3:16, **105**
1:20, **105**

1 John
2:1, **105**
2:27, **125**
3:2, **251**, **256**, **262**
3:9, **175**
4:16, **263**

Jude
1:7, **164**
1:19, **170**

Revelation, 34
1:6, **102**
2:17, **176**
3:12, **262**
5:1, **122**
5:10, **102**
5:2, **128**
5:13, **201**
7:16, **260**
8:15, **262**
14:11, **164**
20:6, **242**
22:1, **64**

Index of Proper Names

Aaron, 101, 169
Abner, 203
Abraham, 37, 100, 126, 145, 171
Achilleus, 133
Adam, 109, 155, 160, 183, 237
Adams, Michael, 14
Aeschylus, 39
Aesop, 245
Agnes, St, 134
Ambrose, St, 104, 109, 141, 217, 219, 224
Amos, 57
Anaximenes, 202
Andrewes, Bishop Lancelot, 59, 69-70, 82, 84, 248, 250
Apicius, 122
Aquinas, St Thomas, 26, 33, 56, 219
Aristophanes, 37, 197
Aristotle, 38, 39, 121, 183, 204, 215, 224
Askew, Reginald,
   Muskets and Altars, 91, 92
Athanasius, St, 248
Augustine, St, 32, 71, 73, 99, 106, 150, 196, 242, 251
Austin Friars, 68

Basil, St, 132, 204, 216
Beckett, Samuel, 28-9, 31
   Waiting for Godot, 31
Bennett, Fr Mark, 14
Blake, William, 24, 25
Boethius, 123
Book of Common Prayer, 13, 19, 70, 83
Bramhall, John, bishop of Derry, 82, 79, 90, 250, 251
Bridges, Joanna, *see* Taylor, Joanna
Browne, Sir Thomas, 81
Burnet, Bishop, 74
Byrd, William, 92, 146

Carbery, Lady, *see* Vaughan, Frances

Carbery, Lord, *see* Vaughan, Richard
Casel, Odo, 13
Catullusm 136
Caxton, William, 79
Charles I, 81, 83
Charles II, 83, 89
Chaucer, Geoffrey, 38
Chrysostom, St John, 38, 71, 73, 132, 248, 251
Cicero, 73, 212, 234, 259
Coleridge, S.T., 49, 71, 86
Conway, Lord and Lady, 88, 89
Cosin, John, 82
Council of Oxford 1222, 67
Cranmer, Prayer-Book of, 11, 19
Cranmer, Thomas, 70, 91
Crantor, 215
Cresippus, 186
Croft, Herbert, bishop of Hereford 73;
   The Naked Truth or, The True State of the Primitive Church, 73
Cromwell, Oliver, 79, 89, 91, 116

Dalstone, Sir George, 218
Daniel, 35, 63, 126, 128
Dante Alighieri, 11, 23, 31, 35-9, 38, 40, 41, 42-4, 53, 56
David, 59, 103, 108, 124, 128, 159, 165, 173, 191, 247
de Worde, Wynkyn, 79
Diogenes, 196
Dionysius Alexandrius, 109
Donne, John, 71, 72, 113, 182;
   Ductor Dubitantium, 16, 18
Duffy, Eamonn, 79, 91;
   The Stripping of the Alters, 79, 80

Edward VI, First Prayer Book of, 70
Eliot, T.S., 12, 34, 35, 40, 42, 43-7, 51, 52, 83;
   'Ash Wednesday', 40, 44-47;
   'La Figliache Piange', 40, 41;

INDEX OF PROPER NAMES

'The Hollow Man', 40, 41;
'The Three Europeans', 35-36, 53;
The Waste Land, 40-4
Elizabeth I, 82, 83
Elizabethan Settlement, 80
Enoch, 100
Epicurus, 190, 193
Erasmus, 119
Eriphyle the Argive, 137
Eudamidas, 119
Euripides, 141
Evangelical Revival Movement, 74
Evelyn, John, 81, 88
Ezekiel, 47, 57, 61, 62

Felicula, St, 134
Ferrar, Nicholas, 81
Fisher, John, 113
Flavia Domitilla, 133
Fourth Lateran Council, 67
Francis, St, 68
Frye, Northrop, 32, 34, 37

Gibbons, Orlando, 146
Goethe, Wolfgang, 32, 33-9 passim, 40, 50
Golden Grove, 146, 147
Gorgonia, 216
Gregory Nazianzus, 38, 216, 219
Gregory of Neocaesarea, 150

Hampton Court Conference, 83
Harrison, Edward, 251
Hegel, Georg W.F., 40, 53
Heidegger, Martin, 48
Herbert, George, 73, 95
Herodotus, 140
Hierome, St, 248
Hippasus the Pythagorean, 246
Homer, 27, 31, 141, 142
Hooker, Richard, 56, 81, 83, 251
Hopkins, Gerard Manly, 31-2
Horace, 203
Hudges, Ted, 35

Ignatius, St, 132, 138
Iphigenia, St, 134
Irenaeus, St, 125, 176
Isaiah, 21, 60, 65, 61, 64

Jacob, 29
James I, 82, 113

James, St, 104, 174, 220, 239
Jeremiah, 57, 61, 62
Job, 30, 100, 170, 242
John the Baptist, 50, 64, 100
John, St, 9, 10, 63, 64, 109, 114, 164, 241, 262
Joseph, 63, 117, 145
Joyce, James, 31
Judas, 10, 191
Jude, St, 164
Julian the Apostate, 215, 216
Juvenal, 138, 139

Kant, Immanuel, 24, 30, 35, 53
Kelly, Kevin, 17
Keen, M., 80
Kierkegaard, Søren, 47
King James Bible, 13, 67, 81, 83, 253
King, Charles, 80

Langsdale, Phoebe, *see* Taylor, Phoebe,
Langton, Stephen, archbishop of Canterbury, 67
Latimer, 80
Laud, William, 80, 82, 83, 182, 250
Libanius, 215
Livy, 141
Lucian, 140, 196
Lucius Quinctius, 244

Macarius, 140
Mackay, Brown, George, 52
March, Frances, 251
Margetson, Archbishop, 251
Marlow, Christopher, 146
Marital, 221
Matisse, Henri, 29
Matthew, St, 134, 156
Maximus the Confessor, 56
McAdoo, H.R., 13, 14, 15-20, 93-99, 180
McAdoo, Leslie, 14
Milton, John, 38, 181, 219
More, Henry, 89, 90
Moses, 61, 101, 127, 142, 169, 248

Naseby, battle of, 85
Newman, John Henry, 76-8, 151;
Parochial and Plain Sermons, 76
Nereus, 133
Newton, Isaac, 35
Nietzsche, Friedrich, 40

INDEX OF PROPER NAMES

Origen, 55, 74, 150, 156
Ovid, 34, 35
Oxford Movement, 75

Paul, St, 53, 101, 102, 104, 105, 106, 108, 122, 123, 126, 127, 129, 130, 134, 142, 145, 171, 177, 182, 187, 197, 219, 226, 240, 241, 244, 270
Perkins, William, 113
Peter, St, 104, 106, 124, 131, 145, 169, 170, 176, 239, 270
Phelbas, 40
Picasso, Pablo, 29
Pickstock, Catherine, 12
Pindar, 246
Pius Quartus, Pope, 83
Plato, 37, 59, 123, 127, 204, 215;
    Republic, 37
Plotinus, 197, 260
Plutarch, 138, 142, 171, 184, 191, 205
Polybius, 203
Ptolemy, 204
Pythagoras, 127

Quintilian, 138

Rahner, Karl, 47, 48-52, 181
Ramsey, Michael, 10, 95
Refauseé, Rayond, 14
Ridley, 80
Rose, Hugh James, 75
Rust, George, 15, 16, 97, 252, 254, 256;
    The funeral sermon of Jeremy Taylor preached by the Most Reverend George Rust, 256-71

Sanderson, Robert, 17
Second Vatican Council, 12, 60, 82, 85
Seneca, 77, 197
Servius, 145
Shakespeare, William, 35, 57, 39-40, 150, 223
Shelly, P.B., 43
Simon Magus, 182
Solomon, 109, 127, 195, 209
Sophocles, 41, 43
South, Robert, 77
Steiner, George, 12, 32, 33, 34, 36, 41, 44

Taylor, Charles, (son), 251
Taylor, Jeremy: life and career, 69-72, 82-90

Taylor, Jeremy, *Works*
    Advent Sunday – Christ's Advent to Judgment, 151-65
    Apology for Liturgy/ Collections of Office, 88, 116
    Apples of Solomon or the Fruits of Sin, 185-92
    Clerus Domini, 93, 96
    The Countess of Carbery's funeral sermon, 220-36
    The Deceitfulness of the Heart, 208-14
    Eniautus, 86, 116, 149, 180
    The Good and Evil Tongue, 200-8
    The Great Exemplar of Sanctity and Holy Life according to the Christian Institution/ The History of the Life and Death of the Holy Jesus, 16, 84-6, 146, 148
    The House of Feasting; or the Epicure's Measures, 113, 193-200
    The Marriage Ring, 116, 133-51
    The Minister's Duty in Life and Doctorine, 99-112
    Preached at the funeral of the Lord Primate of Ireland, 236-49
    Rules and Advices to the Clergy, 93, 94, 96, 98
    Unum Necessarium, 16, 17
    Via Intelligentiae, 114, 115, 118-32
    Via Media, 250
    Whitsunday. Of the Spirit of Grace, 150, 165-79
    The Whole Duty of the Clergy', 93, 96
    The Whole Duty of Man, 20
    The Worthy Communicant or a Discourse of the Nature, Effects and Blessings Consequent to the worthy receiving of the Lord's Supper, 16
    A Yearly Course of Sermons, 86
Taylor, Joanna *née* Bridges (wife), 88
Taylor, Joanne (daughter), 251
Taylor, Mary (daughter), 251
Taylor, Phoebe, *née* Langsdale (wife), 84, 87
Taylor, Phoebe (daughter), 251
Thecla, St, 134
Thomas, St, 239, 255
Thucydides, 215
Tillotson, John, archbishop of Canterbury, 74
Tracterian Movement, 74, 75
Trinity College, Dublin, 114

Ussher, Arnold, 250
Ussher, James, archbishop of Armagh, 73, 82

Valentine, Emperor, 217
Vaughan, Frances, countess of, Carbery, 86, 87, 220
Vaughan, Richard, earl of Carbery, 86, 146
Vaughan, Thomas, 81
Vincentus Lirinensis, 111
Virgil, 31, 141
von Balthasar, Hans Urs, 23, 33, 37, 41, 48, 53-7, 66
    Apocalypse of the German Soul, 40

Walton, Izaak, 81
Wesley, John, 75

Whitefield, George, 75
Wilde, Oscar, 39
Wilkins, John, bishop of Chester, 73;
    Ecclesiastes, or the Gift of Preaching, 73
Wittgenstein, Ludwig von, 30
Wycliffe, John, 69

Xenocrates, 119
Xenpphpn, 243

Yeats, W.B., 25-7
    'The Second Coming', 26;
    'Two Songs from a Play', 27

Zedekich, 191